THE COMPANION GUIDE TO
Jugoslavia

THE COMPANION GUIDES

GENERAL EDITOR: VINCENT CRONIN

It is the aim of these Guides to provide a
Companion, in the person of the author,
who knows intimately the places and
people of whom he writes, and is able to
communicate this knowledge and affection
to his readers. It is hoped that the text
and pictures will aid them in their
preparations and in their travels, and will
help them to remember on their return.

THE GREEK ISLANDS · SOUTHERN GREECE
PARIS · THE SOUTH OF FRANCE
ROME · VENICE · LONDON
FLORENCE · UMBRIA
THE WEST HIGHLANDS OF SCOTLAND
SOUTHERN ITALY · TUSCANY · EAST ANGLIA
SOUTHERN SPAIN · IRELAND
KENT AND SUSSEX

In Preparation
MAINLAND GREECE · MADRID & CENTRAL SPAIN
EDINBURGH & THE BORDER COUNTRY
NORTHUMBRIA · WALES · DEVON & CORNWALL
SOUTH-WEST FRANCE · BURGUNDY · THE ILE DE FRANCE

The Guides to Rome, Venice, Florence and London are
available in the *Fontana* edition.

THE COMPANION GUIDE TO
Jugoslavia

J.A. CUDDON

A SPECTRUM BOOK

PRENTICE-HALL, INC.
Englewood Cliffs, New Jersey 07632

COLLINS
St. James's Place, London

Library of Congress Cataloging in Publication Data

Cuddon, J. A. (John Anthony), (date)
   The companion guide to Jugoslavia.

   "A Spectrum Book."
   Bibliography: p.
   Includes index.
   1. Yugoslavia—Description and travel—
1971-   —Guide-books.   I. Title.
DR1213.C83   1984   914.97'0424   84-3357
ISBN 0 00 211133 0
ISBN 0-13-154824-7 (Prentice-Hall)
ISBN 0-13-154816-6 (Prentice-Hall : pbk.)

ISBN 0-13-154824-7

ISBN 0-13-154816-6 {PBK.}

ISBN 0-13-154816-6 (p)
ISBN 0-13-154824-7 (c)
ISBN 0 00 211133 0 (Collins hardback)

First published in 1968.
Second revised edition published in 1974
in Great Britain by William Collins Sons & Co., Ltd., Glasgow.

U.S. edition © 1984 by Prentice-Hall, Inc., Englewood Cliffs, New Jersey 07632;
William Collins Sons & Co., Ltd., Glasgow; and J.A. Cuddon.

A SPECTRUM BOOK

Printed in the United States of America

10   9   8   7   6   5   4   3   2   1

Prentice-Hall International, Inc., *London*
Prentice-Hall of Australia Pty. Limited, *Sydney*
Prentice-Hall Canada Inc., *Toronto*
Prentice-Hall of India Private Limited, *New Delhi*
Prentice-Hall of Japan, Inc., *Tokyo*
Prentice-Hall of Southeast Asia Pte. Ltd., *Singapore*
Whitehall Books Limited, *Wellington, New Zealand*
Editora Prentice-Hall do Brasil Ltda., *Rio de Janeiro*

Contents

Contents

Illustrations

Illustrations

Introduction

'If God did not exist I should kill thee immediately.' It is a South Slav saying, part of the South Slav legend. Yet whenever I travel in this extraordinarily beautiful and interesting country I am surprised that its people, who are so courteous and tolerant and good-natured, so gifted at maintaining amiable relationships, can be capable of the extreme violence they have often shown.

But Jugoslavia, a land of poets, warriors and shepherds, *is* a country of extremes. The summers are very hot, the winters very cold; the rivers are turbulent or dried up; it is mountainous and hilly or almost dead flat; fertile or barren; covered with forest or bare . . .

As you might expect its people also have emphatic characteristics. The men are virile, the women very womanly; a pleasant change. They are brave, proud and independent and, on the whole, exceptionally good-looking. Their intelligence and admirable sense of humour are soon evident. Like most Balkan peoples they are great plotters and intriguers; they excel at chess, almost a national game, which you will often see the men playing in cafés— especially in autumn and winter. But, again like most Balkan peoples, they are also impetuous and dashing.

The general extremes of contrast subsume a remarkable variety, so much so that Jugoslavia can fairly be described as a microcosm of Europe. The people consist of six major groups: Serbs, Croats, Montenegrins, Bosnians, Slovenes and Macedonians. They have four languages: Serbian, Croatian (these two are very similar) Slovene and Macedonian; and a very large number of dialects. They also have two alphabets: Latin and Cyrillic. Serbian and Macedonian are written in Cyrillic, Slovene and Croatian in Latin. Serbian is spoken in the eastern and Croatian in the western parts of Jugoslavia. Slovene is used in the north-west area; Macedonian, which is half-way between Serbian and Bulgarian, is spoken in the far south.

They have three main religions: Orthodox, Catholic and Muslim.

Approximate distribution of Jugoslav regions and religions

About fifty per cent of the population are Orthodox; thirty-seven per cent Catholic; and thirteen per cent Muslim.

In addition to the six main groups there are numerous minorities, which include Turks, Rumanians, Albanians, Hungarians, Slovaks, Vlachs and Gipsies.

All this makes for diversity, and the difficulty of communications in this very mountainous and forested land, together with the fact that much of it was occupied by the Turks for five hundred years, means that the people of many regions retain highly individual characteristics—especially in the country districts. Jugoslavia is one of the few places in Europe where large numbers of peasants wear costume.

Introduction

It is less than fifty years ago that the regions of Jugoslavia were united into a single state, and it is now a federal republic of six subsidiary states (Serbia, Croatia, Montenegro, Macedonia, Slovenia and Bosnia-Hercegovina) in one of which, Serbia, there are two autonomous regions: the Kosmet and the Vojvodina.

It has taken the South Slavs well over a thousand years to achieve this unity and it is still far from stable. A millennium of resistance against foreign predators and foreign dominion—such a tradition makes a people hardy, resilient, uncompromising and proud. The Jugoslavs have much to be proud of.

And what, as Viola wanted to know, should you do in Illyria? As the country is very unspoilt and full of surprises it is a most exhilarating place to explore. And 'explore' is the right word because there are many parts of it which are completely unknown even to Jugoslavs, almost unmapped. In some regions the people have never seen foreigners, except possibly in the form of invading soldiers.

Most people, however, have insufficient time to venture into trackless country. The more conventional visitor, be he aesthete, hedonist, sportsman or plain tourist, has most things at his disposal in Jugoslavia: excellent swimming and underwater fishing on what is certainly the most beautiful coast in Europe, ski-ing, fishing, walking, shooting, hunting, canoeing, climbing and rafting. There are antiquities from several different civilisations and enough variety of art and architecture to satisfy the most catholic of amateurs and the most expert of connoisseurs. You can also eat and drink very well and live comfortably at a moderate cost. The only person I can think of who might be unhappy here is the urban sophisticate who needs a plentiful range of bright night-life. This is limited even in places like Belgrade, Ljubljana and Dubrovnik.

I have started the narrative at an obvious place on the coast, Rijeka, and followed a course through all the main places of interest down the coast, thence up across Montenegro, south and round Macedonia, up through Serbia to Belgrade and beyond to northern Serbia; then back across the interior of Bosnia and Hercegovina, thence to Zagreb and inland Croatia and round Slovenia, concluding with the Istrian Peninsula and ending within a few kilometres of Rijeka.

Jugoslavia is about the size of the United Kingdom so to make this a more portable book I have been obliged, from time to time, to omit considerable tracts of land and treat others very summarily. But they are areas which only a tiny minority of tourists will ever visit and then, probably, only to pass through with little delay. If the exhaustive traveller suddenly throws up his hands and exclaims: 'Good heavens! He hasn't mentioned Priboj!' then the reason is that I considered that only ·01 per cent of tourists would ever find it—or want to.

I have also been obliged to use a number of relatively unfamiliar words (usually Serbian and Croatian) because there are no adequate equivalents in English. There is some explanation for these in the text. I have not provided phrase-book lists because there are already two good phrase-books: *Essential Jugoslav for Travellers* (Cassell) and *Jugoslav Phrase Book* (Collins), of which the former is the more elaborate. There is also a competent EUP *Teach Yourself Serbo-Croat*.

I have also included details of those fairs, festivals and folklore spectacles which are outstanding. Jugoslavia is a country with a great many traditional events which are celebrated far and near (very often in magnificent costume and whether there are visitors or not) and no trip is complete without trying to see one or two of them. To do so one has to venture off the *autoput* and forsake the well-oiled machinery of tourist plant. This is well worth doing anyway. A journey down the coast, memorable though it is, gives one a very incomplete idea of the sort of country you are in. The real Jugoslavia, 'a land to be reckoned with' as Brian Aldiss has put it, lies inland: a wild and primitive terrain of great beauty which shelters some of man's most remarkable achievements in the process of civilising himself.

Finally, any political comments have been avoided; not from discretion but because they have little place in a book like this. In any case all political scenes are ephemeral and in Jugoslavia they are likely to change even more than in most countries over the next ten or fifteen years.

Up-to-date information to supplement that given in the appendices can be obtained at the Jugoslav National Tourist Office, 143 Regent Street, London, w.1, and at Generalturist, 53 Lancaster Gate, London, w.2; also at the Jugoslav National Tourist Office, 509 Madison Avenue, New York, 22, N.Y.—and at tourist offices of all the main towns in Jugoslavia. The former Putnik organisation has been reorganised and divided into agencies under various names. Mention of Putnik in the text accordingly denotes the tourist office under whatever name it may now be.

CHAPTER 1

The Coast I:
The Kvarner Gulf and Northern Islands

Rijeka—Trsat—the Kvarner Gulf—Krk—Cres—Lošinj—Rab

For thirteen centuries the house of the Virgin Mary was preserved in Nazareth, where it was held in much veneration. So many pilgrims flocked to it that in the fourth century Helena, the mother of Constantine the Great, erected another building over it to protect it more thoroughly. Then, in May 1291, so legend has it (and the Jugoslav littoral is rich in legends), a squad of angels picked up the house and transferred it to a high hill above Rijeka. It was allowed to remain there for three and a half years, until, in either February or December of 1294, the angels again moved it —this time to Recanati in Italy where it forms the shrine of Loreto.

This is not the sort of tale you would immediately associate with a place like **Rijeka** which always seems to me a rough, workaday city of spit and little polish, dirty and noisy, where the hot reeking bars and *kafanas* (cafés) are full of dockers and sailors and a wide variety of seaboard types from all parts of the world. The nearest British equivalent is probably Liverpool or Cardiff. It has not the highly individual character of those places, partly, I believe, because its life has been so miserably disrupted so often. But Rijeka (the Italians called it Fiume, and both words mean 'river') is a more than usually good example of the prey, sport and stake of politicians who, apparently, have had little care for the human beings who have actually had to live there.

The vicissitudes which have befallen Rijeka are in many ways characteristic of much of the country. After the Illyrian-Celtic period the Romans were here and called it Tharsatica. After the Romans came the Croatians . . . And here I must digress for a moment. The Croats, like the Slovenes and the Serbs, were a Slav tribe who moved south and west from the Danube plains (and

13

farther north) between the sixth and the eighth centuries and they have come to be known as South Slavs (Jugo Slavs).[1] It was a great migration and the communities began to evolve a hierarchy along a conventional pattern. In the ninth century the first Croatian dukedom was established and in 852 its ruler, Trpimir, assumed the name of Duke of the Croats. In 910 Tomislav became prince and in 925 was crowned the first king. Tomislav's kingdom covered roughly the same territory as modern Croatia; his successor, Krešimir, enlarged it and proclaimed himself king of Croatia and Dalmatia. All this may seem very remote but Krešimir's descendants are still about. I met one quite recently. She was on holiday from Australia.

In the eleventh century two factions developed: one wanted closer union with the Pope and the Roman population of the coastal towns; the other, the more conservative and nationalist group, cherished the old Croatian customs, rights and privileges against Latin lordship. King Zvonimir became a vassal of the Pope but was killed after a brief reign. However, Zvonimir had married the sister of the Hungarian king Ladislas who, after his brother-in-law's death, shrewdly claimed the Croatian throne. In this he was supported by some Croat noblemen. Another group of nobles elected Petar Svačić, but he was killed in a battle in 1097 while defending his régime. Five years later representatives of the twelve Croatian tribes signed a pact with the Hungarian ruler Koloman and this deed unified the two kingdoms. As a result the centre of Croatian political and cultural life came to be concentrated in what is now Zagreb, but of this more in a later chapter. (See p. 358).

In 1466 the Austrians took over Rijeka and it was not until the eighteenth century that it again passed under Hungarian rule. For a time it was declared a free port with independent status. Then Napoleon's armies occupied it. Then it became Croatian again, then Hungarian. . . . Quite recently it was the victim of one of the more discreditable episodes of political *opéra bouffe*. The villain of this was that corrupt and sometimes felicitous Italian poet Gabriele D'Annunzio about whom Mussolini made one of his

[1] One widely held theory is that the Slavs originated in the morasses of Polesie, a triangular marshland, very nearly half the size of England, whose apices are Kiev, Brest Litovsk and Mohilev. In the sixth century Procopius observed that the Slavs were tall and outstandingly strong people. He also remarked that the South Slavs had reddish hair. Many of them had flaxen hair, and grey or blue eyes. Now most of them are dark and tend to have black hair. Their Celtic characteristics become more and more obvious.

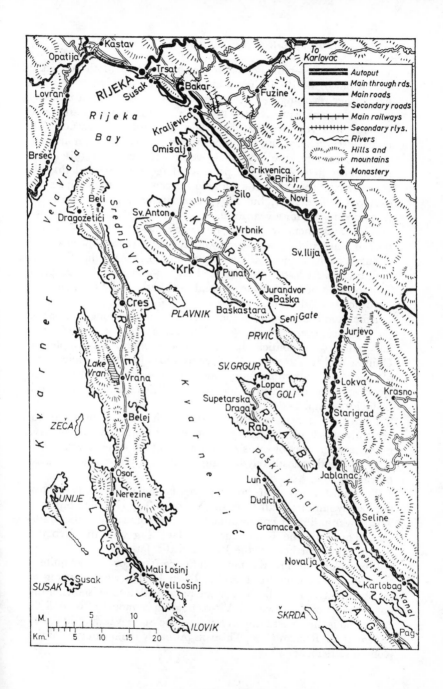

wittier remarks—namely that if you have a bad tooth you either pull it out or fill it with gold. On September 12th, 1919, this bald and rather revolting Fascist marched into the city with a thousand armed thugs and proclaimed it Italian. At this moment an Italian general was representing the Allies as military governor. The embarassed general and the importunate poet came to 'an arrangement'. Although the Italian Government disowned this armed robbery its delegates at the peace conference demanded that the town become theirs. By the Rapallo Agreement of 1920 Rijeka was declared a free state, but D'Annunzio refused to withdraw and remained regent for a year until he was forced out. Three years later another agreement was made by which most of the city became part of Italy and the Jugoslavs were left with the southern suburb —Sušak. When the Italians capitulated in 1943 the Germans took it over. At last it was liberated and re-united with Jugoslavia. The fortunes of Istria, which I shall deal with in the final chapter, have not been dissimilar.

I mention these events in some detail because as one approaches the Balkans (a term, by the way, that comes from the Turkish word for 'mountain') political history becomes about as complex as Chinese and it is as well to be prepared for almost insoluble mazes of chicanery and subterfuge, plot and compromise, alliance and treachery. By comparison the past of Rijeka and its region is pellucidly simple.

I have never been able to decide whether I like the town but certainly it is a good deal more interesting than many people have made out (no port of this size can fail to be of some interest) and anyway it is the most likely starting point for a trip down the coast by car or boat.

The most convenient hotel is the Bonavia (the only central one) a few minutes' walk from the **Narodni Trg** (People's Square). The newer and more comfortable hotels are some way to the southeast. They are the Kontinental in Tito Trg and the Neboder nearby; plus, farther on, the Park and the Jadran.

From Narodni Trg the main sights can be covered in quite a short time. The palace of the Old Town Hall is worth looking at and beside it you will notice a stone pillar with a relief showing the patron saint of the town, St Vitus, holding a model of it. A little farther on is the oldest thing in Rijeka—the Stara Vrata (Old Gate) known as the Roman Gate. This was probably the north gate of the Roman settlement.

If you take the **Supilova Ulica** (*ulica* means 'street') out of the top end of the Trg Republike you very soon see a large pseudo-Renaissance building (where the Hungarian governor once lived and later D'Annunzio and the Italian prefect) which now houses a gallery: mostly nineteenth- and twentieth-century paintings and sculpture. There is nothing of great note but in the **Lapidarium** there is a curious collection of weathered stone carvings, fourteen in all. These figures exist because a rich eighteenth-century merchant of the town called Adamić was falsely accused by his servants and some citizens of gaining his wealth from gold found in burial places on his land. The unfortunate Adamić was imprisoned. When he had established his innocence and been released he ordered the faces and figures to be carved in the likeness of those who had maligned him. They were placed outside his house where everyone could see them: a subtle form of satirical revenge. Nearby is a large park where you will find an excellent Natural History Museum, a small zoo and an aquarium.

From Trg Koblera Marin Držić Ulica leads to **Trg Riječke Rezolucije** where you find the renovated Baroque church of Sv Jeronim (Sv is short for *sveti* which means 'saint'). The municipal offices nearby are a conversion of part of an Augustinian monastery. Moving a little east from here you reach the law courts and the buildings where the main fortifications of the old town stood. Beside them was the only land exit, the Gornja Vrata (Upper Gate) and just inside it was Sv Vid's church.[1] In its stead is a Jesuit, Baroque church—vaguely reminiscent of Maria della Salute in Venice—which has an odd legend connected with it. Like most good legends it is pretty old.

In the thirteenth century a notorious gambler, Petar Lonzarić, was playing cards outside the earlier church and losing. Enraged by this he began to blaspheme, then ran into the church and hurled imprecations at God. Not content with this he snatched up a stone and flung it at the crucifix above the altar. The figure on the cross started to bleed and divine retribution followed a little more quickly than usual. The ground outside opened and swallowed Lonzarić at a gulp—all except one hand which remained thrust from the ground in a valedictory spasm of death. Apprised of the incident the governor of the city ordered the hand to be sliced off and cremated. To commemorate this event a bronze hand dangles from

[1] Vid is the Slav form of Vitus and Sv Vid is an important saint in the Orthodox Calendar.

the foot of the cross above the altar, and the stone (or *a* stone) is attached to the figure of Christ—with an inscription to the effect that the missile struck this spot some time in 1296. The last time I visited the shabby piazza in which the church stands there were four men gambling with cards a few yards from the doorway.

Just to the south of the Koblera Trg is the **Gradski Toranj** or municipal tower which, when it was part of the fortifications, stood at the water's edge. It has been renovated a good deal: the cupola, for instance, has replaced a crenellated top, and the fine clock was added in 1873. The most interesting parts of the tower are the Baroque figures and reliefs—including the busts of the Austrian emperors Leopold II and Charles VI.

If you follow the Korzo Revolucije down to Beogradski Trg and then turn left alongside the Kanal you arrive at Titov Trg. Cross it and the little river Riječina (this was the frontier when the Italians had Rijeka) and just over on your left you will find a very steep flight of steps which leads, eventually, to **Trsat**—where the angels deposited the Virgin's house. The steps were built in 1531 by Petar Kružić: one of the most famous Dalmatian heroes, chiefly remembered for a valiant defence of the fortress of Klis (near Split) against the Turks.

At the top, beyond Frankopanski Trg, is a small church and a monastery. The **Church of Our Lady** has remained a pious spot of pilgrimage and, until recently, was filled with hundreds of votive offerings made in thanksgiving for miraculous interventions and rescues—mostly at sea. Rather like the chapel of Notre Dame de la Garoupe near Antibes it was festooned with an extraordinary collection of illustrations, paintings, sketches, often crude but invariably vivid. I think it's a pity they have been removed. However, the church still possesses the head of Petar Kružić and the remains of a number of Frankopan nobles.

The Frankopans were Dalmatian feudal aristocrats who came primarily from the island of Krk. A turbulent, powerful and ruthless clan, they fortified themselves in numerous castles and owed their dominion to the prudence of ensuring that any likely foe was eliminated before he could act. In company with the Zrinjski family, scarcely less powerful, they held sway over the whole Kvarner area for nearly four hundred years.

A road named after one of the Zrinjskis takes one to **Trsat Castle.** The name comes from the Roman Tharsatica, though then it didn't occupy its present site. Nevertheless there probably was a

Roman fortress here (you can see plenty of Roman masonry in the walls) and before that an Illyrian stronghold. The Frankopans once possessed it and when they died out late in the seventeenth century it passed to the Habsburg rulers. Early in the last century an Austrian general called Nugent (of English and Irish origin) bought the castle and gave it a 'romantic' facelift. He even had himself buried in it, in what looks like a Roman temple.

From its considerable height one overlooks a great gash running up into the side of the mountain, Sušak, much of Rijeka, the southern and eastern coasts of the Istrian Peninsula and the whole of the **Kvarner Bay** in which lie the large islands of Krk and Cres, among many others. It is a magnificent view. Behind, tower the mountains and the barren wastes of the *karst* (appropriately the word comes from a Celtic root meaning 'stony').

I shall have to refer to the *karst* a good many times so it is best to be quite clear what it is. In purely technical terms it is a limestone region which, in Jugoslavia, stretches from Istria in the north to Montenegro in the south: about four hundred miles in length and anything up to sixty or seventy in breadth. It includes the Dinaric Alps and is characterised by high mountains, plateaux and ravines where all rain water rapidly disappears into caves and underground channels so that the whole vast region is honeycombed and perforated. Two remarkable features are lakes which dry up in the summer and fill in the winter, and rivers which burst abruptly from under ground or spring fully-fledged from walls of rock, torrent foaming through gorges, only to vanish as unexpectedly into gaping holes and reappear miles farther on. In Roman times many of these parts were forested but continual depredations for fuel, grazing and building materials—especially for ships—have denuded hundreds of square miles.

But such a summary does not begin to convey the full terror and beauty of this austere and stony desert which, during the long torrid summers, is baked by the sun and, in the equally long and bitter winters, is scoured by howling winds and swept by fierce blizzards. You would hardly expect anything to live in it or on it, yet life there is: scrub, small trees (forests still grow in more protected parts and valleys where soil has accumulated), insects, a few birds, reptiles and wolves which, in winter, rove into the villages. In spring, sometimes, there are flowers like scabious, harebells and flax; and, amazingly enough, all the year round, human beings.

It is a land of death, of fasting and deprivation, the kind of wilderness in which you would expect to find anchorites in the tradition of the Thebaid or those extraordinary early Christian eccentrics who subjected themselves to prolonged marathons of mortification chained to boulders, suspended in tubs or seated on remote mountain tops—and where, in fact, you *do* find peasants of almost incredible hardiness and perseverance. One may well ask why they go on living there and the answer would probably be that their ancestors lived there, that it is their home and they know that life. Indeed, some kind of atavistic affinity and affection for what is known keeps tens of millions in a state of voluntary subjection to the caprices of nature. Why else should people live on the slopes of active volcanoes, above earthquake seams, in valleys long vulnerable to disastrous floods?

Whatever the reasons the peasants of the *karst*, with painful labour and unremitting patience, eke out a precarious existence by cherishing the miserly residues of soil deposited in tiny patches between the rocks. Gradually they clear the ground, terrace it, wall it against the winds. Then they plant, and there is enough soil to nourish a few maize plants and vines; perhaps, occasionally, some grass to supplement the scrub. To these patches, often only a few yards square, they carry water from wells or underground streams— a mile or more. They may possess also a few goats and sheep, a donkey or two. Little wonder that the men and women who inhabit this ferocious wilderness are among the toughest in the world. Yet they are also gentle and hospitable.

The way south and east from Rijeka by boat leads through the **Kvarner Gulf**, so called, probably, because it comes from the Latin name Mare Quaternarium. At all events, the bay is divided into four areas: the Kvarner, the Kvarnerić, the Velebit Channel and Rijeka Bay. A glance at the map shows that there are three relatively narrow straits through which one can pass into the last named—which helps to explain the strategic as well as the maritime importance of Rijeka.

The whole of the Kvarner is a submerged part of the Dinaric *karst* and was flooded in the post-pleistocene era; that is, about ten thousand years ago. On a summer's day its waters are blue, innocuous and inviting and the grey and tawny islands, long scathed by wind and sun, float on it like snoozing monsters. But do not be deceived by this bland appearance. Records down the centuries confirm its treacherous nature.

In the 1770's the Abbé Fortis, that witty, intelligent and well-informed Venetian priest who spent much time travelling this coast, writing of the 'Quarnero', says: 'This channel is exceedingly tempestuous through the violence of the boreal winds, which often, on a sudden, put it in dreadful agitation, raising the waters to a terrible height, and darkening the air by the mist of the sea water elevated and dispersed, in minute particles, by the repercussion of the many rocks and craggy islands, which obstruct and embarrass the channel.'

Hence the number of votives at Trsat, and even today a sizeable steamer can be pitched and rolled like an old tub. However, for most of the summer the waters of the coast are calm and steeped in sun and there is plenty of opportunity for bathing. It would be idle to pretend that these shores are absolutely ideal for this, and you will not find the wonderful beaches of Brittany, the Riviera and the Costa Brava, or England for that matter. But there are several splendid sandy beaches and many tolerable ones of fine shingle. Otherwise most of your swimming has to be done from rocks and cemented promenades where you can also sunbathe. Many parts of the coast, and the rocky islands in particular, provide ample diversion and excitement for the more adventurous swimmer and the under-water swimmer. One of the pleasures of an unspoilt coast is finding little beaches for yourself in deserted coves. For the more restricted there are quite a large number of properly equipped plages. (See p. 416.)

Both Krk and Cres—and Lošinj (they are all well-connected by ship from Rijeka) are interesting places, though I dare say only the more assiduous traveller, or the one with plenty of time, will want to visit them. The names above, like some of the others we have come across, may cause a little difficulty at first, but one soon gets the hang of the pronunciation. Krk is like kirk; Cres like cress; Lošinj like Loshinye, with the j very lightly touched. J is *never* pronounced like a soft g. The other letters that produce most difficulty are: ž—like the s in pleasure; š—like the sh in shoe; č— like ch in church; ć—like the t in picture; dž—like the dg in bridge. It is obviously essential to be able to pronounce the names of towns and villages correctly. You might be quite flummoxed if someone asked the way to Wass-hinge-tone or Brig-he-ton. (For fuller details see p. 452.)

Krk—much of it is as sharp as its name (so many of the names on this coast are abrupt pointed monosyllables like this)—is the largest and most densely populated island in the Adriatic and consists almost

21

entirely of porous limestone. Its mountainous dorsal ridge divides a savage, rocky north-eastern shore, which yet has a rare fringe of forest, from the much more amiable south-west which slopes to good beaches and quite luxuriant greenery of figs, olives and vineyards.

The main town, Krk (a name that has gone through several changes: Illyrian Kurik; Greek Kurykta; Roman Curicum), is an absorbing place. Most of the fortifications that stand are fifteenth century—when the Frankopans renewed them (Krk was their chief base). The main gate now is through the watch tower, above the entrance of which is carved the Venetian lion—a symbol you will see many times on this coast. The pentagonal bastion opposite is part of older fortifications built into the top of which you can see a fragment of an old Roman grave stone, and on this again a star, the Frankopan arms, a signature and the date of the building. Everywhere on the coast one finds this kind of evidence: a mingling of remains as each new civilisation makes use of the rubble of its predecessors.

Immediately beyond the towers a number of crooked, cobbled streets lead off a square. If you dive into this complex you will soon enough find Kamplin Trg and the Frankopan castle. Beside it is the long, Bishop's Palace—which has a collection of sixteenth- and seventeenth-century paintings. There is also a fine triple-naved Romanesque cathedral next to the square, built from the materials of several older churches. The most interesting things here are the chapel of the Frankopans and a number of paintings by Tasco and Paris Bordone. I like the altarpiece especially. Next to the cathedral and above it is another lovely building—an early Romanesque basilica with a flat roof and square capitals.

If you decide to base yourself on Krk for a time (the Dražica and Bor are pleasant hotels) it is relatively easy to reach the other main towns and villages on the island.[1] For instance, there is Omišalj, on a cliff top, which was once a prehistoric fortified settlement. The thirteenth-century Romanesque basilica is well worth seeing. Malinska, now becoming a big holiday centre, runs a Krk Folklore festival during the season. Not everyone enjoys this form of 'cultural' entertainment, but it is something the Jugoslavs usually do very well, and you may live in the country for some time without being lucky enough to come upon traditional ceremony or dancing in costume in a 'natural state', as it were. (See p. 432 for a note on music and dance.)

[1] A large resort complex recently completed. Plus an airport.

Baška, the other end of the island, was once a Roman settlement and a good deal of the medieval town survives. Many of the families here originally came from Senj, on the mainland, during the Turkish invasions. Just inland from it is the village of Jurandvor and the chapel of Sv Lucija. There used to be an eleventh-century church here built by Benedictine Glagolitic monks on land given to them by the Croatian king Zvonimir. The inscription concerning this gift was cut into a stone tablet known as the Baščanska Ploča (Baška Tablet) which is very important as one of the oldest written records of the old Croatian language in Glagolitic script. There is a copy in the church and the original is in the archaeological museum in Zagreb.

This term **Glagolitic** needs some explanation. It is one of the old Slav alphabets and was probably created by Constantine the Philosopher when the Slavs were converted to Christianity in the ninth century. It is different from the other Slav alphabet, Cyrillic (which is largely used in Serbia, Macedonia and Montenegro and, of course, Russia and Bulgaria) and the shape of the letters—a very stylised uncial with rounded forms—is more like the Coptic or Armenian alphabets.

Two forms of Glagolitic developed: the Croatian or angular (called *hrvatski* or *uglata glagoljica*) and rounded Glagolitic (*obla glagoljica*). By the beginning of the tenth century they had spread so much among the Croats that the clergy who favoured Latin made severe attacks on them during two Church Councils at Split, in 925 and 927. Because of the continuous conflict with Venice services conducted in the Slav language and the use of the Glagolitic alphabet became identified with a national struggle against an alien 'Roman' and Latinised clergy. The name *glagoljasi* was given to the pro-Slav priests. It was not until after another Church Council in 1060 that the Latin clergy achieved the upper hand. Even so Glagolitic continued to be used illegally until the nineteenth century —over all the islands, in Istria and as far south as Kotor. One of the first Slav books to be printed was the Glagolitic Missal of 1483, and even today the Slav version of the western religious rite is preserved and used, though with Latin letters.

Very near Krk, the other side of the Punat Bay, is the town of **Punat** where the bishops of Krk used to have a residence and where there are still many graceful eighteenth-century houses with staircases called *ballatura* which lead up to little first-floor terraces. If you go here ask to see *Toš* (Tosh) the old olive mill, and don't miss the egg-shaped island of Košljun in the bay. It has a fortified Romanesque chapel and a Franciscan monastery in whose church there is a polyptych by Girolamo da Santa Croce and a *Last Judgment* by Ughetti.

If you happen to be in Punat on the first Sunday in May you will have a chance of seeing a traditional festivity called *Ples pod trešnjom*—the dance under the cherry tree—performed by young men due to enter the army in the current year. It has obvious affinities with the Maypole ceremony and is probably a descendant of the Roman Floralia. Its contemporary reason looks suspiciously like a case of doctrinaire metathesis. Whatever the latest grafting the rite consists of placing a cherry tree on the sea front where it is attached by ropes to the nearest buildings. The tree and the ropes are garlanded with scarves given by girls. A honey cake and some oranges are fixed on top of the tree and the youngsters dance round it. Afterwards the first girl dancer is given the honey cake and the oranges scattered for the children. Traditionally the young men became eligible for marriage by participating in this rite.

On the north-eastern side of the island there is another village you should certainly see: **Vrbnik**, at the top of steep cliffs from where there is a magnificent view across to the Dinaric Alps. As at Omišalj there was once a prehistoric settlement here. Much of the medieval town survives: steep, twisting streets, tiny squares, high, old stone houses and churches. The parish church is especially worth seeing. It is Gothic but most of the inside is Baroque. To my mind the two are incompatible and it is almost inevitable that the Baroque spoils the Gothic. Hundreds of Gothic churches have been ruined by this taste for excessive decoration.

The picture of *The Last Supper* above the high altar was painted in Venice by an artist from Kotor. There are several Glagolitic inscriptions: one on the sacristy window, another in the Sv Marija chapel, and a third on the back wall of the graveyard chapel. As these are to be found all over the Kvarner and farther south it seems pointless to mention them every time. Once you have seen a few you will recognise them easily enough.

There is a chance of seeing some costumes in Vrbnik, where the commonest form of the women's dresses is plain white with coral and shell ornaments, plus head scarves.

Cres, which is long and thin, is, like Krk, barren on one side and comparatively fertile on the other. It is very near the Istrian Peninsula from which it is separated by a strait called the Vela Vrata (the Great Gate). Krk and Cres are divided by the Srednja

Vrata (Middle Gate) while the Mala Vrata (Little Gate) runs between Krk and the mainland. Between them Cres and Lošinj (they are divided by only a few yards of water) form a huge natural rock barrier between the open sea and the inner Kvarner basin. Because of this and because they guard two channels they have always been very important strategically—as was proved again in the last war.

The town of Cres, snugly sheltered on a wide bay, is delightful: very old and full of an extraordinary medley of architecture— Gothic, Renaissance, Baroque and eighteenth century. Within its Venetian walls, gates and towers, it is, like Krk, a warren of narrow streets and alleys. The two churches worth seeing are Sv Isidor and Sv Marija. In the latter there is a splendid Gothic pietà. You should also have a look at the Arsan-Petris palace—a fine example of Venetian Gothic.

Cres is practically waterless but has in the middle of it a large freshwater lake—Lake Vran. Nobody knows quite why this is here but one theory is that it is fed by some of the rivers which go underground on the mainland and thence travel below the sea-bed. It certainly cannot be supplied by streams or rain on the island.

Just where Cres and Lošinj almost join (the Romans made a canal here) is the small hamlet of **Osor** about which old Fortis was exceptionally rude. 'A corpse of a city,' he called it, 'where the apothecary was the advocate as well and the doctor ploughed the soil.'

It is still tiny and of little importance, yet it is the oldest settlement on either of the islands and for some centuries was the most powerful. It is mentioned in medieval documents under the name Apsarum and some linguists maintain that the original name was Illyrian— perhaps Apsoros—a form used by the Greek geographers who connected Osor with the legend of the returning Argonauts. According to one myth it was here that the Argonaut boats ended the pursuit of Jason and Medea.

The varied history of the town is partly reflected in its buildings. There are a large number of remains from Roman and early Christian times but most of the surviving fortifications are Venetian. You should certainly have a look at the fifteenth-century cathedral (a good deal restored since the last war) believed to have been built by one of the most famous Slav sculptors and architects—Juraj Dalmatinac: George the Dalmatian. The painting above the high altar is attributed to Palma the Younger. There are several other churches and ruins.

Even thinner than Cres (but much more wooded) is **Lošinj**. Viewed from the air it dangles like a rib from Cres's side and at its southern tip disintegrates into a number of chip-sized islands. It was once quite famous for its ship-building but now there are only three places of any size: Nerezine, Veli Lošinj and Mali Lošinj (Great and Little Lošinj). All are very pretty, peaceful spots with good beaches and simple hotels. The palatial houses once occupied by Austrian and Italian nobility flake and crumble now into distinguished decay, their gardens run to seed, weeds prise open escutcheons. Through the narrow streets statuesque Croat women, baskets on head, walk like canephorae into whom life has been breathed.

Both these islands preserve two of the least known Croat dialects: what are known as *ča* and *ća*—this being how the locals say 'what?' On the mainland the Croatians usually use *kaj* and the Serbs use *što* and *šta*.

Susak, a little farther out to sea, is unique in the Mediterranean because it is composed very largely of fine sand. The theory is that it is a sandbank caused by under-water springs a hundred or more feet down. The name means 'the dried up one', from the word *suša*—aridity or barrenness. The women's costumes (now worn less and less) are very attractive and consist basically of close-fitting jackets worn over white linen blouses and short full skirts over numerous pleated petticoats. On festival occasions all the women turn out in costume.

Though most of these northern isles are of the 'classical' and Mediterranean tradition I feel that in part they belong to that sad grey Saxon world so hauntingly evoked by *our* own early lyrical and elegiac poetry, and also by *their* folk ballads and epic poems (*bugarštice*) which are often sung. Many a time when travelling on the small ships which ply between the islands, night or day, you will hear the groups of peasant women, going to or from market, huddled together with their livestock, baskets and produce on deck or in the rough saloons, suddenly begin to sing. One begins tentatively and it is taken up by two or three more. Soon a dozen will be singing in perfect time: long, slow, lamenting songs, in which the tunes are rather monotonous and unsubtle—utterly unlike what you will hear in Serbia, Bosnia and Macedonia. Their subjects are the eternal ones of love and death, of beauty and decline.

The most interesting of the islands in the Kvarner and by far the best known is undoubtedly **Rab** (most of the main steamers call there and you can get to it easily by the ferry which travels from Jablanac on the mainland). A fifteenth-century fortified Venetian city, it is, I am convinced, one of the loveliest places in Europe. I say 'city' but in fact you can walk gently from one end to the other in ten minutes and across it in fewer than five; and this makes it no bigger than an English village. Yet it is a city, of the same lineage and style as Krk and Cres. It has churches and monasteries, museums and libraries, palaces and towers—not to mention a cathedral. The network of narrow streets, whose meshes periodically widen and bag into irregular *piazzette* and *trgs*, is walled by Gothic and Renaissance façades carrying the crests and shields of obsolete aristocracies, both Venetian and Slav. On the seaward side, over the patrician roofs and golden geometries of stone, four slim campaniles rise. However you look at it everything seems to fall effortlessly into proportion. This urbane jewel set irregularly on a narrow finger of rock has been described as a miniature Venice. In a way it is, though much of it was built by Slavs in a gradual way and it has various outward irregularities and disharmonies which addto its beauty.

When you come from the boat alongside the old walls where the palm trees burst like stocky pineapples from their jackets, one of the first things you will notice is the **Prince's Palace** in Tito Square: a thirteenth-century mixture of Gothic and Renaissance with its balcony resting on two lions' heads. Underneath it is the tourist office. The passage next to it leads into Orešković Street, known as Bottom Street (the other two main streets running lengthwise and parallel to it are known as Middle and Upper) which is full of lovely houses. Look particularly for the Marčić–Galzigna palace with its Gothic windows and lions' heads. At the end of this street are the remains of the Nemir palace with a perfect Renaissance Gothic entrance.

Turning back left from here you get into Middle or Ivo Lola Ribar Street. At this end of it you see the **Dominis–Nemir** palace where it is believed that Mark Anthony de Dominis was born in 1560, four years before Shakespeare. By any standards he was rather an extraordinary man who, as far as I know, still awaits a biographer.

He was a writer, a scholar and a philosopher. He was also archbishop of Senj and Split. However, his scientific turn of mind produced liberal ideas which were strongly disapproved of by the Vatican. So he turned coat, became a Protestant and travelled to England where he became Dean of Windsor, Master of the Savoy, and subsequently vicar of West Ilsley in Berkshire! While in London he published his most important work: *De Republica Ecclesiastica*. This was immediately put on the Index, a useful piece of publicity because it very rapidly went through several editions. Later he had doubts about his adopted faith and returned to Rome to discuss matters with the reigning Pope who was a friend of his. Unfortunately this Pope died and his successor was most unsympathetic. The unlucky Dominis was jailed in Castel San Angelo and three months later his dead body and all his works were burned in public. He is alleged to have discovered the solar spectrum half a century before Newton, and the story is that the idea came to him while he was saying Mass. His other contribution to science was his proof of the influence of the moon on tides.

If you go on down this main street you return to very near the Prince's Palace, and arrive at an elegant little Renaissance loggia: the seat of justice during the Venetian régime, one of several on this coast. Near it stands the clock tower and the small church of Sv Nikola.

The street running up to the right and thence to the ridge divides the old part of the town from the new (through which you have just passed). Before you lies the area where Roman Rab stood. Then it was a considerable naval base which later developed into a town with fortifications. Pliny refers to it as Oppidum Arba. None of this remains though many relics have been found: coins, inscriptions and parts of buildings incorporated into later structures. Several of the houses near here are still in ruins because they were abandoned during the seventeenth-century plagues, then burnt out to disinfect them. You will notice that many of their doors and windows have been walled up.

When you have walked straight up the slope to the upper town you come out into a small piazza where stands the tiny cathedral: **Sv Marija**, predominantly a Romanesque church of the twelfth century. Over the door is a remarkable little pietà of 1414. It is an ungainly, clumsy work, yet of great power and there is something deeply moving about that corpse of a fully grown man with its huge hands, its scraggy arms and legs, stretched across his mother's knees. Above, the Madonna's mouth is drawn down and back in bitter pain and grief—yet with her grief is mingled acceptance.

Inside there are several things to see. The marble columns are in perfect proportion, and the stone canopy with its baldaquin is exquisitely light and graceful. There are also some richly carved choir stalls exactly appropriate to their surroundings, a triptych by

Paolo of Venice, and, on the first right hand altar, a fine *St Christo-pher* in silver relief.

According to legend his head preserved the town from Norman conquest in 1075. The cathedral is also reputed to guard the head of a St Catherine: a potent relic whose authenticity a medieval bishop of Rab once doubted. The townsfolk threatened to throw him into the sea for his scepticism so he rapidly wangled himself a transfer to an Italian diocese. The church was also supposed to possess the miraculous heads of Shadrach, Meshach and Abednego, but time and incredulity have disposed of this tradition.

More important than any such beliefs and cults is the church itself and I think Miss Rebecca West has conveyed better than anyone the essential truth about it. 'It recalls,' she says, 'the bone-white architectural backgrounds of Carpaccio and Bellini, that delicate frame of a world which is at once pious and playful, luxurious and simpleminded. Its interior might have been designed by a maker of masks, who with infinite reverence conceived the high mass as the supreme mask.'

The **Romanesque Bell Tower**, easily the finest on this coast, was built on the foundation of a Roman building in the twelfth century. The secret of its excellence lies in the proportion of the windows and the culminating balustrade. At the top there is a great bell at whose making, so tradition runs, the townsfolk gathered to contribute their gold and silver ornaments. There are few mellower peals. Below, the cliffs, bristling with the stiff grey blades of aloes, fall steeply to the sea.

The next church along this street (this also has a notable campanile) is Sv Andrija which belongs to a convent where there are still a few Benedictine nuns. You can get the key by ringing the bell at the main door and it will be put in the hatch. The best things in the church are the Baroque wooden altar and a copy of a polyptych by Vivarini on the gospel or left hand side. The floor is covered with the funeral plaques of old patrician families.

Just beyond the little piazza (Trg Slobode) on one side of which is yet another thirteenth-century palace, stands the church of Sv Justine (the key to which is very elusive) notable for a handsome wooden Baroque altar and a picture of the *Death of St Joseph* which is ascribed to Titian. It is a good painting, but the fact is that works attributed to Titian are almost as ubiquitous as the hairs of the Prophet, the footprints of Buddha and the fragments of 'The True Cross'.

29

The next church is of little interest (the key is available in the house immediately to the left of the main door) but just beyond it are the ruins of an eleventh-century basilica. Beside it is the fourth of the campaniles. From here it is no distance to the inland walls and a park.

One can profitably spend many hours pottering round the rest of the town and almost wherever you look there is something to arrest the eye: a façade one never noticed, a portal in an alley way, a coat of arms, flaking a little, on a honey-coloured wall. And always one is catching glimpses of that fascinating line of campaniles which seem to be for ever shifting their position and grouping themselves in a different way as you change your point of view.

Modern Rab, with several comfortable hotels (I usually stay at the Istra), has spread round the harbour and in the summer it becomes a very mondaine resort. The tourists are well catered for with an open-air theatre, folklore festivals, dancing, regattas and what not. You can eat well, too, and the local wines are delicious— especially Prošek, a sweet, heavy dessert wine (the best Prošek comes from this island) which should preferably be drunk with your coffee and dessert. One exception to this rule is to try it with Dalmatian smoked ham (*Dalmatinski pršut*) at the beginning of the meal.

The rest of the island is well worth exploring. It is much more fertile than most and is ideal for walking. Almost wherever you go (as on Krk and Cres) you will find people leading a way of life that has not been much affected by the encroachments of the tourist industry and has changed little in a thousand or more years. The man in home-made clothes rides his donkey; the woman tends her flock and spins the while on her distaff, or sits at her cottage door and winds silk.

Silk, incidentally, is a traditional culture here and legend has it that it was at Rab that the priest was born who brought the first silk cocoon from the east in a hollow stick.

The road to Lopar takes one near the remains of a concentration camp where, during the last war, about five thousand Jugoslavians were systematically starved to death by the Italians. Lopar (prob- ably the Greek settlement Neoparum and also the birthplace of the hermit Marinus who founded San Marino) is a pretty little fishing village in a sheltered cove. It has one of the best sandy beaches on the whole coast. North of the peninsula are two bare islands: Grgur (Gregory) and Goli (Naked).

Nearer Rab is **Supetarska Draga** where there are a Romanesque basilica and the ruins of a Benedictine monastery. Closer still is **Kampor** around which spreads the Dundo forest, of pine, cork oak and a particularly magnificent evergreen oak, the holm, whose foliage resembles holly leaves.

Such a summary account does not begin to do justice to Rab, which, on its own small scale, seems to me to embody nearly everything that is most pleasing on this coast. Whenever I feel unusually dejected I summon up its image, its palaces and towers, and hear the voices of the ever secluded nuns chanting the Divine Office on a summer's dawn and the song of the nightingales in the woods. Here indeed Viola might have languished for Orsino, and Orsino for her.

CHAPTER 2

The Coast II:
The Croatian Littoral

Bakar—Kraljevica—Crikvenica—Senj—Pag

If you are going from Rijeka on the new coastal *autoput* (a road of which Jugoslavs are extremely proud) you pass through some of the most grandiose scenery on the whole shore. This part, for about a hundred kilometres, is the Croatian Littoral proper (Hrvatsko Primorje) as distinct from what is known as the Dalmatian Coast beyond (most of which is in fact Croatian) and consists for the greater part of a narrow ledge of land between the sea and the stern mountain ranges of the Vapela and Velebit.

Sooner or later you will see one of the solid stone huts with round roofs which abound in this area. These are **bunje**, shelters for herdsmen and so forth (though sometimes they afford more permanent accommodation). Many of the early villages and houses were circular in plan (as you can see in Istria) and the *bunje* are based on a very ancient design which was probably Illyrian in origin.

This word Illyrian needs a little explanation. It was a Greek word used to describe the coast and hinterland of the southern Adriatic; and the Roman Illyricum included territories northwards, as far as the Sava, Morava and Danube rivers. The Illyrian tribes came south from the Danube plains in the Iron Age and by the fourth century B.C. a powerful kingdom had developed. This was overcome by Philip and Alexander of Macedon. In the third century a larger kingdom united Illyria under King Agron and Queen Teuta and for a long time the coastal tribes operated as pirates in craft called *lembi*. They were the forerunners of a great pirate tradition on this coast. The final conquest of the Illyrians was not completed by the Romans until 33 B.C. Thereafter the Illyrian tribes, especially the

Above, the city of Rab, with its four campaniles, soon after dawn. The famous one is the farthest right. Behind, typical *karst* hills, white and barren. *Below*, Maslenica Kanal, looking towards the Velebit. Emerald water in the desolate beauty of white *karst*. The channel (salt-water) links with the enclosed Novigrad Sea

ŠIBÉNIK: the west door of the fifteenth-century cathedral, Sv Jakov; mainly
the work of Juraj Dalmatinac and Nicholas the Florentine. Lions roar affably.
Adam is doleful, Eve cheerful

Dalmatae, provided some of Rome's best troops and also six of her emperors: Claudius, Aurelian, Probus, Carus, Diocletian and Maximian.

The first place of any note after Rijeka is Bakar, tucked inside its huge fiord of a bay. Round here there are many terraced vineyards which produce a refreshing sparkling wine—Bakarska Vodica. Another thing you may notice (these can be seen in many parts of the Kvarner) are tall, sloping ladders which jut high above the water. These are look-out posts for sighting tunny shoals. When the tunny are in the watchers on the ladders give the signal for the nets to be closed.

The unfortunate tunny, a fish of disastrously regular habits, are then knocked on the head, dispatched, carved and usually canned. If you happen to be down here between October and March you may well see a catch being made. Grilled steaks of fresh tunny with a bottle of local white wine make a very good meal. It is a meaty fish and not too oily when grilled.

Bakar itself qualifies as a 'picturesque' old town whose history dates from the first century A.D. The Frankopan castle at the top of the town is worth visiting, and there are two churches the conscientious visitor will want to see: Sv Andrija and Sv Margareta. The former has an elegant bell-tower built by the Benedictines in the twelfth century. Apart from these there are a 'Turkish' type house (very far north for one of these), a 'Roman' house with Baroque arcades, two small museums and a large number of Glagolitic inscriptions built into walls and above doorways. If you happen to notice an unusual number of trimly clad, venerable and weather-beaten old gentlemen the chances are they will be retired sea-captains who abound here, as they do at Orebić farther south.

Kraljevica, round the other side of the bay, is quite as interesting. It is more recent than most of the coastal settlements and isn't mentioned in documents until 1525, though legend links it with the Hungarian King Bela IV about whom I shall say something when discussing Trogir. What is certain is that the town belonged to the Frankopans and then to the Zrinjskis, who each built a castle in the seventeenth century: Stari Grad (Old Castle) and Novi Grad (New Castle). Both stand on the shore. In the courtyard of Stari Grad you can see a well which bears the Zrinjski arms, and in Novi Grad another carries the crests of both families. It is said that the plans for the great revolt of these two families against Austrian suzerainty were hatched here.

For many years both families had worked against the Austro-Hungarian Empire and when Count Nikola Zrinjski died in 1664, murdered by Leopold of Austria's thugs (it looked like a hunting accident) open rebellion was imminent. The Emperor Leopold was afraid and in order to placate the Zrinjskis offered the government of Croatia to Nikola's brother Petar. This would enable him to watch the Croatians' movements. Louis XIV now offered help to the Croatians. Meanwhile the Turks had renewed their attacks on Croatia. Petar, his wife Katarina and Franjo Frankopan, the principals in this intrigue, could all see what Louis was up to. Accordingly an envoy was sent to the Sultan and the Sultan agreed to recognise the rights and freedom of Croatia. The Frankopans and Zrinjskis prepared for rebellion. However, the Emperor's spies at Constantinople had done their work efficiently and Leopold's army was ready. This did not prevent him from inviting Zrinjski to Vienna for talks. Zrinjski went with his brother-in-law Krsto Frankopan, both realising the possibility of treachery: an expectation which proved quite correct. They were executed in April 1671. The estates of the two families were divided by the Emperor and it was the end of an era in Croatian history.

At one time Kraljevica was quite an important commercial harbour and the shipyards were under English firms at various periods. Now they have been rechristened Tito Yard because the marshal worked there as a metal worker when a young man. It was at Kraljevica also that the first bathing establishment on the Croatian littoral was built—as long ago as 1896.

The next town, **Crikvenica**, is the largest resort in the region (except for Opatija and Portorož) and has been used as such ever since the end of the last century. Between the wars it was *the* holiday place on the coast. Not surprisingly. The climate is very mild, there are spacious parks and promenades, and one of the best sandy beaches in the area make it an ideal place to be quickly basted and sedated. If you grow weary of hedonism you can always stroll along to look at the fifteenth-century Frankopan castle or visit the Gothic church of Sv Marija. Alternatively, take one of the regular ferries to Vrbnik or Krk; or a bus to Bribir, a delightful village up in the hills which has a fourteenth-century church and some paintings by Palma the Younger. Bribir was a centre of resistance during the last war and provided one of the heroes of that struggle —Tomo Stržić, whose bust stands in the park. In fact, Crikvenica is sufficiently well sited and equipped to make it a convenient base for a tour of most of the Kvarner area. It is certainly worth making the effort to see Novi Vinodolski only ten kilometres away, and Senj—twenty-two beyond that.

Novi, as it is usually called for short, is a most attractive place, its chief adornment being the Frankopan castle in the old town on the hill. Here, in 1266, an important document was drawn up: the Vinodol Statute (the oldest complete Croatian document). It served as a charter of liberty for the semi-independent district of Vinodol (it means 'wine valley') which lies a little inland behind a chain of low hills. On paper—as it still does in fact—it stretched from above Rijeka right down to Novi. For several centuries it was owned by the Frankopans and after they lost the island of Krk it became their main estate. When the Uskok pirates were active on this part of the coast the Frankopans helped them because they were fighting against Venice. This long, steep green valley is dotted with medieval remains.

From Novi to Senj the road describes one of its most difficult courses over gorges and mountain torrents. The coast becomes wilder, ever more arid and barren. Seawards rises the grey hulk of Krk. Quite suddenly you come upon **Senj**, the oldest and largest town under the Velebit Mountains and at the opening of the Vratnik Pass. Fortis described it quite vividly. 'It lies,' he says, 'on the brink of the sea, on a foundation of concreted gravel, at the mouth of a very narrow valley surrounded by horrid marble hills.' (The word 'horrid', then meant hirsute, bristling or shaggy. The Italian word *orrido* could also mean 'ravined'.)

The history of Senj, always, as now, quite a small town, is closely associated with that remarkable band to which I have already referred: the Uskoks (the name means a 'fugitive' or 'one who jumps over'. The verb 'to jump' is *uskočiti*).

They were originally refugees from the Neretva valley in Bosnia-Hercegovina and when they fled from the Turks they first defended the fortress of Klis, which guards the pass behind Split. When that fell they came to Senj. Though there were never very many of them (the maximum number is generally agreed at about a thousand; though, of course, a thousand is one of those conveniently symbolic numbers like forty) they built a powerful navy and, despite being born landsmen, turned themselves into expert sailors. The craft they built were perfectly suited to the treacherous currents, danger-ous straits and violent storms of the Dalmatian coast. They used light, swift boats which could be easily drawn up on a beach if there was no harbour and with these they harried and destroyed the Turks with the same kind of ruthlessness with which the Partisans fought the Fascists. When Venice gave up the struggle against the common enemy the Uskoks regarded the defection as a gross treachery to Christendom and thereafter the Venetians received the same treatment. Gradually the Uskoks became utterly unscrupulous pirates of whom everyone went in fear. George Sandys, that entertaining English traveller who was in these parts very early in the seventeenth century, said that the pirates 'gather such courage from the timorousnesse of diuers that a little Frigot will often not feare to venter on an Argosie: nay some of them will not abide the incounter, but runne ashore before the pursuer (as if a Whale should flie from a Dolphin), glad that with wracke of ship and losse of goods they may prolong a despised life or retain undeserved libertie.'

The Uskoks became so brutal and extravagant that if they caught a Turk they would nail his turban to his head. They were not even above tearing out the heart of a living man and eating it. Times don't change much. The Četniks used to cut out the hearts of Partisans they had killed, and I have seen photographs of them doing it.

Soon, of course, anything afloat was fair game to the Uskoks and for a long time they were virtually invincible. Desperadoes of all sorts, including numbers of Englishmen (aristocrats and men of fortune) joined their ranks. Criminals accumulated in Senj in such numbers that they spread to neighbouring castles. Twice a year, at Christmas and Easter, they made special expeditions to which every citizen contributed and received in return a proportionate cut of booty. The Church and the priests (who invoked the blessings of God on the ventures) were included in this. Immoral, no doubt, but perhaps they argued that their efforts for the cause of Christendom had been betrayed and rejected.

It wasn't until some way on in the seventeenth century that the Austrians and Venetians managed to overpower and disperse them. Had they not been let down by the so-called Christian Alliance they would certainly have made a much greater contribution towards restricting the advance of the Turks.

One of their greatest warrior leaders, Ivo of Senj, was reputed to have routed fifty thousand Turks with a mere eight hundred men. Such a feat and such statistics clearly belong to the realm of 'heroic' legend and literature, and in fact a well-known heroic ballad includes a kind of elegy for Ivo: His mother dreamt that darkness fell upon Senj, the heavens burst and the shimmering moon fell out of the sky, the dawn rose blood-red and she heard a cuckoo calling . . . Here we have the traditional authentic omens that presage the fall of great men.

When Ivo's mother woke she expounded her dream to a priest who said it foretold her son's death. Even as he spoke Ivo stood before them. His coal black horse was drenched in blood, his body was wounded in seventeen places and he carried his right hand in his left:

> *He rode his horse to the white church door,*
> *And to his aged mother cried:*
> *'Help me, mother, from my horse,*
> *Bathe my wounds in water cold,*
> *And put the chalice in my hand.'*
> *Quickly then his mother obeyed,*
> *Helped him down from his lathered mount,*
> *She bathed his wounds in water cold*
> *And poured out for him the red, red wine . . .*

In response to his mother's questions he then explains how on return from Italy laden with booty he and his band were attacked by three separate posses of Turks. Ivo and his men destroyed the first two posses without loss to themselves, but with the third it was different. They fought fiercely but not one Turk fell, and of Ivo's men not one remained:

> *'Not one, except Ivo thy son,*
> *And him thou seest wounded to death,*
> *Bearing his right hand in his left.'*

As he spoke he died. It is a stirring poem which contains the traditional elements of ballad: simplicity, repetition and rapid action.

Nowadays Senj is a quiet spot where many tourists call but few stay. According to legend it was founded by Tarquin the Proud, but was levelled by those indefatigable barbarians the Avars and the Tartars before, of course, being settled by the Croats. There is not a great deal left of the fortifications now, but as so often on this coast a saunter through the congested streets is rewarding. There are a number of palaces which belonged to well-known Uskok families, a Frankopan castle (which dates from 1340), a Franciscan monastery, and the Cathedral of Sv Marija—rebuilt in the eighteenth century and restored in 1947. Near the cathedral is the Municipal Museum, housed in a Gothic Renaissance palace. Many of the main buildings of note are in or near the central Trg Marka Balena.

On a hill just outside the town rises a machicolated, keep-shaped castle, built by a General Lenković in 1558. In a country full of improbably romantic fortresses sited in magnificent positions **Nehaj** must be among the top ten. Some of the Serbian and Bosnian strongholds precede it in grandeur. You will notice that the embrasures of Nehaj are splayed outwards rather than inwards, a sure sign that it was built in the days of cannon, not bow and arrow. Built out from the battlements at the very top is a natty little roofed lavatory. Incidentally, the name Nehaj is probably a contraction of *ne hajem*—'I don't care', and the word *nehaj* now means 'heedless' or 'unconcerned'. Clearly, then, the occupants of the fortress feared no one. On the way up to the fortress you will see a curious Calvary scene in weathered stone.

The old Abbé Fortis, who had a particularly sharp eye for odd customs, noticed a very unusual one at Senj—namely a ceremonial leave-taking of the dead by friends and relations which involved kissing the corpse: a rite accompanied by spreading a fresh handkerchief over the face of the loved one after the kiss. All the handkerchiefs remained to the heirs; so they might be better off to the tune of thirty or more.

Behind Senj the Jozefinska Cesta (named after the Emperor Joseph II of the Habsburgs) winds away to the forested Vratnik Pass. It is a terrible road, sometimes not much more than the bed of a mountain stream, and it becomes worse and worse; but it has the compensation of passing through splendid scenery and enables you to get into the interior—for example, to visit the Plitvice Lakes (see p. 356).

In front of Senj, between the islands of Krk and Prvić, runs an important strait called **Senj Gate**. When the *bora* wind howls down through the Vratnik Pass the sea becomes very dangerous: a condition the Uskoks often turned to their advantage. This *bora* is very remarkable and deserves comment. It is usually a cold, dry north-easterly wind which corresponds to the mistral and occurs for the most part in winter when atmospheric pressure is high over central Europe and the Balkans and low over the Mediterranean. If there is a depression over the Adriatic it is accompanied by rain or snow. It sweeps across the great central European plain and piles up behind the Adriatic mountains; and the only escape for it is through the passes. It is tremendously powerful. Fortis described it graphically. 'The wind,' he says, 'coming from the bare mountains blow(s) so furiously in that narrow hollow, that sometimes in winter one cannot go out of doors without danger and without the City it is much worse. It happens frequently that children and weak people . . . are lifted up from the ground and dashed against the walls . . . horses loaded with salt are frequently thrown down in the market place, and the roofs of the houses, though covered with very heavy stones, are carried away.'

Fortis does not exaggerate. Its giant breath can derail trains, overturn cars and capsize ships. I have only experienced it once and that was when walking inland from Split in late spring. After walking four miles nearly bent double I could go no farther. I was exhausted. But that day it was well below strength, no more than a prolonged sigh. Other travellers have recorded similar experiences.

To the south, the coast road, cut from the rocky slopes and cliffs of the Velebit, passes through the little village Jurjevo and then climbs and remains at five hundred to a thousand feet above sea level as it hairpins all the way to Karlobag. You will not see much here except minute fishing villages in narrow coves, an occasional sheep or donkey looking for something to eat in the grey desolation of rock, and isolated ruins: an old cottage, a fort, or a chapel in a spinney of cypress. Such solitary relics are a feature of the coast, the casualties of neglect, reprisal and vandalism. One wonders again why anybody chose to live here, unless it was only to make themselves inaccessible to enemies. Human beings, shrunk by the scale of nature, seem mere bugs lodged precariously in seams and crevices between the forces of mountain and water.

By the time you get to Starigrad (*another* Zrinjski–Frankopan castle) the whole eastern coast of Rab is clear. Here I must remark on one of the more beautiful phenomena of the coast: the colours of the sea. There seems to be no end to the nuances of blue it can assume, the gradations of mauve, purple and violet, the shades of grey and green. Often I have watched the light (especially at dawn and evening) play the chameleon as it tinges or suffuses the water and rocky islands so that one minute they look no more substantial than lilac-coloured phantoms floating on mercury, the next like jet black hunks on a lime green silk. There is no need to take mescalin in this part of the world, where few artists would dare to reproduce what they see.

Jablanac (ferry for Rab), a very pretty village, is set in Zavrat-nica Bay which is an interesting example of an inundated *karst*

The Companion Guide to Jugoslavia

valley, narrow and steeply sided. There is not much to detain the traveller here, nor, for that matter, at Karlobag thirty kilometres on. Just before you reach Karlobag you find a turn off to another pass over the mountains, a perilous and hair-raising road built as long ago as 1786 and named after Maria Teresa. It leads via the Oštarijsko saddle to Gospić, but is at present closed for reconstruction.

In the tops of these mountains and the area beyond them (known as the **Lika**) live what are probably the toughest people on the whole coast. They are the Ličani, renowned warriors of great ferocity as the Fascist forces discovered during the last war. The men's costumes are especially impressive, though worn less and less. They consist of tight trousers, embroidered jackets, full-sleeved shirt blouses (also embroidered) and red tasselled caps.

Opposite Karlobag runs the Velebitski Kanal, a narrow strait of sea. Occasionally you see dolphins along here, and the Dalmatian fishermen rigorously obey the ancient tradition that the dolphin is a friend of man and must on no account be harmed. The other side of the strait lies the thin, low island of Pag, known to Pliny the Younger as Cissa and where, according to Fortis, widows were in the habit of tearing out their hair 'in good earnest' and scattering it on the coffins of their husbands—whether they had loved them or not.

When viewed from the approaching car ferry which runs regularly from Karlobag it does not seem that anything could survive on **Pag**. One cannot see a tree, a bush or a blade of grass. It is just stone, pale brown and whitish stone, like a long sliver from the moon. But about five thousand people live on it and it supports a lot of sheep.

The town of Pag lies at the southern edge of an almost landlocked bay, in fact a salt lagoon. It is a medieval agglomeration that survives, but there were certainly Liburnian and Roman settlements earlier—somewhat outside the present site. There are also relics of a submerged town visible in the lagoon when the water is calm and the sky is clear. If you go there (not many people do) you will want to see the fifteenth-century cathedral and the Kneževa Palata (Prince's Palace). Also the costumes. The women's are particularly famous: full, wide skirts with bodices and blouses worked in needlepoint lace (the lace work is much prized), short dark blue or red jackets and starched white linen caps or lace caps (*pokrivača*).

When Fortis went to Pag he was very scathing. He found the

40

inhabitants wild and unpolished 'as if they lay at the greatest distance from the sea and the commerce of polite people. The gentry who pretend to shew their manners different from those of the vulgar are truly grotesque figures, both in their dress, behaviour, and insolent pretensions. The ignorance of the clergy is incredible.'

One can well imagine that things were rough and ready in Pag in those days, especially to a civilised Venetian. Poor old Fortis was even more scandalised because he couldn't find a single medal, inscription or MS. in the whole place; nor, for that matter, a man of good sense. Apparently everyone was so interested in the salt industry that this was their sole topic of conversation.

One thing Fortis didn't mention was the cheese—Paški Sir (*sir*, oddly enough, is the word for cheese) which you will often find in *hors d'œuvres* or served by itself as one. Jugoslavs do not have the habit of eating cheese at the end of a meal. Pag cheese is a piquant ewe's milk product with a distinctive flavour, ascribed to the fact that the island is so flat and narrow that the sea spray is blown right over it—thus heavily salting the grass and soil.

People who are used to French and English cheeses are generally not very impressed with Jugoslavian cheeses. However, *kačkavalja* and *kajmak* are two cheesy products worth trying. The former is a hard cheese usually made from sheep's milk; the latter is the skin of boiled sheep's milk and skimmed off cream which is then salted and left for a time; a form of curds, in fact.

Goats' milk is also used sometimes, and goats abound on this coast as well as in other parts of the country. Herds of fifty to a hundred are not uncommon. Beautiful beasts they are, of many different colours—white, black, liver and chocolate, mottled, brindled, striped and splodged; elegant, fastidious creatures, with their Azmodean eyes, bearded slender muzzles and feathery tails, moving daintily through the scrub and rocks. Their stink, rank and heady, lingers long after them.

Once, jogging a bashful donkey through central Pag, I came upon a herd of them huddled in a rare patch of shade. A little beyond, a ragged shepherd boy was fluting a tune to which five women in white dresses and head-scarves performed a solemn measure. They were dancing a *kolo*: a round or chain dance so ancient that eleventh-century carvings and paintings reveal that even then some of the steps were almost identical to those trodden today. The shepherd was playing a *fuk* (pronounced 'fook'), a reed pipe rather like the Roman *fistula*. The *kolo*, to which I shall need to refer a good many times, is the national dance of Jugoslavia and has hundreds of complex variations. The word means 'a ring', 'round', 'wheel', 'circuit', etc., and as a rule the participants form a circle or a half-circle and hold on to each other. The dance is usually performed to the accompaniment of singing or music. There are basically two kinds: ritual *kolos* connected with old rites and customs and more spontaneous ones which celebrate some joyful event. Sooner or later you are almost bound to see one occurring spontaneously. Everybody knows them and learns the dances of their region from an early age. You will also see them, though less often, in Greece and Bulgaria (see p. 432 for the note on music and dance).

CHAPTER 3

The Coast III : Dalmatia

The road on from Karlobag runs along the edge of by now familiar country to Jasenica, where it makes a sharp turn back to the southwest. At this point it is worth making a detour to visit Obrovac and Novigrad. You can go all the way round the Novigrad and Karin seas (though the roads are poor) and come back to the main *autoput* from Jasenica to Zadar. Ideally the trip should be made by boat.

When the boat leaves the Velebitski Kanal it passes into a narrow channel, the Maslenica Kanal, which is bridged by the Adriatic Highway and whose steep barren sides are pocked with caverns. **Novigrad** lies on the edge of the Novigrad Sea, an ancient city of red roofs surrounded by pinewoods. The Novi Grad built in the thirteenth century stands on the hill above the town: a fairly famous castle because two Hungarian queens, Maria and Elizabeth, were imprisoned here late in the fourteenth century. Both were victims of feudal warfare and Elizabeth was executed here. The church of Sv Kata, which is worth seeing, possesses a valuable embroidered cope presented by the murdered queen.

On the far side of the sea a sinister canyon, whose sheer rock walls sometimes rise six hundred feet from the water, brings one to **Obrovac.** This gorge is one of the more impressive pieces of scenery in Jugoslavia, though the *Guide Bleu* refers to it as a mere estuary. Here, more than in most places, the full terror of the *karst* is manifest. Here man is pigmied and the most mundane forms of life assume an importance. As the steamer chugs slowly up the canyon one might be approaching an entrance of the Nordic abode of Hel.

At last Obrovac, a pretty fishing town, opens before you. It also has a thirteenth-century castle on its hill-top and near it, on the edge of the gorge, is a cemetery which is both Orthodox and Catholic. Dalmatia is, of course, primarily Catholic but there has been a certain amount of Orthodox influence.

The Karin Sea is more difficult to explore because the channel to it will not take any of the large boats, and the only alternative is to travel on the local fishing boats. As a general rule this is one of the most interesting ways of exploring the remoter parts. You can certainly hire motor-boats in Novigrad.

From where you cross the Maslenica Kanal, on a 1,000 foot span of orange Meccano, until you reach **Zadar** there is not much of interest. The hinterland of Zadar is fairly level—a kind of low *karst* with a good deal of cultivation. Zadar itself, a city of great antiquity and beauty, for centuries the most powerful city of Dalmatia, is fitted on to a small flat peninsula with a narrow neck. The people here have great character. They are exuberant and volatile and, I feel, progressive. If you can spare two days to visit Zadar it is time well spent.

It has been in various hands in the course of a long and painful history. The French, Austrians and Italians possessed it in relatively rapid succession; before them the Venetians, for a long time. The Turks reached its walls but never entered. It was in 1202 that one of its more disastrous misfortunes befell it. The city, allied to Pisa, was already at war with Venice when the Doge Dandolo alighted upon the cunning idea of diverting the Fourth Crusade to subdue it. After five days the forces of Christendom broke in, occupied and pillaged it. It was a kind of rehearsal for their iniquitous sack of Constantinople two years later.

As much of the town is closed to traffic the best thing to do is to bear right on arrival near the main gate and drive straight round the edge of the peninsula along the broad Radnička Obala (Worker's Quay). Nearly at the end you will see the Beograd Hotel—a convenient and inexpensive place which serves good food. If you arrive by ship you disembark almost opposite the Beograd. This position has the advantage of overlooking the harbour, a particularly active and interesting one. It is a smaller and more domestic port than Rijeka with its miles of clanging shipyards, its ocean-going tankers and liners. There is a continual traffic of smacks, destroyers, rowing boats, corvettes and small steamers. Dufy would have been delighted with Zadar. The warships are there because Zadar is one of the main ports for the Jugoslav navy which, though small, has a distinguished record and tradition.

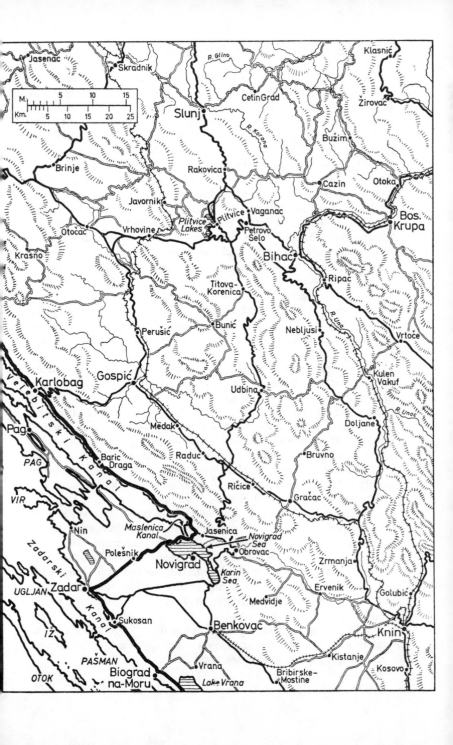

Most nights in spring and summer large numbers of capacious baskets accumulate on the quays, usually containing vegetables bound for Venice and the northern 'Riviera'. To watch the tough and vivacious peasant women loading their baskets and disputing their rights gives one an idea why their fathers, brothers and sons have been and are so formidably independent and strong.

When you come out of the Beograd you have immediately opposite some of the principal bastions of the old defences (you can see how massive they must have been) now converted into a promenade. On this side of the city you can walk a considerable portion of the ramparts. A few steps to the right bring you to the Tri BunaraTrg (Three Wells Square). The building on the western side of this is the eighteenth-century Arsenal, and the little, damaged Baroque church is known as Our Lady of Health (Naše Gospe od Zdravlja). From here the best thing to do is to take the narrow alley, Brne Krnarutica, which brings you to the rather lovely church of **Sv Franje** (St Francis), founded, according to legend, by the seraphic father himself. Whether that is true or not the church was begun in the middle of the thirteenth century and finished thirty-odd years later.

Inside there are seven opulent marble altars. Above the second altar on the right from the main entrance there is a good painting of *St Francis* by Palma the Younger. If you have a careful look at the bottom left hand corner you can discern his signature. On the third altar, right, there is another good painting, this time of *St Anthony*. On the left, in the chapel, is an excellent *Virgin* which tradition ascribes to Vittore Carpaccio who may have been a Slav from Istria.

It must be remembered that there was a constant to and fro of people between this coast and Venice for a very long time and a number of Venetian painters came here to work or had their works brought from Venice. While they were in Dalmatia they would have been helped by local craftsmen and, in turn, Dalmatian artists would have gone to Venice: like Francesco Laurana from near Vrana, a sculptor and a distinguished fifteenth-century teacher. It is thought that quite a lot of the Renaissance artists were Dalmatians who took Venetian nationality and shed their Slav names, possibly from motives of snobbery. Perhaps they thought a Slav name would stigmatise them as provincials.

Before leaving the church of St Francis don't forget to look at the sacristy and also the treasury which contains, among other things, a magnificent eleventh-century crucifix.

The area near the church was particularly badly damaged by one of the many Allied air-raids during the war and this has confused the streets. If you cast about a little you will find the Preradović Ulica which takes you past the Serbian Orthodox church, Sv Ilija (St Elijah) with its slim white bell-tower. Nearby is a high Roman column with a Corinthian capital. Until late in the last century this was used as a pillory (it still has a chain on it) and was once part of the Roman Forum the remains of which, with many of its original paving stones, now open before you. Even in its present disorganised state you can see how splendid it must have been. In fact it was a hundred yards long by fifty wide. Much of the area has been wrecked by bombs and the authorities have seen fit to call it euphemistically Trg Zeleni (Green Square).

On its north-western side, high, narrow, yet massive, is one of the most remarkable churches on the coast, or indeed anywhere. It is **St Donat's,** probably named after the man known as Donatus of Fiesole who died round about A.D. 876. He was an Irishman who is supposed to have arrived in Fiesole just as the bishop died and just in time to fill the see. I have been unable to discover any direct connection between Zadar and St Donat.

Externally the church looks strange because it is circular and has three semicircular apses masked with blind arches in which there are a few tiny windows. It looks more like a castle. Inside it is even more like a dungeon keep. Its two concentric naves are separated by pillars and two spiral staircases lead to a high gallery. As one stands in this twilit, monumental cylinder of stone one is reminded, more than anything, of Piranesi's prisons.

Much of the material came from the ruins of the Forum, as you can see on closer examination—especially round the base on the outside. Extraordinarily enough it has no foundations except the paving stones of the Forum itself and yet it was so strongly built that it managed to survive bombs falling within a few feet of it.

It was put up as long ago as early in the ninth century (we find it mentioned by the Byzantine emperor Constantine Porphyrogenitus in 849) but it is no longer used as a church. Until recently it was a museum and outside it a big statue of Augustus (it was he who gave Zadar the status of a Roman colony) gazed seawards. Before it was a museum it was divided into two stories by a wooden floor and used as a shop. During the struggles against the Turks it served as an arsenal. For the time being it is empty—a rugged tribute to faith, providence and solid workmanship.

Next to it is the **Archbishop's Palace** and behind this (you get there by retracing your steps past the pillory column and turning right up Ulica J. Sundetića) is the **Cathedral of Sv Stošija** (St Anastasia) the biggest church in the whole of Dalmátia and in many ways the most beautiful.

St Anastasia was a Slav who was martyred at Sremska Mitrovica (then Sirmium) near Belgrade early in the fourth century. She may have been a victim of Diocletian's persecutions. Very little is known about her but she is the patroness of weavers and the patron saint of Zadar. Her relics are alleged to lie in the church of Sant' Anastasia in Rome.

Her cathedral was erected in the thirteenth century on the foundations of an ancient basilica and is an almost perfect example of pure Romanesque architecture. The only Gothic influences are the rosettes at the west end and the tympanum above the portal. The west end is superb. The five receding Roman arches of the main door, flanked by two statues of apostles, culminate in the lunette with a bas-relief of the Virgin in the middle; the inscription records the date, 1324, and the name of the archbishop—Butovan.

The triple-naved interior divided by pilasters and columns is—there is no other word for it—majestic. Over the lesser naves you will notice hexaforia and triforia with single windows above these. The proportions are faultless: solidity is balanced by grace, strength by delicacy. An aquarial light dims and softens the bare, austere stone.

Just up on the right hand side a door leads to the remains of the baptistery, first built in the eighth century and destroyed in the last war. The plaque to the left of the door commemorates a visit by Pope Alexander III in 1177 when, it is said, the populace of Zadar gave him a rousing welcome with Slav songs. The fact that Alexander's pontificate of twenty-two years was one of the longest and most distinguished in the history of the papacy and that he was also a doughty opponent of Frederick Barbarossa probably explains this reception.

In the sanctuary there is a noble high altar set on a ninth-century wooden pedestal. Above, rises the ciborium, four centuries younger. It is not quite so flawless as that of Sv Marija in Rab, but nevertheless it is very beautiful. The choir stalls are reckoned to be among the best in the country and the two thrones, for prince and archbishop, make an ideal complement to them. In the apse hung—and perhaps will again when they have been once more restored—six paintings of a polyptych by V. Carpaccio. The work consists of six panels painted *c.* 1495–1500 representing *St Martin and the Beggar*; *St Simeon*; *St Jerome* with the kneeling donor of the high altar, Martin Mladošić; *St Peter*; *St Paul*; and *St Anastasia*. None of them shows Carpaccio at his best, but of these the pick, to my mind, are *St Anastasia* and *St Martin and the Beggar*.

The very high Romanesque campanile just down the street was begun in 1452, but not finished, oddly enough, until 1892. Then it was the work of Sir Thomas Jackson—he who wrote a classic work on the architecture of this coast. You can see easily enough that he modelled the completion on the cathedral bell-tower of Rab.

If you turn left just beyond this campanile you come to Vladimir Gortan Trg and the second most beautiful church of the city— **Sv Krševan** (St Christopher), another specimen of pure Romanesque, a basilica built on the site of a sixth-century church. The façade is rather like that of the cathedral and the best external features are the three apses and the exposed south-eastern wall along Ljubljana Street. There are some interesting fragments of frescoes on the inside of the apses, but the main thing to see, apart from the three naves themselves, with their pillars topped by Corinthian capitals, is the marble high altar decorated by four statues of the patrons of the town: Saints Chrysogonus, Simeon, Zoile and Anastasia. The bones of the first (he was executed by order of Diocletian) lie under the altar.

When you come out of the church turn right and half a minute's walk brings you to a small square. Here is a brand-new museum (at the time of writing not open to the public) which is going to contain the main archaeological relics formerly housed in St Donat's. It is a good collection covering all the main periods. In the city walls here there is the big Morska Vrata (Sea Gate) on the inner side of which a plaque records the reception given to Zadar's fleet after it returned victorious from the battle of Lepanto—when the Sultan's navy was soundly thrashed.

Not far along Ljubljana Street there is a fine Renaissance Palace, the Fanfogna, and almost opposite, on the cross-roads, are two tiny little churches end on to each other: St Marcel and St Peter. The latter is the more interesting—a ninth-century church with two naves, the only example in the country and very rare anywhere. Getting the key for these churches is always a problem and the best thing to do is to agitate at the Tourist office.

If you continue down Ljubljana Street and at the next main

intersection turn left a few paces bring you to the ruins of the old hospital behind which is an amiable market. The other ruin you see nearby is part of a fourteenth-century façade which belonged to the church of Our Lady.

If you retrace your steps, turn left and then take the first main turning on your right you come into Narodni Trg—the main lung of the city, the original medieval 'Platea Magna' and the focus of a very lively **korso.** This is an interesting and ancient custom.

In many parts of the Mediterranean basin townspeople are in the habit of coming out in the evening for a stroll and to take the air. In the Balkans in general and in Jugoslavia in particular this habit is a deeply rooted institution and unlike anywhere else. It is something more than a casual stroll; it is more like a parade or procession with observable patterns of movement and development and even, on occasion, unwritten rules. There is no signal for it to begin or end. It starts about sundown, develops, goes on for anything up to two or two and a half hours and then disperses. Sometimes it begins and ends quite suddenly; and there is often an approximate general agreement about the two spatial points between which it occurs. The girls put on their finery, the young men spruce themselves up and children of all ages are brought out. Practically the whole village or town appears to be involved in it at some stage. The elderly and infirm tend to watch it from their windows and doors or at café tables. It is an extremely sociable and healthy event which gives everyone an opportunity of meeting and generally airs human relationships. Often the main street of a town is sealed to traffic for three or four hours and, even if it is not, you should certainly avoid trying to drive through a *korso*. It can be as dense as a soccer crowd, though incomparably better mannered.

In any case Jugoslavs are still not accustomed to the idea of motorised traffic. The pace of the bullock cart, the horse and the donkey has prevailed for centuries, for ever, as it were, and relatively few pedestrians or cyclists have a well developed road sense. Many motorists are also unreliable. When driving, therefore, one just has to be patient and tolerant and *very* careful—even in big towns like Ljubljana, Zagreb and Belgrade. When on foot oneself one can appreciate the advantages of so few engines, one can actually enjoy one's surroundings without being continually alert to the chance of sudden death or injury.

As there is no traffic in the centre of Zadar the *korso* has full sway and the **Narodni Trg,** now an impressive Baroque piazza, is packed.

Just off it is the Café Central, hub of social life. I recommend this if you feel like a cup of *Turska kafa* (Turkish coffee) or a bottle of beer (*pivo*).

Supposing you visit the Trg in the off-peak period, so to speak, you will find on the left a delightful little municipal Loggia where the principal public business used to be carried out and in front of which the notaries and other officials sat at their tables. Opposite is the Gradska Straža which now houses a small Ethnographical Museum. Its ground floor is devoted to some examples of costume from neighbouring villages in the Ravni Kotari (i.e. the immediate inland surroundings of Zadar). Upstairs there are pots, a potter's wheel, jars and a big loom, plus some women's costumes from nearby islands like Pag and Ugljan. Just next to it on the right are the remains of a small eleventh-century church—Sv Lovro (St Laurence).

From this piazza the best thing to do is to go down Omladinska Ulica which debouches into Zoranićeva Poljana where stands the third most interesting church of the city: **Sv Simun**. It used to be called Sv Stefan but was renamed in 1631 when St Simon's relics were shifted from the church of Our Lady. Inside and out it has been a good deal altered and restored and the façade you now see is what they call 'rustic Baroque' built round about 1705. The main things to look for inside are, firstly, a really splendid bas-relief in marble of the Nativity, just by the third altar on the right. This is a twelfth-century work and seems to have been rather neglected by the historians and critics. Secondly, there is the silver coffin reliquary above the high altar which contains the patron saint's bones. This work was done at the command of the Hungarian queen Elizabeth (the one who was executed in Novigrad) by a Milanese craftsman with the help of local silversmiths. You can get permission for the lid to be lifted (there is usually a nun about in the sacristy) and there see through a crystal glass the remains of the saint's body. It is covered in a pearl-embroidered pall donated by a Serbian ruler to whom I shall need to refer later: one George Branković, Despot of Smederevo (see p. 290). The bronze angels who hold up the coffin were cast from Turkish cannon. Behind the church are the ruins of another beautiful palace, the Grisogono-Vovo.

At this land end of the town there is quite a cluster of antiquities round the Trg Oslobodenja (Liberation Square) which is right next to the Poljana. The big block on the right as you go into it houses municipal libraries and so on and near it is the Tourist Office.

Immediately in front of you, you have another Roman column supposed to have come from the Forum, and just behind that, against a wall, in a ditch, all that is left of a triumphal arch which was almost certainly built in the time of Trajan. If you cross this very agreeable square and go up the steps the other side you enter what is known as the **Terrace of the Five Wells**, and indeed there are five lovely well-heads in it. These were built over a large reservoir in about 1574 and also over what was formerly part of the defensive moat. The big tower on the right is called the Babja Kula, supposedly after a French knight named Beuve d'Antoine captured while fighting in these parts.

A narrow street (Medulićeva) leads from Liberation Square down to the land gate. On the way down do not miss the great Captain's Palace on the right hand side which has a fine courtyard. Part of the palace contains a small art gallery and a natural history museum. On turning left at the end of this street you at once see the huge **Land Gate** built in 1543 by that remarkable military engineer M. Sammicheli. Until a century ago there was a drawbridge across part of the old moat. All that survives of this fosse is a tiny and delightful harbour just south of the gate. The building used to be a custom house and is now a fish restaurant. Beyond stretch gardens and the more modern parts of Zadar which extend some way inland and include a suburb containing an Albanian minority—eighteenth-century refugees from near Lake Skadar. They still speak Albanian and are one of many odd, exiled minorities to be found in the Balkans.

A long straight street, typically Roman, runs from the Land Gate down the peninsula and in it are a number of objects you may be curious about. Almost immediately on the left are some striking ruins of the gutted priory and church of St Dominic, opposite which stands the Gothic Nassis Palace with a lovely portal and windows: rather like those you have seen at Rab and Krk. A little farther on, at the corner of Krstulović Street, is the church of **St Michael,** originally Gothic. The most interesting things inside are the font and a big crucifix. The last port of call before getting back to the Trg Zeleni is St Mary's church and convent. A great many alterations were done to it after its foundation in the twelfth century; then it was very severely damaged by the 1944 air raids. Much restoration remains to be done and it is impossible to say what the final result will be like. If you can't get into it you can at least enjoy its Romanesque campanile, built in 1105 and quite the oldest in

Dalmatia. An inscription round it reveals that it was a gift to Zadar from the Croat-Hungarian king Koloman.

On the seaward side of the town the broad Obala Maršala Tita runs almost the length of the peninsula and from it one gets an excellent view down the Zadarski Kanal to the islands. Near the land end is the Hotel Zagreb where you can eat well. The fish and the local wines are good and, of course, Zadar is the place for Maraschino (Marask)—if you like it. It is a very sweet liqueur distilled from cherries. Behind the Zagreb is an unspoilt part of the old town, mostly dingy alleys and poky shops, full of surprises. I say 'unspoilt' because Zadar is still being rebuilt. I do not think it is always being done with much judgment or taste: many of the new blocks, in the most modern and tedious idiom, are going to look very incongruous. On the other hand it is not easy to see what else could have been done. There would be little point in reconstruction of original buildings and it would have been wasteful to leave the damaged areas merely as gardens and open spaces.

Eighteen kilometres west is **Nin.** The road runs through flat and rather desolate country whose skyline is measured off at quite regular intervals by campaniles. This area, like most of the hinterland of Zadar, is also known as the **Ravni Kotari** (The Level Districts) and is reminiscent of the Roman *campagna*.

Nin is a lonely fishing village at the edge of the plain very near the southernmost tip of Pag. At one time it was an island. Though the water and marshes round it have now been drained so that it is part of the mainland you still enter, from either side, over a bridge. A considerable portion of the medieval walls survives; much more would have remained had not the Venetians razed them to prevent the Turks having a ready-made stronghold. But for their prudence we should probably have inherited something approaching the splendour of Aigues Mortes at the end of the Camargue. Indeed, their situations are similar. When Jackson visited Nin nearly a century ago he was deeply impressed by its solitude. 'A more desolate and deplorable looking place,' he wrote, 'never represented the fallen greatness of an ancient Roman city.'

As he and his companions entered ravens croaked over their heads. Appropriate birds of doom! I cannot say I have ever heard or seen ravens there, but the gull's dirge makes a very fit ing threnody instead. The main gate, immediately the other side of a very old bridge which seems to be sinking into the water, is still impressive (don't miss the little carvings on it, which include a melon and a gourd) and gives on to the main street. If you pursue this you arrive at a large Baroque house, now the Archaeological Museum and worth a short visit. The peasant woman in charge will take you to see **Sv Kriz** (Church of the Holy Cross), the smallest and oldest intact church in Jugoslavia. Battered and dingy, a cruciform church with a tiny cupola, it sits in a little garden at the end of a stony lane. There is nothing inside it but an inscription over the doorway reveals that it was built between 780 and 800 by the *Župan* Godislav. It is difficult to find an exact modern equivalent in English for the title *Župan*. The original *Župans* were tribal leaders. Now the word *župa* means 'a parish' and a parish priest is a *župnik*. Under Turkish rule in, for instance, Serbia, a *Župan* was an official elected by the people (but nominated by the Pasha) who was responsible to the *Kadi* or governor of the district.

Between the ninth and the fourteenth centuries Nin was one of the capitals of the Croatian kings, for, as in Serbia and elsewhere, kings changed their capital regularly in those days. Several of the kings are known by name, for instance Višeslav, Petar Krešimir and Zvonimir. At Nin the oldest known Croatian legal statutes were drawn up (in Glagolitic) in 1103.

Very near the church are the ruins of some palaces. If you turn left just beyond Sv Kriz you get to the fine eastern gate; if right, you reach the centre of the village where it is worth having a look at the church of St Anselm which also has an interesting treasury. The parish priest will very willingly show you everything.

Wherever you go in Nin you will find Roman and early Christian ruins mingled with the gardens and fishermen's houses. Chickens peck across remnants of the old Forum, pigs rout amidst the stumps of the Temple of Diana. Near St Anselm's lies a big Corinthian capital, fortuitously but aptly sited in the middle of a small *trg*. One day I saw a boy standing on it and pretending to be the statue of a Roman emperor.

Nin was once called Aenona, an important town of Roman Liburnia. In the third century B.C. the whole coast from the Kvarner Gulf to the mouth of the River Krka (at Šibenik) was occupied by the Liburni. The Romans, who distrusted sea transport for so long, made full use of the seafaring skill of this tribe and the Liburnian war galley—the *liburnica*—played a large part in naval battles. They are, for instance, believed to have been largely responsible for Mark Antony's defeat at Actium in 31.

There is one citizen of Nin who merits especial mention—that is Grgur Ninski (a huge statue of him by Meštrović stands outside the Golden Gate at Split) who flourished in the tenth century. He has become almost a legendary character for it was he more than anyone who fought for the independence of the Croatian liturgy and the Glagolitic, and in many ways for the independence of Croatia.

A mile away on the Zadar road, a short distance across a vineyard, a cluster of pines gauntly shelters a tiny grey church sitting on a hummock. The hummock was a burial mound and the church of **Sv Nikola**, which is of a very strange design (triple-apsed with a crenellated tower above it), is eleventh century. It is, in fact, a minute fortress, for the circular tower was built in the Turkish wars. Jackson, meticulous as ever, measured the church's nave and found it was a mere 4½ feet long.

From this tump Nin is still visible, a fit subject for elegy. A strange melancholy haunts it. The remote site, the derelict fortifications, the isolated relics of a still ruining splendour in a vast panorama of stone, water and sky. . . . All this evokes a powerful feeling of loss and sadness. Far beyond, the grey lines of the Velebit mountains fade into nothing.

Most of the islands near Zadar (which form the northern Dalmatian archipelago) are fairly small and are not much frequented by tourists. One might spend many enjoyable weeks pottering round them—bathing, fishing and just enjoying being alive. But few will have the time for this sort of dalliance. If you have, the best bets are **Ugljan** and **Pašman** which are quite large, and, farther out, the Kornat group which have strange names like Iž, Žut and Ist. The remains of a good many Roman farms and villas have been found hereabouts, many of them below sea level because the Dalmatian coast has been sinking over the last two thousand years.

The coast road from Zadar goes due south-east and by-passes **Biograd-na-Moru** (*na moru* means 'on sea') once the most famous town on this part of the coast, largely because the Pašman Kanal, which runs between the mainland and the islands of Ugljan and Pašman, was a much used channel—sheltered and fairly easily navigable. There is not a great deal to see at Biograd now but it is a popular resort. Like Nin in the Middle Ages it was a bishopric and a royal town and in the eleventh century was both prosperous and powerful. Then, in 1126, the Venetians sacked it, as the

Turks were to do much later in the sixteenth and seventeenth centuries. The Venetian sack took place on Good Friday and a special Mass is still said every year to commemorate that sad event. There is a legend that on this day a black knight comes out of the sea, as he was reputed to have done in 1126 to save the last Croatian queen in Biograd.

In Biograd, as at Pakoštane a little way down the road, there is a monument to those who died in the National Liberation War. So far I have funked dealing with this matter of funereal masonry and sculpture. If you have come this far you will already have seen many examples, and indeed there are a perfectly astonishing number of memorials, statues, monoliths, busts and obelisks scattered over the whole country. The majority of them commemorate deeds of heroism, particular heroes, executions, unknown soldiers and collective feats of bravery during two world wars, more especially the Second. They vary from one to a hundred feet in height. Nearly every town, and most villages, has at least one.

For a deeper insight into the country one needs to remember that during the last war Jugoslavia lost one in ten of its population, or 1,700,000 killed: that is, nearly double the total casualties for the whole of the United Kingdom and Commonwealth. At any given moment there were *at least* three separate wars going on in Jugoslavia in addition to the principal one against the Axis powers. The Croatians were fighting the Serbs, the Communist forces were fighting the Royalists and the Fascist supporters were fighting all those against them. There were any number of side skirmishes, feuds and wars within wars—not to mention plain murder. By comparison most other campaigns and civil wars have been chivalrous and relatively cheap in blood. In short, it was a typical Balkan situation. Next to Poland Jugoslavia suffered more than any other country. At the end of the war it was in a state of chaos and ruin which probably exceeded even that in Poland.

Some of the worst atrocities in the history of mankind were perpetrated in Jugoslavia by the Germans and Italians. The reprisals and revenges on the part of the Jugoslavians were of unparalleled savagery. In fact, the full tale of butchery and bloodshed between 1941 and 1945 scarcely bears reading. It was the kind of thing that had been going on here on a much lesser scale for centuries, a catalogue of massacres, assassinations, vendettas, rebellions and murders.

It was right that countless acts of bravery, loyalty and love with which human beings ennobled these wretched events should be commemorated in a solid and enduring way. But it is equally true that zeal is no substitute for skill, size no substitute for judgment and the most estimable motives are seldom accompanied by an equal capacity for realising them successfully.

From the artistic and aesthetic point of view eighty per cent of the memorials in Jugoslavia are hardly worth looking at. After one has seen one's tenth or twentieth outsize grenade-thrower or rifleman rampant or Partisan belligerent, or one's thirtieth group of titanic men and muscle-bound women arrested by bronze in undying postures of defiance and aggression, one's perceptions have been more or less bludgeoned into indifference, at best into polite agreement.

Of course, 'Socialist' art of this kind is a form of propaganda and it makes the naïve mistake of supposing that abstract and spiritual qualities like devotion and self-sacrifice can be expressed by Promethean manifestations of physical strength and violence. Only the Michelangelos of this world can deal with the souls of giants, with bulk as well as intensity. Nevertheless I am glad that all these memorials exist. Some are excellent and to those I shall call attention.

A more interesting place than either Biograd or Pakoštane is **Vrana** at the northern end of Lake Vrana. This village, which can be reached easily from either of the other two towns, was also part of the early Croatian kingdom. There was a huge fortress here which Fortis described as 'a frightful heap of ruins'. You can still see the remains as well as those of what was once the biggest *han* in Europe (see p. 200). Fortis gives us an idea of what it was like though even in his time it was in a deplorable state having been abandoned, as he put it, 'to the barbarity of the Morlacchi, who inhabit the neighbouring lands, and carry off whatever materials suit them, to be employed in their wretched cottages.' It was about sixty yards long and sixty deep 'all built of marble, well polished and connected; and the pieces seem to have been brought thither, from the ruins of some ancient Roman fabrick.' The body of the *han* was divided into two courts with the usual galleries and one can still get an idea of what an imposing building it was.

The whole area, which is low and marshy and was once malarial, has a certain sombre beauty. Wandering through the overgrown scattered ruins one has the feeling that at any moment one may stumble upon some rich neglected treasure. I was poking round

57

there one day when I saw a man who was completely black. He addressed me in fluent Serbian and I thought at first he must be a descendant of one of the Negro families that survive in the far south of Montenegro. He turned out to be called Billy Abukawa from Nyasaland and he was reading economics at Zagreb University.

From Biograd to Šibenik is a very short run through low *karst* which is fairly fertile. The fig, the olive and the grape all grow well here. Sometimes you might almost think you are in the south of France, an illusion sharpened on occasions when you see men playing a game which looks very like *boule* and which is here called *boce*, a popular pastime on the coast. (If you are driving remember to allow for getting on and off the ferry to Šibenik.)

CHAPTER 4

The Coast IV: Dalmatia (continued)

Šibenik—Krka Falls—Knin—Vrlika—Drniš—Zlarin

'Kornat's archipelago is closing Šibenik's arkipelago from the west part. Several hundred of inlets are spread and stuck out to the open blue sea forming innumerable channels, bays and droves of rare beautys, especially the inlets posted in front to the open sea, with their rocky cliffs and deep abrasions which are very picturesque . . . and they are only overgrown with aromatic plants usually found in the Mediterranean vegetation. . . . The Bay of Slanica on Murter Island is covered by the finest kind of crystallised sand which is spread out far to the sea and makes bathers enjoy different water games. The beach is enclosed by stony slopes and near by there is a pension dotted with sixty beds, comfortably furnished. . . . In a row unique natural and artistic beauties of the Dalmatian coast, the town Šibenik and its lovely surroundings are occupying a peculiarly interesting place, when considered from touristical point of view. On its district the renown beautys of the Dalmatian coast are further enriched by the most indented coastline with exuberant stony landscapes. . . . The river Krka has enforced its flow through a very picturesque canyon, and from its source to the mouth disposes of winderful waterfalls of rare attractions for the tourists. The canyon is deeply protracted to inland . . . where at the source of Krka is nested a very picturesque town Knin, of great historical value, encircled by a rankness vegetation. . . .'

In its bizarre way this extract from local tourist literature does convey some idea of the region. I cannot answer for the 'droves of rare beautys' or for the 'different water games' but deep abrasions and stony landscapes there are. And the river Krka exists. In its estuary, in an enclosed harbour virtually impregnable from the sea, lies the most interesting town of **Šibenik**. The harbour and the

59

sea are joined by a long, extremely narrow, twisting strait which is very easily defended and which still has a formidable system of fortifications, gun emplacements and arsenals.

Over the centuries, and especially in the last war, Šibenik has had more than its share of hostilities, but the town, like its inhabitants, has survived surprisingly well. It is much better preserved than Zadar and the Šibenčani, who had a distinguished record against the Fascists, are a particularly volatile and energetic people—though not, I think, so pleasant as many Dalmatians. I get the feeling that they have a fairly high opinion of themselves.

Whether you arrive by car or boat you will be very near the two hotels on the quay: the Jadran and the Krka. The Jadran seems to me rather pretentious. The Krka is much livelier and more interesting, as well as being less expensive. Also, the food is usually better there. Immediately outside it is one of the focal points of the *korso*; a very animated one.

The Krka makes a convenient starting point for a tour of the town. On coming out of it turn sharp right to the main square: Poljana Maršala Tita. Cut across the gardens on the left and there you will find the church and monastery of **Sv Franje**. The church has a magnificent seventeenth-century wooden ceiling and a very pleasing organ loft supported on columns with painted capitals.

A narrow winding street with a long name (Narodnog Heroja Pavla Pape Silje) leads from here into the centre of the town, which was nearly unscathed. *En route* you pass the Tourist Office— one of the worst on the coast. As you go down this narrow gorge the *case signorile* of a defunct aristocracy rise on each side of you. Quite soon you come to a small piazza with some wellheads in the form of capitals. If you take the Široka Ulica (*širok* means 'broad' but it is very narrow) you pass the Tobolović Palace. A little farther on the left is **Sv Barbara**, a doll's house mid-fifteenth-century church with some small witty statues on the main façade. Shortly beyond is the old town square. On your right is the **Loggia**, designed by Sammicheli's pupils between 1532 and 1542, which was destroyed in the war and rebuilt exactly as before. On the left rises the **Cathedral**, Sv Jakov or St James's—a masterpiece.

Among all the churches on the coast I feel that Sv Jakov is probably the finest, just beating Sv Stošija's at Zadar and Sv Lovro's at Trogir into first place. The cathedral at Rab is also perfect in its way. Sv Jakov is not perfect but it is fascinating.

It was begun in 1431 by a team of Venetian and Dalmatian

masons but after ten years' work the city council was not satisfied
and decided to employ Juraj Dalmatinac (or George the Dalmatian).
He was also known as Orsini and, in recognition of his work in
this city, as Juraj Šibenčanin.

He laboured on the cathedral until he died in 1473. Then the
man known as Nicholas the Florentine took over and worked on
it until his death in 1505. There were two other important men:
Andrija Aleši of Drač (Durazzo) and Ivan Pribislavić, a Šibenik
man; not to mention, of course, an army of skilled and anonymous
craftsmen. When Nicholas the Florentine died another thirty-one
years were yet to pass before the cathedral was regarded as complete:
one hundred and five years in all. To achieve it the townspeople
emptied their coffers and their purses.

When George the Dalmatian took over he changed the ground
plan and added a transept. He also raised the level of the sanctuary
and built the foundations for the superstructure. He added the

61

sacristy, and designed the baptistery, though some maintain that this was the work of Nicholas of Florence and Andrija Aleši. It is certain that Nicholas of Florence was responsible for the west front and many of the decorations.

When we look at the cathedral from the outside the most remarkable feature is the barrel roof, so made that the top blocks of the west façade are part of the main structure of the roof. Sir Thomas Jackson aptly called it 'the wagon roof'. It is made from huge blocks of mortised stone, as one can easily see whether inside or out, and it is said that no brick, tile or piece of wood has been used anywhere in the construction of the building.

The west front has a Gothic porch (the carvings represent the mission of the twelve Apostles over the globe) with a very large Gothic window above it. The decorations round it are of a later style.

In the north wall, facing on to the piazza (the statue in the corner of the piazza, incidentally, is of Juraj Dalmatinac by Meštrović: by no means one of the master's best works) is a much more interesting doorway which is reminiscent of Radovan's west door in the cathedral at Trogir. It is flanked by two affable lions, above whom stand Adam and Eve on their way out of Paradise. Over them stand the apostles Peter and Paul in their tabernacles: particularly admirable work of Juraj himself. It is worth looking closely at the decorated columns of this doorway which contain exquisite carving of flowers, leaves and birds, and heads on miniature medallions.

The interior consists of three lordly naves whose arches support a frieze and clerestory. All the altars, unfortunately, are seventeenth- and eighteenth-century Baroque. They do not blend with the main design, but they are not too obtrusive. On the right hand side, above the altar nearest to the baptistery, there is a good painting of *SS Sebastien and Fabian*—ascribed to the school of Titian. Over the altar on the gospel side immediately opposite this is a very fine crucifix: a haunting and powerful work. And below it, on the altar, a small fourteenth-century pietà, very moving in its simplicity and grace. All over Europe there are little anonymous masterpieces of this kind which detain you in a state of delighted surprise. If you search further here you will also discover two cherub's heads on a pillar. One faces the light, the other the shadows; one is gay, the other sad: comic and tragic masks. They are beautifully done.

The whole of the sanctuary area is rich in work by Nicholas the

Florentine. At the eastern end of the right nave steps lead down the **Baptistery**—also the work of George—and this compares favourably with the best art of the Italian Renaissance. There is an astonishing amount of intricate detail carved from the solid grey stone of Dalmatia, yet all is as light and airy as a *soufflé*. The leaves, the flowers, the cherubim, the rosette in the roof, the font supported by three cherubs . . . here all is young, exuberantly gay, and perfectly appropriate to the purpose of the chamber. After looking around for a few minutes I am sure you will find yourself smiling. But there is something better yet.

A door out of the baptistery takes you into a narrow alley which leads under the palace to the harbour. Turn left to go round the apses and there you will find a frieze of no fewer than seventy-four carved heads: sculpture of a high order and very probably the work of George the Dalmatian. There is a legend that they represent citizens who refused to contribute to the cost of the cathedral. I find it a convincing idea. It would have been a civilised and witty rebuke in keeping with the medieval tradition that all adornments on churches are by implication to the honour and glory of God.

They are the equivalent in stone of the portraits in the Prologue to *The Canterbury Tales*, a *comédie humaine*. Many of the characters are there; or uncommonly similar ones: cook, friar and summoner; knight, nun and clerk; there are Turks and Venetians, Italians, Greeks and Slavs, slaves, warriors and *condottieri*. They grin, frown and grimace, sneer, gape and stare. Some are in pain, others in tranquillity. Satirical many of the portraits certainly are, the product of shrewd insight, wit and an unerring hand; and (this is what sets them apart from most portraiture), they are the invention of a subtle and compassionate good humour. When passing through Šibenik I always find a few minutes to go and have another look at them. Near them, on an external pillar of the left apse, supported by two especially chubby *putti*, is George the Dalmatian's inscription: *Hoc opus curarum fecit magister Georgius Matthei Dalmaticus*.

After the cathedral the rest of Šibenik may seem a little ordinary, but the bishop's palace and the ducal palace next to Sv Jakov are handsome buildings, and the whole of the old town is full of beauties —a little less obvious, perhaps, than those of Rab, Dubrovnik or Trogir, but after one has sauntered the streets for a few hours there is no doubt that one has received much pleasure.

If you retrace your steps to the piazza with the well-heads and take the Ivana Trubić Lavić Ulica this will bring you to the church of Sv Ivan which has a graceful outside staircase and a bas-relief over the side door. If you then take the narrow alley out of the far left hand corner of the square and then the first on the left you will see high up in the wall another miniature pietà: an excellent piece of work. But Šibenik is full of modest details like this. Just beyond is the church of Sv Mihajlo whose icon is reputed to be miraculous.

There are ten other churches in Šibenik, tucked away in the labyrinth of steep, stepped alleys and streets. Some are closed and threatening to become derelict but most hum with a restless fervour propagated largely by numbers of devout and spirited women. Yet nowhere are the women of Šibenik more animated than in the main market. And especially in the fish market.

High above the centre of the town is a complex of powerful fortifications which consist of three different castles built during the fifteenth and sixteenth centuries. It is worth clambering up these battlements to survey the city and harbour.

Nearly everyone who goes to Šibenik makes an excursion to the **Krka Falls.** I think them a *little* overrated, yet they are well worth seeing once and the trip can be planned to include other places.

You take the main road signposted to Gulin and Drniš straight up the hill from Poljana Maršala Tita (the market is on the left of this road under the trees) and at Gulin, about eleven kilometres out, you turn left and hairpin down through a *karst* that is suddenly wooded to the Krka valley or canyon which runs a long way inland to the source of the river above Knin.

The contrast here between the cruelly harsh grey rock and the almost livid greenness of moss, foliage and undergrowth and the intense ultramarine and emerald of the water is most startling.

Everything is provided at the falls: restaurant, parking place, viewing points. If you clamber about a bit you can find some excellent sites from which to photograph the falls as they spread, spill and drop from level to level seventeen times through thick barrages of trees and little islands. As the brochure so felicitously puts it: it is a 'marvellous site of sublime nature power.'

Not far upstream are some antique water mills where flour is still ground. In this area also (and possibly elsewhere) the locals use a utensil called a *peka* which looks like a small, iron dustbin lid. When dough for bread is laid on embers for baking the *peka* is lowered on top of it. This is very probably the same utensil the Greeks used

SPLIT. *Above*, the southern wall of Diocletian's palace. On the second storey the columns of the original portico are clear. *Far left*, the opening to the south or Bronze Gate which gave immediately on to the sea where the *molo* now is. *Centre*, the top of the mausoleum, now the cathedral. *Background*, the Mosor ridge. *Below*, the peristyle, looking south, as it was in 305. Entrance to the cathedral at left. The arches on the right were filled in in medieval times. The central archway in the background led to the atrium and the imperial apartments

FORTIFIED COASTAL TOWNS. *Above* Dubrovnik: the old port of Ploče (from the south-east). *Below* Korčula from the north-west. The central campanile is of St. Mark's

two and a half thousand years ago—the *pnigeus*, referred to by Aristophanes in *The Clouds*.

If you have got as far as this you may as well go to Skradin and Kistanje and make a round trip through Knin, Vrlika and Drniš. The first two are particularly interesting.

There is not much to see nowadays at **Skradin** though once it was a prosperous inland port and the main market for cattle and wine on this part of the coast. From Kistanje a bad minor road goes down into the Krka valley again to the monastery of the Sv Arhangel: an interesting stop. The main road from Kistanje to Knin runs through the village of Ivoševci near which are the remains of Burnum—the H.Q. of the XI Legion in the first century. A little farther on, near Rudel, you will probably notice two lonely Roman arches known locally as the 'hollow church', and near these are some more falls every bit as impressive as those lower down but seldom publicised.

After another stretch of rocky plateau the road winds down to **Knin,** an ancient medieval town which, as one might expect from its strategic position, has been fought over many times, the last occasion being 4th December 1944 when the Partisans won a great victory.

For a thousand years before this its fortunes had fluctuated. By the middle of the tenth century it was a strongly fortified town belonging to Croatian feudal lords—*Bans* as they were called. The Hungarians possessed it for a time, then the Bosnian kings. It was, of course, captured by the Turks, then by the Venetians, the French and the Austrians—a familiar tale. Amazingly enough most of the enormous fortress on the bluff has survived, a fortress for which, as Jackson observed in an eloquent account of his visit, whole armies had fought and bled, and which, when he went, was guarded by a single soldier. The other place of special interest is the Franciscan Monastery, now an archaeological museum with a good little collection of objects from local excavations. If you can contrive to be in Knin on market day (Tuesday) you may well see some costumes.

East of Knin a poorish road runs along the Cetina valley to Vrlika, a twelfth-century town and once the headquarters of a famous nobleman, Hrvoje Vukčić (see p. 349). You can still see quite a lot of costumes in the Vrlika area which are heavily orna- mented with metal necklaces, belts and pins and strings of coins (*djerdani*).

Near Vrlika is the triple source of the Cetina, the ruins of a Serbian Orthodox monastery (Dragović) destroyed in the last war and the ruins of the church of Sv Spas (the Holy Saviour) in whose graveyard lie a number of Bogomil tombstones—about which I shall have a good deal to say later on (see p. 341).

The road south (a poor one) runs to the village of Kosovo and the Dalmatian Kosovo Polje: not to be confused with its famous namesake in Serbia. Near this is a place called Biskupija, one of the richest archaeological sites in Croatia. There are the remnants of several churches, graveyards from the eighth century, Bogomil tombs and so on. Many of the finds are lodged in Knin.

Thirteen kilometres beyond you reach **Drniš,** a small town between the *karst* and the fertile valley of the river Čikola. There are some Turkish remains here, some houses, a bastion, what was a mosque now converted into a church and the only surviving minaret in Dalmatia.

Several well-known Jugoslav writers were born in this area (though nobody has ever heard of them outside their country) and one famous sculptor of whom everybody has heard—Meštrović. The Božidar Adžija house in Drniš has a collection of his works presented by the artist when he visited his home town from America in 1960. The Dom Kulture in Meštrović Square bears one of his bas-reliefs—*The Ploughers;* and in the public gardens there is another work called *The Source of Life.*

Meštrović came from near a little village seven kilometres from Drniš named Otavice. Above it he built his family mausoleum where he had himself buried at a great age in 1962. He was generally regarded as Jugoslavia's greatest sculptor and he certainly has an international reputation. He was a very prolific artist whose chief influences were probably Rodin and Bourdelle (he studied in Vienna and Paris) and his works are scattered all over Jugoslavia and elsewhere.

I find that he overdoes it in much of his work and he gives me the uneasy feeling that he is striving to be a kind of Slav Michelangelo but without that amazing man's sense of proportion, of controlled power and the elusive magic of being able to convey spiritual qualities.

Meštrović often stuns by sheer volume and, though he undoubtedly attempts to ennoble and dignify man, somewhere in the long and arduous process of creation precisely that ennobling quality evades him. His art is not always equal to the magnitude of his conception.

66

When he works on a lesser scale he is often more successful. He is not much regarded in western Europe now but he was a force to be reckoned with and surely will be again.

From Otavice the round trip to Šibenik can be completed quite quickly and once again you can get on to the Adriatic Highway. (Though it is a most entertaining road I do not recommend the one that runs cross country from Drniš to Sinj and Split.)

The Šibenik archipelago is really a continuation of the Zadar group of islands, collectively the **Kornats,** and what I said in the previous chapter more or less applies again.

Many of them are no more than large uninhabited rocks, baked by the sun, stropped by wind and water. In their crevices a few herbs and shrubs thrive. Some of the larger ones are fertile in places. Among those that support human life and are worth visiting are Murter and Zlarin. The women of **Zlarin** are renowned for their beauty, chastity and fidelity. Just as well they are chaste and faithful because the men of Zlarin have a long tradition as able sailors all over the world in many navies. The women also have beautiful costumes, now dwindling, which consist, approximately, of black skirts and black boleros over white blouses which have red piping on them. They cover their heads with bright scarves.

A number of the islands can be visited on excursion boats from Šibenik. You should on no account attempt to navigate these waters by yourself.

Between Šibenik and Split there are several agreeable small fishing towns by-passed by the main highway. Primošten and Rogoznica are both worth stopping at briefly. The former is the centre of a wine-growing area which produces a pleasant, sometimes fairly strong, red wine called Plavac: good to drink with meat. Rogoznica was very probably a fourth-century Greek colony called Heraklea. It was also one of the main bases for the Uskok pirates.

The whole of the coast between Šibenik and Split via Trogir shows the local methods of cultivation particularly well: the laboriously contrived terraces, the strips and patches of soil painstakingly gathered and irrigated by water carts and cans of water borne by donkeys. Out of bitter, lacerating stone the grapes belly and ripen, olives swell to maturity and the succulent figs become sticky with milk. Once again life survives, in a modest way is even triumphant.

CHAPTER 5

The Coast V: Trogir

Trogir (its name means a goat: from late Latin *tragus*, or Greek τράγσς) is as beautiful as Rab but in a slightly different way. It is more Slav than Rab; more rugged, less urbane. A complex and troubled past has scarred and seamed its features. It is old and mature, but by no means senile.

The town lies on a minute island of the same name and is virtually moored to the mainland by one bridge and to the island of Čiovo by another. Like so many other places on this coast it has been formed by numerous influences, good and bad. What remains is a very small medieval town of tanned and weathered stone, congested with palaces, monasteries and churches, all now deprived of protective walls. From the sea it looks, as Rebecca West has aptly put it, 'like a plant grown in a flower-pot when the pot is broken but the earth and roots still hang together.'

Originally it was a Greek colony founded by the Greeks from Syracuse who had settled on the island of Vis in the fourth century B.C. It was then called Tragurion (Goat Island). After the Greeks, the Romans. For four centuries it was part of the Byzantine régime and for another five under Croat and Croat–Hungarian kings. By the middle of the twelfth century it was developing rather as Dubrovnik was. It regarded itself as an autonomous city state with an aristocratic class who spent much of their time squabbling with Split over the possession of the littoral between them.

Though it escaped the Avars when they pillaged Salona in the seventh century it was not so fortunate when the Saracens came in 1123. They captured and destroyed it and for a long time it was in ruins and almost deserted. However, a good deal of rebuilding had

68

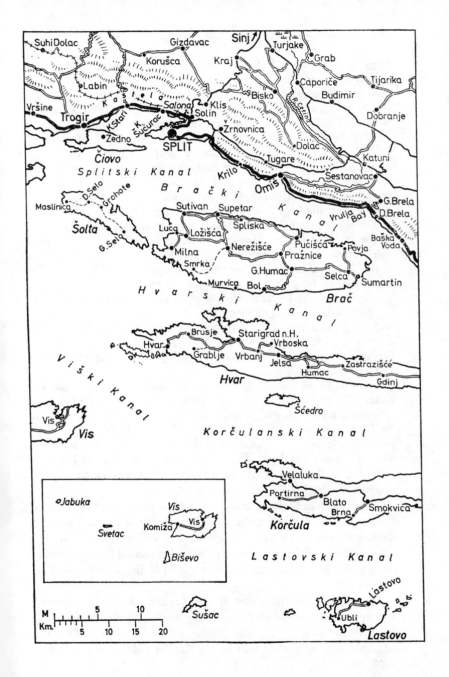

been done by the end of the thirteenth century and from then until now it has been relatively unscathed, even though preyed upon and captured by several powers—including the Venetians, the French, the Austrians and the Italians. People went on living there, breeding, building and creating. The city has shown a certain womanly resilience, a faculty for renewing itself through all misfortunes. Now it is a calm, leisurely place, underpopulated. Amidst the cramped interstices of its alleys and streets a kind of skeleton crew, as it were, keeps it in repair and more or less in working order. It may become prosperous again, but at the moment a certain Jacobean gloom shadows it—even on the sunniest day.

The main **Land Gate** (*kopnena vrata*) into the city is topped by a statue of a St John—one of several dozen St Johns in the Calendar —a Roman by birth, one-time bishop of Trogir and patron saint of the town. At one stage there was a winged lion of **St Mark**. The Lion used to be partly covered by a cypress bush growing out of the walls and the locals foretold a good or bad season for produce by the condition of its foliage.

A very short way from here you come quite suddenly upon the elegant and ample main square. On one side is the Cathedral, on the other the Loggia and tower. Two palaces complete a most civilised quadrangle.

The **Loggia,** which is a beauty, used to function as a tribunal and forum. On the eastern wall a carving by Nicholas the Florentine represents an allegory of Justice. The two saints are Sv Lovro and Sv Ivan, the latter holding a model of the city. Next to the first pillar is the pillory column to which malefactors were chained. The chains are still there. The Clock Tower adjoining the Loggia is part of the old church of St Sebastian, the façade of which was also designed by Nicholas the Florentine.

The big palace at the eastern end of the piazza is the **Communal Palace** or City Hall with the armorial bearing of Trogir above the doorway. Externally it is Romanesque, within Gothic. In the courtyard one of the columns with a Gothic capital bears a head in stone which is supposed to be a man called Gojković—the architect of the hall.

The palace the other end is the **Ćipiko**, a fifteenth-century Venetian Gothic house with one of the grandest façades on the whole coast. It was built by Koriolan Ćipiko, quite a well-known Trogiran humanist and writer. It was in the Ćipiko palace that, in 1650, they found a manuscript of the *Satyricon,* or *The Feast of Trimalchio,* by Petronius: a book that is compulsory reading for all prigs and Puritans. It is a boisterously irreverent satirical romance written by a man who had the rather perilous and hair-raising post of Director of Pleasures (*arbiter elegantiae*) to the imperial court of Nero. He must have been pressed sometimes to invent yet more gimmicks to please the insatiable lusts of his master so I dare say we owe to his professional knowledge one of the best parts of the book which describes a sumptuous banquet given by the vulgar *nouveau riche* Trimalchio to the hero Encolpius.

You should take a look in the palace courtyard where you will see two fine ship's figureheads. The cock was taken from a Turkish ship during the battle of Lepanto in 1571. The goddess Fortune belonged to a Trogiran ship, appropriately called Žena ('the woman') which took part in the same battle.[1]

On the north side of the piazza is the **Cathedral of Sv Lovro** (St Laurence), generally acknowledged to be a masterpiece of Dalmatian art. There is no doubt about it. This magnificent church was begun early in the thirteenth century on the site of a basilica destroyed by the Saracens in 1123 and was dedicated to St Laurence. But for the townspeople it is St John's—and it is his skeleton that lies in the crypt.

The massive main **doorway** was done by a Croat artist, Radovan. It is dated and 'signed' by the artist on the tympanum: 'This door was built in 1240 . . . by Radovan, the most excellent in his art, as the statues and reliefs show, under the bishop Treguan the Tuscan, of the city of flowers.' There is a pleasing arrogance about the self-advertisement which cannot be gainsaid when you have seen how excellent his art was.

The theme of the whole design is *The Fall* and *The Redemption* and the naked figures each side are self-evident. On the columns or receding orders are depicted apostles and saints and the Calendar in allegory accompanied by zodiacal signs. There is an extraordinary profusion of detailed and vivid carving here: various beasts, a stag, a sheep, a goat, an elephant, what looks like a hippopotamus, a flying griffin plucking out the eyes of a pig, a centaur, a seahorse, a mermaid and another griffin demolishing a scroll which bears a human head. There are also various scenes from rural life: a wood-cutter, a leather worker, a man boiling a pot, a man cooking sausages, another man killing a pig, a sheep-shearing scene, a

[1] I was told recently that Žena has been removed.

warrior, and a naked wild man—the sort that Rousseau might have approved of:

> *When wild in woods the noble savage ran*
> *Ere the base laws of servitude began.*

A whole world has been created here, a fantastic and intricate microcosm.

A particularly striking part of the design are the bowed figures supporting the columns. Some are naked and some half-dressed. Two wear turbans, others wear a tunic with a toga. Some are barefoot. One has medieval shoes with pointed toes, another sandals with tied leggings. These, quite obviously, are representations of Croat peasants and Turks of that period.

Above you can see the Nativity: on the left the shepherds with their sheep; on the right the mounted Magi. On the inner arch are the Annunciation, the presentation of the Magi and groups of angels. On the outer arch you can pick out fairly easily various incidents in the life of Christ, though they are not in chronological order: the Flight into Egypt, the Entry into Jerusalem, the Last Supper, the Arrest, the Flagellation, Calvary, the Resurrection, the Three Mary's, the Temptation in the Desert and the Baptism in the Jordan.

One day when visiting the cathedral I was taking a rest in the big porch when a genial and placid man in a broad-brimmed hat and smoking a cheroot strolled up and began to talk. He described himself as 'the chief of criminals' in Trogir—not meaning thereby the head racketeer but the chief policeman. He didn't like the doorway very much: he thought it lacked form and discipline. This seems a fair criticism, yet the incongruities are atoned for by a massiveness and sombre power which make a profound impact. Radovan's artistic vision shows a disordered universe, mysterious, complex and bizarre. In its way it is extremely realistic.

The inside of the church is also sombre. It has the same strength and solidity as the doorway and the light is dim and solemn. Again there is lack of symmetry and order and there is a remarkable variety of workmanship from various periods.

The high altar with the statues of St John and St Laurence is Baroque but the baldaquin over it is fourteenth-century, similar to those at Kotor and Korčula. I think you will notice at once that the choir stalls are exactly like those in the cathedrals at Rab and Zadar.

72

The first chapel on the left is dedicated to St Jerome (who was born in Dalmatia) and contains an interesting polyptych by a fifteenth-century Dalmatian artist and a splendid crucifix above the altar. A little farther along, by what is called the altar of the Holy Cross, you will notice a small space in the wall which contains a reliquary. The hand, held by an angel, belonged to the patron saint.

Next we come to the **Chapel** dedicated to the man known as Sv Ivan Orsini (or Trogirski), built in the second half of the fifteenth century (it took six years) by Nicholas the Florentine and Aleši. The statues, the angels and the figure of St Paul have a vivacity and elegance which are unmistakably the work of a great Renaissance artist. The little cherubs with brandished torches who thrust themselves mischievously round the closing doors may be later but they are perfectly in harmony. As spritely are the cupids romping with chains of fruit and flowers, very like the creations of Luca Della Robbia. Above the altar lies the red and white marble sarcophagus of Sv Ivan with his figure carved upon it.

This man, who was born in Rome, became Bishop of Trogir about 1064 and had a considerable reputation as a scientist. He was also supposed to be a miracle worker. There are various stories of him turning a bad vintage into a good wine, walking on the water, repelling enemies by supernatural means—and so forth. When the Venetians sacked Trogir in 1171 they are alleged to have stolen the body of the saint, but they only pulled off one arm for the sake of the ring which could not be removed from the hand any other way. The arm was then stored in Venice for some years and was subsequently returned by another Doge. The alternative story is that it flew back by itself wrapped in white linen on the eve of the saint's festival.

You should certainly look in the **sacristy** at the end on the left. In it is a superb wardrobe of inlaid walnut as well as several pictures. Those of *St Jerome* and *St John the Baptist* are by Gentile Bellini, that of *St Martin and the Beggar* is the work of Salvator Rosa. The treasury was one of the richest in Dalmatia and a certain amount survives. I think the pick of it is a fifteenth-century monstrance which bears some beautiful interwoven work of foliage and birds. What is described as a coronation robe may have belonged to King Bela IV of Hungary. According to legend he donated it to the cathedral.

This king, like Trogir, had a narrow escape from the Tartars shortly after Radovan had begun work on the cathedral. He took refuge with his court in Trogir and then fled to a small island farther out which is still named Kraljevac (*kralj* means 'king') while the rest of his retinue remained in the city. The story is that when the Tartar hordes arrived they sent a herald on to the little bridge which joined Trogir to the mainland and he demanded the surrender of the king. There was no reply and in due course the barbarians went home. Nobody knows quite why they did this but there is a theory that they had learnt that their king, son of Genghis Khan, had just died. Trogir breathed again.

On the way out do not miss the **Baptistery** at the western end of the big porch. It is a mixture of Gothic and Renaissance design and the energy and realism of the carving is reminiscent of work by George the Dalmatian. From the porch you can get up the bell-tower.

If you leave the piazza by the narrow street next to the City Hall (i.e. at the eastern end) you reach the water-front and a restaurant plus hotel. The accommodation here is fairly limited and not many people actually stay in Trogir because it is the kind of place that can be seen in a one-day excursion from Split. But I reckon two days are essential.

Turn right here and just beyond the rear of the City Hall you find the **Abbey of St John the Baptist** (Sv Ivan Krstitelj) which, after the cathedral, is the most important building in Trogir. It is a thirteenth-century Romanesque church with the remains of some frescoes. It also contains the Čipiko family tomb, designed by Nicholas the Florentine, and a very fine pietà. (This church is usually shut so you must inquire at the tourist office in the main square.)

A little farther on stands the **Convent of Sv Nikola**, founded two years before the Battle of Hastings. It was the discovery of a Greek inscription here that first persuaded historians that Trogir had a Greek past. The convent also possesses the famous relief of Kairos: in Greek mythology the personification of the 'favourable moment' and represented as a young man with wings on his feet, standing on a sphere and holding a razor and scales. The back of his head is shaven to indicate that he can't be caught by his hair once he has passed.

Next to the convent is the other entrance to Trogir: the **City Gate.** The little loggia beside it was built by a sixteenth-century Venetian governor for strangers waiting to enter the town—like the one at Korčula. Now the Trogirans use theirs as a fish market. A short way beyond you find the church and convent of Sv Dominik. The church, lofty and well-lighted, the kind the Dominicans have always liked to build, contains yet another work by Nicholas the Florentine: the funeral monument of the Sobota family. The picture of the *Circumcision* above the high altar is ascribed to Palma the Younger.

From this point the substantial bulk of the fortress, the **Kaštel-Kamerlengo,** becomes more obvious. It is a fifteenth-century stronghold so named because the Venetian official in charge of the town's finances was known as the *Kamerling* or chamberlain. Now it has been turned over to an open-air cinema. Beyond it is the football ground and an object at the end of it which looks like a small covered bandstand and is in fact the 'Gloriette' of Marmont. Marmont was one of Napoleon's more civilised marshals who was proconsul in Dalmatia for five years: a period about which he wrote some entertaining memoirs. Unfortunately for him, his wife, styled the Duchess of Ragusa, found provincial life in Dalmatia too tiresome. She returned to Paris and there denigrated her husband so efficiently that his prospects of higher rank were ruined. The 'Gloriette' is supposed to have been used by the marshal and his officers for card games.

Among the rather tumble-down buildings at this end of the city a solitary campanile marks the spot where there stood the church of St Michael—destroyed by shelling in 1944.

There are still three other churches worth seeing: St Peter's, in the middle of the city; the church of Our Lady of Carmel on the northern side; and **Sv Barbara,** the oldest church in the city, which lies a few paces from the main piazza behind the Loggia. All three contain interesting if unremarkable works of art but mere age plus austerity give Sv Barbara a beauty that more sophisticated and better cared for buildings seldom have. It is little more than a narrow tunnel (the nave is a mere nine feet wide) and in its uncouth simplicity makes a fascinating contrast to the complexities of the cathedral. It may still contain a Meštrović statue of St John as a Dalmatian shepherd and a Romanesque wooden Christ of unmistakably Slav appearance.

But when one has done with the churches and monasteries and convents there is still plenty to be seen in Trogir, especially the many palaces and patrician houses—like the Lučić palace which has now been restored and was once the home of Petar Lučić, one of the

75

notable Croatian humanists, who made an anthology of Croatian poetry in Elizabethan times. His palace overlooks the southern harbour and there is a whole group of comparable ones on the northern side: the Štafilić palace, the houses of the Berislavić and Borgoforte families, and the Garanjin-Fanfogna palace. All are linked with famous Croatian scholars, humanists and artists.

Humanism and religion flourished here without loss to each other, as they did in Dubrovnik; but it must also be remembered that Trogir was a heretical city for a long time, though there is little enough definite evidence to indicate the fact now. Bogomilism and Paulicianism spread into these regions during the late Middle Ages and Trogir must have been one of the many places which helped to transmit the bacilli of these spiritual diseases (as the Church then regarded them) farther west. What are believed to be Bogomil tombs still lie a little to the north near Seget.

The neighbouring island of **Čiovo** was known in classical times as Boas because it was popularly believed that large oxen-eating snakes throve there. While the Roman empire was declining it was used as a place of exile for political prisoners and, much later, for heretics. If you have time it is worth visiting the Convent of the Holy Cross and the church of St Jerome.

Between Trogir and Split (they are well-connected by familiar looking buses that were sold as scrap by London Transport) a road goes through what is known as the **Riviera of the Seven Castles** (Kaštel Riviera) the most fertile district in Dalmatia. The *autoput* by-passes this so you have to turn off for a few miles to see the villages and the remains.

There used to be thirteen of these fortresses which were all built by the nobility of Trogir and Split as defences against Turkish raids. Bar two the surviving seven are named after the families concerned. The first one you come to is Kaštel Štafilić, very close to Kaštel Novi. Little remains of the former but the latter is in good repair. There is also a tiny church dedicated to St Roch in Kaštel Novi. Next is Kaštel Stari (a good hotel here, The Palas) whose fortress, now a ruin, was built by Koriolan Ćipiko in 1476. The fourth one along is Kaštel Lukšić (1487) and here you should also have a look at the church of St Mary which contains a rather fine sarcophagus by Juraj Dalmatinac. Kaštel Kambelovac was put up much later (round about 1566) by the Kambi family from Split and there is still a Kambi palace in Split. At Kaštel Gomilica are the ruins of two castles. Finally you arrive at Kaštel Sućurac. The original fortress here was ninth century. What you see today dates from 1391. Quite as old is a Christmas festivity peculiar to the area (but now, so far as I know, obsolete) called *biranje kralja* ('election of the king'). Experts think it may have some connection with the Roman Saturnalia. In brief, a prominent citizen was elected 'king' and crowned at a 'coronation' ceremony. In return for this elevation he was expected to wine and dine the whole village. The 'reign' lasted a week; quite enough, I should think, in view of his obligations as a host.

Altogether the *Kašteli* make a rather impressive row of fortifications, but unfortunately one cannot see them properly even off-shore because there is so much vegetation and the area has been built over a lot since the war. If you wanted a quiet holiday you could hardly do better than stay at The Palas in Kaštel Stari. There is plenty of boating and fishing and swimming, delightful *kafanas*, good wine and an amiable atmosphere.

You will not have been in Jugoslavia very long before you meet two definite traits in the people about which I feel a word of advice is more or less essential.

When asking for information in Tourist offices, or anywhere else, when shopping, ordering meals and attending to the general needs the traveller has, you will notice that, nine times out of ten, you are not offered alternatives. For instance, you may ask if there is a bus to —— the next morning. If the answer is 'no' it will not be followed up by the information that there *is* one at 2.30 in the afternoon. You must always ask—and go on asking. Very often information has to be extracted by a process of elimination. For example: Is there fish soup? No. Vegetable soup? No. Do you have any broth? No. Lentil soup? Yes, there is (*ima*). *Nema* ('there is not') is hardly ever succeeded by 'but'. By extrapolation the principle involved here applies in a wide variety of circumstances.

Its application is particularly necessary when making inquiries. For instance, to take an hypothetical situation, you are in a Dalmatian town and you wish to make a journey into Macedonia or Serbia. To the average Dalmatian these are different countries, remote, uncivilised, potentially hostile to strangers. All information, therefore, is liable to be coloured by prejudice. It may even be completely inaccurate.

One of the reasons for this is that there is a high degree of regional chauvinism of a much more acrimonious and disdainful nature than one is accustomed to meeting elsewhere in Europe. Provincial and regional snobbery, pride and prejudice are very strong. Even the most sophisticated Serb, Croat or Slovene may be guilty of these. The attitudes are often the result of bitter hatreds brought about by political and religious antagonism. Therefore one should be a little tactful in conversation and even more tactful about any introductions one may make.

I mention these matters at this point because once at Kaštel Stari I made plans to go to Bosnia. The hotel manager looked skywards and produced one of those manual gestures with which Jugoslavs are incomparably eloquent. In this case he drew his fingers across his throat and gave a horrible choking sound. 'They're barbarians,' he said. 'Muslims.' A week later I listened to a Bosnian condemning the Dalmatian Croats as gigolos, thieves and hypocrites. Neither of the men was joking.

CHAPTER 6

The Coast VI : Split

'*Ča je pusta Londra kontra Splitu gradu . . . ?*' (What is mighty London compared with the city of Split?) The query comes in a traditional Split song. No doubt most self-respecting Spličani are quite clear on the matter; certainly the original palace must have surpassed anything that London could boast early in the fourth century.

The land approach is disappointing and gives one no idea of what is in store. After Salona (which I shall deal with later: p. 92, map p. 69) the road swings towards the sea and then through the shabby precincts of an industrial town: grey, dirty and incoherent. It might almost be a development site in a London suburb. New packing-case blocks of flats stand unfinished amidst builder's rubble, vacated shacks disintegrate. Nothing seems to belong to anyone, yet everywhere is the property of wanderer, urchin and squatter.

If you can possibly manage it the best way first to see Split is from the deck of your ship as it docks. Very soon, despite the obstructing and hideous bulk of the harbourmaster's building, you can discern the shape of Diocletian's original **Palace.**

The long grey southern wall—nearly six hundred feet of it—now battered and stained, defaced, reticulated with windows and garnished with laundry and weeds, used to be fronted by a great portico with a line of columns. Centrally, behind the portico, there was a big hall, facing seawards, which led to the imperial apartments where the self-deified Emperor passed his years of retirement. Many feet immediately below, the sea lapped the vast foundation stones. The Emperor had a view that would be worth a fortune these days. On each side and behind the palace stretched forests of pine and oak. Even in Fortis's time the region had been stripped and, as he put it, by its 'horrid bareness' reverberated 'an almost insupportable heat in the summer days.'

Split—Spalato . . . The name is believed to be a contraction of the Greek phrase ἔις τον παλάτιον which means 'into the palace'. A form of Greek was a lingua franca on the coast and it is thought that masons and other workmen bringing building materials would speak of 'going into the palace.' It is easy to see how the Greek could be shortened by the locals. There is another theory that the name came from a Greek settlement nearby called Aspalaton after a fragrant shrub in the locality.

As you disembark amidst an animated crowd of Spličani and groups of particularly volatile and ebullient porters, hotel touts and importunate room-letters, you at once feel a completely different atmosphere which, as a number of people have pointed out, is almost Neapolitan.

Split is a splendid centre for tourism and is well-equipped for tourists. If you have not made any reservation and/or want cheap accommodation by all means make an arrangement with one of the touts; or, go to the Tourist Office (this lies on the broad *molo* or esplanade called Titova Obala which runs beneath the southern wall of the palace) where they will organise it for you. If you make an arrangement on the spot be quite sure how much the room is and how far away—otherwise you may find yourself lugging baggage a mile or more into the suburbs.

Alternatively there are the hotels, usually packed out in the high season. In the eastern suburb of Bačvice there are the Park and the Mosor which are comfortable but too far away from the town centre for my liking. At the western end of the Titova Obala stands the Bellevue, a large and comfortable hotel where many English people stay. Near it is the Marjan, somewhat more expensive but with a good restaurant. Plumb in the centre of the town, in the Narodni Trg, is the Central: interesting but noisy. There are, of course, several others, and the place I usually stay is not so well known as any of them. It is the Srebrena Vrata (with a dependency, the Slavija) a cheap and unpretentious hotel in an ideal position.

If you walk round the harbour and up Hrvojeva Ulica (this lies between the market and the eastern wall of the palace) about half-way up you will come to a great gate (*Srebrena Vrata*—Porta Argentea—The Silver Gate). Step through it and immediately on the left is the hotel, built right up against the original walls and overlooking Tomislav Square which is paved with Roman stones

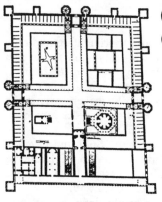

(*left*) Ground-plan of Diocletian's Palace

(*below*) The Palace of Diocletian to-day

1: *Diocletian's mausoleum* (now Cathedral)
2: *Temple of Jupiter*
3: *Peristyle*
4: *Vestibule*
5: *Golden Gate*
6: *Silver Gate*
7: *Iron Gate*
8: *Entrance to Underground Halls of Diocletian's Palace*
9-11: *Corner towers of Diocletian's Palace*

12: *Cindro Palace*
13: *Agubio Palace* (*Ivelić*)
14: *Papalić Palace* (now Split Municipal Museum)
15: *Cambi Palace*
16: *Milesi Palace* (now Maritime Museum)
17: *Old City Hall* (now Ethnographic Museum)
18: *Bronze Gate*

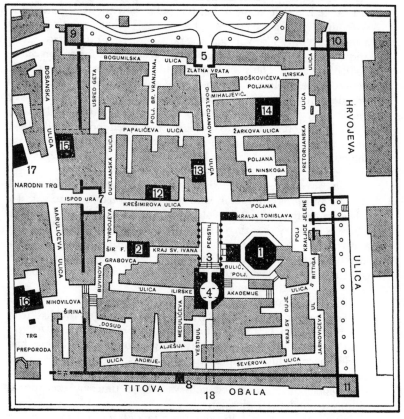

and lined with the bases of columns: a busy thoroughfare and only a little narrower than it was in Diocletian's day—that is, sixteen and a half centuries ago. Here one feels very much in the heart of things even though one is on the edge of the original palace. It is noisy but anywhere in Split is noisy. You will be woken early in the morning, but this is likely in all Jugoslav towns. In any case, who wants to be an Oblomov in a place like Split?

You need at least three days to get an idea of Split and to enjoy it. If you can manage a week with the odd excursion to neighbouring islands and places like Trogir, so much the better. If you cannot afford three days it is wiser not to try and see it at all.

The first thing to do (this seems to me a good rule in most places) is to take a gentle stroll round the palace—without a guide book, without anything except receptive senses. To start with you will almost certainly lose yourself several times. It is rather like edging and working your way through some bizarre rock formation on the floor of a valley. The streets appear little more than clefts and slits between grey columns and blocks of stone which here and there broaden into defiles. High above there are chips and wedges of sky. Suddenly you come to an irregular space, an unexpected slab of light. Then on again into crepuscule pierced occasionally by a tilted shaft of sun. But it is not murky or depressing, merely dense, congested. Repeatedly you have to turn sideways to get past people.

Split owes its existence directly to the Emperor Diocletian, a curious and interesting man who was born nearby in A.D. 245. He was very probably the son of slaves of Anulinus, a Roman senator. There is a theory that the father obtained the freedom of the family and rose to the rank of scribe. Portraits suggest that his son was a stocky, fairly heavily-built man inclined to corpulence, somewhat stiff and awkward in his movements, with a strong, rugged face.

He made himself Emperor in 284 and in 286 divided the rule of the empire with Maximian. In 292 it was further divided with Constantine and Galerius. Thus a tetrarchy was formed. At this period the empire was in a state of grievous decay. There had already been eighteen emperors in fifty years and so it was essential that somebody should try to provide stability, order and direction. This Diocletian more or less achieved, for a time, by exceptional will-power and determination.

He was, it is thought, in some ways modest and tolerant, yet he also exacted worship as a god while still alive and towards the end of his reign he carried out very severe persecution of the Christians. If we want modern parallels perhaps De Gaulle and Stalin both reflect aspects of his character.

He created a powerful civil service and abdicated voluntarily in 305, by which time his palace, which had taken about ten years to build, was ready to receive him. He lived in his palace until he died in 313, and was then buried in it. Tradition holds that he was a keen gardener with a special interest in cabbages. There can be few better examples of a local lad who made good and then returned to his native ground to show how good.

The palace was, and in some ways still is, one of the most remarkable buildings in Europe and it has a particular interest for Englishmen because Robert Adam went there in 1757 and made many detailed drawings which formed the basis of the Adam style and thus greatly influenced Georgian architecture in the eighteenth and nineteenth centuries. It was Split that inspired the Adam brothers to create that complex of buildings known as the Adelphi just below the Strand. Many of the illustrations in Adam's book (published in 1764) were done by Bartolozzi. In fact, it is essential to look at this volume of engravings to get an idea of what the palace used to be like. After that imaginative reconstruction is easy.

We might never have had these, and the architecture of England might be very different, but for the acumen and common sense of an obscure Scot. While Adam was in Split doing his drawings he was arrested by the Venetian governor as a spy. Fortunately the commander of the garrison was called Robert Graeme, a Jacobite general who commanded the Venetian army for a time in the eighteenth century. It was his counsel that prevailed. Nowadays you may still be arrested as a spy if you are found drawing or photographing anything that looks like a naval or military installation.

The original palace was rectangular: the northern and southern walls were roughly two hundred yards long; the eastern and western about two hundred and forty yards. The walls were immense: seven or eight feet thick; seventy feet high on the southern side, getting on for fifty on the other three sides. At each corner there was a keep, but the western one has now gone. There were four other towers along each of the land walls, none of which survives.

In fact, then, the palace was built on the plan of a Roman fort intersected by two main thoroughfares dividing the area into four quarters. The *decumanus*[1] (now the Poljana Kraljeva Tomislava and the Krešimirova streets) ran from east to west; the *cardo* (the 'hinge'—from which we get our word 'cardinal') ran from north to south and culminated in the peristyle or, indirectly, with the small southern gate on to the sea. This is now known as Diocletian Street. Of course these streets are now much narrower than they used to be, except for the section inside the Silver Gate.

The area north of the *decumanus* was occupied by the servants and the garrison etc. To the south were the imperial suites (which took up about a quarter of the total area) plus the public buildings, the temples, the peristyle and the mausoleum.

After Diocletian's death the nucleus of a city began to form within the walls of the palace (today there are about three hundred houses in it and several thousand people) and the northern half became a textile factory for producing Roman uniforms. The Dalmatic tunic was first produced here.

Early in the seventh century those insatiable barbarians the Avars sacked the old Roman town of Salona, whose ruins lie a few miles inland, and the survivors from there took refuge in the palace. Within they built domestic dwellings linked by narrow passages and alleys, many of which survive. You will notice that no motor transport is allowed in them or is even able to pass.

Later still a medieval and then a Renaissance town developed round the palace. In our time Split is still growing. In fact, the post-war development has been intense.

As in so many other towns on this coast nearly everything inside the original palace (a matter of about seven acres) constitutes a museum in itself. And here and there, as you wander, you come upon vestiges of the quondam splendour of the Emperor's conception. Six hundred years after his death so much of its original magnificence remained that Constantine Porphyrogenitus, himself used to the glories of Constantinople, said that even in its ruin it surpassed all powers of description. When Jackson went there 900 years later he found that 'even in its present state . . . overgrown with the mean accretions of fifteen centuries, its vast proportions and solid construction excite our astonishment.' Both would still be impressed.

Probably the best spot to start a detailed tour is the central,

[1] So called because the main entrance of a Roman camp was known as the *porta decumana* where the tenth cohort of the legion was stationed.

southern gate from the *molo*, the **Porta Aenea** (the Bronze Gate). This leads at once into an area of cavernous basements which, until quite recently, had been filled with refuse and rubble accumulated since the seventh century. Some of the chambers are still full of it. Superbly built they were and they roughly correspond in lay-out with the imperial quarters which once stood above them. Now they are used for art exhibitions.

You pass through a broad, central basement hall and into a smaller one which supports what was once the **vestibule**. From here recently discovered steps lead up into the **peristyle**: the palace's main courtyard. The granite columns with Corinthian capitals are open on the eastern side but were unfortunately closed on the west in the Middle Ages to provide the outer walls of houses.

Behind you steps rise to the **ante-chamber,** circular, with high walls curving to what used to be a domed roof. A short passage leads to the only remnant of the Emperor's apartments, the vestibule. Beyond that there used to be an atrium, a huge 'nave' lined with columns, and so on. Eventually, after being passed from one set of minions, in ascending order of rank, to another, you would have arrived in the august presence itself.

It is almost certain that Diocletian, who had been much impressed by the pomp of eastern despotism, sought to make himself very inaccessible: partly from egoism, partly from fear. He wanted the trappings of power and by surrounding himself with elaborate ceremonial he aimed to emphasise the idea of his divinity and inspire ever greater awe and respect. And there can be little doubt that the individual, at last granted permission and having made the long journey to the remote 'god' throned in splendour in the innermost fastness of his castle, was well-nigh overwhelmed when the moment came to prostrate himself.

But my final impression of Diocletian is of a lonely, sad and anxious man, with many enemies and few friends, apprehensive lest someone should try to kill him, suffering from disease, fearful for the fate of his daughter, uneasy about his wife (who, ironically, became a Christian), viewing the inevitable demise of the empire, contemplating suicide (which he may have committed) and probably wondering whether, in the end, it had all been worth it.

On the east of the peristyle is Diocletian's **mausoleum,** which was converted into a cathedral towards the end of the seventh century. It may have been then that the Emperor's sarcophagus and body were removed or destroyed, but it seems more likely that it vanished at the end of the fifth century. One of these days, as Rebecca West has suggested, it will probably turn up 'in the cellars of some old and absentminded family of Split.'

Near the entrance to the mausoleum is a regal Egyptian sphinx in black granite (there used to be two) which was part of the original decoration but at least fifteen centuries earlier than Diocletian. Such objects help to put glory in perspective.

The mausoleum was built on an octagonal foundation and consists of an eight-sided *cella* surrounded by a colonnade. Its carved **wooden doors** are well worth a close scrutiny. They depict twenty-eight scenes from the life of Christ and were the work of a local thirteenth-century artist called Buvina (possibly Guvina). On the left, starting from top left, you have 1. The Annunciation, and next to it, on the right, 2. The Nativity. The sequence, always moving from left to right, down to the bottom and then up again on the right hand side, is as follows: 3. The Three Wise Men travelling. 4. The Wise men worshipping. 5. Massacre of the Innocents. 6. Flight into Egypt. 7. The Presentation. 8. The Baptism. 9. The miracle at Cana. 10. The Temptation. 11. Healing the man possessed (?). 12. Christ and the Woman of Samaria. 13. Healing the lame and the blind. 14. The raising of Lazarus (?). 15. (?). 16. Christ weeping over Jerusalem. 17. The Entry into Jerusalem. 18. The Last Supper. 19. Washing the Disciples' feet. 20. Agony in the Garden. 21. The Betrayal. 22. Christ before Pilate. 23. The Flagellation. 24. The Crucifixion. 25. The Deposition. 26. The Entombment. 27. The Last Judgment. 28. The Ascension. The whole thing is a remarkable achievement: detailed, delicate and animated, and one of the best pieces of medieval wood-carving in existence.

Inside there is a certain amount of confusion and discord, largely because so many diverse periods have added something. The most outstanding objects are: the hexagonal pulpit, beautifully carved and generally regarded as one of the most accomplished things of its kind in Romanesque art; the circular frieze under the dome which includes bas-reliefs of Diocletian and his wife Prisca (unfortunately it is very difficult to see these); the painting of the *Virgin and Saints* by Palma the Younger; the altar in the north-east alcove: another work of vividly realistic carving by Juraj Dalmatinac, especially in *The Flagellation*. Lastly I mention the choir stalls which are magnificent and need close examination. These may also be by Buvina (or someone of his school). The intricate carving and lattice-work are fascinating.

Underneath the mausoleum is a crypt, now a chapel dedicated to St Lucille. The campanile was built between the thirteenth and seventeenth centuries but was in a very imperfect state until Jackson restored and completed it between 1882 and 1908. I recommend a climb to the top, from where you will get an excellent bird's-eye view of the palace.

From the peristyle (sometimes used as a theatre in the summer) the narrow Dioklecijanova Ulica, flanked by Gothic and Romanesque buildings, goes north. The main one of note is almost immediately on the left hand side: the de Agubio palace, with a noble doorway and courtyard. The next main turn to the right is the Zarkov Ulica. A short way along it stands the **Papalić Palace,** a lovely Gothic building designed by George the Dalmatian. After the war it was converted into the City Museum. There is nothing very remarkable in it—mostly weapons, documents, coats of arms and some interesting pieces of medieval sculpture in the lapidarium.

If you return to Diocletian Street and go on up it you very soon arrive at the great land gate, the **Porta Aurea** (Golden Gate, *Zlatna Vrata*) the principal entrance to the palace and the end of the Salona road. You will notice that the projecting arches above are purely decorative. They are a possible origin of the pensile arcades of Lombardy and a design used repeatedly in Serbian and Byzantine architecture. Just south-west of it is a magnificent medieval palace whose eastern façade is Romanesque, while its northern is late Gothic—once again the work of George the Dalmatian, and properly regarded as the master's best creation in Split. Now it is part of the Workers' University.

Above the Golden Gate, somewhat to its left as you look at it from within, there was built in the ninth century a long, thin chapel, known as the **Chapel of Sv Martin.** You can get to it by some steps from Bogumilska Ulica. In this very unusual chapel, which really occupies a scissure between the two main walls, you will find a stone altar screen of exquisite grace and delicacy: the work of a very early anonymous Croatian artist.

Immediately outside the gate is Meštrović's colossal and rather grotesque statue of **Grgur Ninski,** which used to stand in the peristyle and was removed from there by the Italians during the war. Though this was a rude gesture it seems to me to have been sound aesthetically. Apart from anything else the peristyle was much too small for it. The ruins in the garden beyond the statue are the remains of an eleventh-century monastery of which the basilica groundplan is still clear. The Gothic chapel of St Arnerius nearby was another work by the prolific George the Dalmatian.

From inside the Zlatna Vrata turn east and you find a small piazza (**Boškovićeva Poljana**) which also serves as a theatre on occasion. From here Ilirska Ulica runs into Pretorian Street and this goes right down to the Silver Gate and the Poljana Tomislava. There is not much to delay you in the north-east and south-east corners of the palace but they are certainly worth exploring.

If you again take the peristyle as your starting point and set off westwards, you pass the seventeenth-century Cindro Palace on your right and then arrive at the west gate (Porta Ferrea, Iron Gate) in the upper story of which (you can reach it by the outside staircase just to the north of the doorway) is a tiny church—**Gospa od Zvonika** (Our Lady of the Belfry). This is a pretty little pre-Romanesque building which has some crude, recent decoration within. From this position one can get a good semi-aerial view of the immediate neighbourhood.

Turn left inside the west gate and a few strides bring you to a small clearing and the back of a slight and graceful temple, known variously as the Temple of Jupiter and the Temple of Aesculapius. Very early on it was transformed into the **Baptistery of St John.** Outside it there are three objects of interest: another Egyptian sphinx, a fifth-century column and, built into the wall of an adjacent house, part of a pre-Romanesque arch. Inside there are several curiosities. Firstly the font, whose front panel shows what is probably a very early Croatian king on his throne. At his side there is some kind of attendant who, as Jackson pointed out in a scathing comment on the whole scene, appears to be suffering from stomach ulcers or something of the sort, and at his feet grovels what may be a subject doing homage. It is a naïve and crude work, yet pleasing. The sarcophagus at the back on the left belongs to Archbishop Ivan of the seventh century, the first prelate of Split and organiser of the Church there. That on the right belongs to Archbishop Lovro of the eleventh century. Between them stands Meštrović's statue of St John the Baptist—one of his more successful works. The block of Romanesque and Gothic buildings in the immediate neighbourhood has been converted into classrooms etc. for the Workers' University, 'an excellent example', as one of the guides points out, with the complacency of official publications, 'of the way in which premises unsuitable for habitation can be both conserved as historical monuments and hygienically adapted to a daytime use.'

From the front of the temple a mere crack of a street leads back to the peristyle.

Immediately beyond the west gate lies the medieval town and the **Narodni Trg**—the social heart of Split. Most evenings in the summer it is so densely thronged for the *korso* that one might be in a football crowd. There is an old and curious tradition connected with this *korso*: everyone moves along on an east to west line, but the young walk on the north side and, as they age, so, gradually, they move southward.

As for the Split personality, Spličani are a vivacious and even, on occasion, turbulent people. They also have a reputation for a particularly caustic humour and both the men and the girls are unusually good-looking. If you take part in the *korso* or just sit and gaze you begin to get an idea of them all. The Café Central is *the* place for discussion and meeting and no trip to Split is complete without a visit there.

There are two buildings of note in the *trg*: firstly, the big Clock Tower, high above the west gate, to which was added an ornate clock in the sixteenth century; secondly, the little Gothic palace, built in 1433, which now houses the **Ethnographical Museum.** This has a modest but interesting collection of costumes, instruments and other items of peasant workmanship. The two plaques outside record the liberation of the city in October 1944 and the first meeting of the Croatian Federal Government in 1945.

A number of narrow, irregular streets branch from this lung of the city. If you try the Domaldovo Ulica out of the north-west corner you will soon discover the church of the Holy Ghost (Sv Duje) and a gateway which gives on to the ruins of an eleventh-century convent.

From the south-west corner Šubić Ulica, which has some lovely buildings in it, (including what is called the small Papalić palace, refashioned in Gothic by Juraj Dalmatinac) runs into two small squares: Radić and Preporod. The two big towers in front of you (the Hrvoje) were part of fortifications built by the Venetians. On the left is the Milesi Palace, formerly the home of the noble Milesi family, now the **Maritime Museum**—an extremely well arranged and rewarding one. In the middle of the square is another work by Meštrović, a statue of one of the more famous early Croatian writers —Marko Marulić, who flourished between 1450 and 1524.

From here there is an opening on to Titova Obala which has some pleasant cafés and a number of shops and agencies devoted to the tourist's needs. Here also are some kiosks where you can buy English newspapers—a great rarity in Jugoslavia. They are seldom obtainable even in Belgrade. This scarcity can be frustrating for some people but a diligent beat round the foyers and sitting-rooms of 'A' category hotels will sometimes put up a *Times* or *Telegraph* that is not too out-of-date.

At the western end of the *molo*, just beyond the hotel Bellevue and the very handsome **Trg Republike** (more like a parade ground than a square and a favourite resort in the evenings) is the Franciscan church which contains the tomb of the poet Marulić and also that of the Archdeacon Thomas, the thirteenth-century chronicler of Split; a most important figure in its history. He was born in 1200 and as a student in Bologna in 1216 heard St Francis of Assissi preach. He describes how most of the city came to hear this man who was ugly, unkempt and of contemptible mien. Thomas became archdeacon in 1230 and for the next thirty-odd years was continuously involved in civic and religious affairs. He sounds a typical Spličani—active, exuberant and a trenchant critic of power and injustice.

If you walk along the edge of the harbour for about another ten minutes you will discover on your right the temporary Museum of Croatian Antiquities: an important collection with a great deal of medieval sculpture, including objects from Nin and Knin. This museum may shortly be re-housed elsewhere.

The high wooded hill—part of a peninsula—which lies west of here is the **Marjan.** It used to form part of the Emperor's hunting grounds. Now it is a public park and there is a zoo at the top. If you have an afternoon to spare there is a good walk right down the peninsula, through Meje, on the road which winds close to the shore. You can come back on the upper road along the edge of the woods. About half-way to the Marjan Point (where there is an oceanography institute and an aquarium) you will discover the **Meštrović Gallery;** a private villa which the sculptor presented to Split in 1952, containing a collection of his work. A little farther on is a large group of buildings surrounded by a wall, the Kaštelac. The chapel contains Meštrović's New Testament cycle of bas-relief woodcarving, thought by many to be his best work.

An alternative trip is to go via the upper road and return on the lower—along which there is a regular bus service. If you settle for this take the Lenjingradska Ulica from beyond the taxi rank at the end of Titova Obala and carry on until you reach the steps, then climb. Or you can go round the harbour, as if to the Museum of Croatian Antiquities, and take the Brajevica Ulica which again leads to steps. When you reach the top go straight ahead and you will find the tiny church of **Sv Nikola,** over a thousand years old and probably the best example of a cruciform domed Dalmatian church of its time. Another flight of steps brings you to near the zoo. You may need a drink by this stage; if so there is a café on the terrace with a splendid view over the city.

From the western end of Titova Obala a broad street, Marmontova Ulica (named after Marshal Marmont) goes straight up to **Bulatov Trg,** in the middle of which is yet another statue by Meštrović. This is of a nineteenth-century poet called Botić, a native of Split. The large building the other side of the square is the National Theatre. The whole area west of Marmont Street, known as **Varoš** (the suburb) is worth exploring at leisure. It is full of medieval buildings and old churches. In Marmont Street there is a café/restaurant called the Bastion on whose terrace they perform national and Dalmatian dances. The spectacle usually occurs on a Wednesday evening and should not be missed.

Northern Split, as I have suggested, is rather a mess. Amongst the confusion, however, there is one more museum which is more or less essential for the conscientious traveller. From Bulatov Trg take the Zrinjsko Frankopanska Ulica and at the end of it, on the left, you will find the **Archaeological Museum** which contains a valuable collection of prehistoric, classical and medieval objects. The things to look for particularly in the garden are an Egyptian sphinx, somewhat younger than that by the Mausoleum, some luxuriantly decorated sarcophagi (one showing Phaedra and Hippolytus, another Meleager and the hunt of the Calydonian boar) and some bas-reliefs of Pan. In the building there is a good statue of Diana, another of Venus, and an accumulation of jewellery, pots, coins, etc. Near here, in Lovretska Ulica, is a big, less important gallery with a fairly comprehensive collection of recent Dalmatian sculpture and painting and some early work by Meštrović.

If you strike out into the country beyond the archaeological museum (it is impossible to give clear directions: the only thing to do is to go on asking the way) you will eventually reach a rural Franciscan monastery called **Gospa od Poljuda,** a tenth-century foundation, though most of the present buildings are fifteenth. It has two paintings by Girolamo di Santa Croce. One, which was at the east end of the church but may have been moved during recent restoration, represents the *Virgin and Child* surrounded by angels and saints; the other the *Virgin and Child with St Peter*. In addition, do not miss the portrait of the bishop Thomas Nigro by Lorenzo Lotto. There is also an odd picture which shows famous writers who have praised the Virgin. Among them is Mahomet. This painting is supposed to have preserved the church from desecration by Muslims who actually used to visit it to do homage to their prophet.

From the monastery you look across the bright waters of Salona Bay to the Seven Castles and the fertile slopes beneath the Mosor range. If you return to the museum and then take a narrow street opposite (Sutrojičin Put) a few hundred yards brings you to the ninth-century church of the **Holy Trinity**—a pre-Romanesque building with six apses, which is fairly unusual.

The eastern portions of Split are rather dull and I think only the most assiduous visitor will take the trouble to explore them. But do not forget the animated market outside the eastern walls, and if you have time and like Baroque pop into Sv Dominik's church opposite the Silver Gate. This is a thirteenth-century foundation, restored in the seventeenth. The altarpiece is by Palma the Younger.

Within easy distance of Split there are several places eminently worth visiting.

A few kilometres north, just off the main *autoput*, are the widely scattered ruins of **Salona**—where Diocletian was probably born. *En route* (if you haven't got a car take one of the plentiful buses; the walk is tedious) you will see away on your right all that remains of the Emperor's aqueduct.

The old city, beyond the River Jadro, is spread across a slope dotted with shrub, small fields and trees. The ruins, among the most important in Europe, were excavated by the great Dalmatian archaeologist Monsignor Bulić between 1883 and 1932 and it is very appropriate that he should be buried near the site of his immense labours. Even now only a tenth of the area has been properly examined.

There was a Greek colony here in the third century B.C. on the site of an Illyrian settlement. In the Roman period it was an important town with a population estimated at sixty to eighty thousand. In the fourth century it became a vital centre of early Christianity and there survive the remains of at least thirty churches and basilicas. Whether you are an expert or not it is necessary to have a guide in order to get the best out of a visit there and the safe thing to do is to hire an official guide from the tourist office in Split. However, I suspect that most people are content with a stroll and an inquisitive poke about. You will have little difficulty in recognising a number of the exposed buildings: some of the temples, for example, the churches, the amphitheatre, baths, cemeteries and so forth. As one rests on an empty sarcophagus or in the slim shadow of a cypress and watches the lizards slip and flick between the carious walls, and the maroon and yellow hornets zooming from fig to fig, one becomes aware of what a very agreeable desolation it is, just the kind of place that evokes an elegiac and moralising mood in the *ubi sunt?* tradition. Almost certainly, as you relax, you will hear the raucous protest of a braying ass.

The road north from Salona ribbons up to the wind-scathed, scarred fortress of **Klis** which is clearly visible on the saddle of the pass into the interior. The name is believed to derive from the Greek κλεῖς or the Latin *clavis*, meaning a key. It is an apt name because strategically Klis is the key to Split and the whole area round it.

The immense fortifications, whose cracks and crannies support any number of growths like rosemary and lavender, would make a formidable stronghold even today. From its topmost dizzying heights one has an incomparable view of Split, the coast, the islands of Čiovo, Brač, Šolta and even Vis.

In fifteen centuries this fort has changed hands many times. The Avars and the Turks, the Venetians and the Austrians have all held it. Now once again it is Slav. Probably its greatest remembered hero was in fact a Slav—Petar Kružić whose tomb, as I mentioned earlier, is at Trsat. It was he who defended it against the Turks in 1523 and 1537.

Twenty-four kilometres beyond Klis—once more one is reminded of the comparative urbanity and ease of the coast and the sternness of the interior—you come to a green oasis in a grey wilderness of *karst:* the town of **Sinj.** Apart from a Franciscan monastery and the Roman remains of Aequum (near the village of Čitluk just north) there isn't a great deal to see in Sinj. But on August 15th or thereabouts each year it is crowded out with visitors to see one of the great spectacles of the Balkans—the **Alka Sinjska.** It is an anniversary which has been celebrated for two hundred and fifty years.

On August 13th 1715 a chronicler recorded that at noon all was quiet at Sinj. It was hot but the weather was uncertain. The streets were deserted. At sundown urgent activity began . . .

A mile or so away lay an army of Turks, including thirty thousand cavalry. Their tents were clearly visible from the town. The Pasha's envoys had already delivered a demand for surrender and this had been rejected disdainfully. The inevitable battle lasted two days—and ended in a Turkish defeat. The Pasha himself was unhorsed and had to leg it for safety, leaving his weapons and his mount Yedek on the banks of the River Cetina.

The *Alka* tournament was then instituted to commemorate a resounding victory. It is in fact a kind of jousting competition for which only citizens of Sinj and the Cetina March are eligible. The preliminary and eliminating rounds take place some time before and the preparations for the big event have brought everyone to a most intense pitch of excitement and anticipation by the time it is due. On *the* day, when everybody, even by Jugoslavian standards, rises inordinately early, the whole of Sinj is one exhilarating seethe and hum. The villagers come in from miles around. Large quantities of liquor are consumed.

Before combat comes a ceremonial procession through the streets. The contestants, looking rather handsome and cavalier in eighteenth-century costumes (a kind of hybrid of Cossack and the full dress of the Royal Horse Artillery) liberally lashed with gold and silver braid, and accoutred with a miscellany of arms—swords, daggers, rifles—march through Sinj accompanied by their mace bearers (*buzdovanari*), shield-bearers (*stitonoša*) and squires (*alkarski momci*). Part of the procession s a horse representing Yedek led by two youths from the Cetina March.

As they process to the sound of cacophonous and enthusiastic bands dozens of shots are let off in jubilation, mostly into the air. It is very much a Montenegrin-type entertainment, though here we are far from the Black Mountain.

The actual contest is exciting. Spectators sit crammed each side of the jousting area and run-up. A cloaked, fur-hatted 'knight' gets his charger into position. The trumpet sounds and he is off at a gallop, lance levelled, down the hundred and forty yard run which must be covered in not more than thirteen seconds.

At the end of it an iron ring (the *alka*) is suspended from a rope stretched fairly taut about nine feet above the ground. This (the details are important) has a diameter of six inches and contains another ring with a diameter of two inches. The two rings are joined by two horizontal pieces and one vertical—thus forming one upper half and two lower quarters. If the jouster pierces the inner ring he is awarded three points; if the upper half, two; if one of the lower quarters, one. All competitors have three rounds. At one side stands an official who informs the black-clad judges of the result. If the maximum has been scored a band plays a triumphal march and more shots are fired.

The victor's prizes are a sash and a silver shield, plus an inestimable amount of kudos in the neighbourhood. When it's all over the contestants and the young men of Sinj escort him to his home and an evening of Homeric conviviality follows. Eventually one returns to Split, elated and a little hung-over—partly from anticlimax.

The road south from Split, which runs through quite fertile land along the edge of the sea, takes you to the small town of **Omiš**—a fishing port and seaside resort. On the way you pass near Stobreč, the site of the ancient Greek colony of Epetion which was once linked with Trogir and Vis.

At Omiš the River Cetina runs out through the kind of gorge that invites mythical explanation. It is a gash of titanic proportions back into the mountains and thus produces the sort of wild scenery that always enchanted 'Romantic' landscape painters and illustrators. Most appropriately Omiš, which lies the far side of the swift, deep green Cetina, was once a prominent pirate stronghold for centuries impregnable. The Pope himself preached a holy war against the freebooters in 1221 because they were sacking the crusaders' ships. The Venetians spent a fortune trying to dislodge them and when they finally capitulated many of them merely moved north to Senj where they carried on their buccaneering for another two hundred years.

The predecessors of the people of Omiš were the Neretljani who were pagan until long after the majority of Slavs had been converted. In fact, Omiš, like Trogir and many other towns on this coast, was believed to be a heretical city. The existence of a number of Bogomil tombstones in the graveyard helps to support this theory.

Now Omiš has become a quiet and balmy spot. It even has a couple of paste factories and another for knitted goods. Most of the old walls have gone, but it still has a Baroque church, a distinguished bishop's palace and a number of aristocratic houses adorned with sculpted coats-of-arms. There is a harsh reminder of its turbulent and violent past in the remains of the original corsair fortifications built inaccessibly up the side of the mountain behind the town. The

95

main tower tops a pinnacle of rock. About three thousand feet higher there is another castle, Starigrad, now a complete ruin and a perfect accompaniment to a grandiose scene.

What you should certainly do is to take a stroll up the chasm alongside the Cetina. Quite soon it opens on the right into a marshy plain. Beyond are the Gubavica Falls and a huge hydro-electric station. Creeping up the main road to the interior the lorries look no bigger than bugs.

In the mountainous district away to the west, known as the **Poljica,** there existed a small 'rustic republic' until as late as 1807. It was then that Napoleon's troops, for no very good reason, slaughtered the inhabitants.

These people had no town but they lived in a dozen or more scattered villages each of which was governed by a *knez* ('duke' or 'prince') over whom presided a *veliki knez* (grand duke). The hierarchy consisted of three ranks: the highest consisted of about twenty families who claimed Hungarian descent; next were families descended from Bosnian nobility; third were the peasants or plebs. Lower still, not even qualifying as a rank, were the serfs: obviously the delta class. Even lower, at a social perigee of uncouthness not far removed from the brutish, were the slaves: clearly the epsilons; or even, as Aldous Huxley once called the Hollywood film moguls, 'semi-minus epsilons'.

Annually, on St George's Day, the great council assembled to elect their leaders. The *veliki knez* was nearly always chosen from the Hungarian ranks; the others from among the Bosnian 'nobles' by the peasants. If present at all, the deltas and epsilons formed an unsuffraged audience.

Fortis, who visited them in his travels (what an intrepid traveller he must have been!) remarked that the elections seldom went by without violence because there was usually more than one candidate. In which case, he says, 'one of the boldest partizans lays hold of the box containing the privileges of the community, which is the deposite annually committed to the care of the great count; he runs with the box towards the house of him for whom he is engaged, and every member of the diet has the right to pursue him with stones knives and firearms and may make use of their right to its full extent.'

One can well imagine that they did so. However, if the man took 'his measures well' (I presume that by this Fortis means 'ran like hell') and arrived safely at the proposed house with the box the

DUBROVNIK. *Above*, façade of the Rector's Palace. Probably based on designs by Michelozzo, but largely executed by another Florentine — Salvi Michele. In the middle background, the Sponza Palace. Both façades show the mixture of the Gothic and Renaissance styles typical of this coast. *Background*: Mt. Srdj, 1,200 feet. Just visible, the French fort built in 1809. *Right*, the capital of an arch on the Rector's Palace (fourth from right in upper picture)

Above, Mt. Lovčen Kotor. The lonely tomb and funeral chapel of Prince Njegoš, 5,000 feet above the Gulf. *Below*, Gulf of Kotor: the islands of Sv Juraj. Where the annual *fašinada* takes place. On the left the remains of the twelfth-century Benedictine monastery; on the right Gospa od Škrpjela (Our Lady of Chisels)

'grand duke' was duly elected and nobody could gainsay him. Very occasionally the *veliki knez* was chosen from among the Bosnians. If this happened it was not a good omen. And it was a long time before people forgot that the last *veliki knez*, when the French troops arrived, was a Bosnian.

They had many strange customs; among the oddest was the punishment of a murderer. The *knez* of the village plus his retinue was allowed free quarters and provisions in the offender's house for as long as he pleased. The *veliki knez* could then follow him, if there was anything left, and do likewise. Particularly grave murders were punishable by fines.

CHAPTER 7

The Coast VII : Dalmatia (continued) and Central Dalmatian Islands

Makarska Riviera—Neretva Delta—Narona—Šolta—Brač—Vis—Hvar— Korčula—Lastovo—Orebić—Ston—Trsteno—Mljet—'Pompey's Narrows'

It is 230 kilometres from Split to Dubrovnik and the *autoput* runs along a coastline full of variety and very often beautiful. It is a stretch that, for the traveller by car, can be taken at a good pace with a few stops.

After Omiš the first place of note is the small village of Mimice where the lower slopes of the mountains are hatched and terraced very neatly with vineyards. Somewhat beyond lies **Vrulja Bay**— which means 'boiling bay' because underwater springs fed from inland gush up and cause a considerable disturbance, especially after heavy rain. Here, through the Dubci Pass, the *bora* blows almost as fiercely as it does at Senj. If it happens to be blowing while you are about take care, otherwise you may take off.

From Vrulja Bay the coast for the next fifty kilometres is known as the **Makarska Riviera** and here, perhaps more than anywhere else, there is an absolutely consistent clear-cut contrast of sceneries. On the land side the Biokovo Mountains rise in abrupt precipices: whitish grey, beautiful and, for the most part, utterly barren. The narrow and fertile coastal strip is a succession of gracile, silvery golden beaches, pine woods, olive groves, and fig groves interspersed with small villages. Beyond is the ever blue, seductive Adriatic sea and, successively, the shores of Brač, Hvar and the Pelješac Peninsula. It is the kind of scenery that very few painters could handle without finishing with a mush of colour.

After Vrulja Bay, Brela—which is in two parts: Gornja Brela (upper) and Donja Brela (lower). The former is high above on the mountain face and its little church is surrounded by a number of

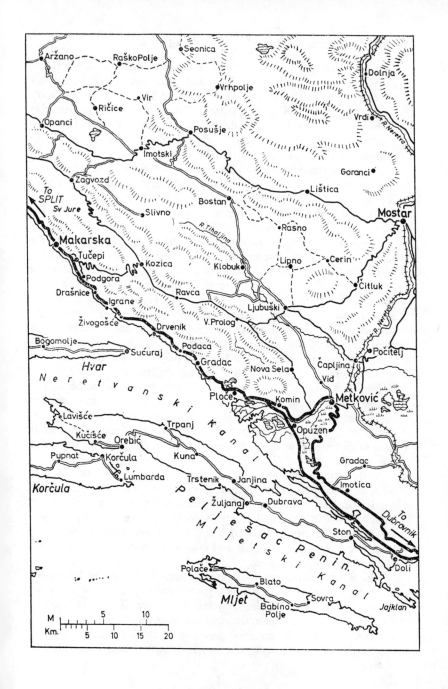

Bogomil *stećaks*. The latter village was born when the pirate threat was more or less removed and the mountain people felt it was safe to come down. There is a good beach at Donja Brela and some decent small hotels and private villas. I am told by Jugoslav friends that it is an excellent place to have a quiet holiday. The same can be said of Baška Voda, a little farther on. Both are well-connected with Split and Makarska.

By Dalmatian standards **Makarska** is a modern town, probably not more than a thousand years old; though the Romans had built a place called Muccurum nearby—which was duly destroyed by the Avars. Makarska and its region were eventually settled by the Neretljani.

There are few antiquities here though, of course, there are the usual architectural remains of various rules: Croatian, Turkish, Venetian and Austrian; by this stage you will have little difficulty in distinguishing one from another. On the harbour promenade survives a sixteenth-century Franciscan cloister and a church that was used as a mosque. The statue on the quay is by a relatively obscure sculptor called Rendić and represents a much more obscure popular poet of the eighteenth century called Kačić-Miošić.

Makarska, therefore, which is well-equipped with good hotels, is a very suitable place in which to contemplate one's navel, stroll, swim, bask and allow the benificent sun to soothe some of the effects of the thousand shocks we are heir to. It is easy to excurse to Split, neighbouring islands and other places I have mentioned. If the labours of sybaritism become tiring you can always don a stout pair of shoes and walk up to the summit of Sv Jure, six thousand feet above.

At Tučepi, not far on, there survives an eleventh-century chapel, with more Bogomil tombstones. At **Podgora,** which means, aptly, 'under-the-mountain', several hamlets are loosely joined along the road. On the hill overlooking the harbour you can hardly fail to see an immense monument called *The Gull's Wings*. This is one of the hundred foot high memorials and commemorates the heroic efforts of Partisans from this area.

There are several small villages between Podgora and Gradac— a most pleasant spot on a rocky promontory. From here the long mountainous ridge of the Pelješac Peninsula is clearly visible. Beyond Gradac the mountains dwindle and the road moves inland through rolling rocky country, past the six Baćinska Jezera (lakes) which are all linked, and joined to the sea by man. This join has produced the unusual situation that they have both fresh and salt-water fish.

Soon you are in **Ploče,** a large new port on the edge of the broad marshy delta of the Neretva River. There is something Chinese about this scene, an impression which is sharpened by the illusion of paddy fields, in fact reed beds, through which the locals get about in odd boats called *tupice* (*tupica* is a trunk). This delta is being gradually drained and will then provide hundreds of acres of fertile ground.

The *autoput* goes straight across the delta to **Opužen,** so called because the Venetians erected a fort there named Opus in 1716. Each side of the Neretva there are roads running up to Metković—a small, busy port even though it is twenty-odd kilometres from the sea. Metković is dull. Even the Jugoslav guide books say that the only thing of interest there is a collection of stuffed birds.

But a few kilometres north of it, near the village of Vid, are the remains of an important Roman colony: **Narona.** This was next in size to Salona. They were both razed by the Avars about the same time and in later centuries the region became the centre of those warrior tribes to whom I have referred—the Neretljani, described by Porphyrogenitus as Paganoi. They were an extremely indepen-dent people and, like those at Omiš, resisted Christianity until very late. The Venetians did not manage to defeat them until about A.D. 1000. Narona has hardly been touched by the archaeologists, but the expert and the amateur can both find something of interest. People are constantly discovering things on neglected sites like this.

Forty-five kilometres north of Metković is Mostar, in Hercego-vina: one of the loveliest towns of Jugoslavia. But this I deal with in a later chapter (p. 339).

From Opužen, across the *karst* plateau, there is nothing out-standing to divert you until you reach Rudine, near the neck of the Pelješac Peninsula, where there is a road back to Ston while the *autoput* carries on to Dubrovnik.

So far I have not said anything about what are known as the **central** and **south Dalmatian islands** which, with the exception of Rab, are the most interesting of all on this coast. This, therefore, is a convenient point at which to return, as it were, to Split, before carrying on from Ston.

Getting about in Jugoslavia always creates interesting problems, not least on the coast though here the communications are better than anywhere. The main difficulty on the coast is to decide how much to use the road and how much the ships. Whether you have a car or not the ideal compromise is to boat one way and drive the other. If you have a car and cannot or don't want to do this, one answer is to leave your car at, say, Split, and make excursions to Brač and Hvar. Then you can drive on down the coast along the route already summarised and visit Korčula from Pelješac. More southerly islands like Mljet are better reached from Dubrovnik. An excellent if somewhat expensive alternative is to take your car with you on the boats and have it put off at Brač, Hvar and Korčula. From Korčula you can return to the mainland at Orebić on the ferry. I put these forward as more or less obvious suggestions which, in the final analysis, have to be implemented and refined by a careful study of the map and the latest timetables.

Šolta (see map on p. 69) is only a short journey from Split, a smallish island which, like Brač, was once used by the Roman emperors to dispose of political exiles. Later they were found handy for keeping dangerous heretics out of the way.

Šolta is very fertile and so far unspoilt by tourism. Its main villages are Nečujam and Grohote, but Nečujam is about the only place that caters for the visitor. If you go there for a day excursion take some provisions with you. There is very little in the way of antiquities but it is an ideal place for a long walk. Unfortunately the Italians destroyed many of the villages during the war and either massacred or deported much of the population.

Brač, an ellipse in shape, and the third largest island on the coast, is much more interesting and extremely beautiful, though still little known. In the past it has been renowned for its goat's milk cheese, which Pliny extols, and for its wines, which Fortis praised. The reputations hold good today. The dark, purplish red wine of Bol is particularly delicious. There are also Vugava, from the area of Nerežišće, a golden white wine, and Murvica, a red. In fact Brač is a very fertile island and to be recommended to anyone who enjoys walking and who likes to get off the beaten way of the tourist.

There are many enchanting villages, especially Selca, Milna, Sutivan and Supetar, which is the largest town. Both Milna and Sutivan have good beaches. At Supetar you should certainly make a point of seeing the noble mausoleum of the Petrinović family done by the sculptor Rosandić, himself a Dalmatian. He was a much less prolific artist than Meštrović. The Petrhović family, incidentally, came from Supetar and a number of them emigrated to Chile where they made fortunes in the nitrate fields.

The quarries of Brač are famous for a very fine stone, much prized and used all over the world. Diocletian's masons used it for his palace. Trogir cathedral was also built of it; as, for example, was the Canadian war memorial on Vimy Ridge. It is a very white limestone and scarcely ever tarnishes. Naturally enough many of the houses on Brač were also made with it.

Much farther out to sea is **Vis,** said to have derived its name from Issa, a girl from Lesbos loved by Apollo. Vis, which is visited even less often than Brač, is a very small island with a benevolent climate. It rises nearly two thousand feet to Hum peak (*hum*, incidentally, has much the same meaning as 'hummock') and consists of a rocky shell protecting a fertile core of vineyards and flowery vales, orange and lemon groves, scenes which no Dorian Greek or Theocritus (who might easily have come here from Syracuse) could fail to celebrate in eclogues. During the last war it was used as an H.Q. for the Partisans and the British Military Mission and about this phase of its life there is a good account by the leader of the Mission, Sir Fitzroy Maclean, in his book *Eastern Approaches*: essential and first-class reading for anyone with more than a cursory interest in the country.

This was by no means the first time the island had been used as a base. It was originally colonised by the Greeks from Syracuse (when it was known as Issa) from whence they established themselves at Trogir and Stobreč. In those days, as now, Vis was famous for its wine, Opol, a quite outstandingly good light red (this is also produced near Trogir). There are also Black Vis (*Viško crno*) a strong heavy red wine which can even be drunk with tunny; another form of Vugava, a strong, heavyish white; and Plavac—purply, dark and also strong.

During the Napoleonic period the British seized Vis, as well as Korčula, and used it as a base for transporting goods to central Europe. When a French admiral tried to stop this he was defeated by Hoste and a British cemetery commemorates the event. Later the English gave the island to the Austrians and there was another big naval battle in 1866 when the Austrian navy, largely manned by Jugoslavs, trounced the Italians, an engagement in which one of the early iron-clads was used.

There are several interesting villages on Vis, especially Komiža, a fishing village with a sardine industry. In fact the whole region is very rich in fish and all round the rocky coasts of these outlying islands there are large numbers of crab and lobster. After the crustacea have been caught and before they are sent on to Zagreb, Belgrade and elsewhere, they are temporarily stored in a huge, roofed concrete basin, so big that a rowing boat is needed to go out and select the 'catch'. Komiža also has a couple of churches to which are attached strange legends. One of them is called Gospa Gusarica (Our Lady of the Pirates) because it contains a miraculous picture of the Virgin once stolen by pirates. However, every time they tried to go out of harbour the spell of the picture held them back. It wasn't until they threw it overboard (it was later recovered by 'miraculous' intervention!) that they were able to move on. The other church, Sv Nikola, was reputed to possess the relic of all relics; the head of Christ. Sensibly enough this tradition has been allowed to lapse, like that of Meshach, Shadrach and Abednego.

There is a small island nearby called **Biševo** where the descendants of the original vines still survive because it was one of the few places that did not catch the phylloxera plague which devastated the vineyards of Europe in 1866. (After this disaster Europe was restocked with vines from America.) Biševo, which was first settled in the eleventh century by the Benedictines (their church of St Silvester still stands), also possesses a rather fine Blue Grotto (Modra Špilja)—which is about as impressive as the one at Capri. If you can arrange to visit it between 10 a.m. and noon you will see a dazzling chromatic display. There is another cave called by the locals Medvidina (Bear's Cave) because the seals like to shelve there. The islanders call them 'she-bears of the sea'.

If you were to base yourself on Vis (and it would make a most unusual and interesting place for a holiday or part of one) you could easily get to the other small islands in the vicinity: Svetac, for instance, a thousand foot high rock, covered with pine and scrub and whose ruined fortifications are alleged to be Illyrian; and Jabuka Island which is composed almost entirely of iron ore (havoc to compasses!); and the Isle of Brusnik (the whetstone) where there are small lavender-coloured dragons, and where I have certainly seen a strange, black, fork-tailed lizard.

There is no doubt that living on small islands steeped in sun, especially when they produce good wine, promotes a certain disposition. Even after a few hours' romancing over the bottle with the natives of Vis and thereabouts classical mythology becomes quite reasonable and the stories and superstitions of sailors and fishermen are as rational as the apophthegms of Bacon.

There are a number of places on this coast about which it is not easy to speak temperately. **Hvar** (pronounced whar) is one of them. Like the Peljesac Peninsula and the islands of Mljet, Brac and Korcula, the island of Hvar (which is quite long: about seventy kilometres) is obviously the top of part of a submerged mountain range lying at a slight tangent east-west from the mainland. The principal towns and villages (with the exception of Hvar itself) overlook the Hvarski Kanal and a shore of Brac. People have been living here for at least three thousand years. At Starigrad-na-Hvaru, for example (Old-town-on-Hvar) there are a number of pre-Illyrian remains—more particularly the so-called 'Cyclopean Walls' built of gigantic blocks of stone. There are comparable walls at Mycenae and Troy and the Greeks believed they must have been built by the giant Cyclops. At Jelsa there are the remains of Illyrian and Greek fortifications. Scattered about the island you can discover other vestiges of ancient tenancy. Most periods of its history are represented. (See map on p. 69.)

When the ship comes round the headland and you suddenly see the town of Hvar itself, as golden as the honey the island is famous for, you realise why the ancients thought of it as one of the Isles of the Blessed—that half-mythical paradise or Utopia that has haunted the consciousness of western civilisation for centuries. All expectations are fulfilled. For once the posters and the photographs have not exaggerated.

It spreads across the hill, round the harbour, a yellow, old palimpsest, patched, carelessly splashed with the black interjections of cypress. Through the interstices, across the rucks, there are splodges and scrolls of colour where the fig burgeons and the oleanders exfoliate into curly doodles, and the bougainvillæa runs purple and waxy like broken seals.

The climate, like that of Korcula, is perennially benign—so benign that the hoteliers, whose establishments overlook the harbour, won't charge for any day in winter when there is fog, snow or a temperature at or below freezing point. In addition they offer a fifty per cent reduction for any day on which there is more than three hours' rain between seven and five. They are nearly infallibly safe concessions. I have seldom seen Hvar but it is basking gently between an immaculate blue sky and an almost flawless blue sea: idyllic but never monotonous—as sometimes the idyllic can be. As you might expect the hotels at Hvar are pretty good and it also claims one of the best plages in Dalmatia. I recommend the Palas and the Dalmacija, but Hvar, like Korčula and Dubrovnik, is a most suitable place to take a room in a private house. The name Hvar, incidentally, has caused a certain amount of disagreement. One school of thought maintains that it comes from the Greek for a lighthouse—*pharos*; another that the first Greek colonisers came from the island of Pàros.

The town is small so you will not have been there very long before you discover a beautiful and unusual town square, almost triangular, at the apex of which stands the sixteenth-century **Cathedral,** Sv Stjepan, alongside its Romanesque belfry. The façade is eighteenth century. You will easily be able to distinguish the blend of Gothic and Renaissance styles so typical of this coast. Inside there are some lovely marble altars and some equally fine carved choir stalls, plus a painting over the high altar attributed to Palma the Younger representing *St Stephen and a Pope.* You should certainly ask to see the treasure in the sacristy. Look especially at the crozier or Bishop's staff: a masterpiece of delicacy and ingenuity by an early sixteenth-century goldsmith. The ruins behind the cathedral were a Gothic Venetian palace.

The combination of the white and wheat-coloured stone, the irregularity of the design and the variety of the handsome buildings make the whole piazza one of the most pleasing on the coast, and down at the base of the triangle, near the harbour, a wide opening with a rounded arch reveals the sixteenth-century Arsenal which was converted into a theatre in 1612. This makes it one of the oldest in Europe and it is still used for plays and concerts.

The Clock Tower opposite is a beauty, and so is the **Loggia** built by the great Sammicheli between 1515-17 and now part of the Palas Hotel. The terrace above is a congenial place to lunch or dine and sample the astringent white wines of Hvar with lobster or mullet and the local Prošek with dessert. While you are indulging your palate the eye can feed with a more ascetic voluptuousness on the shells and skeletons of palaces and noble mansions which rise irregularly up the hill opposite. The hill culminates in a large, very well-preserved fort built by the Spaniards in 1531; above it is another, equally well-preserved, which was made by the French in the Napoleonic period.

It is well worth climbing up the stepped and narrow streets to the very summit. On the way you go under the old town gate by the Arsenal and you will see almost immediately on your left what is the most superb Gothic façade in the whole place, all that survives of the house of the Croatian poet Hektorović, chiefly famous for a poem called *Ribanje* (Fishing) which was published in 1555 and gave an idyllic picture of the Dalmatian fisherman's life.

Hvar is full of aristocratic ruins like this, most of which were caused directly by a particularly barbarous corsair called Uluz-Ali who burnt the city in 1571. After this catastrophe there was not—and never has been—enough money to rebuild them. According to legend Uluz-Ali was a renegade monk from Calabria who burnt every place which contained a church. But, as so often, one is more than surprised that anything has survived the vicissitudes of conquest after conquest.

At the other end of the town, a few minutes' walk, is a small **Franciscan Monastery** whose refectory, not used as such now, harbours one of the best collections of painting on the coast. (Ring for entrance and a monk will guide you, but probably only in French.) The principal pictures are by Francesco di Santa Croce, Palma the Younger and one of the Bassano family—they say, Leandro. Those by Santa Croce are supposed to have been presented by a noble family of the town who either brought the pictures or invited the artist from Venice. There is also a small portrait of a saint which I was assured is by El Greco, but I have been unable to confirm this from any source. However, the pride and joy of the monastery is a large painting of the *Last Supper* which occupies the traditional position at the end of the refectory and fills the whole wall from the dado to the ceiling. The figures are very nearly life size and it is a most vivid and accomplished work. It is ascribed to a Florentine, not very well known, called Matteo Rosselli. It is said that he was crossing the Adriatic from Italy to Dubrovnik when he fell ill and was looked after by Franciscans. The painting was his gift of gratitude.[1]

You should also have a look at the church which has some fine choir stalls by Dalmatian craftsmen. The excellent *Madonna and Child* in the lunette above the west door is reminiscent of della Robbia's china work. From the point beyond you have a good view of the Pakleni Otoci (the Islands of Hell), an archipelago of large

[1] According to Professor Siriščević it is now more than likely that it was the work of Matteo Ingoli, of the Venetian school.

rocks round which there is some of the best underwater fishing in the Mediterranean.

If you decide to explore the island, which is tolerably well supplied with public transport, you ought to try and see the villages of Starigrad, Jelsa and Vrboska, especially the last. It is a very pretty village, at the end of a narrow bay, surrounded by pine woods and vineyards. There are two churches there and one is both church and castle, a kind of citadel for final refuge in war. It is crenellated and has embrasures for cannon. It possesses several pictures; one of them is ascribed to Paolo Veronese; another (according to local tradition) to Titian, a third to Leandro.

Three hours away on the boat down the Korčulanski Kanal lies the town of **Korčula**, (see maps on pp. 68 and 99) at the eastern end of the island. In size it approaches Hvar but is much more compact, built on a tiny, bud-shaped, humped promontory and surrounded by the remains of massive fourteenth-century fortifications. Its name probably derives from the Greek 'Korkyra melaina' (Black Korkyra), the name the Greeks gave the island because it was covered in thick, dark woods. For the Romans it was 'Corcyra Nigra'. You can get a complete superficial impression of the place in an hour or two, but it is worth spending two days there: one for the town, one for excursions. There are two hotels: the first, immediately opposite when you disembark, is the Korčula; the second is The Park, about two kilometres out of the town. This has five annexes or pavilions, as they call them. The Korčula is simple and inexpensive and has the advantage of being handy.[1]

The design of the town reveals an interesting feature. It is like a fish skeleton (except at the tip) with the backbone running the length of the hump, but nearly all the streets which rib it are slightly curved and also off-set where they join. This reduces the effects of wind and is thought to be the original Greek plan.

If, on leaving the Hotel Korčula, you turn left and walk along the quay you almost at once find a splendid stone stairway, and then the old Loggia which for centuries gave shelter to travellers arriving after dark when the town was closed. A few paces on are the shipping office, then the tourist office, and in a couple of minutes you have arrived at the neck of the peninsula and the main City Gate to the old town (the newer parts stretch away on your right) which was erected in the seventeenth century to celebrate the Venetian victory over the Turks at Lepanto in 1571.

[1] Now also the Marko Polo, and Bon-repos tourist settlement.

This gateway gives on to the **Glavna Ulica**—the spine. Immediately on the left is the sixteenth-century Town Hall with an elegant loggia. The building the other side is the church of Sv Mihovil (St Michael). The Glavna Ulica leads one directly to the main *trg*, if anything so irregular as this may be called a square. It has always been a focal point for the citizens, for society, diversion and even sport. Historians record that it was used by the Korčulani for ball games, even some form of soccer. One of the better known stories relevant involves a certain Jacopo Faganeo, a Florentine monk with a great reputation for erudition and for eloquence in the pulpit. On a visit there he took part in a game of football and distinguished himself. When it was suggested that he should preach in the Cathedral the canons were scandalised and refused to allow such a sportive monk in their pulpit. A few years later Faganeo was appointed Bishop of Korčula and, apparently, was a great success.

On the left of the square are two Venetian Gothic palaces which used to belong to the patrician Gabrieli and Arneri families. The former now harbours the **City Museum;** a modest but pleasing display of local objects which includes a plaster cast of an important fourth-century Greek inscription found at Lumbarda, a seaside village a few kilometres distant. This is Korčula's oldest written record. The museum also has a display which records Korčula's ancient craft of shipbuilding, for which a great deal of timber on the island was used. A century and a half ago there were more than a hundred shipyards and though there are only a few left the tradition is very strong. Quite a lot of ships are turned out each year. Early documents show an odd British connection with Korčula; Korčulani and Britons fought together against Napoleon's armies. At one time there was a British naval H.Q. on the island.

Opposite this palace stands the former **Bishop's Palace,** which houses another museum: a delightful small collection of works of art, in the care of Father Matijaca: a priest whose admirable taste is matched by his warmth and courtesy. Knock at the right hand door and he will show you in.

Everything is well-labelled in French as well as Croatian. Apart from early manuscripts, Gothic chalices and medieval embroidery there are a number of good paintings and a curious statuette of Mary Stuart, beautifully carved and rather like a Madonna of Mercy: the skirt opens out to reveal kneeling men and women. Nobody I have asked has an explanation of who the people are or how the statuette got there. The best pictures are *An Unknown*

Man by Carpaccio, a *Madonna and Child* by G. Bellini, *An Unknown Knight* from the school of Bassano, and a *Virgin and Saints* of the school of Titian. There are also some fine studies of hands by Tiepolo. Altogether this comprises one of the most agreeable small art collections one is likely to come across in this part of Europe.

Next to the bishop's palace is the **Cathedral of Sv Marko,** the principal work of art in the town. It was started in the thirteenth and finished in the sixteenth century (once again one marvels at the continuity of the craftsmen of those times) and is a mixture of Gothic Romanesque and Baroque, though it was a fifteenth-century Korčulan, Marko Andrijić, who was responsible for most of what we see now.

Space was too valuable to allow a large piazza so one cannot get far enough away from the façade to view it properly. Nevertheless it is lovely and the most striking feature is the balance between large blank areas and details of great richness and complexity: the door, the window, the gable. On either side of the main door are the figures of Adam and Eve, somewhat less dignified than their counterparts at Šibenik and Trogir, supporting couchant lions. On the ornate cornice are some curious beasts among which are two alleged to be elephants. The rose window is splendid and so is the elaborately carved gable with its strange female bust about which there has been much speculation.

The interior is very irregular, yet somehow harmonious. The main works of art to look for are the Tintoretto, behind the high altar, showing St Mark, patron saint of the town, and the ciborium over the high altar which Andrijić did himself. The Gothic baptistery, the choir stalls and the thirteenth-century font are also worth examining.

In the cathedral's baptismal register there is an entry of 1520 in the name of Polo, and there are still Polos living in Korčula. The island has a rival claim to Venice as the birthplace of Marco Polo. As many of Venice's naval commanders came from Dalmatia the Korčulese claim may well be just. What is called 'Marco Polo's House', a curious machicolated building, stands a little beyond the cathedral. There is nothing to see in it but the tower affords a pleasant roof-top panorama.

Polo was captured with his Doge in 1298, just off the island, during a great sea battle with the Genoese—who held Korčula for some time. While he was in prison in Genoa he wrote his *Travels,* one of those books that I suspect a lot of people imagine they have read. It was in 1271 that, with his uncle and father, Marco set off on an embassy from the Pope to the Grand Khan of Tartary. They visited the Emperor of China and spent seventeen years in the territories of the Grand Khan. Eventually they returned by sea via the Persian Gulf and reached Venice after an absence of twenty-four years.

If you retrace your steps from the cathedral *trg* (the standard, incidentally, was erected as a flagpole in 1515 and afterwards served as a pillory) towards the triumphal arch and take the last turn but one to the left and walk down to the end of the street you will find a small church called Svih Svetih (All Saints) which was built about 1300. Inquiry at one of the houses opposite will produce a caretaker (*čuvar*)—probably an old lady who speaks beautiful Italian—and she, with a good deal of pride, will invite you to look at a collection of Byzantine icons, a magnificent fifteenth-century silver cross and a large pietà. A coffer in the sacristy contains costumes worn during the procession of the three religious brotherhoods every Good Friday. I have not been able to see this but I am told it is a memorable spectacle.

Long after one has done one's duty by the accredited monuments Korčula remains a town in which it is a continual delight to stroll and gaze. It is built of the same beautiful stone as Hvar and Dubrovnik, for instance, and at high noon it looks quite white. As the light changes it acquires subtle golden hues, shades of amber and mead, the illusion of a patina. To be in it is like walking about in the rare fabric of a shattered honeycomb, a Cyclopean comb—not indeed fashioned with the discipline and geometrical forethought of the bee, yet with a grace and strength, an acute perception of the fair proportions of things and the virtues of stone, that give an inestimable pleasure.

There are any number of deserted mansions, empty palaces. Orange trees and lemon trees fill their courtyards. Fig trees prise open cracks in the masonry. Bougainvillæa purples over balconies and balustrades. At every turn there is a Gothic or Renaissance window, the armorial bearing of some extinct family or order, knockers, crests . . . There is a kind of elegant desolation in these buildings which is not in the least depressive. They have been so well constructed that I am sure they will survive until there is ample money to restore them.

Every year, on July 27th, there is an event at Korčula which should on no account be missed. This is the **Moreška;** a traditional

III

spectacle at least a thousand years old, which also used to be done at Vis, Budva, Dubrovnik, Split and Zadar. It is performed by the young men of the island, the boat-builders, the masons and farmers, and is basically an amalgam of dance, masque and melodrama. One form of it symbolises the war between the Christians and Arabs in which there is a more or less peaceful ending; the other a struggle between the Moors and the Turks at the end of which the Moorish leader is conquered. The latter episode is the one which you can see at Korčula. It used to take place below the city walls near the Loggia but is now usually presented on the basket-ball arena near the Hotel Park. (You should book seats as far ahead as possible and find out whether or not there are extra performances on other days—now almost certain in view of the increasing number of tourists.)

The spectacle begins with the kidnapping of Bula (a word which in Turkish means a 'veiled woman') who is believed to symbolise the town of Korčula, by the Moorish king Moro. All his followers are clad in black with white embroidery and trimmings. Bula is the betrothed of the Sultan Osman who, exotically clothed in red (his followers are also in red with yellow and white trimmings) arrives to rescue her. Then the two principals fight until Moro is defeated. While this is going on Bula tries to intervene to save the Sultan. There then ensues a highly intricate and exciting 'dance' in seven different figures and a symbolic battle between the two sides. Each combatant has two swords: one symbolising attack, the other defence. The two forces, in an inner and an outer circle, move round each other crouching, weaving and interchanging in a series of stylised patterns. It is half march, half ballet. There are several passages of arms in which the rhythms become faster, the clashing of swords more violent. Sparks actually fly. It is a skilled and potentially dangerous conflict. A faulty stroke, a missed parry, and blood flows.

Of course, this spectacle has many parallels in traditional European folk drama and not a few in the fertility rites of most parts of the globe. The Sword Dance is often a survival or a development of an initiatory rite and the men of Korčula are only perpetuating a tradition that, according to our earlier records, was practised by the Maruts and the Kouretes. There are obvious similarities between their ceremonials and those of the Roman *Salii*, and somewhat less obvious parallels with those of the Grail knights. In Britain the nearest analogies in dramatic form are the Revesby Play (a folk drama of Lincolnshire), the Plough Monday Play (from the east

Midlands), the Sword Dance and the Mummer's or St George (or Sir George or King George) play which is fairly widespread in these isles and in which the main contestants are St George (or king or sir), a Turkish knight, Captain Slasher and a doctor. These plays appear to be more closely connected with fertility rites than the Moreška, though I should think it is possible that the Moreška incorporates elements from a time prior to the Turkish threat. They are nearly all linked with rituals that symbolise the death and resurrection of the year.

Another festivity to be seen on the island is the **Kumpanija** or *ples od boja* (battle dance) which recalls a time when Saracen pirates harassed the island and celebrates a victory over them. As in the Moreška there is a balletic conflict (to the accompaniment of bagpipes and drums) which includes stylised figures under the sword and over it and ends with a decapitation. Finally all the performers do the *starinski tanac*, an old Korčulan folk dance. The decapitation looks like a direct link with fertility rite. Curiously enough a Turkish knight (Turk, Saracen and Moor were all regarded as infidel and many of them were pirates) is a stock character in English folk plays and appears, for example, in a Midland Mumming play in which he is killed by St George. He is subsequently brought back to life by a doctor—another stock character. The symbolism of rebirth is obvious. In the Moreška and the Kumpanija it is a matter of delivery rather than rebirth.

The Kumpanija occurs every April 23rd at Blato (it means 'swamp' or 'mud') a village in the middle of the island. I once saw four black men here and again I thought they must be Negroes from Ulcinj. But they turned out to be four Germans covered in black mud.

There is no doubt that the whole island of Korčula, like Hvar, is a most rewarding place to explore if one has the time. A few kilometres east of Korčula is the small village of Lumbarda with some pleasant sandy beaches. On the way there you pass the Vrnik quarry which has been supplying stone for Dalmatian buildings since the time of Christ. Round this part is also produced an excellent wine called Grk (Greek), a pale, amber-coloured, aromatic dessert wine, fairly dry. At the other end of the island lies Vela Luka where there are two small hotels. On the way you pass several pretty villages; particularly Zrnovo and Cara. I was once wandering about in a desolate part of the centre of the island when I saw two unfamiliar creatures, which I later discovered were jackals. In fact, Korčula is one of the last haunts of the European jackal, a rather scruffy looking animal like a cross between a dog and a fox. The theory is that most domestic dogs have descended from wolves and jackals.

The smallish island of which you may catch a glimpse south-east of Korčula is **Lastovo,** where, according to legend, Calypso detained Odysseus for seven years. You can reach it by the occasional boat from Korčula or Dubrovnik and, though there is not much to see in the way of antiquities, it is a beautiful island, very thickly wooded, and the town of Lastovo itself is a most amiable place where you can see some interesting costumes. These are most unusual and worn as a rule on festive days. Basically they are red and black, decorated with gold braid. The men wear bowler hats and bow ties and have broad yellow stripes down their trousers. This is the only place in Jugoslavia where I have seen bowlers— though once I found a Macedonian farmer wearing a very motheaten, faded brown bowler. Heaven knows where it came from.

At Lastovo we again find a number of legends and traditions connected with the Turks and pirates including one of particular interest called the **Poklad** or Carnival. It is a ceremonial pageant performed in the streets (in much the same way as the Mystery Plays were) action and dialogue being supported by song and dance. The procession, with an effigy of a Turk, moves through the town, stopping at various points to present different scenes. These are always improvised because there is no text, and in any case everyone knows the plot. The cast includes the Turk's mother, a doctor, his assistant, a vet (!), an admiral, a standard bearer, a musician who plays the lyre, and what are known as the *pokladari*: men representing the Lastovo forces. The effigy of the Turk is eventually tried and burned. While it is burning the townspeople sing and the church bells are rung.

The historical and semi-legendary origin of this rite was a siege of the island by Turkish pirates, one of whom was sent as envoy to demand surrender. Instead of surrendering the men fought and after a storm had dispersed the pirate fleet the unfortunate envoy was burnt at the stake. There are clear similarities between this ritual and English Mumming plays—especially in the function of the Turk, the mother and the doctor.

One delightful excursion from Korčula is to the densely wooded nearby island of Badija where there is a fifteenth-century Franciscan monastery (there are records of a Benedictine foundation in the tenth century) which has probably the most beautiful cloister on the coast. It is a miracle that there is anything left, because the wretched Uluz-Ali sacked the place in 1571, no doubt by way of revenge after failing to subdue Korčula. Other barbarians did the same thing nearly a century later, but it and a few monks survived.

Opposite the town of Korčula one can see quite distinctly the white houses of **Orebić** on the long mountainous thrust of the Pelješac Peninsula: a particularly fertile part of the coast and an increasingly popular resort. Orebić is famous for its retired sea-captains one of whom runs a small hotel called the Bellevue where you may still be able to do yourself pretty well for very little. In the middle of the village is a pink house belonging to a Mr Matko, a lawyer with a long ancestry of sea-captains, and this has been turned into a museum which gives one a good idea of a middle-class family's tastes and interests over the past hundred years or so. Most of the houses of Orebić have lovely gardens, full of flowers and palm trees, and the whole area, thanks to the very temperate climate, is rich in vegetation: forests of cypress and pine; orchards; almonds, figs and what not.

West of Orebić are some of the pleasantest small resorts on the whole coast: Kučiste, Viganj and Lovište. The people round Viganj are known locally as the Farauni or Pharaohs. The names of their villages are interesting ethnographically because they suggest a former gipsy settlement. Viganj itself means a 'bellows', Nakovan, an 'anvil', Kovačevići, the 'smiths'. In the Balkans smiths are very often gipsies and are still frequently to be seen plying their trade, though I have only seen them in Serbia and Macedonia. A further curiosity is that gipsies are sometimes known as Pharaohs.

High above the villages soars the peak of Sv Ilija, a mountain whose sides are thick with pine forests, also inhabited by jackal (jackal shooting is a local sport), and this provides magnificent if somewhat strenuous walking country.

The road from Orebić to Ston is spectacular. Sometimes you careen along the mountainside hundreds of feet above the sea, sometimes stoop to cross comparatively level plains. You soon pass through the village of Dingač, which gives its name to one of the better known exported wines: a strong, rather heavy, red vintage to be avoided in the heat of the day.

Half an hour or so farther on lies the interesting town of **Ston,** little known to tourists, a powerfully fortified and ancient outpost of the republic of Ragusa or, as we now call it, Dubrovnik. In fact, Ston was about the northernmost point of the old republic. It is here also that for the first time on this coast we come into contact with the peripheral nerve-ends, as it were, of Serbia and Montenegro and their histories. Outside the town of Ston, which has some imposing Gothic and Renaissance mansions, there stands a tiny church called St Michael's, which contains the portrait of an eleventh- or twelfth- century Serbian *župan* supposed to be the founder of the state which grew into Montenegro and which was formerly called Zeta. In the neighbourhood are the remains of several other early Christian churches. From now on the influences of the Turks and the Serbian empire become gradually more apparent.

Beyond Ston you leave the Pelješac Peninsula and run through hilly country which superficially resembles parts of Scotland. The rocky ground is covered in pine woods, tamarisk and juniper scrub. There is nothing much to detain you until you reach Dubrovnik except the small and pretty village of Trsteno—an agreeable spot to stop for some refreshment, perhaps some Dalmatian ham and a glass of Prošek.

There are a couple of truly colossal plane trees in **Trsteno** by the main road which are supposed to be the largest trees in girth in Jugoslavia and also to be at least five hundred years old. It may be so, but trees, like carp, have a tendency to acquire reputations for longevity. Anyway, they are splendid trees and near them a tablet commemorates the thousandth anniversary of Croatia's first king— Tomislav. The circular cemented area next to it is a dance floor. There are quite a lot of these in Balkan villages and they are circular because that is the shape of the threshing floor, often the only flat area to be found in villages—especially in the hills. The threshing floor is believed to be the probable origin of the Greek theatre's shape.

Trsteno was the home of a number of celebrated and affluent men of Dubrovnik some of whose houses survive. One of the better known families were the Gučetić, reputed to have entertained guests as diverse as Titian, Byron and Marshal Marmont. The house stands and its gardens have been turned into an arboretum.

All the way from Janjina to Ston you run parallel with the north-west shore of Mljet, the other side of the Mljetski Kanal, the only other island of much note between Korčula and Dubrovnik. **Mljet,** seldom visited by tourists, is long and narrow, but somewhat smaller than Hvar and Korčula, and there is a very strong tradition indeed that St Paul was shipwrecked here on the way to Rome—an event of which there is that vivid description in Monsignor Knox's version of *The Acts*: 'For several days we saw nothing of the sun or the stars, and a heavy gale pressed us hard, so that we had lost, by now, all hope of surviving; and we were much in want of food . . . On the fourteenth night, as we drifted about in the Adriatic Sea, the crew began to suspect, about midnight, that we were nearing land . . . When we were safe on land we found that the island was called Melita. The kindness which the natives showed to us was beyond the ordinary.'

If Mljet was Melita and not Malta (Adria can be taken to mean the central Mediterranean in general) then the fact that St Paul was bitten by a viper becomes more relevant. Malta has no poisonous snakes and may never have had any; Mljet has always had them, so many in fact that at some time mongooses were imported to reduce them. There are still plenty of mongooses and some snakes on the island.

If you go to Mljet you will find the natives as courteous and hospitable as they were to St Paul and his mariners. Like Čiovo and Brač it once served as a place of banishment. One of the exiles built a palace which survives and round it has developed the village of Polače. What most people go to see are the three sea-water lakes surrounded by antique forests. At the southern end of the Veliko Jezero there is a small island on which stands a twelfth-century Benedictine monastery which has been converted into a hotel.

There are several more small islands, close to the mainland and easily reached from Dubrovnik, the chief of which are named Koločep, Lopud and Šipan: all amiable places and geared to tourism and excursions. Between Šipan and Jakljan runs a strait called **'Pompey's Narrows'** to which is attached the kind of apocryphal tale the Dalmatians are fond of. Guides will tell you that Pompey was trapped in the Bay of Šipan by Caesar and escaped towards Egypt through the strait. Do not believe them. It is almost certain that it was from Dyrrachium (now Drač, the main port of Albania) that Pompey made his flit.

CHAPTER 8

The Coast VIII :
Dubrovnik and region

Dubrovnik—Trebinje—Cavtat

The pages of many guide books and travel reminiscences which deal
with **Dubrovnik** (it means 'a wooded place') are always clogged
with the superlatives and banalities of excessive adulation. . . .'The
loveliest place God ever made' . . . 'The fairest gem in the crown of
imperial Venice' . . . 'The pearl of the Adriatic' . . . 'The empress of
Dalmatia' and so forth. Even Bernard Shaw, in a fit of uncharac-
teristic lyricism, said that those who are in search of an earthly
paradise should see Dubrovnik. For a very long time Dubrovnik
has been receiving the unmitigated applause and admiration of
nearly all who behold it.

It is certainly difficult to find fault with it. Seville may become
too hot, Florence too oppressive, Paris too noisy, Venice too smelly,
but Dubrovnik is never too hot (or too cold), it is seldom noisy, its
smells are aromatic, its buildings civilised—and its people are
amiable, harmonious and urbane. This in itself is fairly remarkable
since they belong to what is undoubtedly one of the most popular
tourist 'processing plants' in the Mediterranean.

It is also a most animated and vivacious town and it is obviously
the people who give it this vitality—and always have done. In fact,
Dubrovnik improves as it ages, and I think the visitor appreciates
it more as he ages. Every time one visits it the spells are recast more
potently.

If you arrive by boat or train in the suburb of Gruž (not a very
prepossessing introduction) you are about four kilometres from the
old town. If you come by car from the north you also come through
Gruž, but remember, if you are car-borne, that in the high season
Dubrovnik is packed and it is often very difficult to find a parking

place near the town; and it is almost impossible to find shade, which is necessary in this part of the world because the very hot sun has a bad effect on fabric and tyres.

Car-less travellers must take a tram or taxi from Gruž to Pile, at the edge of the old town. You pass through a delightful suburb of villas and gardens, reminiscent of the French Riviera. At **Pile** are the Atlas Tourist office and the agencies, a cab rank and the departure point for coach excursions. If you want a private room Atlas will find it. If you want a hotel there is a substantial choice.

There is only one hotel in the old town—the Dubravka—which I recommend, partly because it has an excellent and, for Dubrovnik, inexpensive restaurant which is the shop window, as it were, of a catering school and where you can sample real Jugoslavian cooking. On the other side of the town, in Ploče, near the shore, stand the rather swish and dear Argentina and Excelsior. In these you are more or less on the international circuit: monotonous, efficient and rather characterless. However, they are reckoned to be among the best (possibly *the* best) hotels in the country. In Pile, very near the Atlas, is the Imperial—capacious, comfortable and of Edwardian vintage. For many years it was regarded as *the* principal hotel and I have always found it a pleasant place to stay. On the Lapad Peninsula there are a large number of hotels and pensions. If you want peace and quiet, bathing, etc., Lapad is the place to go: its disadvantage is that you have to travel in and out of the town.

For a tour of the city the best place to begin is the **Pile Gate,** a double gateway—a small castle in itself—set in the immensely powerful fortifications. The statues above the gates represent Sv Vlaho (St Blaise) the patron saint of the city. The one above the inner gate is the work of Meštrović. As you pass below there opens before you the great **Placa**, the main thoroughfare and *korso*, a long broad street whose pearly white stone has been smoothed and polished by feet for three hundred years.

There is nothing quite like this Placa anywhere, and the most agreeable thing to do right away is to walk down it and then do a little pottering. It is flanked by big, aristocratic buildings on whose ground floors are shops, cafés, etc. Most of the shops are devoted to tourist bric-à-brac, not in keeping with the surrounding dignity. The fabric of Dubrovnik is tremendously solid, yet at the same time there is a sensation of grace, lightness, airiness. Many streets and alleys grid it in a most regular fashion and these let in abundant sun. There are also a number of squares and piazzas, all irregular.

Quite soon one becomes aware of the benign but by no means indolent atmosphere that pervades the town. This is partly communicated by the inhabitants. They have not the aplomb and hauteur with which the Venetian view their *serenissima*, but they possess a most appropriate air of pride and independence plus a relaxed and genial serenity—and serene one's disposition should be under these clement skies and fruitful suns. They look content without being complacent, cheerful without being nervy or frivolous; in short, mature.

But Jugoslavs are, in many ways, mature people. They have suffered a great deal. They know how to enjoy the good and simple things of life: each other's company, water, wine and just walking about looking at things. But there is nothing simple about them. In fact they are extremely complex people and full of variety. If there is such a thing as a national character and if it is instructive to look for it then I should say South Slavs are intelligent, passionate, individualistic, devoted to principle (to the point of obduracy), impulsive, capable of being very gay and also very sad and reflective. Sometimes they are really sombre. At times they are very devious and impenetrable, at others implacably bloody-minded. They are morally and sexually healthy and they usually have beautiful unfussy manners.

I do not suggest for a moment that the people of Dubrovnik epitomise all that is best in the South Slav character but, like the people of Hvar, Korčula and Kotor, for instance, they possess many pleasing qualities and virtues in an unusually concentrated form.

By the time you have scouted about a little and imbibed some of the beneficent essences and graces of the town you will be ready to address yourself with equanimity to its history, objects and culture. The past of this remarkable place and its inhabitants needs to be looked at in a certain amount of detail.

Originally the site of Dubrovnik consisted of a rocky island divided from the mainland by a narrow channel. Refugees probably began to settle here in the third and fourth centuries but in the seventh (possibly round about A.D. 640) there was an influx from what was then known as Epidaurus (now Cavtat a few kilometres down the coast) when that town was sacked by Slav invaders. In the first place, of course, Epidaurus was a Greek city (one of three by that name) subsequently taken by the Romans.

Later, Slavs occupied the ground immediately opposite the island and there then followed a perilous time of consolidation against repeated attacks by pirates, Arabs and Saracens. This was the early trial by fire and sword which tempered and strengthened the communities. From 1186 to 1190 they were ruled by the Normans and when they were evicted the communities agreed to fill up the intervening strait. This filling in was the foundation of the modern Placa. Afterwards they built a defensive wall. The original Dubrovnikians, then, were presumably a mixture of Slav and Graeco-Romans. The town came to be called Ragusa, by which name it is still known in Italian and French. The word 'argosy' merely means a ship of Ragusa. The name Dubrovnik (from *dubrava*) is supposed to derive from the woods of oaks that grew on the mainland. It did not come into use until late in the seventeenth century.

In 1180 the citizens elected a prince and in the course of the next fifty-odd years this miniature state expanded and developed intensely. This was the next vital stage in the growth of what was to become a powerful maritime republic. It is fairly clear that it was achieved by a people whose principal worldly virtues were a quite exceptional commercial shrewdness and diplomatic acumen, plus intelligence, courage and a capacity for hard work.

A series of trading agreements and political treaties were made which brought wealth, power and influence and set the pattern for the next five hundred years. First was a peace treaty and agreement with Nemanja, the *župan* of Serbia, which gave Dubrovnik trading rights in that land. Next came a trade agreement with the Governor of Bosnia which provided a monopoly of the sale of salt and also trade throughout Bosnia as well as in other Balkan territories. In 1190 the citizens made a very astute 'alliance' with the pirates of Omiš which guaranteed freedom of trade to Dubrovnik in return for which Dubrovnik supplied the pirates with goods and weapons against the old and mutual enemy—Venice.

In the following year Dubrovnik had developed an oligarchical régime. Previously all agreements had been signed in the name of the people of the city, the assembly of the inhabitants. Now are mentioned a privileged class of *nobiles*. It was this nobility which eventually attained almost complete control over the city. A very few of their descendants survive.

In 1205 the old enemy conquered Dubrovnik. However, almost at once there was a revolt and in order to maintain his power the Doge was obliged to win over the aristocratic families with promises to recognise their rank and their right to rule the city. For the next 153 years there prevailed an odd situation. In most respects the city was autonomous yet presided over by a Venetian governor. But the citizens were already developing a genius for accepting alien influences and turning them to their advantage.

In 1358 their diplomacy was put to the test again. The Venetian governor was 'asked to leave' and sent on his way with full honours appropriate to his rank and Dubrovnik came under the formal sovereignty of the Hungarian king. The city paid him tribute and maintained its internal freedom. The main principle of the policy was now clear: it is better to negotiate with and buy off a potential enemy than fight him.

By the end of the fourteenth century the Dubrovnik merchant empire was established and represented all over the Mediterranean and Near East and as far north as London. It had the best intelligence service in the world and it was extremely rich, yet still its home territories were quite small. They stretched up the coast to Ston and Pelješac and down south to include the Konavli Valley and the Sutorina Mountains.

But the city had yet to achieve its most astute diplomatic victory. When the acquisitive and energetic Turks, advancing north, finally routed the Serbian armies on the plains of Kosovo and occupied Serbia and Macedonia it became obvious that the most potent threat to the future security of Europe were the forces of the Sultan and the Prophet's religion. In 1430 Dubrovnik, whose agents and diplomatists were already working where it mattered most, made the first treaty with the Turkish empire and the Sultan's charter guaranteed her trading and maritime rights in return for tribute. Fairly soon after the fall of Constantinople (probably in 1526) Dubrovnik recognised the supreme overlordship of the Sultan and every year a procession of nobles laden with rich gifts and ducats set off on the long road to the Sublime Porte in Istanbul.

So the city continued to prosper and build while periodically having to repel renewed onslaughts from the envious Venetians and other less virulent foes. Though all her wars were defensive her navy had become probably the best in the world. But the South Slav sailors have always been outstandingly resourceful and skilled. Their only superiors have been the English.

After the city had survived for so long against the hand and aggression of men it was more than ironical that a great natural disaster should begin its demise. On 6th April, 1667, a fifteen-second earthquake ruptured the walls, destroyed three-quarters of the buildings and killed nearly two-thirds of the population.

Promptly a Venetian fleet set sail to polish off the victim and eleven days later arrived outside the port. A sailing ship, carrying a delegate of the Republic, Nikolica Bunić, went to meet the Venetian flagship. Bunić handed to the captain a letter in the name of 'the Prince and Senate of the Republic of Dubrovnik' though there was neither prince nor senate at that moment, and precious little republic. The Venetians expected submission and were met with a welcome. The Venetian commander explained he had been sent by the Doge to offer help to the stricken city. Bunić thanked him for the offer and reminded him that the government of Dubrovnik had sufficient strength to resist any attempts at foreign penetration, and as far as the offer of help in connection with the earthquake was concerned the government had already taken the necessary measures. Bunić concluded by thanking the Doge and Venice for their solicitude. Bluff, aplomb and resolution carried the day.

Not long after the Pasha of Bosnia demanded a 'loan' of a hundred and fifty thousand ducats, and a delegation, led by Bunić, went to negotiate. Their instructions were as follows: 'To violence you will reply by renunciation and sacrifice. Promise nothing, give nothing, suffer everything. The Republic is watching you. There you will meet a glorious death, but here the land will be free. In case of difficulty, delay. Be united and reply that we are free men, that this is tyranny and God will judge them.'

They went. After months of negotiation Bunić died in a Turkish prison, but Dubrovnik did not pay a ducat and remained free. There is a tablet to the memory of Bunić in the hall of the Grand Council and it is the only memorial to an individual nobleman in the city. There is something lordly and grand about those orders, but, like the Byzantine Greeks, the people of Dubrovnik were capable of the superb gesture.

For ordinary people the earthquake would have meant the death of the Republic and dispersal. But the survivors gathered, the patricians assumed control, suggestions to move the site of the city elsewhere were rejected; they rebuilt. They rebuilt and succeeded in driving off renewed attacks by the Venetians. For well over another century Dubrovnik, by employing exactly the same methods as before, remained free and prosperous—though never again so powerful and wealthy.

It was not until Napoleon occupied the city in 1806 and in 1808 dissolved the Republic by a decree annexing it to the province of

Illyria that it finally lost its independence. The decree was read out by a French N.C.O.

Even after this strenuous efforts were made to revive it and when Napoleon fell it was re-established—but not for long. Soon it was annexed to Austria, and it was then that the remnants of the nobility vowed not to marry or have children because it was dishonourable to live under occupation. Thus, most of the aristocratic families dwindled and died out. A proud and drastic measure.

Such a terse summary does not begin to do justice to one of the most civilised 'city states' ever to evolve. I say 'civilised' because the ruling families who might easily have become corrupt and decadent through so much wealth and power set an unusually high standard of urbanity and moral healthiness, an example followed by the citizens.

They were very progressive, as a few instances will indicate. By 1347 Dubrovnik had a municipal Old People's Home. There was an orphanage there by 1432. Slave trade was abolished early in the fifteenth century, long before most people had even entertained the idea. Torture was forbidden even earlier. By the fifteenth century public assistance was available for people in want. There was a public health service, a town planning 'institute' and numerous schools. The level of education was high and the Republic which, at its zenith, numbered thirty thousand souls at the most (in the city and outlying districts) produced numerous scholars, writers, artists and scientists. In fact it was an enclave of humanism which was also devoutly religious.

To continue our journey from the Pile Gate: just inside on the right is a large **fountain** (rather too large, for its surroundings) which has been a traditional meeting place for the young for centuries. It reminds me of the cupola from an Arab mosque and was built by a Neapolitan called Onofrio della Cava as a memorial to the construction of an inland aqueduct and sewage system in 1436.

Immediately opposite is the minute church of **Sv Spas** (St Saviour) erected as a votive offering after an earlier earthquake in 1520. It was designed by the Andrijić brothers from Korčula. At its left is the main entrance to the **City Walls** which you can walk all the way round: a trip I strongly advise you to make at some stage. It gives you a series of fascinating views of the city and also an idea of the skill and industry of the previous inhabitants.

For bulk, strength and splendour these ramparts have few equals.

On the right, behind the Onofrio Fountain, is what remains of the Romanesque convent of Sv Klara (St Clare) first built in 1290 (it contained the orphanage later) and rebuilt after the 1667 catastrophe. Now it houses what is called a Workers' Hall and a pleasant restaurant named the Jadran: a good spot to eat or merely refresh yourself.

Next to Sv Spas stands the **Franciscan Church and Monastery** which is still occupied by monks. The church is largely Baroque now though it was completed in 1343, except for the steeple. Look out for the monumental south door and the pietà above it done by the Petrović brothers, local craftsmen. Inside the church is the tomb of Ivan Gundulić, the city's most famous poet. He died in 1638 but is still much read and was first introduced to me by a head waiter in Dubrovnik many years ago. At one stage we were discussing the hazards of marriage and I asked if he was married. He gave a laconic smile and quoted Gundulić: 'It is better to be hungry than in prison'.

One of the oldest parts of the monastery is the **cloister:** the work of one Miho, from Bar in Montenegro, who died in 1348 during a plague. It is quite small and very graceful, with a garden and fountain in the middle of it. The coupled columns are exquisite, with capitals profusely decorated with heads and figures and grotesque creatures. The far side of the cloister is a small museum and treasury (no entrance fee, but it is usual to leave a dinar or two in the plate provided). The main things to look for are: a picture of Dubrovnik painted at the end of the sixteenth century, a silver reliquary alleged to contain one of St Sergius's (or St Blaise's) hands (very good relief work on this), some fine chalices and a Gothic silver cross made by John of Basle who spent part of his life in Dubrovnik. The Apothecary's shop (the original was founded in 1317 and was one of the oldest in Europe) contains a large number of villainous-looking instruments and many portly decorated jars and pots. The modern Apothecary is near the entrance to the cloister where pretty girls in white serve most of the city.

At the other end of the Placa, where it broadens into a square, is a spritely monument called **Orlando's Column,** raised in 1428 at a time when the Republic was particularly oppressed by enemies and misfortune. In an effort to revivify the citizens' dejected spirits it was decided to put up this as a monument to freedom, a curious gesture. It was named after the legendary hero and knight-errant

Orlando, who was much revered in Dubrovnik. On the column is the figure of a medieval knight in armour. But it had a practical as well as a decorative and patriotic use: the clenched right hand and forearm of the figure was an official measure of length in the city—known as the 'Dubrovnik Elbow'. At the foot of the column are three steps from which, for hundreds of years, the edicts of the state were proclaimed. The lowest step was used for announcing mundane municipal matters; the middle for the more important ones; the topmost for momentous decrees involving peace and war.

Near this is what they call the Little Fountain of Onofrio, a vivacious piece of work done at the same time as the big fountain the other end of the Placa. An Italian sculptor, Pietro di Martino, helped della Cava with this.

The elegant building at the end of the Placa on the left, just before the big gateway, is the **Sponza** or Divona, originally erected as a customs house and subsequently used as a state mint and an academy. It is the work of several artists (including the Andrijić brothers) and you will notice the contrast between the wide arches of the portico, the decorated Gothic style of the first floor and the reversion to a late Renaissance style on the second. (The statue in the niche is of St Blaise.) I think the combination of architectural styles is successful but there is disagreement about it. The courtyard inside is lovely. Nowadays the Sponza is used to house the state archives and for art exhibitions.

Next to the big inner **Ploče Gate** is the clock tower. The green bronze knights strike the hour. At the beginning of the century the whole tower began to list alarmingly so what we see today is the result of a complete rebuilding.

Immediately opposite the Sponza, the other side of the square which is a favourite gathering point for tourists and citizens and is invariably cobbled with hundreds of pampered and corpulent pigeons, there rises the Baroque church of Sv Vlaho (the original church was burnt down) who is believed to have been an Armenian (or Cappadocian) bishop. He became the patron saint of the city as a result of a premonitory vision vouchsafed to a canon of the cathedral. It happened some time in the tenth century when a large Venetian fleet was anchored near the city. The Venetians, apparently, were friendly and a number of them were entertained in the city. However, late one night, the worthy canon was at his prayers when suddenly the church was filled with soldiers. Amidst them stood the venerable Sv Vlaho, the bishop and martyr who lived at the turn of the third century. He told the canon that the Venetians were going to attack. The canon warned the Council. The attack was foiled and the martyr accepted as the patron saint. Every year on his feast day, February 3rd, there is a considerable ceremony: High Mass, processions in full national costume, bands, banners, gunfire and—the climax—exposition of the relics (of which there are rather a lot) in their gold and silver reliquaries. It is still a colourful spectacle, though not on the same scale as what a M. Poulet saw in 1658 when no fewer than three hundred reliquaries of gold and silver were paraded, a display followed by carnival festivities, jousting tournaments and so forth.

St Blaise is still invoked, particularly for diseased animals and against infections of the throat. I clearly remember attending church as a schoolboy on February 3rd and putting my neck in a cleft of crossed candles as the invocation was uttered. The sore throats I have suffered ever since are the result of heavy smoking rather than lack of intercession.

There is little to see inside this church except a rather fine statue of the saint in gilded silver. According to custom he is holding a model of Dubrovnik which is of special interest because it shows (like the picture in the Franciscan museum) individual buildings as they were before the great earthquake.

Just opposite the church is the **Town Hall,** the Gradski Kino (city cinema) and the Gradska Kafana (city café)—all in the same building. The café is one of the main foci of social life and has a pleasant terrace overlooking the old harbour. All this was erected in 1862 to replace the Hall of the Great Council burnt down in 1816. This was an outstanding disaster because the original hall formed a superb group in company with the **Rector's Palace** (Dvor) next to it.

Under the old régime the Republic was governed by a Grand Council composed of all male members of noble families who were of age. The Grand Council elected fifty-one of its members to the Legislative Council and eleven to the Little Council. This last managed day-to-day affairs according to policies laid down by the Legislative, while the Grand Council made decrees, fixed tariffs, etc. At the head of the Republic was the *Knez* (or Rector) elected from among the members of the Grand Council. This representative lived in the palace, but his office only lasted for a month and his power was very limited. He could hardly ever leave his palace, was cordoned by protocol and barriered with custom and ceremonial.

To the citizens he looked like the embodiment of power but the *real* power was vested in the nobility and landowners who went through the motions of reverence to him. When he had finished his month's office he could not display any emblem of his former rank until his death. Then they were placed on his coffin.

The first Rector's Palace was a fortress with turrets and when this was destroyed by an explosion reconstruction was entrusted to Onofrio della Cava with the help of other artists. Thirty years later this was also destroyed by an explosion. It was then that the great Florentine, Michelozzo Michelozzi, who had then been employed to work on the fortifications of the city, was commissioned to draw up plans for yet another palace. He did so but the plan was rejected. Nevertheless it is generally agreed that the magnificent **Loggia** of wide arches in the front is based on his designs. These arches with the decorations on the capitals reward close examination. The other architects were very probably della Cava and Juraj Dalmatinac.

The portico leads to a small gate with a smaller one beside it called the Gate of Mercy because it was in front of this that the needy used to gather to receive public assistance. The State Gate was only opened on special occasions. Its archway has some most interesting ornamentation of mythological creatures and angels concealed in interwoven leaves and flowers.

In the forecourt is a porch with stone seats round which the Rector and members of the council used to sit on state occasions. In the atrium stands a bronze bust of Pracatović done in 1638 by order of the Senate, because this man, who was not a noble, did much service to the state and left his fortune and lands to it. Such a memorial was a rare if not unique tribute.

The upstairs rooms, many of which can be visited, are only a shadow of what they used to be. Fire and the French and Austrian occupations all helped to destroy their riches. Now they are given over to an Historical and Ethnographical Museum which is well worth visiting. You can buy a room plan as you go in.

Beyond the Dvor are the Bishop's Palace and the Baroque **Cathedral of Our Lady,** a building on the site of an older cathedral erected, legend says, with money donated by Richard I of England who was supposed to have been ship-wrecked on the isle of Lokrum a little south of Ploče and the old harbour There are some rather fine pictures in the cathedral, more particularly the painting of *The Assumption* over the high altar: yet another attributed to Titian. Titian's or not, it is an impressive work. On the left of the sanctuary

Above, Stari Bar, Montenegro. The ruins of the old town, destroyed when the Montenegrins expelled the Turks in 1878. The spectral figures in the left foreground are Muslim tombstones. *Below*, the old fortified fisherman's village of Sveti Stefan, now transformed into a vast hotel

Above, Budva; a settlement traditionally founded by Cadmus. The ramparts are medieval. *Below*, Lake Skadar with a characteristic boat. (See p.129)

is a *Head of Christ* by Pordenone, a minor north Italian painter. On the right, a copy of a Raphael *Virgin*. There are several other good pictures in the church.

The Cathedral treasury is very rich and its most valuable relics are the skull and a hand belonging to Sv Vlaho, both encased in gold and silver, plus relics of St Stephen, the martyr, and St Augustine. There is a silver cross by a sixteenth-century Dubrovnik goldsmith, Matov; and a magnificent jug and basin of gilded silver worked with a marvellously intricate design of lizards, tortoises and snakes in clusters of seaweed and coral. There are many other objects of craftsmanship, and relics claimed to be the head of St Laurence and a hand of St Peter.

A narrow street from the rear of the Cathedral leads one to **Gundulić Poljana,** behind the Dubravka Hotel. This is the main vegetable market which, like all markets in this country, starts very early in the morning (the sole argument against staying at the Dubravka). It is nothing like so interesting as many markets in Jugoslavia (those in Bosnia and Serbia, for example) but it has a style and animation of its own. In any case a market is a most instructive place and wherever I am in Jugoslavia I never fail to visit them.

After you have been in Dubrovnik for a day or less you will almost certainly have seen some women in local costume, though hardly ever will you see male costume except on festival occasions. Unfortunately we are saddled with this term 'costume' which always suggests something artificial and theatrical. Applied to the clothes worn by Jugoslav peasants nothing could be more inaccurate. It is true that there are a number of places where traditional 'costume' is worn on special occasions for particular celebrations, but for the most part ordinary home-made clothes, especially in the country districts, are worn all the year round.

In the market you have a chance of a picture or two. The business of photographing people always raises problems of courtesy, which are exacerbated if one cannot speak the language. On the whole Jugoslavs don't mind posing and very often they enjoy it, for the good reason that it is a complete novelty to them. However, only in the most exceptional circumstances should anything be given by way of return—and *never* money. Jugoslavs are very unmercenary people and would be most insulted to be rewarded like this. Usually one has the greatest difficulty in persuading people to accept anything. If you snap children then some chocolate or sweets may be appropriate (chocolate is still a luxury) and if you take adults then probably the only thing to do is to thank them very much. In the more unsophisticated and untravelled parts you may well be asked to send a copy of the photograph. This can become expensive. I cannot offer any general rule except to be as tactful and polite as possible on all occasions and to remember that Muslims (especially Muslim women) often object strongly to being photographed because their faith forbids representation. If you speak the language a little (or can communicate in another language) all such problems are diminished. You can offer the men a drink and a cigarette and you can chat with the women. But offering drinks also has its hazards (especially in towns) because the codes of hospitality are very high —except in the most tourist-ridden areas—and the men will invariably insist on buying you a drink in return, and then you feel obliged to repay them and so forth. Before you know where you are you will find another drink in front of you and when eventually you manage to detach yourself you will probably discover that everything has been paid for without your knowing. And no amount of remonstration will change matters.

Jugoslavs don't expect foreigners to speak their language because, as they freely admit, it isn't much use outside their country, but they are always most interested and helpful at the slightest pains anyone takes. In fact, they are pretty good linguists themselves, especially in German, Italian and English and, to a lesser extent, in Russian and French. But do not assume that a Jugoslav speaks another language and under no circumstances address somebody in one without first asking whether or not they speak it (e.g. '*Molim vas* (if you please) *govorite li Engleski, Nemački, Francuski*? etc.). Now, back to the **costumes**.

The women wear long, plain, rather high-waisted skirts (or a kind of chemise-frock all in one piece) but over them they often have attractive aprons—dark blue, striped or spotted. The belts are red or black with yellow stripes or red with white bands (or black with light blue or green silk bands) and pinch the waist right in so that there is almost the effect of a pannier dress. The top half of the costume has embroidered panels in front which feature lozenge-shaped patterns in pale silks (they've probably grown the silk themselves) like lavender, pink and purple. Sometimes there are red facings to the bodice and red stripes on the sleeves. What looks at a distance exactly like a yellow chrysanthemum at the bodice turns out to be a tasselled bobble. The bodice or *jelek*, is a kind of sleeveless waistcoat.

The head-dresses are particularly graceful. Unmarried girls wear a small round maroon or red felt hat sitting snugly on top of coiffured, towered hair—very Renaissance and dignified. Sometimes a light veil trails from this behind. Married women have wide, white head-dresses starched and turned back from the face. Widows and elderly women occasionally wear this free on the shoulders and widows may wear it with a black dress. The general effect is extremely stately if a little severe. Somehow it combines the uniforms of nun, nanny and nurse and can make them look slightly forbidding.

For festivals men wear blue trousers, baggy to the knee and then fitting the leg. White shirts are tucked into a waist scarf or belt, usually a kind of red cummerbund which used to serve to tuck in knives and guns. You can see variations on this in many parts. The *jeleci* may be very gay, adorned with silver buttons and worked in gold and silver braid. The headgear consists of a small, round, flat-topped cap.

The statue in the middle of the market square represents the poet Gundulić, a work by the nineteenth-century sculptor Rendić. The city's other most famous writer was Držić, a sixteenth-century Croatian Molière, whose plays are often performed in the open-air summer drama festivals.

The rather imposing balustraded steps leading out of the far end of this square go up to another one: Boškovićeva Poljana. In it are the building that once housed a grammar school and the Jesuit Church—a late seventeenth-century building, designed by a north-ern Italian called Andrea Pozzo who became a Jesuit lay brother. He was an expert in *trompe l'oeil*. There are a lot of pictures in this church and the one showing the *Apotheosis of St Ignatius Loyola*, the founder of the Jesuit Order, seems to me to be one of the most interesting.

If you take the narrow street which runs from the north-west of this church you will soon come to the **Rupe** which was built as a grain store in 1590 and now shelters an interesting collection of Romanesque sculpture, embroidery, jewellery, costumes, etc. It is called the Rupe (*rupa* is 'a hole') because it has several openings into it. If you strike north from here you will have little trouble in finding your way back to the Ulica od Puča which runs parallel with the Placa and contains a large number of old merchants' and crafts-men's shops well worth exploring. Some way down it is the Serbian Orthodox Church and next to it an old house which has a small museum of Byzantine and Russian icons.

On the northern side of the Placa, again parallel, runs the Prijeka Ulica (it means 'across street' or 'beyond street' because it is the other side of the old ditch) with many ancient high houses with splendid doorways and balconies. Forty or fifty feet above the gossip is lobbed to and fro through the swagging of laundry.

When you go out through the inner Ploče Gate by the Sponza and enter a narrow cavernous street you will shortly find a flight of steps on your left. Go up these and at the top is the entrance to the **Dominican Monastery** where there are still many monks. Very striking they look, in their white habits and black scapulars, strolling round the cloister.

The whole group of buildings is somewhat cramped and folded into this corner of the city, and with the fortress towering above it looks as if it might almost be part of the defences. The cloister, which is graceful and airy, was the work of several artists and exhibits again that blend of Gothic and Renaissance design so frequent on this coast. I think the church is easily the best in Dubrovnik: a lofty, spacious building of the early fourteenth century which contains a lot of pictures. The painting immediately on the left as you go in represents *St Mary Magdalen and St Blaise* and other figures; this is definitely by Titian. There is another picture by a sixteenth-century Dalmatian artist of the *Virgin and St Blaise*, and again the saint is holding a *maquette* of the city.

There are two other little churches nearby. The one alongside the Dominican church is **St Sebastien's** which has been used, among other things, as a prison and a warehouse. Close to the Ploče Gate is the **Church of the Annunciation,** another work by the Andrijić brothers.

I have, of course, only mentioned the principal churches in this city. There are several other small ones (there used to be over thirty altogether). Some of the survivors are disused and were attached to convents—of which there were formerly eight. Quite clearly the place once swarmed with nuns, a plurality explained by the fact that the Dubrovnik nobility tended to give a dowry only to the eldest daughter. All the rest, round about the age of fourteen, were dispatched to the nunneries.

Beyond the Ploče Gate is another of those patriotic monuments on a terrace which affords a fine view of the coast, the isle of Lokrum and the Old Harbour. The enormous block which juts into the harbour on the far side now contains an Aquarium, the Maritime Museum and an Ethnographical Museum.

Lokrum is a worthwhile excursion in one of the little motorboats. It is very fertile and heavily wooded and is an excellent spot for a walk and a picnic. For a long time Benedictine monks were virtually the only inhabitants and their monastery has survived to be converted into a biological institute.

From the Ploče Gate I suggest you walk on towards the Argentina Hotel. Some way up the road on the left is an art gallery, mostly devoted to modern art, which will give you an idea of recent Jugoslavian painting. The especially interesting things to look for here are: Milosavljević's *Makedonka*; Gvozdenović's *Red Studio (crveni atelier)*; a *St Francis* by Meštrović; and some icons from the Gulf of Kotor (Boka Kotorska) School, from the end of the seventeenth to the middle of the nineteenth centuries. They continue the icon tradition of Serbian monasteries. The more important painters came from the family of Dimitrijević-Rafajlević at Risan. You will notice the distinguishing features of huge eyes, very long noses and exaggerated nostrils.

I think it is also a good plan to take the road outside the city land walls which leads back to Pile. Beyond the big moat, now often used to 'park' donkeys and mules, soar the colossal fortifications.

There are any number of pleasant excursions to be made, and the most interesting local ones, apart from the isles of Lokrum and Lapad, are to climb to the top of Brdo Srdj above the city and to take a bus from Gruž to the mouth of the underground river **Dubrovačka**, which you will have passed if you came by road. This is a beautiful luxuriant valley caused by an earthquake and filled by the sea. In the old days it was a favourite summer resort for the nobility, some of whose mansions and villas survive. At the very end of the inlet, under the branches of the overhanging trees, the river emerges from the base of the cliff. It is a continuation of the River Trebišnjica which flows through Trebinje towards Metković and then vanishes into the ground about thirty kilometres from where you are.

What you should not fail to make are trips to Trebinje and Cavtat. The former, which is in Hercegovina, lies about thirty kilometres away on a good road. You branch left at a clearly marked junction five kilometres out of Dubrovnik on the way south-east. The road curves and switches through furrowed and jagged *karst* and then dips to a big, fertile plateau encircled by bare mountains. **Trebinje** is at one side of it, very green, and between its trees and roofs a few minarets still rise like white missiles. (See map, p. 137).

The Leotar (the only hotel) is comfortable and cheap and from here you look across what appears to be a wide moat and is in fact the river Trebišnjica. Beyond, peeling, stained and dilapidated, the old houses and what remains of the defensive walls sink into their reflections: a momentary illusion of an aspect in Venice or Delft.

When you cross the bridge into the town a broad street, bordered by impressive 'Venetian' façades, runs straight. Each side of them and beyond sprawl spacious gardens and parks and a number of Austrian public buildings. As Trebinje is a big military depot there are several large barracks.

The old town lies immediately to the left of the main street and contains what is in effect a small fortified village whose walls and gates are still in quite good repair. Most of the buildings inside them are decayed. The mosques are shut and neglected and the spiders weave their shrouds over windows and wrought iron—a moribund outpost of the dead and almost forgotten Ottoman empire.

You may see an occasional old man in breeches and faded fez or a half-veiled woman leaning through a lattice window but if you want to see a really bright array of clothes you should come here on a Saturday (which is market day). The men ride in from the outlying mountain villages in their homespun breeches and stockings and coarse linen shirts, on their heads fur hats or sometimes fezzes or little, circular flat caps wound with coloured wool. The Muslim women may be in bloomers and colourful head-dresses, and the Christian women in white dresses with vividly striped aprons bearing heavy fringes. Over these they sometimes wear a kind of long coat with sleeves which fall nearly to the ankles. There are a very large number of variations, which will increase as the regional and village distinctions gradually die out. Indeed, in many parts you can see vestigial costume combined with off-the-peg, mass-produced clothes.

It is not such an impressive market as those you will discover in parts of Bosnia and Serbia but it is certainly a sight not common now in Europe and will probably be extinct within the next decade or so.

Cavtat (the name may be a corruption of *civitas vetus*) is only twenty kilometres from Dubrovnik and is an exceptionally beautiful place even by Dalmatian standards. I think the best way of getting there is by boat, for the coastline is a continuous pleasure when viewed off-shore and you get some more objective views of Dubrovnik itself.

Almost nothing remains of the Greek or Roman settlements and most of the houses that stand were built during the supremacy of the Republic—often enough by the rich nobility who wanted a change of air.

The main items of cultural interest are the house and library of Valtazar Bogišić, a nineteenth-century lawyer and scientist, and the house and paintings of the artist Bukovac, who was born here. On the topmost point of the peninsula is the **Račić Mausoleum,** by Meštrović. The Račić family were wealthy shipowners from Cavtat and this mausoleum is reckoned to be one of the maestro's best works.

It is austere and simple though it has quite a lot of decoration. The bronze doors between the caryatids show the four Slavonic Apostles: Cyril, Methodius, Gregory and Sava. The figure with the dog is St Rock, or St Roch, who, according to legend, was succoured by a dog when stricken with the plague. Other figures represent members of the Račić family.

On the whole, though, I don't think many people go to Cavtat to do much more than relax in its Arcadian surroundings and benign climate and bathe in its voluptuous waters—beneath which, incidentally, you may catch a glimpse of large blocks of stone supposed to be the remains of the original Epidaurus.

Quite near Cavtat a small, unspoilt fishing village called Mlini straggles along the rocky shore amidst the pine and palm and cypress. It possesses two comfortable old hotels, the Mlini and the Astarta (plus other accommodation) and is an ideal spot for a simple, restful holiday.

CHAPTER 9

The Coast IX: Gulf of Kotor

Čilipi—the Gulf of Kotor—Hercegnovi—Risan—Perast—two islands: St George and Our Ladv of the Chisels—Kotor—Prčanj—Lovćen Pass

There is not much to stop for on the road between Cavtat and Hercegnovi, and if you are at sea there is less of interest than usual because the mountainous coast is bare and exposed and there are no islands. Behind the mountains the *autoput* runs down the Konavli valley, one of the most fertile parts of Dalmatia and particularly beautiful in spring when the red soil seems to impart something of its colour to the flowers and leaves. The people of the valley are goodlooking and dignified and the women quite often wear costumes of the kind you will already have found in and immediately round Dubrovnik. If you can contrive to be in the village of **Čilipi** on a Sunday morning you will see a fine array as the locals go to Mass. In fact, the Dubrovnik Tourist office organises coach excursions specifically for this spectacle.

Quite soon you arrive at Hercegnovi at the entrance of the first of the four bays of the **Gulf of Kotor,** the Boka Kotorska. This is one of the most remarkable natural phenomena in Europe, the climax of the whole coast, and the most awe-inspring entrance to the Crna Gora (the Black Mountain—Montenegro). Whether you enter it by sea or by one of the two main land routes the sight of it will last a lifetime.

Hercegnovi was new as long ago as 1382 when the Bosnian king Tvrtko I founded it in order to try and break Dubrovnik's monopoly of salt. It is a pretty little town, straggling along a slope, a leafy, mild place, thick with orange trees and cactus, palms, aloes and oleanders, a great profusion at the base of grey mountains. In summer the bougainvillæa spills voluptuously over its crumbling walls; and in their season the trees are bright with oranges and lemons. In fact it has such a benign climate that it makes a holiday resort all the

136

CHURCHES I. *Above*, Poreč, the Basilica of Euphrasius, a sixth-century foundation whose mosaics belong to the period of St. Apollinare and San Vitale at Ravenna. The conch shows the Virgin enthroned and flanked by angels. *Below left*, Nin, Sv Kriz, believed to be the smallest and oldest intact church in Jugoslavia. It was built between 780 and 800 by the *Župan* Godislav. *Below right*, Nin, Sv Nikola, a tiny fortified church built in the eleventh century. The crenellated tower was built in the Turkish wars

CHURCHES II. Zadar, St. Donat's. A most unusual ninth-century church raised on the paving stones of the Roman forum. The rotunda style is Carolingian. There is no other church like it on this coast

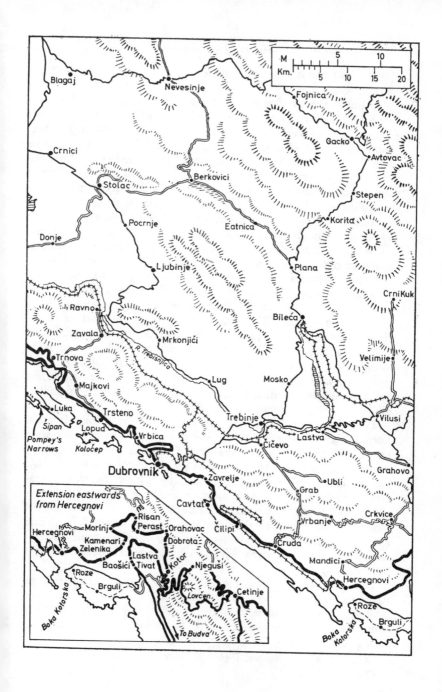

year round and is a useful centre for excursions round the Gulf and farther south.

About a century after its foundation it was captured by the Turks who held it for two hundred years—from whom, in turn, it became the property of Venice and Austria, among other nations. All these influences have left some marks, including a Turkish clock tower and fountain. The Austrians, who quickly divined the commercial merits of its climate, built the Hotel Boka; this is the best place to stay.[1] Like much of the town it has the indefinable air of a spa establishment. The food is good and the cellar well-stocked.

All the antiquities can be seen in a couple of hours. If you turn left from the hotel five minutes' walk brings you to a signpost to the town museum which houses a small ethnographical collection. If you turn right you are in the town centre where are the clock tower and some churches which are always difficult to get into. But you are not missing much if you do not. Above the town (and it is worth clambering up to look at them) are the ruins of two picturesque forts, Turkish and Spanish. The Spanish were yet another nation at one time keenly interested in possessing the great natural harbour beyond.

Igalo, not far away, is quite a well-known spa, with a decent hotel —the Igalo. The dark mud of the Igalo shore has potent curative properties which, apart from being good for rheumatism, neuralgia and articular complaints, are also a remedy for what are enigmatically described as 'women's diseases'.

Two kilometres out of the town to the south-east you will see a hospital sign on your right (H Bolnica) and immediately opposite a notice and path to the **Monastery of Savina** which is supposed to have been founded by Sv Sava in the thirteenth century, though most of the present buildings are much later. This is a Serbian Ortho-dox monastery and from now on we shall see an ever-increasing number of these. There are still one or two monks here one of whom will very willingly show you into the church, which has a fine iconostasis, and also the treasury in the small eleventh-century chapel next door. About Sv Sava I shall have a good deal to say at a later stage (p. 183).

You will probably have noticed by now that the characters on signposts, official notices, above shops and on plaques, etc., are doubled. The unfamiliar ones are Cyrillic (*Ćirilica*, a word which comes from the name Cyril). Rather beautiful characters they are, strong yet graceful.

[1] There are also the Riviera, Topla and Igalo.

SS Cyril and Methodius were two brothers who lived in the ninth century and were known as the Apostles of the South Slavs. Cyril, the younger, taught in Constantinople for a time. They both became priests and were sent to preach in Moravia where they had considerable success. St Cyril is believed to have been the inventor of the Cyrillic alphabet (similar to Glagolitic) many of whose characters are obviously related to the Greek. On the other hand Cyril's followers may have invented it. At all events the system bears his name and very probably it was at Ohrid,[1] in the far south of Macedonia and one of the most interesting places in the Balkans, that the alphabet was first worked out and the first church books written in it.

Zelenika, a naval base, is the first town of any note after Herceg-novi and then you come to **Kumbor,** a small pretty village which gives its name to the strait it overlooks. Djenovići, Boašići and Bijela are all rather dull. Pierre Loti spent some time at Baošići when he was a young officer in the navy and there fell in love with a local girl. In *Fleurs d'Ennui* he wrote a vivid if somewhat rhapsodic account of the great gulf.

At Kamenari you reach the ferry which gives you a short cut to Kotor. The strait here is narrow enough for it to have been sealed by chains in the past in order to discourage enemies—hence the name Verige Strait. Here, if you are in a car, there is quite a difficult decision to be made. If you take the ferry and turn right the other side you can continue on the *autoput* to Lastva and Tivat—thence to Budva and the rest of the coast. If you go left round the mountain you pass through several interesting villages and reach Kotor. But the most interesting way is not to cross but to drive right round the gulf. You can, of course, get on from Kotor to Budva and Cetinje.

The road, a fairly good one by Jugoslav standards, is a narrow ledge between the base of the mountain and the deep waters of the gulf. From it you get a succession of magnificent views. Just beyond Kostanjica a bridge crosses the **Sopot waterfall** which leaps straight from the rock and plunges a hundred feet or more. The hole in the rock is the plughole, so to speak, of an underground river. Nobody knows where it rises, but it has rushed through many a twisting limestone tunnel and cavern before its final gush into the light.

At Morinj you swing north-east to Risan out of which a stony track winds to the uplands of the Krivošije region where gaunt weatherbeaten shepherds in homespun cloaks pasture their flocks the summer long and where nothing has changed for centuries—if

[1] See pp 217-22.

ever. No doubt the shepherds are descendants of those half-legendary 'shepherd kings' of the early Middle Ages about whom Keyserling wrote; here, as in other mountainous districts, their mien and appearance at once suggest a royal lineage.

Risan, which was founded by the Illyrians, is the oldest town in the Boka Kotorska and, like so many other places on the coast, once served as a pirate stronghold. As far back as 400 B.C. it was important. Unfortunately, earthquakes have destroyed many of the early settlements but it is possible to see some of the ruins below the water. The Illyrian queen Teuta is supposed to have lived here.

A little farther on is **Perast** and I recommend you pause here. Perast was famous much more recently and is still a beautiful little town of deserted palaces and patrician houses among which the fig and Judas trees and wistaria thrive luxuriantly. A millennium ago it was one of the leading maritime states and for four centuries its sailors were famous throughout Europe. In fact the whole gulf had a great reputation for its seamen which it has by no means lost.

The principal houses of Perast belonged to the Smaki, Bugović and Zmajević families and one of the more famous Perastians was Matija Zmajević, commander of Peter the Great's Baltic fleet which trounced the Swedes three times running. Perast was to Europe what Greenwich was to England and it was from here that Peter the Great, like the Venetians, drew most of his ablest sea-captains. Often enough foreign powers sent their men to be trained there. But the glories of Perast are gone, though you can gather a little about them from a good museum (now installed in the old maritime school) and from looking at the magnificent Venetian Gothic buildings.

Almost opposite, in the middle of the bay, are two tiny islands: **Sv Juraj** (St George) and **Gospa od Škrpjela** (Our Lady of the Chisels). On the former are the remains of a twelfth-century Benedictine abbey and a sailors' cemetery. The latter island was built, according to legend, by the Perastines themselves. Originally it was supposed to be no more than a rock on which, one stormy night, a shipwrecked sailor clung and vowed that if he survived he would build a church there and dedicate it to the Virgin. He did survive and thereafter the sailors of the gulf made a point of dumping stones which eventually formed an island. The church was built in the seventeenth century and inside it, on the high altar, is a picture of the Virgin reputed to have miraculous powers. There is another version that on July 22nd, 1452 two brothers were fishing near a rock in the bay when an illuminated icon of the Virgin appeared on the rock. The brothers took it and put it in a church in Perast, but mysteriously it returned to the rock. It was then decided to make an artificial island and erect a church.

To commemorate July 22nd, the people of Perast observe the **Fašinada**. Just before sunset a procession of garlanded boats loaded with rocks sets sail to the island. In the first boat is a costumed choir and prominent citizens. The rocks are dumped to reinforce the walls and surrounds of the isle and an evening of feasting and merry-making ensues. At a late hour everybody rows back rather drunkenly, the lights bobbing and winking in the waters and the singing voices echoing round the mountains.

On August 28th there is another celebration to commemorate a great victory against the Turks in 1654 when the Virgin is supposed to have put the enemy to flight by appearing in a monstrous shape. The holy icon of the Virgin is taken to the cathedral of St Nicholas (one of the boats contains armed men as a reminder of the former Turkish threat) and is later returned to the island.

The festivities of the day include a sport called *gadjanje kokota* (shooting the rooster). The luckless fowl is tied to a plank and floated about five hundred yards off-shore. The best marksmen of the town then improve their aim and the winner is the hero of the day.

Curiously enough it was Gospa od Škrpjela on which the German painter Böcklin based his strange vision of *The Isle of Death* and sometimes, when the sun is obscured and the waters lie like black glass between the austere mountains which here rise six or seven thousand feet, the whole bay looks profoundly sinister and forbidding in a Gothic gloom.

The next places you pass are Orahovac and Dobrota, both o. which still supply numerous sailors for the Jugoslav naviesf Dobrota is virtually a long narrow city—row after row of noble Venetian palaces and churches. Many of them are gutted—partly as result of fierce guerrilla warfare against the Germans and Italians. If you pause here there are several churches worth seeing: the eleventh-century Sv Ilija (Elijah); Gospa od Vrta (Our Lady of the Garden) of the fourteenth century; and an eighteenth-century Baroque church dedicated to Sv Eustahije (possibly St Eustace) which possesses several notable paintings by Italian and Croatian artists.

Finally, surfeited by scenic splendours, you reach the head of the fiord and **Kotor:** a tiny, walled medieval town, laced by narrow streets and alleys which suddenly open into cramped piazzette. Above it the Lovčen mountain soars almost sheer for six thousand feet. Up the side of it, barely visible, twists and loops the hair-raising road which leads into the savage and rocky fastness of Montenegro. When you look up the side of the mountain it does not seem possible that anything could be built on it; yet there it is, and to go up or come down it is a memorable if somewhat alarming experience.

But first Kotor: a site and a city attacked, captured and pillaged by one enemy after another: by the Romans, the Saracens and the Serbians, by the Tartars, the Hungarians and the Bosnians, besieged by the Turks in 1538 and 1657, partly destroyed by earthquakes in 1563 and 1667, afflicted by the plague in 1572, and at one time or another the objective and possession of the Venetians, the French, the Russians and the English. An extraordinary record even by the standards of the Dalmatian and Montenegrin coasts. Yet there survives a city many of whose buildings date from the late Middle Ages.

There are two things particularly that give Kotor a continuity: one is the Seamen's Guild of the Gulf of Kotor (the Bokeljska Mornarica) whose records go back to 809—possibly even earlier; the other is the Catholic Cathedral of Sv Tripun (St Tryphon) which was consecrated in 1166 on an older foundation—also of 809 or thereabouts.

Sooner or later you will stroll along from the Hotel Slavija (the only hotel, it lies outside the main town at the extremity of the bay) down by the harbour until you reach the gate into the walled city. (as you go under it don't miss the gay bas-relief of the Virgin on the right.) Having passed the gate you enter the main L-shaped square where there are tourist offices and cafés and a fine Clock Tower, originally the city's torture tower. The Tourist Office is just on your right and beyond it is an interesting little lapidarium. On one stone is carved one of the last winged lions of St Mark and Venice that you will see going south.

If you take a narrow street leading out of the square's farthest right-hand corner you will eventually arrive at the cathedral (*en route* look out for a lovely arcaded house with a balcony). The **Cathedral of St Tryphon** is a really outstanding example of twelfth-century Romanesque architecture, which Kotor owes to Benedictine monks. St Tryphon is the patron saint of Kotor and, according to tradition, the townspeople acquired his head in 890, part of a cargo of relics being carried to Europe. It cost them three hundred pieces of gold. February 3rd is the anniversary of the deal, an event always celebrated by dancing and merrymaking. St Tryphon is a saint little known in the Latin church but he is much venerated in the Greek. He is one of three martyrs (the others were Respicius and Nympha) whose feast is celebrated in the Latin church on November 10th. He was supposed to have been born in Phrygia and as a boy was a gooseherd. He was put to death in Nicaea about 250 and is the patron saint of gardeners.

The west front of the cathedral, flanked by twin towers, is most imposing and possesses the rare feature of a single wide arch which spans the porch between the towers—all of which were added some time in the seventeenth century after the 1667 earthquake. The interior is lofty and spacious and is based on the basilical plan of nave, aisles and triple apse. The eye instantly homes on the **ciborium** or baldaquin above the high altar and the silver *pala* behind it. This is reminiscent of those in Trogir and Korčula cathedrals and is a masterpiece. The proportions of the twin colonnettes alternating with the statuettes are faultless. An angel crowns it. If you look closely at the carvings on the architrave you will see that they depict the legend and history of St Tryphon. The work on the *pala* and the altar are by the artist known as John of Basle. A figure of the patron saint holds a model of the original cathedral—which also had twin towers.

A guide will show you the treasury which possesses a number of relics (mostly arms and legs) of which the pick is St Tryphon's head. Hanging on one wall is a large wooden crucifix alleged to have been given by the daughter of Baldwin II, the last Latin emperor of Constantinople, to the widow of the thirteenth-century Serbian king Uroš I. I find it a most disturbing and powerful work, horrific in fact. Natural decay has accentuated the cadaverous appearance of the body and the features which depict the most dreadful agony. It is such a sombre *memento mori* that Sir Thomas Jackson may well have been right in attributing it to a fifteenth-century artist—which would, of course, dispose of the earlier account.

When you leave the cathedral take the alley running out of the opposite right-hand corner of the square. This brings you to another small piazza and the **Maritime Museum,** housed in an old palace. It is a most interesting museum and gives you some notion of the history of the Seamen's Guild, the organisation that more than anything else made Kotor famous in the days when, like Dubrovnik, she relied on trade and diplomacy. She was a close ally of the first Montenegrin kingdom and the Nemanja dynasty of Serbia. As Kotor was the nearest port for both those kingdoms it was very much in their interest to maintain cordial relations.

The passage running along the left of the museum in due course produces another square and a delightful little church: Sv Luka. It is not much more than a stone box with a dome at the centre which was built in 1195 or 1196. It is important because it is one of the very earliest examples of the church architecture that was to evolve in Serbia in the Raška 'school', about which I shall have a great deal to say shortly (see p. 168). Sv Luka carries its years lightly. Alongside it is a tiny chapel dedicated to St Spiridion. The iconostasis here and the wooden Christ are impressive. The church beyond is the Orthodox Cathedral which is not of much interest. If you press on through the narrow streets you will soon find the Catholic parish church and the defensive battlements on the northern side of the town.

The two cults, Orthodox and Catholic, have thriven here in tolerance and agreement for centuries. In fact, not far away, at Sutomore, there is a church with two altars where the different masses are solemnised alternately. In the time of Tvrtko I of Bosnia's rule there were Bogomils in Kotor and there are records of co-operation between all three creeds. It seems that some broadminded people have long anticipated the recommendations of the Oecumenical Council. Perhaps the fraternity of the sea raises men above religious bigotry.

Hemmed in as it is by mountains Kotor can be very oppressive in the summer, and is in shadow quite early in the afternoon. But it is a most enthralling place in which to pass a day or two and from which to excurse. It is also a good region for walking. If you feel really energetic you can walk all the way round the bay to Perast, or go by bus and walk back. Or you can clamber up the precipitous walls to the fort above the town—which is a good deal more difficult than it looks. Or you can go round the other side of the bay to the village of Prčanj which was a prosperous town two hundred years ago (as the decaying mansions witness) and produced a large number of famous sailors, including the first Slav, Ivo Vizin, to sail round the world. The ship was made locally. Alternatively go up the hill behind Kotor on the Budva road and from the top of the saddle you will have a splendid vista across the Zupa Plain and an even better one back up the Gulf. When thunderstorms brew over the mountains, as they often do in late summer, the scene becomes almost frightening. The peals crash and ricochet round the immense walls of the fiord like the proclamations of some cosmic upheaval and the lavish thrusts of lightning appear to carve open the very mountains themselves.

From Kotor you have a choice of route. You can cross the saddle I have just mentioned and take the Tivat road across the Zupa Plain which puts you back on to the *autoput* to Budva, or you can take a deep breath and ascend the **Lovčen Pass.** It is the latter course I recommend. You can always get to Budva from a road the other side of Cetinje and between Kotor and Budva on the *autoput* you miss nothing.

When you have climbed the Lovčen Pass Kotor looks no more substantial than a patch of bright gravel and you will almost certainly want to stop and gaze. Not far on you reach the village of **Njeguši** where the nineteenth-century monk, poet and prince of Montenegro, Petar II Petrović-Njegoš was born in either 1811 or 1813. I shall have a good deal to say about him in the following chapter. This village is one of the starting points for his mausoleum. Three hours' walk away on the summit of Lovčen he lies in a white marble tomb in a chapel, probably the loneliest and windiest grave in the world. From this eminence you can see across the Gulf of Kotor to Hercegovina, over the Adriatic and Montenegro and even as far as Albania.

'If it were not for the wind spiders would mesh over the heavens,' says an enigmatic Jugoslav proverb. Up here, on these gale-torn peaks, in the glitter of light, you are on the symbolic summit of the most fiercely cherished purity of freedom known. Njegoš, who more than once compared himself with the eagle, could hardly have chosen a more appropriate site for his bones.

CHAPTER 10

The Coast X:
The Montenegrin Littoral

Cetinje—the Biljarda—Gorski Vijenac—Budva—Sv Stefan—Stari Bar—Ulcinj.

'May no gun hang on your wall.' If a Montenegrin pronounces this malediction upon you it is a very serious matter. It is tantamount to saying that you deserve to die, or at any rate that you are scarcely fit to live. However, the traveller or tourist who earned such a curse would be exceptionally unlucky, for the Montenegrins are among the most extravagantly open-handed and amicable people alive.

You might not expect this to be so when you first see the bleak lineaments of their old capital **Cetinje,** but here, or anywhere else in Montenegro, provided that you come with friendly intent, you will find that it is true.

The Grand Hotel, the only one in Cetinje,[1] is a large, shabby and rather dingy establishment of considerable character. It is the only hotel in Jugoslavia, for example, in which I have found hot water in both taps. It is the only hotel anywhere in which I have met a waiter who was familiar with *The Canterbury Tales.* And it is probably the only hotel in a capital city (even though quondam) anywhere in which you would see a man draw a gun and shoot a mad dog dead in the dining-room. The Grand also makes a convenient starting point for a tour of this unusual city.

Cetinje, known as 'the stony throne of freedom', lies in a plateau at two thousand feet and is encircled by a serrated rim of rocky peaks. You get the feeling you are in the top of a filled in crater. It is very isolated and in winter is virtually snowbound from October to late February. I have been there in mid-April and seen drifts ten feet deep which had been melting for weeks.

[1] There is now also the Park Hotel.

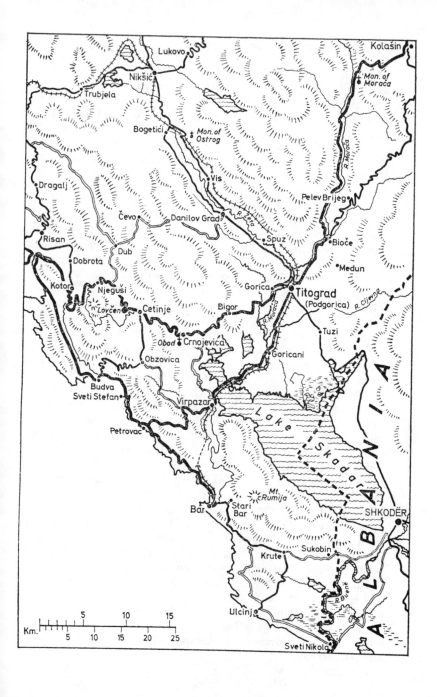

It is a very clean place, washed by rain and snow, swept and scoured by winds. The air and the colours and the light are quite different from the coast. The houses are grey and unadorned. The roofs are grey. The lines of every object are clean and sharp. It is a frugal town—in ways reminiscent of some towns in the Cévennes— and the people are frugal. Their lives have been simple and austere. A tragic and turbulent past, the close traditions of the family hearth and the clan, and the most exacting codes of honour, have all helped to create an atmosphere of sobriety and asceticism.

But Cetinje is by no means Puritanical or depressing. The Montenegrins themselves make sure of that. The women are vivacious and often beautiful and the men must be among the handsomest in the world, even better looking than the Bosnians and Hercegovinians. They are often very tall and straight and one gets the impression that the *average* height is about six foot—if not more. And there is a kind of lazy arrogance about them, a lordly but good-humoured hauteur, which is most striking. They are proud and stubborn but not at all well disciplined. Such mundane activities as work do not appeal to them. Though they can and do work very hard if it is absolutely essential, they usually accomplish it with a certain tolerant nonchalance. In fact they belong to a sort of aristocrat warrior class and to see them at their best you probably have to watch them fighting to defend their Black Mountain which (this is one of their proudest boasts) has never been subdued—not even by the Turks. Then they are heroically courageous, epically grand. In the absence of war I suspect that their favourite occupations are hunting, shooting and conversation, and so forth. And, of course, just *being* Montenegrin. At that they excel.

Mr Lovett Edwards, who has a deep knowledge and understanding of this country, says that 'the Montenegrin outside his own country either rises rapidly to a position of trust and influence, or becomes the most morally corrupt of all the Jugoslavs. It is a matter of character and education. Those who have the character to apply their code of honour and heroism to the complexities of the modern world become great men; those who forsake it rapidly acquire a Western polish and Western vices, but little else.' This is very shrewd and has certainly been borne out by my own experiences a number of times. You are much more likely to be fiddled by a Montenegrin than by any other Jugoslav (except, possibly, a Hercegovinian) and no one but a Montenegrin is capable of such positive generosity and self-sacrifice.

The frugality and austerity of their past is nowhere better symbolised than in the former **Royal Palace** of Cetinje (a short walk from the Grand)—a royal palace without any trace of luxury and extravagance. It was built by the prince-poet, Njegoš Petar II and has always been known as the *Biljarda* after the billiard table that was brought with enormous difficulty at the prince's command all the way from Kotor and up the Lovčen Pass on what was then no more than a mule track. The precious slate was installed in 1830. Unhappily, it has not survived.

The **Biljarda** is a long, low two-storied building, like a barrack, in a walled enclosure, with round towers at its corners. It is almost as plain inside as it is without and is now a first class museum in three parts: one is devoted to an ethnographical section; another to what is called The People's Revolution—that is to say, the struggle for liberation in the last war; a third contains the private apartments of the former princes. The plan consists of long corridors with rooms opening off them.

The ethnographical section has a variety of objects like wooden ploughs (you still see a lot of these in use in Jugoslavia), fine Montenegrin costumes and some beautiful carved *gusle*—a one-stringed fiddle which produces a monotonous wail and might be called the national instrument. They were played primarily by *guslari*, wandering minstrels, often blind, who travelled from village to village reciting the deeds of heroes in heroic lays that had been passed down in the oral tradition from century to century. You will see plenty of these instruments in Jugoslavia and you will quite often hear and see them being played.[1] If you are extremely fortunate you will come across a *guslar* reciting, but I shall have much to say about this later (see p. 254). I have only been lucky enough to come across two in the remoter parts of Serbia and Macedonia and one in Bosnia.

In the 'Liberation War' section, which is very well laid out and documented, there is a big collection of items: proclamations, newspaper reports, *maquettes*, weapons, uniforms, sad personal

[1]Its origin is unknown. In appearance it is a cross between a lute and a Turkish tambur. In some regions it has two or more strings—in which case it has a different name. For example, in the Srem and Bačka districts of Serbia it is known as a *gege*. It may be made of many different materials: usually of wood (especially maple) but sometimes of baked clay, metal and even stone. The basic shape has altered very little over the centuries, but each end and the bow have lent themselves to a wide variety of ornamentation—very often in the form of human, animal and reptile heads. In the past many *gusle* players made their own instruments.

relics of dead warriors, and hundreds of photographs—many of them gruesome. In the struggle against the Fascists practically the whole population of Montenegro took part and they gave more lives for the cause of freedom than any other region. There is a gallery of photographs of national heroes and heroines, many of them looking like film stars from the thirties. There are also extraordinary pictures of heroes at the moment of execution, facing death almost carelessly, which are very moving. There are numerous museums like this in the country. Every town has at least one, and a good many of the villages.

Centuries of bloodshed, massacres, revolutions and feuds have accustomed Montenegrins to death in its most violent and painful forms. If you want some insight into their history and customs you should read some of the work of one of the most famous Montenegrins of this century—Milovan Djilas, formerly a colleague of Marshal Tito. In *Land Without Justice* Djilas tells how, for centuries, the republic's social and political life was organised on a patriarchal, tribal basis in which the *bratstvo* (the family ties) was vital. Relationships in the *bratstvo* and tribe were regulated by many archaic customs, the most deep-rooted of which was the blood feud which demanded satisfaction by death for injury, insult or murder. He describes how his own family suffered from these barbarous traditions. His brothers, his father, an uncle, his two grandfathers and his father's grandfather were all killed in the payment of debts of honour. This may seem incredible in one family, but it was by no means uncommon and was quite recent. In fact feuds were still going on after the last war.

But, as I say, the Montenegrins have always been warlike. A vivid observation by an English traveller called Paton, who was here in the 1840's, emphasises the point further. He records that 'even when a child is baptised, pistols are put in the infant's mouth to kiss, and then laid in the cradle beside him; and one of the favourite toasts drunk on this occasion is "May he never die in his bed". ' Alas, that wish has too often come true.

The apartments of Prince Njegoš contain a number of portraits, some furniture and his library. From the portraits and several extant accounts by those who visited him it is quite clear that the Prince was an outstandingly handsome man. He was six foot eight tall, rather pale, and had long black hair and a black beard. His voice was gentle and charming. Often he used to wear a red fez, a scarlet fur-edged pelisse, a white coat, blue breeches, white stockings and a crimson cummerbund crammed with weapons. An odd looking bishop, but he was a highly civilised man who spoke and wrote German, French, Latin and Russian. Under his rule the Montenegrins made much progress. As was fitting in the prince of such a people, he was a good shot. One of his favourite parlour tricks was to have a lemon thrown by an attendant into the air—whereupon he drew and shot it down. Another English traveller, Sir Gardner Wilkinson, actually witnessed this and remarked that it was a 'singular accomplishment for a bishop'.

Petar II became *Vladika* in 1830 and thus continued a tradition that had already existed for over a hundred and fifty years. The word *Vladika* means 'bishop', so the prince was spiritual as well as temporal leader of his people.

Montenegro's earlier history was very confused but its people were mainly concerned with keeping out the Turks. In the late Middle Ages it was under the rule of Serbia and the Nemanjić kings (the people are Serbs as well as Montenegrins, as, for example, the Welsh are British as well as Welsh) and it received Christianity from both Catholic and Orthodox Churches. Eventually it became predominantly Orthodox and adopted the Cyrillic alphabet. When the Serbian empire disintegrated the Montenegrins were left on their own and the Turks managed to conquer part of the country and impose tribute.

Nevertheless, Montenegro remained the one free state of Serbia. It upheld its banners against the so-called infidel and preserved the traditions of the Serbs to the extent of repeopling Central Serbia (known as the Šumadija) ruled by the Crnojević family—a member of which founded Cetinje in 1485, nearly a century after the disaster at Kosovo. This family reigned until 1697 when it was succeeded by the Orthodox bishops: the beginning of the theocratic autocracy which culminated in its greatest representative, Petar II.

Unfortunately, many Montenegrins, especially in the south on the borders of Albania, became Muslims. This defection produced friction and civil war and eventually led to one of the most important events in Montenegrin history: the Montenegrin Vespers, a revolt which broke out in 1702 at Virpazar, a village not far from Cetinje on the shores of Lake Skadar (Scutari) apparently as a reprisal for Turkish devastation of the monastery in Cetinje and also because the bishop Danilo had been maltreated and imprisoned by the Turks. The Montenegrin Muslim renegades had been given a choice: death or Christianity. There was a huge slaughter.

Petar II, Njegoš, who is rather misleadingly regarded by some as the Jugoslav counterpart to Shakespeare, wrote his greatest work, an epic poetic drama, about those Vespers. It was called *Gorski Vijenac* (The Mountain Wreath), a most interesting work in a metre which closely resembles that of the national epic lays: a ten syllable line with four stresses, very difficult to render into English. The drama consists of a series of scenes in the form of dialogue and soliloquy and is primarily a play of ideas, a dispute. Its characterisation is good but it is seldom dramatic, in the proper sense of that term. It is to be read not acted and, as a play, has precisely those defects typical of nearly all the nineteenth-century poets who attempted verse drama, especially writers like Browning. However, *Gorski Vijenac* contains many profound observations on human nature and is much quoted by Jugoslavs.

Njegoš wrote two other works which are much less famous. One was on the theme of the Fall of Man. It is Miltonic in spirit and Njegoš may have known *Paradise Lost* in a Russian translation. The other was about an extraordinary character called Šćepan the Small who actually lived and whose career was of the kind that probably could only happen in a place like Montenegro. This man came to live on the coast, when he was about thirty, in either 1766 or 1777. He stayed mainly near Budva and made a living as a quack herbal doctor. There were some rumours that he was an itinerant monk of Polish birth, then others that he was the Russian Czar Peter III (husband of Catherine) who was dethroned in 1762 and believed to have been murdered.

The Montenegrins had always been on good terms with the Russians and much admired them. At that time the ruling bishop, Sava, was senile and his deputy inexperienced and it occurred to the Montenegrin chieftains that if they put this man into a position of authority he would carry out their orders. No doubt Šćepan was an adventurer and a confidence trickster and perhaps he had that quality of hypnotic plausibility which can reduce the most sceptical

CHURCHES III *Above*, Ohrid, the cathedral of Sv Sofije, one of the most important sacred antiquities in Jugoslavia. It belongs to the Greek and Byzantine traditions as developed between the eleventh and fourteenth centuries. It was built on the ruins of a fifth-century basilica and subsequently transformed into a mosque by the Turks. The frescoes inside are among the finest that survive in Macedonia. *Below*, Nerezi, Sv Panteleimon: a beautiful example of a tiny rustic church of the Macedonian and Kosmet schools, built about 1164. It looks like many Greek churches.

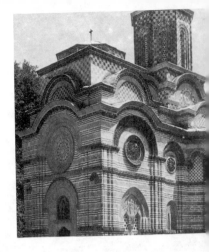

CHURCHES IV. *Left*, Dečani (1327–35). Designed by a Franciscan monk from Kotor, this is one of the finest examples of the Raška school, characteristics being the arcaded 'frill' under the eaves, the Romanesque windows and doorways, and elaborate carving in marble. *Right*, Kalenič, the monastery church. This is the culminating achievement of the Morava School, characterised by lateral polychromatic brickwork, and intricate carving round doorways and windows. *Below*, Gračanica: the monastery church. Founded in 1321 by King Milutin, this is generally regarded as the *chef d'oeuvre* of the Macedonian and Kosmet schools. Its frescoes are among the best in Serbia

and hardheaded person to a state of acquiescence. Perhaps, also, the Montenegrins *really* believed he was the Czar. At any rate they made him their prince and he very rapidly achieved respect and popularity. Once installed and secure he solemnly declared that he *was* Czar Peter III but, out of modesty, preferred to be known as Ščepan the Small.

When the Empress Catherine heard she was embarrassed and angry and a special Russian mission was dispatched to Montenegro. Its leader attempted to denounce Ščepan as an imposter but there was a lot of support for him. The mission left and Ščepan remained as leader. However, the Turks, who feared any kind of unity among the Montenegrins, decided he must be disposed of and the Vizier of Skadar succeeded in bribing Ščepan's barber to cut his throat. This was done and the barber escaped. And so, in 1773, ended the short and happy reign of King Ščepan the Small, in whose time not a little had been achieved because, by all accounts, he was a wise and good ruler, though, apparently, illiterate. It all sounds like serio-comic opera, like a good many other events in Montenegrin history, but in substance it is true.

Adjoining the Biljarda, in a glass building, is a big relief map of the whole of Montenegro, made by Austrians and Italians. There is a 'bridge' across it and you can walk most of the way round it. This is a remarkable model and gives you a good general picture of what kind of terrain you are in.

A few yards from here is an enormous chestnut tree under which the first and last king of Montenegro, King Nicholas I, dispensed justice, rather as the Grand *župan* must have done in the rustic republic near Omiš.

Behind the Biljarda is the **Monastery** founded by Ivan Crno-jević in 1484. There are still a few monks here and one of them will very willingly show you round the tiny church and treasury. In the church is buried one of the early members of the Petrović—Njegoš dynasty, Danilo; and his brother Mirko, a famous national hero. It also contains the relics of Petar I, the poet's uncle. The treasury has an impressive collection of icons, vestments and jewellery, one superb cope and—*pièce de résistance*—one of the first books, if not *the* first, to be printed in the Slav language. Various dates have been given for it and the latest is usually 1493; that is, only twenty years after Caxton's first publications.

Above the monastery is the stump of an old tower which, when it was whole, used to be decorated with the heads of Turks stuck on to stakes. Round about the ground was strewn with skulls. When Sir Gardner Wilkinson visited Petar II he remonstrated with the bishop over this barbarous kind of exposition. The bishop explained that the Turks did precisely the same with the heads of Montenegrins. If one side desisted the other would infer that it was weakening. In fact the Montenegrins usually decapitated their own dying and maimed men lest the Turks should mutilate them.

A couple of minutes' walk from the Biljarda is the former **House of King Nicholas** (now the State Museum in the care of a very civilised and courteous curator) which has been preserved in more or less exactly the same condition as it was when occupied by the monarch. The bedrooms, sitting-rooms, studies and so forth are full of Victoriana, *chinoiserie*, portraits, paintings by Jugoslavs like Bukovac, costumes, banners and arms. There are some splendid pictures of Montenegrin warriors, fiercely moustached and hispid with weapons, gathered round their chieftain—their king.

King Nicholas, like Petar II, was a cultured man. He was also a good soldier and an able politician. Unfortunately he became despotic and unscrupulous to the point of treachery. Nevertheless he reigned for fifty-eight years before finally abdicating in 1918. He then fled to France and died at Antibes in 1921. Here and there in his 'palace' you will discover links, very near home, with Queen Victoria and Roosevelt. There is a letter, for instance, from George V, to his 'dear brother' the King of Montenegro. Europe shrinks. One can hardly imagine George V sitting under a chestnut tree in St James's Park dispensing justice to the warring tribesmen of Lancashire and Yorkshire.

Except on special occasions you will not see many costumes in Cetinje nowadays, or anywhere else in Montenegro except at Ulcinj, though there were a good many about until the late thirties. The highlanders used to be clad, not unlike their famous *Vladika*, in a red embroidered waistcoat, a white coat (useful disguise in snow or amongst the *karst*), black or dark blue breeches and white leggings. On their heads they wore round caps with a red and gold embroidered crown and a black rim. Over their shoulders hung a long brown, heavily tasselled plaid (rather like our highlander's plaid) which served as blanket, overcoat and camouflage. They were always well-armed and in their belts carried a pistol (ready for immediate use) an assortment of knives and a ferocious looking *yatagan*—a curved, double-bladed sword.

You will still occasionally see old men wearing the breeches and embroidered waistcoats, plus belts or cummerbunds; and, more frequently, the traditional rimless hat. This often goes with ordinary modern clothes. The black is said to represent mourning for the defeat at Kosovo, the red the blood that was spilt, and the gold, everlasting glory.

Many of the old men (this applies in Serbia and Bosnia as well as other parts) sport luxuriant moustaches: either great bristling whiskers or bushy, old-fashioned soup-strainers. They usually look rather splendid and are still revered. There is a good and perfectly credible story about these moustaches told by a French colonel who wrote some account of his time as governor of the Province of Kotor between 1807 and 1813. Then it was obligatory to wear a moustache and if anyone touched it or spoke of it disparagingly this was deemed the greatest possible insult, as two Italian soldiers once discovered when they entered a café where a Montenegrin was having a drink. One of them went up to him, took hold of his moustache in an affable manner and said: *Dobro jutro, brate* (Good morning, brother). The Montenegrin shot him dead on the spot and walked out.

A little way south-east of Cetinje (I advise you to ask about the route) you swing right for the road to Budva. In a moment the city has vanished, lost in the troughs and crests of turmoiled rock. The scenery calms, expands and you reach an unexpected climax as you arrive at the edge of the mountain. At Braići there is a derelict fort away on your left and a little church with a belfry. . . . About three kilometres later you swing round a corner and suddenly, with almost the impact of a physical blow, the coast and the sea are spread before you in an immense panorama two thousand feet below: Sveti Stefan like a mailed fist on an azure ground, Budva a chunk of greyish-brown stone.

From here the road descends in leisurely swoops and curves until you are running across the level, broadened shore.

Budva, a good centre for excursions into the Crnagora, has some claim to be the oldest settlement on the whole coast. According to legend it was founded by Cadmus, an unfortunate man who was supposed to be the king of Phoenicia and whose sister was abducted by Zeus, exercising his *droit de seigneur.* It was Cadmus who sowed the teeth which turned into warriors who all killed each other except for five who helped him found the city of Thebes. After that he married one of Aphrodite's daughters, but their children led them such miserable lives that they begged the gods to relieve them of the burden. Whereupon Cadmus and his wife were turned into serpents.

At any rate Budva was certainly a Greek colony by the fifth century B.C. The Romans had it for a time; and it belonged to Venice for nearly four centuries—during which period many of its present buildings were erected. It is a small, wall-girt town, originally an island, and there is not a great deal to see there except for a couple of churches: Sv Ivan of the ninth century and the Orthodox church of Sv Sava. The battlements are impressive and you can walk most of the way round them. The humped island with scalloped slopes opposite is Sv Nikola and makes an enjoyable half-day trip.

In the high season Budva becomes a mondaine and popular resort which is being exploited more and more. The Hotel Avala (which has an underground night-club attached) is large, fairly comfortable and, to my mind, tedious.[1]

A few kilometres south, on a tiny island connected to the mainland by a causeway, is the old fortified fisherman's village of **Sveti Stefan**—now completely renovated and transformed into a vast hotel. It was obviously a brilliant idea to do this and it is now the showpiece of the Jugoslav Tourist Industry. What is more the transformation has been done with a good deal of ingenuity and taste. Each cottage and house has been renovated and they now form self-contained apartments with all mod. cons.—133 suites in all. There is a large restaurant, a night-club, a church, hairdressers, etc. It is an expensive place but during the high season it is packed out. It lies in scenery which is magnificent by any standards. The slopes of the mountains are covered with orchards and pomegranates, olive groves and cypresses. Dotted among them are many old Orthodox monasteries. Near Sv Stefan is the Miločer, formerly a royal residence and now converted into a comfortable hotel.

If you enjoy pseudo-romantic evenings under star-jewelled skies where the multi-lingual waiters arch obsequiously over your table at your slightest behest, and the dark and glittering Adriatic laps lazily below you while a smoochy band reproduces the latest imported tunes, then Sveti Stefan is your best bet. But don't deceive yourself that you are seeing Jugoslavia.

Petrovac, not far on, is a fairly well-equipped resort with several hotels, of which the best is the Palas. North of the bay is the old fortress Lastva, and in the bay the Katić Islands which make an agreeable excursion. Sutomore, which I mentioned in

[1] Now at least eight other hotels and ample private accommodation.

connection with the Orthodox and Catholic cults in Kotor, is the next port of call. Here you can still see the church which has the two altars for the separate sacrifices. This village has only two hotels: the Sozina and the Južno More. Both are comfortable.[1]

Ten kilometres beyond is Bar in a wide and sumptuous bay with a shingle beach. There is little to detain the traveller in Bar anyway, except the old Turkish castles Haj and Nehaj (Fear and Fear Not) which overlook it remotely.

The scene becomes more tumultuous and austere than ever as the road swings up into the mountains. Soon, on the slopes of Mount Rumija, you reach **Stari Bar** which is in two parts. The upper town is now a complete ruin. The first record of its existence is ninth century. For a time it was under the rule of Byzantium. Thereafter the medieval Serbian kings possessed it (and, it is thought, some Serbian nobles). When the Venetians took over the coast they used it as a strongpoint until 1571. That year the Turks captured it, and kept it for over three hundred years. In 1878 the Montenegrins destroyed it while they were expelling the Turks from this part. Amidst the ruins (directions are impossible, but you will be able to figure out the details) are a number of interesting remains: a palace, a Turkish bath, an aqueduct, two Gothic churches dedicated to St Veneranda and St Catherine, an early medieval chapel, and the Cathedral of St George (probably thirteenth century and erected upon an earlier foundation—conceivably a basilica). The fortifications that survive are mostly Venetian and Turkish (the earliest from the eleventh century) and are in a better state of repair on the northern part of the hill.

All over this region there are vast olive groves which date from pre-Christian times. Only in Greece have I seen bigger groves or more venerable trees. The locals say that some are anything up to 2,700 years old. I believe it is true that olive trees can flourish and bear fruit for fifteen centuries or so and their longevity would help to explain why so many customs are attached to them, customs that in some cases approach worship. Round these parts there is still a tradition that a man may not marry until he has planted a certain number of trees.

Thirty kilometres from Bar is **Ulcinj,** one of the more interesting of the smaller towns in the Balkans. *En route* you will see men in a fez or a turban, and, more frequently, women and girls (gipsies and Muslims) who wear flowing robes in gaudy colours. The gipsies

[1] Plus, now, the vast hotel complex the Zlatna Obala.

wear long draggling skirts. High on the mountain slopes the sheep, looking no larger than grubs, nibble the meagre vegetation. Here and there a blob of colour reveals their shepherdesses.

I first went to Ulcinj many years ago with the specific intention of seeing the Negroes who, I had been told, were the descendants of slaves brought by Turks and by corsairs from north Africa. I had been there a whole day without seeing one and early in the evening was obliged to take shelter under a doorway from a thunderstorm. I had stood there some minutes when a man who had arrived from behind me asked for a light. I turned towards him. In that instant there was a vivid, quivering annunciation of lightning. By it I saw that he was an elderly Negro, completely black. The only language he spoke was Serbian and he had some vague idea that his ancestors had come from Africa. It was a memorable moment. He was a descendant of a sixteenth-century slave and, as such, a member of a unique minority in Europe.

That same evening I saw several portly Negresses clad from head to foot in billowing white silk, veils drawn across their chins (more than a shadow of the *yashmak*), wafting silently like great moths through the narrow streets. After that I seemed to see them everywhere, though there are probably not more than a few dozen left in Ulcinj and a few round Stari Bar.

At the moment there are two hotels here: the Galeb and the Jadran.[1] The latter, simple and inexpensive, is high on a wooded point which forms one horn for the bay. The Galeb, more expensive, lies somewhat behind amidst pine trees. From this promontory you look north over the harbour to the old, shattered citadel which adorns another point and south down the broad coastal plain which continues along the shores of Albania. These hotels are no place for gourmets but the food is quite good and both red and white wines are very drinkable.

All the other towns you have seen so far (even Trebinje) have been formed by Western, Latin and Christian influences. The principal forces in the making of Ulcinj have been oriental and Muslim. It was probably part of the Illyrian empire originally and the Romans were there for a time (Pliny mentions it as Olcinium) though virtually nothing commemorates their tenancy. Then, in the eighth century, it was captured by Saracens who held it for about two hundred years and began its long career as a pirate stronghold. Thereafter it was possessed by Slav rulers (again nothing survives of

---

[1] Plus, now, the Albatros, Bellevue, Lido, Mediteran and Olympic.

a superficially Christian era) until 1571 when it was taken by the Bey of Algiers, Uluz-Ali, an ally of Sultan Selim II in his war against Venice. From then until 1878 it was the headquarters of a particularly strong buccaneer force. Most of them were Moroccans, Albanians and Turks, plus a certain number of Serbs.

As one might expect there is little of 'artistic' value except some mosques and what we usually describe rather misleadingly as 'Turkish' houses, but we are stuck with this word now and I shall continue to use it when necessary. As you will see this type of building all over southern Serbia and Macedonia and in parts of Bosnia-Hercegovina we may as well establish its basic characteristics. They are very graceful, usually two-storied, wide-eaved houses whose deeply waved tiles ripple from a short ridge down shallowly sloping roofs. There is a central chimney (normally it has a little roof or lid of its own) which is slotted to emit smoke. One side of the upper story opens in a broad verandah or overhanging balcony, so you have in effect a long, airy room. The small windows are normally latticed, at any rate half-way up, or shuttered. The ground-floor windows are smaller and there are fewer of them so that this part of the house looks defensive, withdrawn. Quite often there is an outside staircase. The houses are built of mud and laths, or mud bricks and are whitewashed. The floors are wooden but the ground floor may often be flagged or consist merely of hard-packed mud.

The Turks have always loved gardens and so their domestic quarters became arbours. Sometimes the houses are built round a courtyard which is also a garden and the big houses often stand in fine walled gardens, fertile and well-irrigated. There was another reason for this seclusion and comfort: their women were seldom allowed out and always forbidden to show their faces, and so it was necessary to protect and conceal them.

There is a good deal of disagreement about the origins of this type of domestic architecture. Some say that the Turks brought the style with them, others that they adapted what they found. It is most likely that it came from China and Central Asia. A number of towns in Serbia and Macedonia are very Chinese in appearance.

Another feature of Ulcinj, as of all 'Turkish' towns, is its irregularity which is an extension of the subtly irregular shapes and positioning of the houses. It sprawls each side of one long main street and the buildings are linked by winding paths and tracks. The whole effect is of an unobtrusive and harmonious disorder which gives continuous pleasure.

The market goes on in and alongside the main street, somewhat haphazardly. Some villagers ride in on mules, donkeys and horses; others walk, herding their stock. It is usually the men who ride and the women who walk (this applies to much of the country) and often enough the women carry their bundles and baskets on their heads. The farther south you go the more you see this method of transport which is both graceful and dignified and of course produces the kind of carriage dreamt about in young ladies' academies. But I have seen women carrying enormous loads on their heads in the main streets of Belgrade and even Zagreb. The Muslim women are nearly always dressed gaily, the Christians with more sobriety and restraint—and you will see many fascinating contrasts and blends in costume. . . . Especially on the occasion of a Muslim wedding when all the girls turn out in ravishing fineries of white silk and coloured ornaments and several hundred people join in animated celebration. Dancing usually takes place on the threshing floor, the *gumno.*

The **Citadel,** high on the bluff that juts into the bay, is a battered and spectral place, almost as derelict as Stari Bar. Some of the stone houses within the shattered battlements are still occupied and, incongruously enough, are supplied with electric light. There is not much of interest here except for a Turkish fountain and a ruined mosque which was once a church and is now littered with smashed stonework and complete cannon balls. The *mimbar* or 'pulpit' still stands. An eerie desolation of decaying houses surrounds these relics.

South of the town an ample sandy beach stretches for six miles, so it is clear that in the next few years Ulcinj is going to become a very popular resort. Behind the beach the flat land is very marshy and there are extensive salt pans over which the road is carried on a causeway. Albanian fishermen down here use primitive equipment: wide square nets which are lowered into the water and, when a fish is seen swimming over them, hauled up again by a curious contraption made of supple branches. Beyond lies Albania, behind a heavily guarded frontier. Not so long ago it was imprudent to be seen too near it and even now, if you happen to stray far off the usual routes and are near the frontier, do not tempt fortune or, more accurately, the aim of some bored Albanian sentry for whom you may provide an irresistible target and a much needed diversion in the dreadful monotony of remote outposts.

When you have seen Ulcinj there is nothing for it but to return to

Crnojevića Rijeka, near where the river enters Lake Skadar. The bridge is probably Turkish

A 'deep romantic chasm', the Rugovo Gorge leading to Peć. One of the wildest and most beautiful regions of Jugoslavia

Petrovac and the new road to Titograd. You *can* turn off outside Bar and go across the Rumija range, and it is a most entertaining trip, but the road is appalling. And now that we are approaching the wilder parts of Jugoslavia a word about roads and maps is timely.

The fact is that apart from the main *autoput* roads there are still not *so* many good roads in this country; but they are being rapidly improved in all parts and the situation changes for the better from month to month. It has certainly improved out of all recognition in the last ten years, and many places that were inaccessible except on foot or horse now have good roads to them. Maps, too, are much better than they used to be (See Appendix p. 414).

As soon as you get off the main trunk routes you may find anything, but usually stones, dust and axle-breaking potholes. The worst roads are those that consist of a kind of eroded macadam broken down by snow, ice and rain and by the weight of buses and big lorries. It is the heavy transport that does a lot of the damage and therefore you will often discover that the most remote roads are the best because they never carry anything heavier than horses and ox-carts.

However, if you do not go off the main routes you will never see anything and I am bound to offer as encouragement and consolation the fact that in the course of travelling well over twenty thousand miles in this country by car and bus I have only known two punctures and two breakdowns. If you *do* break down you may be in serious trouble but the Jugoslavs are extremely helpful and sympathetic to all travellers and in the countryside they have a keen sense of obligation to the guest.

Before making journeys on minor roads or into remote parts always make careful inquiries, or you may find that a road is up for construction or a bridge down for rebuilding. Then you will have to make a detour of many miles. The bus drivers are always exchanging information like this. As a general rule all information about travelling facilities should, so far as possible, be checked twice, before settling for the majority opinion. Much information is supplied out of a kind of spontaneous desire to please and may be very unreliable. In this respect the Jugoslavs are rather like the Irish (after all, the Celts came from this part of the world) and they tell you what they think you would like to know. Even the staffs of Tourist offices sometimes have a distressing habit of providing you with totally inaccurate facts. Countrymen know their own district intimately and their information will usually be accurate, but it will only cover a small area. All this, of course, makes for more entertaining and diverting travel and may produce splendid surprises—but it can also lead to violent frustrations and loss of time. This is a commodity to which many Jugoslavs are more or less indifferent. When you have plenty of it at your own disposal that indifference can become very winning. *Ima vremena* ('there is time') is a phrase you will often hear.

CHAPTER 11

Inland Montenegro

*Lake Skadar — Virpazar — Crnojevića — Obod Monastery — Titograd —
Nikšić—Žabljak—Mt Durmitor—Morača Monastery—Serbian art—Gorge
of Tara—Pljevlja—Mileševa Monastery—Čakor Pass—Rugovo Gorge*

As you cross the mountains you begin to see the expanse of **Lake
Skadar,** a third of which belongs to Albania. It is a strange
greeny blue surrounded by bare *karst* mountains which plunge
abruptly into it. The blue is water; the green, reed beds, lily plants,
algae and other growths. In the swelter of summer, haze and mirage
play the oddest tricks with this lake. Denuded peaks appear to
float in air above the motionless water, colour and shapes acquire
an intensity which belongs to the visionary world of the mescalin
taker. (For map, see p. 147).

The northern end of the lake is dotted with small islands on some
of which are derelict monasteries and squalid fishing villages; and
the shores are indented with numerous coves many of which conceal
other fishing hamlets. In fact fishing is the principal source of livelihood here among a people who are very poor. Fortunately fish are
plentiful, especially the lake sardines, *ukljere* and *skobalji,* which
spawn in the Adriatic and return by underground river. Obviously,
the Little Egrets and Great White Heron who breed here are well
supplied.

There are other peculiarities about this lake. In spring acres of it
are covered with a kind of aquatic lotus which bears very sweet blos-
soms. In August the women of the villages, clothed in black, mysterious, go out in big flat-bottomed boats and gather a lake fruit
called *kasaronja.* This is a kind of knobbly chestnut whose leaves float
on the water and whose roots grow in the lake bed only a few feet
below the surface. Curiously enough, in a year of drought it never
bears fruit even though there is ample water in the lake.

Quite soon you reach **Virpazar** (it means, approximately, Whirlpool Bazaar and was the flashpoint of the Vespers) a small brown and white village connected to the mainland by dykes. It is still the main market place, even though neighbouring villages are ten times larger, and the locals still speak of going 'to town' when they visit the market.

There is little in the way of antiquities to see here but **Crnojevića**, only fourteen kilometres away, on a river which runs into the lake, is an interesting spot. They call it the Venice of Montenegro and indeed it has boats that resemble gondolas, and two lovely bridges, one of which the Turks built. King Nicholas had a modest summer palace here and nearby are the remains of the monastery of Obod, founded by Ivan Crnojević in 1493. Crnojević, a militant foe of the Turks, became the hero of numerous legends and there is a cave near Obod where he was supposed to sleep in the arms of the fairies (the '*vile*') who would one day wake him so that he could expel the enemy and join Kotor to Montenegro. Thunder is still interpreted as the wrath of the old man, and the Rijeka Crnojevića which flows into Lake Skadar a few miles from the cave was supposed to have been formed from the tears he shed over the misfortune of his people. At Obod, also, the first Slav printing works was set up (with equipment brought from Venice) in 1493 which produced the first books printed in Cyrillic. But it didn't last long. After some years the lead had to be melted down for bullets: an apt footnote to Montenegrin history.

You can reach **Titograd** easily from Crnojevića or Virpazar but it is not a place in which one wants to remain long. If you happen to arrive there by train I must warn you that the railway station (easily the most uncomfortable one in eastern Europe) lies a long way from the town.

Titograd used to be called Podgorica but this was almost completely destroyed during the war. Out of its ashes rose Tito's town, of which Montenegrins are rather proud—and justifiably so. For them it represents progress and symbolises modern Jugoslavia. Some of the public buildings and the packing-case blocks are striking. They are particularly proud of their 'A' category Crnagora Hotel which is palatial and lavishly designed. When they built it the rest of the country thought it was a megalomaniac act but it is used a good deal and I think is much overrated as well as too expensive. However, the cooking has always been good whenever I have stopped there. Most nights in the summer there is an orchestra and singers on the terrace, a form of entertainment which you will find in many small remote towns where tourists never go. At Titograd it certainly *is* for visitors and the Montenegrins suffer such innovations with a disdainful patience. Not so long ago a clan chief would have pulled out his gun when he wanted silence, and if he didn't get it would have fired a round or two into the air.

Of antiquities there is almost nothing in Titograd, except, beyond the river, some old stone houses, a few with pendent balconies and wide eaves, the remains of two mosques and a Turkish clock tower near the bus station. I should think that most of these will be demolished in the next few years.

From here there is an interesting trip to be made to Nikšić, high in the mountains to the north, where the men and women appear to be taller and better looking than anywhere else in Montenegro. They are also very courteous and hospitable.

Soon after leaving Titograd you pass the confluence of the rivers Morača and Zeta where lie the remains of the Roman town of Dioclea, a name which is believed to come from the Illyrian tribe Docleati. It was an important city and there are relics of substantial walls, a bridge, columns and sarcophagi. After running through the valley for some way you begin a long, steep, twisting climb, and you will soon see, far to your right up the mountainside, a white blob. This is the monastery of Ostrog which can be reached by a road signposted near the top of the pass. It stands in an almost impregnable position with precipices rising hundreds of feet immediately behind it. It is a pilgrimage spot because it harbours the body of the Orthodox Saint Basil, a Montenegrin who flourished in the seventeenth century but about whom little is known. He has a reputation for miracles.

The whole region between Titograd and Nikšić is strewn with monuments to the dead of many bloody struggles against invaders. In the last war, in either folly or cynical wisdom, the Germans allocated Montenegro to the Italians, who were not able to compete against mountain tribesmen with at least six centuries of fiercely guarded freedom behind them. Unhappily the Italians committed many barbarous atrocities here, as they did on the coast. Naturally enough the Montenegrins got their own back with interest.

After you have crossed the pass the road curls down and then straightens to **Nikšić,** more or less in the middle of an enormous plateau which has a few rocky bumps on it and is encircled by high grey mountains, barren except for scrub. Nikšić (its Hotel Onogošt is good) is a typical Montenegrin town and a good deal bigger than

Cetinje. It was built on the site of a Roman town, Anagustum, and has passed through several hands since: those of the Goths, the Byzantines and the Turks, for example and none of whom have left much mark. Near the railway station on the west are the ruins of old ramparts and towers which walled the medieval city. On the eastern side, the principal church, Sv Petar, is clearly visible on a small hump. In the modern cemetery alongside it there are, incongruously enough, a few well-preserved Bogomil tombs. The other side of the church, on the edge of the park, you find a rather shabby-looking building which was a royal palace and is now a school. If you go round to the back you will see a door, in a corner of the right wing, which lets you into a small museum. This has some costumes, Turkish and Montenegrin, on the ground floor and some interesting photographs of Bogomil tombs found in the vicinity. Upstairs is a section devoted to the Revolution and Partisan activities. A few kilometres from the town (you must ask for directions in the Tourist office) are the remains of the Gothic settlement of Onogošt and a bridge which is thought to be Roman.

From Nikšić, but only in the summer, you can drive on to the **Žabljak** region and **Mount Durmitor**—one of the most popular resorts in the country. The lofty mountains are dark with spruce and pine forests through which torrents rush. On the high green plateaux big flocks of sheep pasture. The hunting and the fishing are good and it is, of course, matchless walking country. On the high slopes of Mt Durmitor you will probably notice groups of small wooden huts, called *katuni*, which are used by the Montenegrin shepherds and cowherds during the summer. They are furnished with dairy equipment and the bare essentials of life. The older women do the milking and make the butter and cheese, the men tend the flocks. Day by slow day the seasons turn, pass, piped by the shepherd's flute, tolled away by the sheep bells and cow bells.

Occasionally the shepherds join for a form of highland games: wrestling, stone-throwing, long-jumping, hurling stones at a target, shooting, and a local sport called *gudžanje*, related to golf.

Žabljak itself is a small town with a good hotel, the Durmitor, which has become the ski-ing and tourist centre of the Montenegrin equivalent of the Lake District. If you happen to be here on July 13th (anniversary of the Montenegrin uprising in 1941) you will see an assembly of Montenegrin warriors—many of them in costume. This is also the day of the Crnagora Derby, on the plains of Njegovodja.

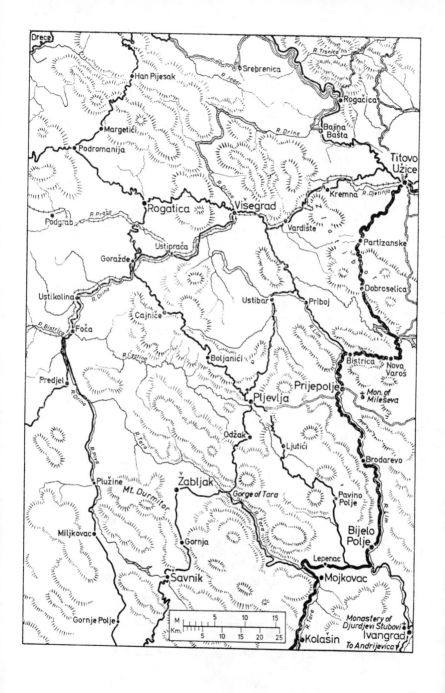

If you have got as far as Žabljak it seems a pity not to go on to the famous **Gorge of Tara** (Djurdjevića Tara). The River Tara rises far to the north-west not far from Sarajevo and runs down to the Morača near Titograd and among all the extravagant gestures of Jugoslavian scenery the gorge qualifies for three stars. It is between two and three thousand feet deep and the river is crossed, not far from Žabljak, in three hops and a bound, by a noble bridge.

Here there is another difficult decision to make. You can climb the other side of the gorge and drive over the uplands to Pljevlja and Prijepolje and the monastery of Mileševa (an essential visit, in my view) and on into eastern Bosnia (parts of which I shall deal with later) or you can turn south-east and drive down the gorge to Mojkovac and Kolašin. Both are exciting journeys. A further alternative is to omit Nikšić from your itinerary and take the other main road (a very good one) north from Titograd and travel up the Morača valley. If you do this you can still see the other places I have mentioned above and make a splendid round trip. For simplicity's sake I shall follow this line temporarily.

You leave Titograd from the north of the main *trg* and for 110 kilometres you climb steadily to three thousand feet along the sides and through the valleys of massive hills and high mountains which are often covered in dense forest containing a good many wild animals. Villages are rare and small and you will notice fairly soon that a lot of wood is used in building. Even the roofs are made of overlapping slats which, when weathered grey, look like slabs of thick slate. These are common all over Bosnia and Montenegro. About twenty-five kilometres short of Mateševo you can hardly fail to see the **Monastery of Morača** which is just below and right up against the new road. There is a sign to tell you you are approaching.

As this may well be the first Orthodox monastery of any note you come across some introduction is necessary to the subject of medieval Serbian architecture and art, a vast subject that has exercised the skill, love and care of many artists and scholars for a long time.

Three 'schools' can be distinguished: the Raška, the Central Serbian and the Morava. The 'Raška School' corresponds roughly with the realms of the early Nemanja princes of Serbia in the twelfth and thirteenth centuries and includes the monasteries of Mileševa, near Prijepolje; Djurdjevi Stubovi and Studenica, near Novi Pazar; Žiča, near Kraljevo; Peć, in the Kosmet; Sopoćani and Gradac, near Raška itself.

The 'Central School' in southern Serbia and Macedonia (also

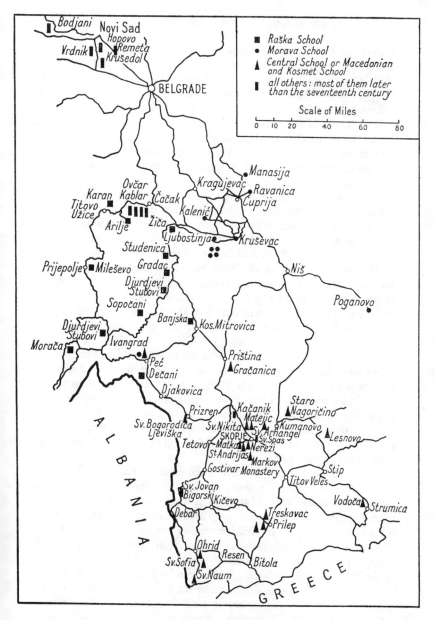

The rough distribution of the principal Orthodox churches and monasteries

known as the 'Macedonian and Kosmet School'), belongs to the thirteenth and fourteenth centuries and includes Gračanica, near Priština; Lesnovo, near Štip; Markov Monastery church, near Skopje; Nagoričino and Matejić, also near Skopje—and several others in the region; as well as churches at Prizren.

The works of the 'Morava School' (named after that river near whose valley most of the buildings are to be found) are mostly fourteenth century and include the church of Lazarica at Kruševac and the monastery churches of Ravanica, Ljubostinja, Manasija and Kalenić.

This is a very rough, working classification to help simplify an extremely complex subject. I have omitted a good many of the churches I shall mention later. Some of them are in towns but most of them belong to monasteries in the country, of which there are more than three hundred in Serbia and Macedonia.

Though they all look different externally and internally, nearly all monastery churches have certain things in common: they are small (some of them are tiny); they are tucked away in remote valleys and mountain fastnesses; and they were nearly all ordered and paid for by royalty or nobility. In other words, they were princely religious foundations (*zadužbine*) in which the donors wished to be buried. Many of them contain portraits of the donors. They were built and decorated, for the most part, by Serbs and Greeks who were completely familiar with the forms of Byzantine architecture and art. The more southerly churches show pronounced Byzantine influences; the more northerly and westerly have much more in common with the Romanesque and west European traditions. Here and there one meets fascinating mixtures and, as always, exceptions to the rule.

Under the Byzantine Comnene emperors in the twelfth century and earlier there was a unity of style in fresco painting in the southern Serbian and Macedonian provinces, especially in the Ohrid region and near Skopje. The main influences had come from Constantinople. In this connection two of the most important churches are Sv Sofije in Ohrid and Sv Panteleimon outside Skopje, whose paintings precede chronologically those mentioned in the three 'schools' above. A case can be made that they are the forerunners of the work done in the later Central Serbian School.

The style of the late Comnene period spread to Raška towards the end of the twelfth century. From Raška there were links to Dalmatia, Zadar in particular. But the unity was broken by the

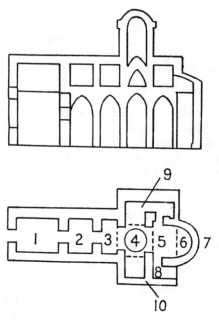

1. Exonarthex
2. Narthex
3. Esonarthex (this is rare)
4. Dome or cupola
5. Naos (the area under the dome is also part of the naos)
6. Iconostasis
7. Apse
8. Diaconicon
9 & 10 Transepts. There may be lateral chapels here.

Plan to show principal features of an Orthodox Church

sack of Constantinople in 1204, and thereafter, for fifty years, little or nothing was produced in that city. The Macedonian provinces retained the Comnene idiom and mannerisms, but the Raška School developed its own. When the Greek emperors returned to Constantinople half way through the thirteenth century there began a minor renaissance in the arts under the Palaeologues. Late in the thirteenth century we see the main results of this renaissance in the works of the so-called 'Serbian School'.

The whole matter is beset with the complexities typical of the Balkans. At the same time we can say that all the painting was an attempt to describe, explain and order a vision of the world and the relationship between God and man: in short, to create a unity which was part of a greater and higher unity. Here I cannot do much more than point out and recommend. For decisions one must go to the experts on the subject.

The Morača monastery church is rather important. It is an engaging white building with a cupola topped by a cone, and has an altogether stylish simplicity about it. Its proportions comply with the formula of the 'golden cut': height plus width equals length. Like most of the churches in the Raška School it has three divisions: narthex, naos with a dome and the chancel area with its apse screened by an iconostasis. Occasionally there are transepts and lateral chapels. It was founded in 1252 by Stefan, a son of the *Župan* Vukan. Most of the frescoes are sixteenth- and seventeenth-century work, traditional in style and rather dull. It is a feature of this art that later painters went on repeating what had already been done in a very stylised idiom. They did not solve, or perhaps attempt to solve, problems of perspective and arrangement. The same can be said of much icon painting. However, of the original frescoes there survive a *Virgin and Child* in the tympany of the west door and, inside, in the diaconicon (a room attached to or enclosed in the church which in early Christian times was used for the reception of offerings and served as a vestry and library) some scenes from the life of Sv Ilija which are excellent and most important in the history of Serbian art, more especially in the development of the Raška School. Morača comes after Mileševa and Peć chronologically, but before Sopoćani, and the monumental style and subtle harmonies of these few original frescoes show the distinctive features of the court painters. The treasury contains some interesting icons and a very early printed book, a liturgical work that may have been done at Obod (see p. 164)

This seems an opportune moment to say something about the art of fresco painting. The word, of course, means 'fresh' and there are two kinds of fresco painting. One is *fresco secco*—namely paint applied to dried plaster; not much more than a higher form of decorative distemper which flakes off fairly soon. The second is what they call *buon fresco* or true fresco, a most durable medium, as the paintings of Jugoslavia demonstrate very clearly.

The processes involved are approximately as follows: the wall is rough plastered and then a coat called *arricciato* is applied. The whole drawing is then traced on to the wall and an area sufficient for a day's work is covered with another layer of plaster which must be damp. The original cartoon is re-drawn over this so that it joins with the uncovered parts. The paint mixed with lime-water or plain water is then put on the damp plaster. The pigments become integrated with the wall itself so that flaking and scaling cannot occur. At the end of the day's work the unpainted damp plaster (called the *intonaco*) is cut away and the following day a new layer of damp plaster is re-laid. Microscopic scrutiny of the fresco shows the joins in the plaster and from this evidence it is possible to calculate how many days a work has taken.

It is an exacting medium, one that requires speed, deftness and an outstanding sense of proportion—especially when working on curved and angular surfaces, in poor light (many of these churches are very dark) and from extremely awkward positions.

When you reach Matešsevo I suggest you diverge to make a tour of central Montenegro, which can include the Gorge of Tara. You take the road to **Kolašin**, a small austere market town surrounded by forested mountains and with the same atmosphere of almost chilly frugality that characterises Cetinje. Yet the region, like much of interior Montenegro, is fertile to the point of luxuriance. The thick green pile of the grazing lands, and the orchards hung with succulent fruit are a banquet after the strict fast of rock and stone. In fact the Kolašin area is like an improbable mixture of Kent and the Lake District.

Twenty-three kilometres farther you reach Mojkovac and turn north-west up the Tara valley: a lonely, wild gorge where everything is dwarfed, even the hundred-foot pines that cling like sprigs in the clefts and on the pinnacles of sheer rock faces. All the time you receive quick, glancing kingfisher-blue gleams of the river as it darts far below.

After the graceful acrobatic of the bridge comes a very arduous climb of about three thousand feet. The road from here to Pljevlja is quite good for much of the time and to start with winds across pine-forested plateaux, then into more open and rolling country. It is like being in the Canadian outback up here and there are plenty of wolves in the forests. Apart from the occasional hamlet of half a dozen grey wooden houses, a shepherd or shepherdess with a flock, the odd horseman, there is little life. You won't see a car or lorry in these parts for days on end. Everybody rides or walks. Sometimes I have seen a hundred or more saddled horses tethered at rails or grazing loose in a village where the men of the district have ridden in for some meeting.

Gradually you descend to **Pljevlja,** a small, Turkish-looking town in an ample valley. It is an interesting mixture architecturally. Quite a lot of post-war building is mingled with traditional, solid stone houses and a profusion of Turkish houses with gardens, which here are not surrounded by walls. There are several mosques of which one, with a fountain, is very elegant. In the triangular public garden lies a solitary Bogomil tomb next to a recent monument.

The only hotel, the Tara, has considerable character. It serves good simple food and the white and *rosé* wines of the district which are excellent. Most nights the café part of the hotel is packed out to listen to the band and singers. These are sometimes supplemented by a well-upholstered *chanteuse*.

Monday is the best day to be in Pljevlja for then there is a great gathering for the weekly market. In their hundreds the inhabitants of the remote villages ride or walk in with their flocks and fowl. Many of them come ten or fifteen miles and return the same distance in the evening. You will not see a great deal in the way of specific national costumes (the Montenegrins have been quicker than most to shed these) but the people are so magnificent to look at and wear their clothes with such style that this is more than enough.

From Pljevlja a bad road runs across wild uplands to Prijepolje. Here, as in so many other parts, you will find lonely women guarding their flocks and nearly always spinning or knitting as they do so. Montenegro is the land of eagles and black widows . . . weather-beaten crones crouching at the roadside like birds of ill omen, like witches, Cassandras of doom and sorrow, gaunt women, with lean faces and fierce unflinching eyes, who can lope for miles with the supple ease of fit animals. They have lived lives of incredible hardiness and suffering and share with their men such a spirit of stoical and absolute resolution that one cringes a little to think of it.

There is little to see at Prijepolje but you have to go there to reach **Mileševa.** When you come into the town go through and then take a turn slightly to the right just beyond the Turkish clock tower, (*sahat kula*). This is a poor road and after five kilometres there is a turn to the left. Very soon you come to the church and monastery on the slopes of Mt Zlatar at the entrance to the gorge through which a main road from the Adriatic to Istanbul used to run. There is still a road (very hazardous) to Novi Pazar a hundred kilometres away. Far up the gorge you can see the ruins of a medieval fortress and the gleam of a swan-white mosque. Not much is left of the monastery buildings and there are only a few monks attended by some middle-aged 'nuns', one of whom will show you round. The last time I went there on a perfect summer afternoon I found two monks in the paddock. They were heavily bearded, as most Orthodox monks are, and their dark hair fell in rich tresses from beneath their high, black cylindrical hats and curled luxuriantly over their cassocks. One, a cheroot dangling from his mouth, leant negligently against a barn and read a newspaper. The other sat under a tree and chatted with some children whose mother was spinning wool on her distaff. Sheep nibbled and pigs rooted for early windfalls in the orchard. Beyond, three hill-men with long white moustaches were loading their mules.

The church is very plain and modest outwardly: whitewashed, with sloe-coloured cupolas and roof. It looks like one of those simple parish churches in neat little villages where next to nothing happens in a hundred years. But this was a royal foundation once ornamented in pure gold. An Orthodox king was buried here, a Catholic king was crowned here, and the body of Sv Sava, the greatest saint in the history of the Serbian Orthodox Church, once lay here—until the Turks desecrated and burnt it. When you are shown through the low narrow door at the side and you catch your first glimpse of the frescoes you realise it is far from ordinary.

The church was founded and built in 1234 by King Vladislav, one of the earlier monarchs of the Nemanjić dynasty, and the frescoes were executed about the same time by three men whose names have been found recently in inscriptions: Dimitrije, Djordje and Teodor. They were very probably Serbians.

First the programme: in the cupola, on the north side, is the *Birth of Christ*; on the south, the *Descent from the Cross*; on the pillars, the *Presentation in the Temple* and the *Entry into Jerusalem*; on the south wall you see Vladislav being presented to Christ by the Virgin; above that is the *Resurrection*, just to the left of the little window. On the wall just to the right of the chancel (usually separated from the naos or main sanctuary of the church by an iconostasis) is the *Virgin of the Annunciation*. On the west or back wall of the naos is the *Dormition of the Virgin*, the customary position for this subject.

On the north wall of the narthex (the narthex is the transverse vestibule of an Orthodox church; there may also be an exonarthex which is outside and precedes the façade and, less frequently, an esonarthex which is between the nave and the narthex)[1] you find portraits of the kings Radoslav, Vladislav and Stefan; on the south, Constantine and Helena who appear very often in the Serbian frescoes; in the north-east angle of the narthex, Sv Sava and Sv Simeon and Stefan Nemanja (founder of the dynasty); on the west wall, the *Betrayal* and the *Agony in the Garden*. The exonarthex contains a notable but rather faded *Last Judgment* scene and some curious figures who look as if they are wearing pyjamas.

It is almost miraculous that all these paintings survive because the church has been burnt out, reconstructed, exposed to the elements without a roof and even used as stables by the Germans during the last war. Their survival is a tribute to the technical excellence of the artists. Originally, and for the first time in wall painting, the backgrounds were coloured in gold of which you can still see traces. This was a blending of the mosaic tradition with fresco technique.

Most of the paintings are monumentally large and well spaced and this monumental quality characterises the Raška School. I personally prefer these to the rather overcrowded walls of places like Dečani. *The Deposition*, though a little difficult to see, is a masterpiece, the personification of sacrifice and suffering. The serene gravity and beauty of the Virgin in the *Annunciation* has seldom been surpassed in any other fresco. If you look closely you will see that she holds a slim distaff and is spinning wool: as far as I know this is the only time Our Lady has been shown in this way. Better, even, than this, is the ravishing white angel of the *Resurrection*: a marvellous figure of mystical beauty and radiant grace. The features are epicene yet of great power.

The group which shows King Vladislav being presented to Christ is chiefly remarkable for the naturalism of the king's face. The group of the three kings and the three saints in the narthex is also naturalistic and shows considerable insight and compassion in the rendering of the different features. The portrait of Sv Sava is particularly striking. That of Constantine is also very good but unhappily the face of the empress has been disfigured.

From Prijepolje there is a splendid run down the **River Lim valley** to Bijelo Polje. The areas round here are devoted to sheep rearing and the shepherds have little movable huts on runners. They

[1] See plan on p 171.

are about six foot long by five in height, made of branches or boards mortared together, and they can accommodate one or two men. They enable the shepherds to keep constant watch over their sheepfolds and guard against wolves.

Shortly beyond Bijelo Polje you reach a fork: the right road takes you back to Kolašin, the left down the Lim valley to Ivangrad and Andrijevica and the main road to Peć. Though it means you miss some superb scenery between Mateševo and Andrijevica it is probably best to go via **Ivangrad** (see map on p. 181), a small town founded by the Turks on an earlier site as recently as 1862. Northwest of it (ask for directions) is the monastery of Djurdjevi Stubovi: the Pillars of St George (not to be confused with the one near Raška). It has an imposing fortress-like church with a double narthex divided by a tower. It belongs to the Raška School (it was built about 1220) and a few excellent frescoes survive. However, this is not an essential visit and as there are so many other much more important churches and monasteries you would be well-advised to press on to **Andrijevica** (a well-known centre for fishing and hunting expeditions) where there is a mixture of substantial stone houses and wooden ones. Like Kolašin and so many Montenegrin towns it is rather bleak. When you reach Murino I recommend a diversion up into the Prokletije massif. Only eleven kilometres away on quite a good road you come to the pretty village of Plav on the banks of the **Plavsko Jezero** (Lake Plav) which lies like a big blue dew-pond cupped 3,000 feet up in the mountains which soar far above it another three or four thousand feet into a series of peaks.

The lake is well known for its excellent trout. Twenty-six kilometres farther on, in austere and awe-inspiring scenery, lies the small frontier town of Gusinje. The mountains form the Prokletije range through which runs the Albanian-Jugoslav border. The principal peaks (all well over 7,000 feet) are Bogićevića, Maja Rozit and Djaravica. Beyond stretch the Highlands of Albania and one of the most inaccessible and unknown regions of Europe. Here live the Gegs (predominantly Muslims) whose clan and chieftain system is similar to that of the Scots and many of whose separated brethren live in the Kosmet (see next chapter). The Gegs, like the Montenegrins and the Gurals in the High Tatra of Czechoslovakia, are magnificent guerilla soldiers, warriors of legendary courage and prowess. You must not stray near the frontier. Every Geg is a crack shot, capable of picking off a cabbage white at a hundred paces.

From Gusinje one is obliged to return to Murino via Plav and rejoin the main road (for map, see p. 181).

Beyond this town the scenery becomes more extravagantly wild and grandiose the farther you go. You creep up huge hills and crawl down the sides of vast valleys until the route reaches a climax at the **Čakor Pass** which is well over five thousand feet up. Across the mountains are pastures where shepherds spend the whole summer and build little huts (like those near Bijelo Polje) which form a temporary village called a *bačilo*.

Having reached a sublime height on the roof of Jugoslavia there is every incentive to stop. There is nothing to disturb the immense silences of these lofty peaks, except the drifting tinkle of sheep bells, the wind, and the croak of buzzard or raven. Njegoš, in some lines reminiscent of Wordsworth, wrote how a hundred times he had watched the fleeting clouds that sail like phantom ships high off the sea and anchor on the mountain range, of how he watched them break in flashes of lightning and ominous rumbling, the heaven's artillery, while he basked in the sun.

> *'I saw and heard how they rent the skies;*
> *Squalls of hostile hail poured down,*
> *Plundered the earth of her fertility.'*

This contrast of light and darkness, this war in heaven, symbolises the past of Montenegro, a past he wished to transcend in his efforts to bring peace—which now there is.

A long and profound descent follows through country as awe-inspiring as anything one is likely to see in Europe, and all the time you are on a route that was only a track until 1925. Ten years before that the second Serbian army, with a rag-tag of destitute refugees in its wake, retreated here to Albania and Corfu. They did it in midwinter with appalling loss of life. So many survivors died of plague and malnutrition on the isle of Vid near Corfu that the Serbs still call it the Isle of Death.

Soon you enter the **Rugovo Gorge** which narrows and narrows to a jagged twilit canyon four thousand feet deep, where the dark, dripping rocks almost close over your head and down which the River Pećska Bistrica hurls itself in a foaming, boiling fury.

CHAPTER 12

The Kosmet and S.W. Serbia

Peć—Kosmet—Monastery of Visoki Dečani—Djakovica—Prizren—the road to Skopje

Suddenly the gorge ends. The valley widens. The plain begins to unfold, and **Peć** lies scattered before you: the Rome of the Orthodox Church. But the comparison is only nominal.

Near the south of the gorge, in a walled paddock below the road, the plump cupolas of the **Patrijaršija** (the Patriarchate) are just visible. You have to keep a sharp eye open otherwise you drive straight past it.

The original headquarters of the Serbian Orthodox Church was at Žiča, some way north near Kraljevo. However, this proved to be too near what was then the Hungarian frontier and the seat of the Church was moved to Peć—probably in 1345, but perhaps earlier. It remained here until the Turks abolished the Patriarchy in 1766. Virtually nothing remains of the original bishop's palace and monastery, but there are still a handful of monks and nuns in the conventual buildings that exist.

The 'cathedral' consists of three churches which really form one, with a common narthex and, alongside, a small chapel. The central and oldest building is the **Crkva Svetih Apostola** (Church of the Apostles); that on the north the Church of Sv Dimitrije (St Demetrius); and the southern one is dedicated to the Virgin. The tiny chapel is St Nicholas's. Parts of the Church of the Apostles were built in the twelfth century or even earlier. Between them they form the Canterbury of Serbia but the whole group would fit into Canterbury Cathedral five or six times, and in St Peter's would look no bigger than a summer house. From this modest establishment one of that oligarchy neatly described as an 'œcumenical syndicate of Popes', ruled.

Entering the broad dingy narthex is more like going into a tomb than a church. It is a matter of atmosphere rather than lack of light, for few of these churches are well-lit. However, some of the frescoes, in company with those at Mileševa and Sopoćani, are masterpieces of thirteenth-century Serbian art and when the lights go on a sombre splendour is revealed.

In the central church the outstanding and important work is *The Ascension* in the cupola, plus the paintings on the north, south and west arches under it—which include the *Descent of the Holy Ghost*, the *Doubting of Thomas*, the *Mission of the Apostles*, and, below, the *Last Supper* and the *Raising of Lazarus*. This series also includes heads of the prophets and the four evangelists.

All or nearly all these frescoes were done by a man or men who belonged to the same group of painters who worked at Mileševa and Studenica. If you have seen either of these two churches first it is fairly easy to recognise certain elements. You will notice the same liking for monumental figures, the very bold vertical strokes, the harmonious blending of tones, the highly imaginative and naturalistic arrangement of figures and groups of figures. There is also the emphasis on youth: in fact, almost an apotheosis of youthful beauty. This is most noticeable in the Apostles and the angels.

In some respects the paintings of the Raška School portend an increasing realisation of the dignity of man (a realisation that was to become common in Europe during the fourteenth century and thereafter). The attempts at apotheosis were the prelude to so-called 'humanism', and the increasing secularisation of a society suffering from the need to assert itself against the traditional laws of contingency and the very limiting notion that man was only a little superior to the beasts. Plausible philosophers like Pico della Mirandola gave some intellectual respectability to the painter's humanistic concept of ennobled man. The conception, to start with, was concerned not so much with physical beauty as with the beauty of essence and spirit, the outward rendering, if you like, of inward grace. We have only to compare the work of great artists like Giotto or the court painters of the Raška School with that of people like Bacon to see what has become of the original ideals.

The Virgin in the *Ascension* group is probably the most remarkable figure of all. The Virgin of the *Annunciation* at Mileševa has a lyrical grace and spiritual serenity which inspire wonder and respect. The Virgin in Peć is a buxom, peasant beauty, a stunningly healthy and beautiful girl; almost, if one may say it without irreverence, sexually desirable. No symbol of the bodily church has ever

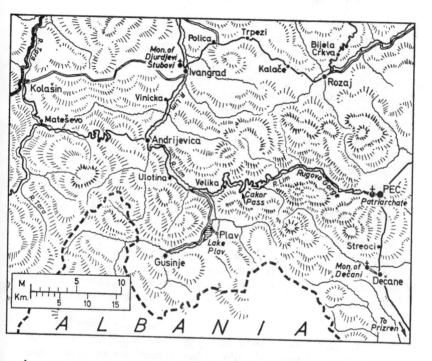

been represented in such an earthy and earthly fashion. The other most important painting in this church is the *Christ in Judgment*, in company with the *Virgin and St John the Baptist*, in the apse.

The flanking churches of St Demetrius and the Virgin were built near the beginning of the fourteenth century and it was then that the common narthex was made for all three. The most important paintings in St Demetrius are the cycles illustrating the legends of the saint and the great feasts of the Church. Among the best paintings is the *Birth of the Virgin*. Look particularly at the young woman carrying the amphora. On the west wall of the Church of The Virgin there is a good portrait of the founder, Archbishop Danilo II, holding a model of the church. There is also a sequence (in the chapel north of the altar) which illustrates the *Life of St Arsenius*, the founder of the monastery. In the chapel outside the main block the *Legends of St Nicholas* are depicted. This work is late seventeenth century and you can see how ordinary it is by comparison with, for example, the *Ascension* scene.

The narthex has three interesting paintings: the comprehensive and splendid *Last Judgment*, the *Cycle of the Calendar* with a composition for each day of the year, and the *Procession of the Nemanjić dynasty* which begins with its founder Stefan Nemanja and finishes with Csar Dušan.

This seems the opportune moment to give an extremely brief and simplified account of the complicated period of early Serbian history up to the end of the fourteenth century. I mention only those key names and dates which are likely to recur at regular intervals. If one can grasp these it is a great help; repetition begins to fix them securely.

Before the Nemanjić dynasty was established the history of the Serbs had been similar to that of the Croats. The various tribes which came south elected *župans* or tribal leaders. The districts over which they ruled were known as *županije* and were often named after rivers and mountains. There were no kings, but class distinctions based on landholding and kinship began to evolve and by the end of the eleventh century some families were pre-eminent. The traditional process of natural selection resulted in a kind of aristocracy. *Vojvoda* was the title of a military leader; a *knez* was a noble or knight.

The basic and typical South Slav unit had also evolved by this time. It was the **zadruga**: a family group of father, brothers, sons, etc. with their wives and children living together communally in a group of buildings (they had one main dwelling-house) and cultivating their land and stock. The leader, the *domaćin*, was the oldest male (occasionally the oldest female). The average number of people in a *zadruga* tended to be between fifteen and forty. Sometimes they numbered up to a hundred. The system had obvious advantages: mutual protection, shared work and responsibility, the unifying force of powerful blood ties.[1]

The *zadruga* system developed and throve throughout the late Middle Ages, survived the Turkish occupation and was functioning as late as 1945. In remoter parts remnants of the system are still to be found and I have seen a number of large farmhouses occupied by fifteen or more people who were living in a manner that has scarcely altered in a thousand years. But there was nothing primitive

---

[1] It is possible that the Serbian *zadruga* developed as a result of the East Roman taxation system, in which the *kapnikon* or hearth tax formed the separate unit of taxation. Some scholars maintain that the *zadruga* system was not properly established until the Turks had over-run Macedonia and Serbia.

about the people. Like many South Slav peasants they had the effortless dignity and courtesy of civilised aristocrats.

Cohesion of the early tribes under their *župans* was first developed in the Raška area and the dynasty was founded by Stefan Nemanja in 1169. Stefan abdicated in favour of his second son in 1196 or 1199 and then retired to Mt Athos where he became the monk Simeon. His youngest son, Rastko, was already there. His eldest, Vukan, was governor or 'king' of Dalmatia, Bosnia and Montenegro. Stefan II (known as *prvovenčani*, the 'first-crowned') reigned until 1228.

Shortly after his father's arrival on Athos, Rastko (his monastic name was Sava) returned to organise the Serbian Orthodox Church of which he become the first archbishop in 1219. All accounts of Sv Sava show that he was a very remarkable man: intelligent, astute, humble, a first-class organiser and a skilful and experienced diplomat. On top of all this he was well-educated and saintly. A more formidable array of qualities can hardly be imagined.

He saw clearly that a Serbian national state could only be created through a Serbian national church. He therefore set up his headquarters at the monastery of Žiča and from there organised the church until 1233 when he resigned in favour of his young pupil, Arsenius, and set out on a pilgrimage to the Holy Land. He died in 1235 or 1236 at Trnovo in north Bulgaria and from there his body was taken to Mileševa where it lay until the Turks committed their atrocity with it in 1595. In his fourteen years as archbishop the saint gave the Church that faith, purpose and structure which was to tide it over centuries of trial and persecution. It is a measure of his greatness that he is venerated by all creeds and to this day receives much devotion as one of the most outstanding saints in the Orthodox Calendar.

His brother's son Radoslav reigned until 1233 and was then dethroned by his younger brother Vladislav (whose portrait you have already seen at Mileševa). Vladislav only lasted nine years (he usually looks a weak, confused, rather bovine man) and was then deposed in turn by his younger brother Stefan, Uroš I, in 1242.

A somewhat sinister pattern has begun to establish itself by this stage and it takes no great effort of the imagination to envisage these unruly, virile and belligerent Serbian nobles quarrelling violently over who should rule and how it should be done. But Uroš had a long spell of thirty-four years and was shrewd enough to marry an excellent wife in the shape of a French princess: Helena of Anjou, a niece of Baldwin, the first Latin emperor of Constantinople. Though puritanical, Helena was an accomplished woman who introduced western culture and knowledge and founded schools, churches and public libraries (even fortresses) while her husband increased the territories of Serbia.

Uroš was eventually dethroned by his son Dragutin in 1276. But Dragutin didn't last long and retired in favour of his younger brother, Milutin (Uroš II) who ruled until 1321. Milutin, a militant despot, lecher and careerist, has more than once been compared with Henry VIII. They have certain common characteristics. The fresco portraits of Milutin are not misleading. He was the kind of man who had to prove himself—and so he did. He defeated a number of foreign powers and expanded Serbia considerably. He became very rich and devoted much of this wealth to religious foundations. He made an oath that for every year he remained on the throne he would build a church to the Lord. He reigned for 42 years and built 42 churches. A number of these were outside Serbia, as far afield as Constantinople, Sofia, Salonika and Jerusalem. Most of Milutin's foundations were Byzantine in their architecture because of the Greek influence at court caused by his second marriage to Simonida, the teen-age daughter of the Greek emperor Andronicus. Had Milutin lived in our day he would undoubtedly have become an industrial magnate or a newspaper proprietor and founded, instead of churches, hospitals and university colleges.

Milutin was succeeded by his son Stefan Dečanski (Uroš III) whose second name was taken from that of the monastery at Dečani which Stefan founded as a thanksgiving offering for a great victory over the Bulgarians at Kustendil. Unfortunately, he also married a Greek princess for his second wife and this led to the formation of a Greek junta at court which tried to declare the son of the second marriage heir to the throne instead of Dušan, the son of the first. This was the kind of 'Byzantine' situation that was very common at the time. The result in this case was a tragic mixed blessing. Dušan and his supporters rebelled and with his connivance his father was murdered. However, the reign of Csar Dušan (Uroš IV) was the summit of Serbian power and glory.

Dušan was a military and administrative genius whose ambition was to found an empire which would incorporate all Serbians, Greeks and Bulgarians. Between 1331, the year of his accession, and 1347 he fought a series of successful campaigns which greatly increased Serbian territory. Having done this he applied himself to the business of governing it properly. Law, custom and ordinance were laid down in what is known as Dušan's Code (the *Zakonic*) the most important document in the history of Serbia.[1] He then assembled an army to conquer the Byzantine Empire and, at the height of his power, died—in 1355.

Probably only Dušan could have dealt with the advancing Turks and the Hungarians who now began to overrun the country. The Serbian empire started to disintegrate. Dušan's heir and successor, Uroš V, was a weak, ineffectual man who struggled on till 1372. When he died the Nemanjić dynasty was extinct. The Turks had already administered a severe defeat to the Serbs in 1371 and eighteen years later came the death blow at Kosovo which began five centuries of Turkish domination.

The town of **Peć** (it gets its name from the *pećine* or caves nearby which once served as cells for eremites) is a large, amorphous place whose twisting streets are crossed by brooks and overhung by old Turkish and medieval houses. The Turks always arranged to have a number of streams running through their towns to irrigate their gardens and cleanse the streets, and a most civilised idea it is; except, of course, that it can produce a lot of mud. There is one particularly interesting form of architecture in Peć and other parts of the Kosmet called a *kula*—a keep-shaped fortified dwelling usually built of stone or brick with small windows and loopholes set high up. These are clearly for shooting from. The *kula* (it means 'a tower') is normally surrounded by a high wall. One of the best examples in Peć is the Jaša Pasha's tower near the women's market (the *ženska pijaca*). These buildings, plus several mosques, *konaks* in leafy gardens and orchards and the presence of numbers of costumed women (including gipsies, Serbs and Montenegrins) give Peć a distinctly oriental appearance.

There is also a tradition that some aristocratic line of beautiful

---

[1] A few extracts from the Code will serve to illustrate its scope and nature. Article 10 deals with heretics: 'If a man be found to live as a heretic among Christians, let him be branded upon the cheek and driven forth; and if any man conceal one such let him also be branded.' Article 69 is devoted to freemen: 'Let there be no gatherings of freemen, and if any be found in such a gathering, his ears shall be slit and his eyebrows singed.' Article 72 applies to those in distress: 'If any in distress come to the court of the Csar, justice shall be meted out to all, except to the slave of a feudal lord.' Article 95 admonishes swearers: 'If a man curse a bishop or a monk or a priest, he shall pay a hundred gold pieces; and if it be found a man has slain a bishop or a monk or a priest, he shall be slain and hanged.'

Amazons survives in Peć. For evidence I can only adduce the fact that one morning I became aware of a succession of tall, Grenadier-straight beauties strolling negligently through the town. It may have been a Coleridge type vision inspired by wine or the *vile* or the sort of euphoric *schwärmerei* that occasionally overtakes one in this part of the world. I have never seen them since but others swear they exist.

Now to more practical matters. . . . The best place to stay is in the centre of the town: the large new Metohija hotel, an interesting piece of modern architecture which blends Moorish and Byzantine styles externally. It is comfortable and inexpensive and has a good restaurant which is particularly well run because the hotel combines a catering school.

Jugoslavs are always complaining that they have no tradition as restaurateurs to compare with the Austrians, Swiss and Italians, but my impression after eating in several hundred Jugoslav restaurants of all sorts and descriptions is that the Jugoslav waiters and waitresses are good. They try hard to please without any mercenary intent; they are courteous, helpful, patient with foreigners who are in perpetual difficulties with their language, and most appreciative of any gesture in return.

There is one curiosity about waiters and waitresses in this country. Almost wherever you are they will be in the traditional garb: white jacket and black tie; black dress and white apron and, quite often, a white cap. All this is an odd survival of pre-war days. It is even odder when you see a country girl tricked out like an English parlourmaid nipping to and fro amidst the fur-hatted, sheep-skinned warriors in town for the weekly market.

Indeed, market day in Peć (a Saturday) is not to be missed. The peasants come in many miles from the hills and forests and the plain, and the streets are crammed with an extraordinary agglomeration of costume and produce. There are many Muslims and Albanians in this region (as in other parts of Serbia and Macedonia) because it is one of the principal towns of the autonomous district of **Kosmet** (Kosovo-Metohija), a post-war creation towards solving the problem of the Albanian minority; a problem which has been acute in the past. Many thousands of Albanians settled outside their country during the Turkish occupation and repopulated a deserted Serbia. The population of Albania now is rather more than a million, but there are well over half a million Albanians living outside their country. In the Kosmet they have their own schools and newspapers.

The men, lean, tough and handsome, are easily recognisable by their baggy, home-spun white trousers (slung very low on the hips) braided with thick black and brown stripes. They also wear black *jeleci* and skull-caps of white wool. The older men often wear turbans wound round these. This outfit, which is completed by their thick home-made stockings and leather *opanci*, makes them look very splendid. They are upright, haughty in mien, rather contemptuous of strangers unless you are their guest and then they are most courteous and hospitable. Probably their most outstanding characteristics are their fatalistic stoicism and their immense strength and stamina. In a country that produces the toughest and the fiercest guerrilla fighters in the world the Albanians are probably pre-eminent.

Those of the Kosmet are called *Šiptars* (their own word is *Šqipetar*) and many maintain an old tradition of going to the northern cities for seasonal work—especially in the autumn and winter. But you will often see two or three of them, moving with that athletic and tireless lope so typical of Albanians, in many different places at any time of the year. The work they do is wood-cutting for fires and they carry their equipment with them: folding trestles, hatchets, bow saws and a skin for water.

A short drive on the main road south from Peć brings one to the important monastery of **Visoki Dečani** (founded, as I mentioned, by the father of Csar Dušan) which lies at the entrance to another forested gorge a couple of kilometres from the village of Dečane. The roads are good and well signposted.

Like so many of the monasteries in this part of the world it lies behind walls which were originally built for protection as well as seclusion. Wild animals, bandits and invaders were common enough and livestock still needs protection against wolves.

Dečani was designed by a Catholic monk, Vid, from Kotor and is one of the loveliest buildings in this part of Jugoslavia—at any rate from the outside. There is not much left of the monastic establishment and only two or three monks survive but the modest yet solid church has an indefinable quality of great age which is somehow still youthful. Externally it is covered with pale pink, grey and white marble, colours which combine in subtle harmonies. Inside it is covered with frescoes, more than a thousand different paintings in all.

The building was started in 1327 by command of Stefan III but wasn't finished until 1335. It must have been an odd sensation for Dušan to order the completion of a church begun by his murdered father. Thirteen years later the frescoes were added.

In the tympanum of the west door there is an impressive *Christ between Two Angels*. The south door is adorned by the *Baptism of Christ* and the inscription of the architect in Cyrillic lettering. These are unusual features for an Orthodox church; and there are others, no doubt ascribable to the fact that Vid was familiar with western and Romanesque architecture. The doorway and the windows are Romanesque, and architects have observed that the north door is very similar to one at Semur-en-Brionnais and that the apsidal window is similar to one at Aulnay-en-Saintonge. The corbelled arches remind one of those on the Golden Gate at Split. The pilaster strips are characteristic of Lombardic churches. The concentric arches of the doorways are a common feature of Norman architecture. It is, therefore, a very interesting mixture of the Western and Byzantine traditions. In its main lines it belongs to the Raška School, but its paintings do not. They are crowded, complex, narrative, and reveal a number of crude attempts at developing the art of perspective. In this they show a definite effort to advance from the formalism of Byzantine art.

The narthex is dedicated to St George and a number of paintings depict his legends. Here, also, three hundred and sixty-five separate compositions illustrate the Calendar. There are also some excellent *portraits* of the Csar Dušan, his wife Jelena and their son Uroš, plus the Nemanjić family tree with a portrait for every member of the dynasty.

No space is wasted and the same is true of the naos. The lower parts are covered with more than two hundred and fifty paintings of saints as well as a number of pictures of kings and celebrities connected with the Church. The rest of the frescoes illustrate much of the New Testament and many legends of the saints. One can profitably spend a whole day moving slowly round this vast cartoon which in the end has an almost epic quality. It is an 'encyclopaedia' of the Middle Ages, a vivid and silent universe. There is the added pleasure of working out the sequences of the plot, as it were, and solving the relationships. No doubt many artists contributed but the name of one only survives: Serge Grešni, who, like the architect, came from Kotor.

A curious detail of the Crucifixion sequence in the naos (barely visible, owing to its height, without some aid) are flying objects which were supposed to represent the sun and moon, but in fact look just like primitive spaceships with pilots inside, their arms and hands clearly occupied in a steering motion. They zoom across the sky, much to the consternation of some angels who are holding their noses and ears. The good monks maintain that these sputniks symbolise the sun and moon in eclipse, but Christ Himself, rising from the dead, is encased in what looks very like a rocket.

The church possesses a number of icons made between the fourteenth and sixteenth centuries and also what is said to be the tomb of the founder which now, apparently, enshrines only one hand. No doubt the rest of his corpse has been rifled at some time or another by devout relic-mongers. The tomb, covered with an embroidered cloth, lies near the iconostasis and the locals say that certain rites performed by it will cure them of diseases. It is an oddity that Albanian Muslims as well as Christians visit the tomb with similar expectations.

Happily, Dečani suffered very little under Turkish rule and legend relates that its survival can be ascribed to the intervention of providence . . . After the Battle of Kosovo the Turks wanted to turn it into a mosque, but just as an *imam* was standing outside the west door and bowing towards Mecca a piece of stone carving fell on his head and killed him. This was interpreted as a sign that Allah did not wish Dečani to become a mosque.

But about these ancient buildings all sorts of stories accrue—and not only stories . . . Nearly thirty years ago an English writer reported a swarm of bees near the west door, and when I was last there a couple of years back there was another swarm. In fact they quite often swarm in the churches. Monks of all orders have always been great bee-keepers but it may be that the Orthodox monks have a special magnetism. Their bees are regarded as holy and the candles used in their churches may only be made from bee's wax.

You will notice that all these Orthodox churches contain iron stands with an upper and a lower tray filled with sand in which lighted candles are stuck. The candles in the upper tray are for the living; in the lower, for the dead.

From Dečani to Prizren there is a road of very variable quality over fairly level ground, but by the time you read this there may well be a completely new road.[1] On the way you pass several interesting small towns and villages. The biggest of these is Djakovica, a predominantly Muslim town with several mosques and an adequate hotel, the Sloboda. I find **Djakovica** a diverting place to pass a day or so in. They are beginning to modernise it but there is still a wide variety of Turkish houses as well as the *kule* you have seen in Peć.

[1] The road is now good.

Traditionally it is a town of craftsmen, a number of whom survive in their booths and shops. A few potters still use primitive hand-operated wooden wheels and turn out a type of black pottery (the chimney flue soot mixed with water is used for darkening it) in various shapes. Ware of this kind is very cheap in Serbia and Macedonia and you can often pick up original workmanship. Market day is on a Monday. Other villages you would find interesting are Biztražin (beyond which you cross the river Beli Drim—the 'White Devil'—on a fine six-arched Turkish bridge) Zrze and Kruša. Not far beyond Kruša you approach the big range of mountains called the Šar Planina at the foot of which is Prizren, a large and fascinating Muslim town each side of the Prizrenska Bistrica river. There is a comfortable new hotel (the Theranda) in the centre and I recommend a full day here.

Prizren (see map on p. 191) is a town of brown roofs, white walls, and green gardens. Brown, black and white are the colours of the costumes, with the occasional streak or blob of deep mulberry red or burnt orange. It is among the most beautiful of the Balkan towns and in the old *konaks* behind the high walls set with stout, studded doors and ornamental knockers, a traditionally patriarchal way of life is still strong. If you ever have a chance of visiting any of these houses don't miss it. Their construction, decoration and furnishing belong to a rapidly vanishing world.

Nearly everything has been done by local craftsmen and craftswomen: the carved rose ceilings, the bright goat's hair carpets on the walls and floors, the ottomans, the long low seats below the windows, the big carved cupboards for storing mattresses and quilted eiderdowns stuffed with fleece (you'll often see these being made in the markets), the *mangals* (a type of open brazier), the pewter and brass ware, the *sofre* (low wooden tables) and dozens of other things. . . . Even Turkish baths in closets.

Among the first settlers were the Romans whose town was called Theranda. After their decline and the Byzantine revival Prizren became prosperous in the thirteenth and fourteenth centuries when it was a seat of the Nemanjić kings the remains of whose formidable fortress, the Ribnik, spreads on top of the jutty hill south-west of the town. There are several mosques and several notable churches, especially the monastery of Sv Spas (the Saviour) clearly visible on the hill to the right of the castle. This was founded in 1348 by Csar Dušan. There are also the ruins of the monastery of Michael the Archangel. But *the* church to see in Prizren is **Sv Bogorodica**

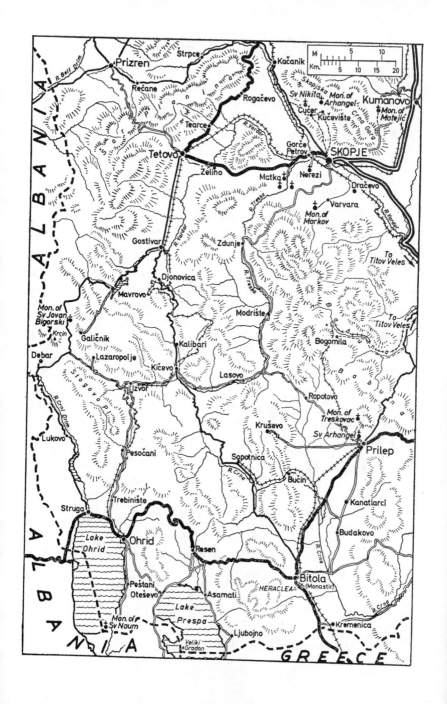

Ljeviška (the Virgin of the Falling Asleep). It is an interesting mixture of Serbian, Greek and Romanesque styles, built with five cupolas, an exonarthex and a belfry. It was one of King Milutin's forty-two foundations and work on it was started in 1307 or thereabouts on the site of an earlier basilica.

Unfortunately, under Turkish rule it was transformed into a mosque and all its frescoes were covered in plaster. In 1913 the Turks were finally expelled and it was reconsecrated, but it was not until 1950 that restoration began. Restoration revealed (as elsewhere) the disastrously efficient iconoclasm of the Turks. Every few inches there is a white scar on the paintings giving the effect of a heavy snow-storm. This was done to make it easier for the walls to take plaster.

However, between and behind the flakes of this 'blizzard' one can still see the frescoes which are among the finest of the fourteenth century. Very probably there were two painters at work here and the name of one of them is known from an inscription in the exonarthex. (On the arch is the inscription which gives the name of the architect, Nikola; and the artist, Astrapas.)[1] In fact this part contains some particularly interesting work and I suggest you look carefully at the realistic *Last Judgment* on the southern wall and the scenes of the *Glorification of the Virgin* on the northern. The *Allegory of Lust* in the former composition is outstanding.

The narthex has some good portraits of interest from an historical as well as an artistic point of view. On the west wall above the entrance there is a painting of Stefan Nemanja; to the left Sv Sava; on the right King Milutin and Stefan Nemanja's second son who, like his father, became a monk. On the northern part of the eastern wall there is a splendid portrait of Milutin looking, in fact, every inch a king.

On the west wall of the naos, as usual, you find the *Dormition of the Virgin*; in the cupola, *Christ Pantokrator*—that is, Christ as ruler of the world. In the apse are Church fathers and above the arcade a fine painting of the *Communion of the Apostles*.

I was in here one afternoon when two elderly Albanian tribesmen

[1]Astrapas is one of the most important artists of the period. He did a great deal of work for King Milutin at the end of the thirteenth century and the beginning of the fourteenth. His name means 'like lightning', and it is an apt one because of the intensity of his vision: the vivid contrasts, the bright colours, the unusually animated features in the portraits. Two other painters, known as Mihajlo and Eutihije (see p. 206) were his followers and there is a theory that Mihajlo was his son. When Astrapas died these two developed his style and techniques and improved upon them.

PAINTING I. Eleventh-century fresco in the apse of the cathedral Sv Sofije, Ohrid (see plate facing page 192). Stylistically the frescoes here are related to those in St. Sofia at Salonika and to the mosaics in St. Sofia at Kiev.

PAINTING 11. *Above left*, detail of pietà in Sv Panteleimon, Nerezi (near Skopje), about 1164. The figures are nearly life size. This is one of the most famous paintings in Balkan art. *Right*, a twelfth-century icon in Sv Sofije, Ohrid. *Below*, the birth of Christ's Mother, in the King's Church, Studenica. A fresco of the more naturalistic Raška School of the thirteenth century

came in. They wore turbans, black *jeleci*, striped woollen trousers and the traditional turned up leather *opanci*. They spent a long time there, strolling round, looking at the frescoes and discussing them. They were almost certainly Muslims but I was much impressed by their reverence and sense of propriety and the proudly unassuming way in which they viewed works of art alien to their religion yet a cherished element of their past. Outside, their ox-carts, with a few sheep huddled in them, remained in the care of a boy who was eating *burek* (see p. 429).

The day to be in Prizren is a Wednesday, the occasion of the weekly market. From an early hour the neighbouring villagers (mostly Albanians) come in thousands: pedestrians, riders on mules, horses and donkeys, caravans of bullock and buffalo and ox-carts, cavalcades of traps, buggies and gigs, droves of sheep, pigs and cattle . . . By eight in the morning the streets are clogged. About half the town is given over to the market, but the main concentrations are in the centre each side of the river. The stock market spreads out to the north-west.

The range of costume is spectacular. The men's gear is similar to that at Peć, Priština, Djakovica and other 'Albanian' towns. The women have about four different basic get-ups: (1) Black with white head-dresses; bloomers and black sateen dresses. (2) A white head-dress with an embroidered 'cowl'; another scarf wound right round under the chin; white dresses with delicate embroideries in pale green, violet and pink; a dark brown apron; black woollen stockings. (3) White head-scarves, bright blue 'tops' to the waist, long black skirts. (4) An elaborate head-dress of scarves, largely red; pannier bustle dresses; red aprons caught up at the waist; velvet and embroidered waistcoats; long white dresses and under those red dish pants or bloomers. (Most of the women who wear this last mixed rig-out have very noticeable eagle-like features with raven hair.)

From Prizren you can go across the Šar Planina direct to Tetovo and a most exciting trip it is through very wild country; but the road is poor. However there is now a very good road to Skopje via Grlica and Kačanik. I recommend this course. There are several small interesting villages *en route* and the scenery is splendid, especially through the Skopska Crna Gora along the Lepenac valley. On the way into Kačanik you find on your right a curiosity in the shape of what can only be described as Baroque Byzantine: probably an eighteenth-century church, it is done in the decorative manner of the Morava School.

CHAPTER 13

Skopje and district

Skopje — monasteries — Nerezi — Markov — Sv Matka — Sv Andrija — Sv Nikola — Kučevište — Sv Arhangel — Sv Nikita

At a quarter past five in the morning in late July 1963 a considerable part of **Skopje** collapsed on and about its inhabitants. About a thousand people were killed, three thousand injured and approximately a hundred thousand left homeless. As most of the station disintegrated one minute later the big clock stopped. When I last visited Skopje the hands were still at 5.16—a laconic footnote to a disaster which the Macedonians, more than most people, could ill afford. It has now been decided to leave the clock as a kind of temporal inscription and memorial.

There have been a good many minor earthquakes in the area over the centuries, but the biggest was as far back as A.D. 518, a catastrophe which destroyed the nearby town of Skupi. Fortunately I had visited Skopje twice some years before the 1963 earthquake and have clear recollections of what it was like.

There is no doubt that it is much changed, and will be even more so in the future. A big new town is spreading round it: originally as temporary quarters, but it is already obvious that it will become permanent. Indeed, many of the inhabitants are better off than they were before. The houses (the work of international co-operation and money) are well built, with modern facilities, gardens, well-lighted streets and nearby shops. When you go round the old town you can see how many of its people used to live—in wretched poverty.

In the centre of the city many buildings are so damaged that they will have to be demolished and there will be even more spaces available for rebuilding: operations which will probably take about ten years. Ironically, more damage was done to modern structures than to the old. Reconstruction has continued steadily, but there is still much to be done.

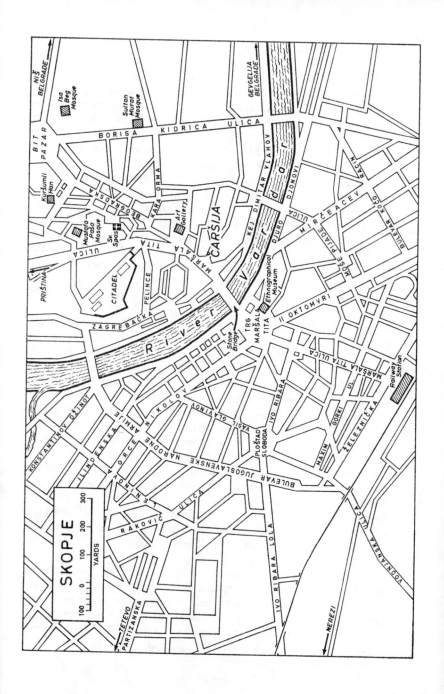

The town, capital of Macedonia and a university seat, crouches in a great valley more or less surrounded by mountains. It divides itself quite definitely into halves and the line between them, spanned by an ancient bridge, is the River Vardar. On one side stands the twentieth century and occidental civilisation; on the other the antique and the orient. Macedonians are proud of the former but, quite naturally, the traveller's main interest is the latter.

The station makes a convenient starting point to stake out the territory for you (directions for entering the city by car would be too complex to be useful) and when you come away from what was the main entrance, beside the exequial clock, the broad Maršala Tita Ulica stretches straight before you—down to the Trg Maršala Tita, the main square. The principal hotels and shops lie in this area. Indeed I don't think there are any hotels beyond the river, though there may be a squalid inn or two. I usually stay at the Turist or the Park. They are both inexpensive and the food is quite good.

During the evening *korso*, one of the most remarkable in the whole country, the populace spills into Tito's street and round Tito's *trg* and achieves the density of a cup-final crowd. On the far right corner of the *trg* is the Ethnographical Museum of Macedonia which was founded between the wars. Unfortunately many of its objects were destroyed during the last war, but what survives is a small and well-presented collection of costumes, pottery and furniture.[1] A temporary hotel has been erected on the far left of the square.

When you cross the narrow stone bridge over the Vardar, a bridge believed to have been originally built by Csar Dušan in 1348, the character of the city alters abruptly. Almost at once you enter a maze of cobbled streets and alleys which crook and wind up and down between ramshackle workshops and houses and ordinary shops pulsating with every kind of activity. This is the **Čaršija** or bazaar. It is like the one in Sarajevo, but is much bigger than that and comparable with what you will find in North Africa, in Istanbul and other parts of Turkey.

Nearly every street belongs to a guild of craftsmen. The mattress-makers and the carpet-makers and the quilt-makers squat on raised floors which are open to the street and closed at night with iron shutters. there are tailors, hat-makers and saddlers; tin-smiths, copper-smiths, jewellers and furriers. Outside the shoe-makers

---

[1]There is also an excellent display to illustrate the way of life of the upland shepherds in the Vlach country.

dangle clusters of *opanci*. Many of the tradesmen and craftsmen have shops that are no bigger than cupboards, mere wooden niches in which they crouch. Among the shops are wedged innumerable cafés and a superabundance of barber's shops. There is also a street of Advokats, but they are not lawyers; they are scribes, which is not surprising in a country where until quite recently more than half the people were illiterate.

It is almost impossible to give directions for finding your way round this area, nor, I think, would they have much point.[1] The Čaršija is a place of jostle, din, animation, banging, hammering, clanging, of inexhaustible interest, in which to stroll and discover things at leisure. At the end of a morning the main features are clear and you will probably be glad of a rest for in full summer the heat is severe. By noon the mountains are hazed and the sun throbs and glitters like a golden gong through a fine veil of dust.

Near the entrance to this quarter, on the right, you will see the solid form and rounded humps of the **Daut Paša Hammam,** the baths built in the fifteenth century by order of Daut Paša, the Grand Vizier. They are certainly the most important of the Balkan baths and are virtually intact. In them is the Umetnička Galerija (Art Gallery). Most of the objects are paintings and sculpture by contemporary artists, but, to be quite honest, they are not of much merit. There is also a collection of medieval icons. Occasionally they have a special exhibition. The trouble with so much twentieth-century Jugoslav art is quite simply that it is only very recently that the culture of the west has been accessible. This is especially true of southern Serbia and Macedonia.

Above the old Citadel (see p. 198) a large new art gallery has been built and is in the care of the enterprising Professor Petković. On my most recent visit (1972) there was a more or less permanent display of paintings and sculpture, for the most part by modern Jugoslav artists. There was little of great note but it is worth looking at.

Beyond the Čaršija, in a wide open space surrounded by the ruins of many buildings and some very precarious looking mosques whose minarets have lost (or are about to lose) their conical tops, is the main market with long lines of booths and stalls and vendors of every conceivable ware: pottery, filigree, melons, carpets, cheese, pictures, phonographs with curved horns like bizarre black lilies, bales of wool, baskets—plus the ubiquitous Birmingham trash.

[1]Even more difficult now because of reconstruction.

A colourful miscellany of gipsy women also trade here. Some of them squat day in, day out, under their gay umbrellas, selling combs, beads and pocket mirrors: the kind of thing Mungo Park and company used to take on their explorations for bartering. The question that always comes to one in a place like this is: How do they all make a living? The answer is, I fear, that they hardly do. In such a society a few dinars are a great deal of money.

The **costumes** here and throughout Macedonia are among the most interesting you will see anywhere. The women from the Black Mountain (Crna Gora) near the city—women with a great reputation for militant heroism over several centuries—wear a coarse stiff smock and a sleeveless tunic embroidered with black or dark blue geometrical patterns. White coifs cover their heads. Dresses are often embroidered in red. Muslim women wear white head-dresses and baggy trousers of calico. Often enough they look as if they have been made from curtain material and table cloths.

Macedonian costumes are a subject in themselves. They vary a lot from village to village, the commonest colours being white, black and red. The intricate designs of the embroidery (often geometrical) are reminiscent of Arabic and Moorish patterns and they contain ancient symbols which the women regard as secret. Some of the more obvious ones are the half moon which signifies fertility, the circle which represents the sun or life, and the small green circle which is against the evil eye. As a rule the women wear wide-sleeved blouses and long, full, white skirts over which hang embroidered aprons. Sometimes they have metal ornaments round their necks. The men are sometimes to be seen in white woollen trousers, as in the Kosovo-Metohija region, a short black jacket or *jelek*, purple or maroon cummerbunds and sheepskin hats. A few Muslims wear fezzes and the Albanians have the white skull-caps.

On the far side of the market place are the mosques of Isa Beg and Sultan Murad and the big clock tower (Sahat Kula). From any point in this vicinity, looking back across the Čaršija, you can see the big bluff on which stands the Citadel, or what is left of it. The first fortifications were erected in the sixth century and later Csar Dušan had his palace here. You can reach this directly from the old bridge by walking on up the Maršala Tita Ulica. Unhappily the earthquake accounted more or less completely for the fort and quite destroyed the archaeological museum, though they managed to salvage a part of the very valuable collection which one day will be displayed again. Nevertheless it is well worth climbing up here because you can obtain a splendid panoramic view of the whole city and the country outside. Far beyond the rambling suburbs the long columns of fastigiate poplar march into the plain.

An even better view is to be got from the *muezzin's* balcony on the minaret of the big **Mustafa Paša Džamija** (a *džamija* is a 'mosque') which is quite close the other side of the road. But you need to be reasonably fit and sure-footed to climb the narrow spiral staircase which will probably be thick with debris. I had a chat with the *imam* here one afternoon and he told me that you can't get *muezzins* these days and it is too much of a strain for the old men to clamber up and down the minarets

However, let us assume that you have climbed the spiral, stepped through the little doorway which traditionally faces towards Mecca, and that you are on the vertiginous platform of the *muezzin's* balcony: an incomparable point from which to proclaim that Allah is great and there is no god but Allah. On the long wooded hill to the north-east is a big Muslim cemetery and on top of the hill the *turbeh* ('tomb') of Gazibaba, a holy man believed to have died in battle in the sixteenth century. Farther north is the French military cemetery from the First World War. This exists because in September 1918 a brigade of French cavalry captured the city in a dashing attack and thus helped the defeat of a huge Bulgar-German army.

Farther north still, not visible, but no more than twenty minutes' walk from where you are, lies the **gipsy quarter.** This should certainly be visited. It is a kind of shanty town, like a small *favela* in the purlieus of Rio. The farrago of mud huts, shacks and hovels are painted blue and pink and daffodil yellow. The streets, swarming with children, are of mud and stone. It is a gay, animated place and the people support their poverty with an admirable fortitude.

There are quite a lot of gipsies in Serbia and Macedonia and they are a source of unease to the orderly minds of indoctrinated planners and bureaucrats in Belgrade. Verminous and dishonest, parasitical and undisciplined the gipsies may be, but any tribe that postpones a world of regimented yes-men should not be discouraged. Nevertheless, if you visit the *cigani* in Skopje you ought, as usual, to watch your pockets.

Bringing your eyes back from noon to six, as it were, you will soon pick out almost immediately below you the **Kuršumli Han.** This was one of the finest *hans* ever built and still shelters a rich archaeological collection.

The *hans* or *caravanserai* were a kind of hotel for merchants and are scattered all over the Balkans and across the Near and Middle East. In Istanbul alone there used to be well over a hundred of them and many have survived. Some of them were immense (the Kuršumli Han is fairly large) some quite small: strongly built, barrack-like buildings of stone consisting of two or three stories round a courtyard. The stabling for camels and horses was on the ground floor, plus rooms for doing business. On the upper floors galleried chambers accommodated merchants and their servants. They were strongpoints as well as hotels because, after all, these land-borne convoys often carried much wealth and were tempting prizes for brigands.

Some maintain that the Kuršumli was built by merchants from Dubrovnik in the Middle Ages; others that it was put up by the Turks. There is a third and unlikely theory that in origin it was Roman. There is certainly a link with Dubrovnik because Skopje was a centre for collecting goods from all over the East. It was thus part of a vast commercial network and in a way reflects the great antiquity of the town which was firstly the capital of the Illyrian province of Dardania and then a Roman city two centuries before Christ. Justinian was born here and it was an important city under the Byzantine régime. In 1189 it was seized by the Serbs and became the residence of Csar Dušan. After the battle of Kosovo it remained in Turkish hands until 1912.

There was a smaller *han* in the Čaršija called the Suli Han, no less handsome than the Kuršumli (which was wrecked in the 'quake but has now been completely rebuilt), and several badly damaged mosques which are now closed. There is only one church of interest and that is the tiny one of **Sveti Spas** (the Holy Saviour) just below the bluff of the Citadel but on the Čaršija side of Maršala Tita Ulica. Its foundations are well below ground level because of the Turkish decree that no Christian church might be higher than the roof-tops of their houses. It was built in 1689: cramped, irregular and dark, like so many Orthodox churches. The episcopal throne is a splendid object but the masterpiece here is the **iconostasis.** It was carved by three brothers, craftsmen from Galičnik, near the Albanian frontier, in the eighteenth century and it took them twelve years. That is not surprising when you examine the marvellous intricacy of the workmanship which shows a naïve and yet accomplished skill. It illustrates many Bible stories and often the figures and features are those of peasants of the time. Salome, for example, wears a Macedonian costume and the executioner is obviously an Albanian.

At the north-west corner of the open market area there is one of the few intact mosques. It is the most used mosque in central Skopje. About 11.45 a.m. any day the faithful begin to gather; a hundred-odd men, mostly elderly. Supple, with loping stride, slightly stooped, as if they had borne great loads on their backs in their time, these old warriors of Islam come. Dignified, grave, they salaam to each other, touching their foreheads and then their breasts with the right hand. They take off their shoes to wash their feet in the covered fountain. They converse and smoke. They wait. Near noon, an old *muezzin*, fobbed and chained and wearing a frock coat, a gold Mecca scarf wound round his fez, stands on a parapet and intones the midday call. It is a moving scene, and one which, in Europe, will be rare in the near future.

Skopje makes an excellent centre for excursions into the neighbouring hills in which is hidden a constellation of beautiful monasteries. You need at least four days to visit these. All are difficult to get at but the effort is amply rewarded. It is impossible to give detailed directions so you should first inform yourself at the Tourist office. Better still get hold of someone who knows the locality—by inquiry at one of the museums or at the University.

With one exception it is more or less essential to have one's own transport. The few taxi drivers are very reluctant to go out of the city and even if they can be persuaded they charge a lot. I begin with the exception—**Nerezi,** which lies about six kilometres, if you go across country, to the south-west. There is a good road if you have transport (and there is the occasional bus anyway) but the most interesting way to get there is to walk. At the station end of the Maršala Tita Ulica turn right and after a few hundred yards turn off to the left. Then you must start asking. If you are fit you will be able to walk there in about two hours. The climb is steep, along paths and rough tracks through vineyards, and it will probably be extremely hot.

Nerezi consists of a minute, rather derelict old Muslim village, inhabited by a few families, high on the mountainside. It has a mosque with a stumpy wooden minaret and a communal fountain. The women here are still veiled and keep their backs prudently towards any man. But this is not uncommon in the remote districts of Macedonia.

A little beyond the village is a paddock and orchard which contains the ancient **Monastery of Sv Panteleimon.** There is little left of the monastery but the tiny rustic church is complete. The new road has given greater accessibility and the increasing fame of the church means that coach parties are common. The authorities have built a pleasant restaurant on the edge of the paddock and an open-air café below it. In fact Nerezi is now a major tourist attraction, a development which will happen more often in similar isolated spots over the next few years.

The church exhibits most of the characteristics of the Macedonian and Kosmet Schools, a development of later Byzantine architecture. They tend to have a central square space on which a cupola is raised. Four vaulted arms form a cross, so that a cruciform structure rises above a square ground plan. Four supplementary cupolas rise at each corner. The churches usually have one or three apses and a narthex. Nerezi, a demurely small foundation of pink brick and plaster covered with curly tiles, has four pepper-pot cupolas and one central one. It is barely fifty feet from the entrance to the apse, and the naos at its widest is twelve yards.

It was built in 1164 by Macedonian masons at the command of the Byzantine prince Alexis Comnenos and is one of the best examples of medieval Macedonian art. The interior is covered with frescoes, most unaltered from the twelfth century though some were restored later. The most outstanding paintings are those of the *Deposition* and the *Virgin embracing her dead son*, a profoundly moving picture and one of the most famous frescoes in Jugoslavia. You should also note particularly the *Warrior Saints* and the *Entry into Jerusalem* on the north wall; on the south the *Resurrection of Lazarus*, the *Transfiguration* and the *Presentation of Jesus in the Temple*. The west wall bears the *Nativity of the Virgin*. On the right of the iconostasis there is a fine *portrait of Sveti Panteleimon*, the patron saint. You should also note, in a conch of the cupola tower on the north side, another splendid *portrait of the Virgin*. This is easily overlooked but in my opinion is one of the best of the many portraits of the Virgin in this part of the world.

The other side of the mountain, south-east of Skopje, is **Markov Monastery,** to which there is now a good road. From the end of Maršala Tita Ulica you take the road to Kisela Voda—a suburb to which anyone will direct you. You then follow a long steep hill to Sopište, and go on to Rakontinci and Dobri Dol, from which you climb steadily before going down once more on a long hair-pinned descent which eventually brings you to the Markova river. You bear right for the small village of Sužica. Not far on is the monastery.

The monastery site is spectacular. Above and beyond rise massive mountains and thick forests where there are a few scattered villages connected by mule and goat tracks. The monastery is surrounded by solid walls and entered by an iron-studded gate. A number of the conventual buildings survive: ramshackle, balconied edifices joined by wooden staircases. There are still one or two monks in residence. The outbuildings contain a venerable stone bread oven and, next so it, a cellarage, where they make brandy. Below that is a fine water mill of great antiquity.

The monastic church was started in 1345 by King Vukašin during the reign of Csar Dušan, and was finished by his son King Marko Kraljević. Over the west door there is an impressive figure of St Demetrius bearing the figure of a man reputed to have repaired the church during the Turkish occupation. The mounted figure is surrounded by angels and beneath the hooves of the white horse lie the remains of a Turkish soldier with broken sword and spear. The legend of St Demetrius always represents him as a great warrior saint of the same ilk as St George.

The frescoes inside the church are the work of two artists, or two groups of artists. One, the earlier it is thought, worked in the time of Vukašin; the other in the reign of Marko Kraljević. In the lower half the *procession of the angels* is particularly fine; in the upper zone the masterpieces are the cycle of *The Passion* and the *Lamentation of Rachel*. The latter is a most moving and intensely imagined work.

To reach **Matka Monastery** you follow the main road to Tetovo and about twelve kilometres out take an unsignposted road to the left. A little way up this on the right (invisible from the road) lies the monastery, which was built about the same time as Marko's. A walled paddock surrounds some rather ruined but beautiful conventual buildings. A few monks and some locals inhabit these. The church of Sv Bogorodica (the Virgin) is minute, dingy, smoke-blackened and mysterious. Unfortunately many of the frescoes (some of which have folklore motifs) have been severely damaged by the pious peasants who stick lighted candles to the walls below the figure of the saint whose aid they wish to invoke. Actually these paintings are not of great merit, they mostly date from towards the end of the fifteenth century.

From here you go on up the road along the side of the Treska valley with stands of poplar stretching away across it. High on the hill-sides are small Muslim villages with red-roofed houses, each settlement marked by the spike of one gleaming white minaret. These villages are only approachable by way of rough tracks.

A little farther on, the River Treska, which rises far to the south in the wild Stogovo Mountains, has been dammed at the entrance to a magnificent gorge three thousand feet deep. Here you forsake transport and follow the path which runs alongside the new lake. Soon you reach a small clearing where there is a rest house and café and another tiny church Sv Andrija: an elegant combination of an elongated trefoil on the inside and a free cross on the outside. It is triple-apsed and above the central area rises a cupola on pendentives. This church was erected by Andrea, second son of King Vukašin, in 1389 (the year of the Battle of Kosovo) and is named after its patron saint. This is all that remains of the monastery.

The interior is frescoed in three horizontal zones outstanding for their stylistic and artistic merits and also because, in their arrangement, the painters have departed from the normal Byzantine iconographical programme. For instance, the scenes from the life of the Virgin, the miracles of Jesus and the Communion of Apostles, usually to be found in the main apse, are not there. The artists have also made singularly successful attempts at realism (noticeable in the features of the *Warrior Saints*) and at perspective (notable in the scenes depicting *The Passion*). The best paintings are, I think, *The Last Supper*, the *Washing of the Feet*, the *Agony in the Garden* and the *Deposition*.

High above the other side of the lake, on a small plateau, you can just see the walls of **Sv Nikola.** An old *Šiptar* is (or was) the caretaker and if he happens to be about he will take you across in his boat. If he isn't, walk back down to the dam, cross below it and then take the forest path up. This will take about three-quarters of an hour and is a steepish climb.

At the top is a little church in a semi-fortified compound. This was part of the Ševevski monastery and consists of two buildings: the eastern a single-aisled church with apse; the western a narrow cross with a cupola. In the dingy interior you find three layers of frescoes. The oldest are on the north and south walls of the sanctuary. In the eastern part they are fourteenth century. Those on the west wall and the cupola belong to about 1630.

From up here you get an eagle's eye view down into the gorge to Sv Andrija and up the gorge where, across the precipitous cliffs gashed and holed with caves, real eagles float and spiral like fragments of burnt paper. One afternoon I counted ten of them.

There remain some monasteries and churches to the north-west of Skopje. These are harder to find. Take the main road from the new bridge over the Vardar and go up Ulica Boris Kidrić. About seven kilometres out of the city is a sign on your right to Doli ('lower') **Sv Ilijah.** A hundred yards up a lane stands a peaked gate into a paddock. The small, stone cruciform church is modern and of little interest. The former buildings of the monastery are now a farm. The main building,which has a magnificent balcony, is now a restaurant which specializes in Macedonian food. At the back of the farm, in what looks like a small outhouse, you discover a whitewashed church, a little bigger than the average bathroom. A few ugly modern icons adorn it. This primitive and rustic temple is probably one of the oldest churches in the region.

From here you follow the pavé road towards Kučevište, and after about three kilometres reach the village. As you arrive, just by the bridge, there is a turn up to Sv Arhangel. About three kilometres up the valley (the road is good), as the green, rugged hills begin to swell across the sky, you at last reach the white-washed walls of the **Monastery of Sv Arhangel**, sited above a burbling stream. It is more like a fortified farm than a monastery and makes one of the most idyllic rural scenes imaginable. The spring water here is much prized by the locals who come miles to drink it.

There are only one or two monks here, plus three sisters or 'nuns': a Bosnian, a Serb and a Montenegrin—all remarkable women. They organise a large farm, grow most things they need and run a water mill which produces electricity and grinds the corn and maize of the nearby villagers.

Here, as in many parts of Serbia and Macedonia, the domestic pigs have been crossed (usually by accident) with wild boar. The hirsute, brindled pigs (some are so hairy that they possess thick matted fleeces) are the cross breeds. Often the wild boar drink with the domestic swine at the stream. In winter stock has to be looked after carefully because the wolves become bold, though there is always danger from both wolves and bears.

As in most Serbian and Macedonian monasteries you will probably be offered some hospitality, as you *always* will when asked into a private house. In the latter case you may not leave any money, but in monasteries I usually contrive to leave something for the church. The 'nuns' at Sv Arhangel make a delicious, dark, purplish wine. In other places it may be Turkish coffee or *rakija* or *šlivovica*. But the traditional and commonest form of hospitality is *slatko*—a dish of jam or preserves accompanied by a glass of water and a spoon. You take a spoonful of *slatko* and then a sip of water.

In the farmyard of the monastery stands a tiny church (it has some features of the Morava School) which was built, very probably, near the end of the fourteenth century. The frescoes date from about 1700 and are of small importance. The colours are pale, though the drawing is emphatic. Two of the best compositions are Christ appearing to St Thomas and the man being cured of the dropsy.

From here one must return to Kučeviste, a primitive and attractive village where the way of life has not changed much in several hundred years. At this point you are on the perimeter of a big range of hills and mountains, the Skopska Crna Gora, about sixty miles long by thirty broad. There are few roads across them, and few villages in them. The densely forested valleys are the habitat of wolves, bear, lynx and wild boar. If you choose to ride or walk through this country you need a guide, and, possibly, a gun.

In the middle of Kučeviste, near the main threshing floor, is the remarkable **Church of Sv Spas,** dedicated to the Blessed Virgin (Sv Bogorodica). This odd amalgam of structures lies in a walled compound and you will probably have to cast about for the key.

You enter a long, low-roofed narthex supported by wooden pillars and then go down into another narthex, also mainly of wood. The original church, comprising a cross inscribed in a rectangular space with a high cupola on four columns, was built in the 1340's. There is a variety of frescoes dating from the 1340's to the seventeenth century. The most notable ones depict the *Washing of the Disciples' Feet*, the *Lamentation* and the *Virgin and Christ*. Most of the frescoes have been badly damaged. At the end of the inner narthex there is an amusing nineteenth-century portrait of Csar Dušan which represents him as a perky, moustached Turkish magnifico. Above the narthex rises a little chapel dedicated to St Nicholas, also of the fourteenth century, where there are more frescoes from several periods. Those illustrating the *Life of St George* and the *Last Judgment* are the best.

The village of Kučeviste has many handsome Turkish houses and walled gardens. If you happen to be in this area on June 26th you will coincide with a *sabor* (an 'assembly' or 'gathering') when the peasantry meet for feasting, dancing and jollifications.

Seven kilometres east of Kučeviste, via the village of Ljubanci, you turn up a steep road to the **Monastery of Sv Nikola**. The site is beautiful. There are some rough conventual buildings, a bell tower and a tiny church, about thirty feet by twelve. There is nothing of merit inside it but this minute spiritual outpost is worth visiting for the tranquillity alone.

From this point it is best to return to Kučevište, pass through it and rejoin the main road. About a kilometre down it (on the way back to Skopje) there is a signposted turn on the right to Čučer and Sv Nikita. Čučer is a delightful little village of white-washed walls and curly tobacco-coloured roofs, and half an hour's walk up a steep hill beyond it (the road is quite good) lies the **Monastery of Sv Nikita;** another miniature church in a walled paddock.

This church was founded by King Milutin at the beginning of the fourteenth century (*c.* 1307-8) on the site of an earlier foundation and was decorated by the artists responsible for Sv Kliment in Ohrid and Staro Nagoričino near Kumanovo. They were Mihajlo and Eutihije (or Michael and Eutychios), both believed to be Greek rather than Slav Macedonians—I make the distinction because Macedonia was under considerable Greek influence for a long time—who probably did a lot of work farther south in Constantinople and may have helped to paint the Protaton on Mt Athos and the Church of St Demetrius in Salonika. They were active round the turn of the thirteenth century when it became more customary to sign work. You can see the signatures of Mihajlo and Eutihije at Sv Nikita (on the shield of the warrior saints on the south wall).

It is an odd fact that most medieval art, like much medieval literature, was anonymous. The so-called Renaissance brought a change of view and more and more people signed their work. Few of the great monasteries and cathedrals of medieval Europe can be ascribed to an individual. They were the result of corporate effort. To this day many monks are buried in nameless graves. The more materialistic a society the more its members wish to be remembered.

The best paintings on the dingy walls of Sv Nikita are the *Marriage Feast at Cana, Christ Expelling the Money-lenders*, the *Washing of the Feet* and the *Last Supper*: all on the south wall. The *Dormition of the Virgin* is also fine, as is the cycle Christ's miracles.

From here one must return to Čučer and the main road (incidentally, there is a pleasant modern restaurant quite near Čučer.)

CHAPTER 14

Western Macedonia

The Vlach—Tetovo—Gostivar—Galičnik—Sv Jovan Bigorski—Lazaro-polje—Debar — Struga — Trebenište — Ohrid — excursions — Sv Naum—Kolos—Resen—Lake Prespa—Bitola—Prilep—Marko Kraljević—Monastery of Sv Arhangel—Kruševo—The Bogomils

'What a year has not given you,' says a Macedonian proverb, 'a day will bring you.'

The Jugoslav people possess a great hoard of proverbs, maxims and fables which every child is brought up to know. They are constantly used to comment on or illustrate a situation. This is also true of Greek and other peoples but the tradition is almost defunct in England. Though we have hundreds of proverbs you seldom hear young people (or anyone) use them nowadays. Fables are even rarer. When used they are nearly always importations.

After you have been in Macedonia for a few days you begin to see the sense of the proverb above. It smacks of the earth, and grievous hardship. It also embodies a statement about patience and will-power before which the panoply of empires, the rigmaroles of cunctatory law and the boot of armies are insubstantial.

'What a year has not given you . . . ' It suggests a kind of passive and feminine optimism and Jugoslavs say that if one had to plump for the main influence in this part of the world, then it is to the women you would probably look first for it is they who have cherished the tradition of freedom of faith and worship with the utmost tenacity and privacy: at their hearths, in their small lonely villages, in their secret, hidden churches.

Nowadays when we speak of Macedonia we tend to mean Jugo-slav Macedonia but it is really a territory which, after much exploitation and squabbling by interested foreign powers, is now spread over Jugoslavia, Albania, Greece, and Bulgaria. Bounded on the west by the Šar mountains and on the east by the Rhodope mountains it extends well down into Greece as far as Salonika. Over all these parts Macedonian is spoken (a language a good deal different from Serbian) but there are large numbers of Albanians, Greeks, Turks, Jews and Gipsies in the Jugoslav part and therefore large numbers of people who speak Albanian, Greek, etc. The presence of Turks is explained by the fact that Macedonia was the only Slav land where Turkish peasants came as settlers. They were given small holdings of twenty or thirty acres, but a lot of the land was held by absentee landlords and managed by tax farmers. These tenancies were called *čiftliks* (or *čitluks*); Christian *rayah* worked on them but were so exploited that many Macedonians emigrated or worked abroad for long periods.

Most of the Illyrians and Celts were absorbed during the Slav migrations or fled to the mountain retreats. Some descendants who were not absorbed became the inhabitants of Albania. Others, who were Romanised but who never adopted the Slavonic language and traditions, were the Vlachs (the name probably comes from the word Wallachia) whose descendants still live as nomadic herdsmen in the Macedonian mountains and in Rumania where many of them went. They take their flocks to the high pastures in summer and bring them down in winter. The Macedonians call them *Vlasi* and they have their own language, Vlaški (sometimes known as Armanesti). There is a fascinating legend that they are descended from the Vth Legion and as a result of this they are also known as *Cincarski* (pronounced sinsarski). The main concentration of *Vlasi* is round Bitola (farther south), Kruševo and Nižopolje, but some are to be found as far north as Istria, and it is very likely that there are others in the wild mountains of northern Greece. The Greek word for Vlach is *vlahos*, a term of abuse popular among bus-drivers whose vehicles collide on narrow roads. *Vlahos* means 'a man who has never seen the sea'.

'I think it is in Macedon where Alexander is born: I tell you, Captain, if you look in the maps of the 'Orld, I warrant you sall find in the comparisons between Macedon and Monmouth, that the situations, look you, is both alike. There is a river in Macedon, and there is also moreover a river at Monmouth . . . ' Sitting over a book or a map in a library or in one's own home Macedonia and its history does seem remote, vaguely linked with resonant names like Philip and Alexander and about as misty as Fluellen's surmises. But when you actually find yourself looking at a Vlach shepherd, in his brown homespun cloak, walking along with a crooked pastoral staff at the heels of two hundred head of baaaing, tinkling sheep in the austere, spacious uplands of interior Macedonia, two millennia seem momentary.

Tetovo is a benign and soothing spot that spreads out into the plain and stacks itself up against the lowest slopes of the Šar Planina. It has a pleasant new hotel (the Nova Makedonija) in the main street and in winter becomes base camp for a number of popular ski-ing slopes in the locality which are well-supplied with cable cars and chalets. A lot of Jugoslavs come here but few foreigners as yet. (See map on p. 191.)

The centre of the town has been gutted and flattened to make way for some unusually ugly and pretentious buildings, but I have no doubt that they are more comfortable and better-equipped than their predecessors. Many Macedonian and Serbian towns now have these concrete centres which are quite out of sympathy and harmony with their surroundings and at the same time aggressively demon-strate the Jugoslav desire and intention to catch up with the west European drive towards a more or less soul-less and functional geometry produced by third-rate creative minds. Its most bigoted enthusiast can hardly claim that it is more than the beginning of a contemporary idiom. Some otherwise short-sighted French travellers have wittily called it the Uniprix style. Occasionally, but only occasionally, it has come off; but not in Tetovo.

What you find round and beyond all this is a quaint and lovely town whose broad streets twist between ample *konaks* and green luxuriant gardens irrigated by numerous streams. Everywhere the textures and colours detain the eye: the choppy ripple of russet tiles, the rough flakiness of outer walls topped by peaked roofs and set with grilled apertures and studded doors, rutted streets duned with ochreous dust, the scraped pinks and jean blue of house walls and shutters ... Tetovo (like Prilep and Štip and several other towns in Macedonia) is a tobacco town and in late summer when the crop is picked the women crouch in rows on the verandahs and in the wide-eaved shadows as they grade and string the leaves on wires. Some-times the whole family gets down to it. As each wire is completed it is strung in a wooden frame. Some of these frames are quite small, tent-shaped or like hinged clothes' horses; some are enormous squares and rectangles (twenty by thirty feet). In August and September the whole town is decorated with garlands of tobacco festooned at the edges of streets, on frames leaning against walls and strung in row upon row along the sides of houses like the shirred silk curtains of Venetian palaces. The latest picking is a crisp, succulent green, the oldest a wrinkled and fragrant looking Corona colour. In between there is an infinitely subtle range: green Chartreuse, quince yellow, a sere umber and the rusted gold of maturity.

As you will already have noticed in places like Peć and Prizren, the people are poor. Most children, many women and some men go barefoot. Their clothes though clean, are patched, frayed, often ragged, but life in Macedonia is more primitive than in any other part of Jugoslavia. For instance, a pregnant woman will often work in the fields up to the last minute. When her baby is born thus another woman wraps it up, brings it home and washes it. The mother follows later. The baby's placenta is the object of several curious practices. For example, some women bury it, others dry it and keep it swathed in a garment as a good luck charm.

Sooner or later in your wanderings round Tetovo you will come across what is called the **'Coloured Mosque'** which lies just the other side of an old bridge over the River Tetovska on the road to Gostivar. By the bridge there is a Turkish *hammam* which, like so many neglected monuments in Europe, has been turned into an unofficial public lavatory.

The 'Coloured Mosque' or Šarena Džamija is a lovely and unusual building with a tiled roof, no cupola and a portico painted with clusters of flowers. The outer walls are 'panelled' and covered with painted lozenges and stars. Inside there are painted arabesques, views of Istanbul, fountains, gardens and groves: a frivolous and almost boudoirish prettiness, very rare in mosques where most decoration is severely geometrical and abstract.

There is also a small museum in Tetovo (in the Haki Paša Konak) and another in the most interesting group of buildings of all—the **Tekija** or Whirling Dervish Monastery on the south-west perimeter near the funicular station and beyond a spacious and neglected Muslim cemetery.

All the Tekija buildings, which are scattered in an orchard, are more or less intact. The lay-out is rather like a *zadruga*, with sleeping, eating and recreational quarters, store rooms, stables and so forth. The Dervishes were not celibate monks and their harem was conveniently near the *selamlik* or male apartments. The more interesting structures are the ornate pavilion round a fountain in the gardens, and what they called the 'common room': in Western monastic terms, a calefactory. This is now a war museum.

Part of the male apartments have been devoted to an ethnographical and costume museum. The 'whirling' house contains a few Roman remains and some rather sinister manacles and irons.[1]

There used to be Dervishes at Priština, Prizren, Bitola, Skopje, Peć and all the large Muslim towns, but as far as I know the Tetovo Tekija is the only complete one that survives in Jugoslavia; and I believe Dervishes are extinct now anyway.

The fact they existed at all is a little odd because the Prophet forbade monks. But as early as A.D. 657 (only twenty-five years after his death) a sect was founded which rapidly increased and at one time there were about a hundred and fifty different sects. Each rallied round a central idea and had its own ritual. Usually the members carried 'rosaries' bearing thirty-three, sixty-six or ninety-nine beads, the last bead being much larger than the others. Allah had ninety-nine beautiful names.

Basically there were two kinds of Dervish: the Howling and the Whirling. Very often their rituals overlapped but the Howlers howled, wailed, moaned and ululated and the Whirlers concentrated on the dance. Their costumes varied but they usually wore the costume of the district (at any rate in Jugoslavia) plus a high fez of soft white felt with a dent in it. Some sects wore long white robes.

A typical ceremonial began by the Dervishes squatting on their heels in a circle in the whirling house, their leader either in the centre or at one side. They began to chant and sway and bend. Intermingled with the chant came groaning noises. These limbering-up operations, no doubt designed to induce the kind of controlled hysteria desired, were followed by a whirling, circular dance accompanied by drums, cymbals and tambourines. Faster and faster they went in giddying revolutions, and as they revolved they formed a wheel within a wheel, until finally they passed into a kind of trance. At the climax some sects were in the habit of stabbing themselves in their cheeks, necks and sides with daggers. This, apparently, did little damage. Very probably their quasi-ecstatic condition made them immune. After the 'orgasm' there might be a gradual unwinding and slowing down or an abrupt withdrawal.

It seems the Dervishes never agreed about the exact meaning of the ritual. The Prophet was supposed to have leapt up and gyrated many times when in a state of intense excitement and fervour and it may be that the Dervishes imitated him. Whatever the reason the dance has always been an essential part of religious and cosmological belief and ceremony and it is very likely that the Dervishes' circular

[1] A pleasant modern restaurant has been built in the grounds.

motions represented the traditional emblem of perfection and also the concordant stellar spheres.

The peasants in the villages round Tetovo believe that the tomb of the Dervish who founded the Tekija and who died in 1785 is that of the prophet Elijah and early in the morning of his feast day (August 2nd) numbers of them come to the monastery to light candles at the tomb, put offerings on it and spend the day in holiday in the grounds, feasting and dancing the *kolo*. This is rather a good example of the elision of beliefs and the compression of time. The true peasants have little conception of time or distance, which accounts for their inability to give accurate directions and their comparative immunity to the discomforts of delay . . . *Ima vremena*. And don't miss the tomb of 'Elijah'. It has some delightful decorative scenery behind it.

From Tetovo you journey up the Vardar valley until you reach Gostivar, a Turkish town with a clock tower and one particularly elegant mosque. Market day is traditionally Tuesday and well worth seeing. Away to the west, above the magnificent forests of chestnut, soar the barbaric splendours of the Albanian mountains; bluish-grey streaked with pink, like veined marble.

Not far on you come to **Mavrovo** and one of the more outstanding instances of recent Macedonian progress: big, artificial lakes, Mavroska Jezera, part of a hydro-electric scheme which it is hoped will bring thousands of people from a condition of extreme poverty to subsistence level.

If you have time you should make a diversion up a steep, twisting mountain road to the remote village of **Galičnik** (with a small hotel) which is the market centre of an important agricultural area. You will see some costumes here and, possibly, variations of the old long white homespun coat with, over it, a brown woollen jacket and a red cummerbund or sash. The trousers are rather like those worn in Peć, Prizren and areas round Skopje. Sometimes reddish-brown or black caps are worn (like the men's in Hercegovina) with black tassels. The women's clothes vary a lot. The long chemise frock is a basic and this is often heavily embroidered in red and magenta designs. Over this they wear a *jelek* which may be magenta or purple and embroidered in red and gold and decorated with silver buttons. On top of this some women still wear a long white coat, the *klasenik*, also embroidered in red, gold and black. Fringed belts of a dark red or magenta and aprons of the same colours (sometimes double aprons) more or less complete the outfit. Some women also wind round their middles broad silk scarves with fringes which are worn like aprons. You might think that in a country where the summer temperatures are usually well over 85°F and often nearer a 100°F this would be sufficient, but they also adorn themselves with wide metal belts fastened with big buckles and a variety of coin jewellery. On their heads they wear scarves, sometimes double scarves. Despite this heavy and elaborate regalia they walk easily and gracefully.

Galičnik is even better known for its marriage customs. In times past the men travelled far and even emigrated to make more money to send home. The women had to do all the work in their absence. However, the tradition grew that once a year, in July, all the men returned from wherever they happened to be. On St Peter's Day, July 12th and the days immediately after it, all the marriages were celebrated, so there was a multiple wedding feast. The ceremonies are not so elaborate as they used to be but they are still interesting.

On St Peter's eve there is a torch-lit procession of brides to three fountains where water is drawn for a lustral purification ceremony. Elaborate clothing rituals are then accompanied by song and music. The wedding ceremony itself is quite complex and has one very curious feature: brides, bridegrooms and guests knock each other's heads together. The first marriage night consists of a complicated hide-and-seek game and the newly-weds do not sleep together. On the second day there is a great feast accompanied by dancing and singing. The bride, at first reluctant to take part, eventually sings a rather beautiful song which begins:

> Sokol me leta visoko . . .
> (*The eagle flies high up with me,*
> *Holds me fast in his lap!*
> *Wide and high as sorrow reaches,*
> *The sorrow of love . . .*)

On the second night husband and wife sleep together and consummate the marriage, but before they do so there is a little ceremony involving two apples which have been placed in the bride's wedding chest. They take an apple each, halve them, exchange one half and eat the other. The apple is a pledge or symbol in a large number of love rituals and there is a taboo that apples must not be eaten before St Peter's eve.

From Galičnik you have to return to the main road and about twenty-five kilometres farther down you find a sign on your left for the monastery of **Sv Jovan Bigorski**. I recommend a diversion here. The road winds steeply through exotic scenery until you are confronted by stone walls and a big wooden gate. For a moment, as at some other monasteries, you might imagine that you have arrived at a Tibetan retreat. Beyond the gate, a yard, the church, and the lofty conventual quarters (reminiscent of Bačkovo and Rila in Bulgaria) once inhabited by more than two hundred monks. Now there is one *čuvar*.

According to well-established tradition the monastery was founded by Stefan Nemanja in 1200. If it was so nothing has survived. The present buildings, including the church, are eighteenth- and nineteenth-century. The object of the pilgrimage lies within the church—the **iconostasis**: a masterpiece of the same tradition and style as that in Sv Spas, Skopje, and very probably by the same artists. It is about ten feet high and divided into seven panels separated by pillars. Each panel represents traditional biblical scenes and the pillars swarm upwards with a profuse existence of their own: animals, birds and human figures. The panel on the extreme left shows the artists at work—as at Sv Spas. The panels are surmounted by icons and predatory eagles and above these is a luxuriantly elaborate foliage of acanthus leaves mixed with two rows of icons depicting church feasts and the apostles. The eye continues to ascend this wooden wall thronged with jostling life— to the akroterion, the icons of St John and the Virgin guarded by voracious dragons. It is a rich and bizarre microcosm of amazing complexity; almost as if Breughel and Dostoievsky, combined in one being, had amalgamated their visions and taken up knife and chisel.

The Galičnik region has a long-established reputation for its master wood-carvers who were continually commissioned all over the Balkan peninsula. They worked (and still work) in hard woods, usually walnut, and applied their skill to many different objects besides iconostases: pulpits, for instance, ceilings in houses, window frames and furniture. A good many buildings in Prizren, Tetovo, Ohrid and elsewhere have been enhanced by them.

Some kilometres south of Sv Jovan (you can also approach it from the main road nearer Debar) is quite a famous co-operative farm called **Lazaropolje** which is well worth visiting. You can be shown over it but it is advisable to prepare the ground for this with the tourist authorities in Skopje.

A story which verges on legend explains Lazaropolje's existence. Three hundred years ago there was a village the other side of the hill which was one day raided by the Turks. The inhabitants took refuge in a tunnel in the hill-side. In the stampede one girl was left behind, an idiot. When the Turks entered the village she laughed at them and said that all the villagers had escaped into the tunnel. So the Turks found the tunnel and lit fires in the entrance. All the villagers bar one were asphyxiated and the survivor only got away by forcing his way down the tunnel which became the bed of a stream. When he emerged the other side he founded a new village and married a girl from Galičnik. The man's name was Lazar.

The next place of any note is **Debar,** a beautiful Albanian town tiered up the hillside and dominated by two mountain peaks: Velivar and Krčin, both a little over seven thousand feet. There used to be a Roman town here called Deborus and it was Byzantine until late in the thirteenth century when King Milutin took it. For centuries its craftsmen were famous, especially its goldsmiths and silversmiths. Now it seems a sad and subdued spot. Many of the houses are ruined and the bright minarets belong to neglected mosques. However, on a Saturday you will see an interesting market and costumes and, with luck, some of the traditional head-dresses of the women: white veils adorned with crimson circles in which are worked purple crosses. Ten kilometres away is a small spa called Debarska Banja whose waters have remarkable curative powers for rheumatism.

Should you be in the Debar area (or in the neighbouring village of Rajčica) on May 6th you will be able to witness the kind of *sabor* they have at Kučevište and Banjani. Many of the women don their best costumes for this event.

From Debar to Struga is one of the most exciting drives through some of the most prodigal scenery in Europe. You ride along the valley of the River Crni Drim (the Black Devil), a turbulent fisherman's stream whose energy and zest are certainly diabolic but whose colours are of a seraphic jasper and turquoise. The road is good but there is no point in hurrying.

At last the valley broadens and you bump into **Struga,** a place which two much debased words fit well: it is pretty and charming. There are many Muslims here and every Saturday there is a gathering for the weekly market which should not be missed. One market is in the centre of the town for produce of all kinds; the other in the northern purlieus for livestock.

Oddly enough for the kind of provincial town it is it possesses a very good natural history museum in which the local fauna are particularly well represented. It is the creation of a Russian refugee who personally collected and mounted everything in it. If you have had any doubts about the existence of bears and wolves in Jugo-slavia you will see some goodlooking specimens here, together with heron, pelican, scorpions, snakes and so forth. There are plenty of brown bears round **Lake Ohrid** and sometimes they come down into the vineyards to gorge on the grapes.

The devilish river slips unobtrusively and placidly out of the lake at Struga by a sandy beach, and round this part a lot of eels are caught—a delicacy much prized by Balkan gourmets. The presence of eels here has a really extraordinary explanation, so extraordinary that it might be culled from one of the more bizarre anecdotes of Herodotus or Polo or even Sir John Mandeville. Every year the eels travel to the Sargasso Sea to spawn. From here the elvers make the return trip of getting on for seven thousand miles as the crow flies, so to speak. As the eel swims it must be a good deal more. This in itself is scarcely credible but it has also to be remembered that Lake Ohrid is more than sixty miles from the nearest sea by the most direct route imaginable. How does the eel do it? The answer is that it travels the length of Albania by river through the mountains before it finally wriggles into the pellucid waters of Ohrid. So, having swum the breadth of the Atlantic and a considerable part of the Mediterranean it then has to 'climb' two thousand feet, for that is the height of the lake above sea level. I don't think I could ever eat an Ohrid eel.

The town of Ohrid lies along the margin of the lake and on the way there you find a turning to **Trebenište,** a quaint and friendly village not far from the narrow gauge railway that goes all the way from Ohrid to Skopje. Connoisseurs of train travel will enjoy this trip through the wilds of western Macedonia. You average ten miles an hour for 120 miles.[1]

On the nearby hills east of Trebenište (about an hour's hard walk) is a very ancient pre-classical site which, curiously enough, was first excavated by Bulgarian troops in 1918. The excavations were continued in the early thirties when the archaeologists found an Illyrian necropolis and a priceless collection of gold masks, jewellery, vases, ear-rings, agraffes and so forth—all of which can be seen in the Belgrade museum. The big find was a sixth-century vase which not only tallies exactly with a vase described in detail by Herodotus but is also a smaller version of one found as far away as Vix on the Côte d'Or.

Like Rab and Dubrovnik Ohrid survives effortlessly all the encomiums lavished upon her. Here, more than in most places, one

[1] I am reliably informed that this railway has been closed.

is aware of a great antiquity. It is so old, so mellow, that its essences must be imbibed very gently. Indeed, there is no incentive to haste. The great bowl of blue water encircled by mountains, the profuse vegetation, the beneficent sun, the buxom air—everything conspires to induce ambling leisure. According to local legend the lake was caused by absent-mindedness. At one time there was only a tapped spring from which a young bride was in the habit of drawing water every evening. One evening she forgot to turn off the tap—and the next day there was a lake.

Its beauty is celebrated in a famous folk song: *Biljana platno beleše, na ohridskite izvori* (Biljana was bleaching her linen by the springs of Ohrid)—a theme which was appropriated by the composer Hristić for his ballet *The Legend of Ohrid*.

Ohrid is the main tourist resort of Macedonia and one of the principal resorts in Jugoslavia. Quite a lot of people spend their whole holiday here and the summer long there are large numbers of Jugoslavs. It is certainly worth spending two or three days, or even a week—using it as a base for easy day-excursions. There are several hotels a few yards from the lake (which is quite suitable for swimming) plus pensions and annexes. I can recommend The Palace which, though grand, is comfortable, well-organised and has a good restaurant.[1]

Two centuries before Christ Ohrid was an important town on the Roman road, the Via Egnatia. It was a bishopric as early as A.D. 300 and many of its buildings, like those in the neighbourhood, are at least a thousand years old. It has been described as the cradle of Slav Christianity and there are still about forty churches in various stages of decay and repair scattered round it. In the days of Csar Dušan there were reported to be more than a hundred. The total number in the early Middle Ages has been put at well over three hundred. It was obviously a spiritual power-house on the same scale as Athos, to which there has been no counterpart in western monasticism.

Even the lake trout have been famous for centuries and, according to ichthyologists, belong to a singular group also found in Lake Prespa and Lake Baikal. The Sultans themselves had special courier services to take them fresh to Istanbul, over five hundred miles by road. To this day they make excellent eating, cooked and stuffed by traditional recipes. It is a dish you can get in most

[1]There is also the less expensive and pleasant Riviera, and any amount of private accommodation.

restaurants. *Pastrmka à la Ohrid*. With it try some of the local white wine. Macedonian wines are not outstanding but some of the white ones are quite good and I personally like the Ohrid *vins ordinaires*. Good red wines are rare, but the *rosés* are drinkable.

There is a new and an old town in Ohrid and the latter lies congested along the foot of a high hill topped by the ruins of an enormous castle. Everything here seems immutable: like the ungainly high fishermen's boats which looked just the same, if the evidence of the Belgrade Museum is to be believed, a millennium ago; the huge plane tree in the central square round which a *kafana* is built; the cavernous medieval bakeries that open on to the street; the very manners of the people. If you can manage to be in Ohrid on a Monday, the market is worth seeing. An interesting variety of people come in from the neighbouring hills and some of their costumes are exotic; especially the women's. The women from the nearby village of Peštani are striking. The older ones wear a white head-dress, a long white linen robe and blue and white striped aprons. The men are tending to shed their traditional garb, but there is a good variety of hats: black fezzes, *šubare*, and high white wool hats (reminiscent of old-fashioned night caps and the Dervish head-gear).

In the centre of the old town there are several small churches. It is worth looking at Sv Bogorodica Bolnička (with a rich iconostasis and frescoes) and Sv Nikola Bolnički (also with some good frescoes). They are both fourteenth-century foundations. Near them, in a handsome, balconied nineteenth-century house, you will find a small museum which gives you some idea of the prehistoric and Graeco-Roman period and also possesses an ethnographical section.

The three most important monuments are the church of Sv Kliment, the church of Constantine and Helena and the cathedral of Sv Sofije. **Sv Kliment** sits on a small plateau well above the town *en route* to the castle. It is a highly ornamented brick church built in 1295 which contains a large number of frescoes by Mihajlo and Eutihije. They are believed to be their earliest known work. In my own view they are not as good as those at Staro Nagoričino (near Kumanovo; see p. 244) but some of the paintings of the saints are very fine and so is the pietà. There are also several icons in this church: the *Virgin and Child* is one of the best.

St Clement, whose fierce and theopneustic features are vividly portrayed, was a man of courage, learning and tenacity. He became the first bishop of the area. Theophilactus. his biographer, remarked on his energy. He was never idle, he wrote, 'He either taught children, and that in various ways—showing one the shape of a letter, explaining the meaning of what was written to a second, and guiding the hand of a third as he wrote, and not only by day but by night as well, or he conducted prayers or was absorbed in reading or even writing a book.' In his thirty years of pastoral work he is believed to have taught 3,000 pupils—a plausible figure, even in terms of the modern teacher's curriculum. We can only guess at the obstacles the saint had to surmount.

Not only human beings responded to his fervour. Legend has it that his sanctity was so potent that the very birds and beasts were inspired by him with a kind of divine talent for site-spotting and were in the habit of showing him the best places to raise altars, churches and monasteries.

Behind Sv Kliment, near the school building, you find the minute church of Constantine and Helena, founded in the fourteenth century by a monk called Partenije. There is a portrait of him on the south wall holding a model of the church. Near him are his mother and son.

The **Cathedral of Sv Sofije** lies in the centre of the old town; a lovely and venerable building comparable with the finest of the Greek Orthodox churches and one of the most important ecclesiastical buildings in Jugoslavia. The original foundation was a fifth-century basilica, fragments of which were incorporated in what we see today: a structure that dates from the eleventh to the fourteenth centuries. It is a triple-apsed church of three naves, separated by arcades and columns, and a spacious narthex. When the Turks took Ohrid they turned it into a mosque and it remained as that for five hundred years. A minaret was added, the frescoes were painted over, and the pulpit was converted into a *mimbar*. The *mimbar* remains but the minaret has gone.

The whole church might have gone after the war because, for a time, there was a lunatic and fanatical iconoclastic movement which desired to destroy as much evidence of a Christian past as possible. This was typical of the South Slavs who never do things by halves. A fierce crusading zeal surges through them, quite possesses them, and usually only immolation and a holocaust will sublimate it. Luckily, on this occasion, reason prevailed and the frescoes have been gradually exposed. Many of them date from the eleventh century.

All the paintings that survive here are intensely imagined and exciting and are a natural transition to the early Italian masters.

They are grandly vigorous and bold and yet there is also much delicacy and grace in them. In the narthex there is a splendid *Last Judgment* and on the west wall of the naos a vast *Dormition of the Virgin*, one of the great works of Serbian art. On the southern wall in front of the apse the most outstanding fresco is the *Sacrifice of Abraham*; opposite, on the north wall, a scene depicting the story of *Jacob's Ladder*. The entranced figure of Jacob and the small angel on the ladder are very vivid. The other most notable paintings show the procession of angels moving eastwards to do homage to the Virgin in the apse, and the *Ascension of Christ*.

It is well worth climbing up to the castle. The first fortifications at Ohrid were erected in the fifth century but most of what we see today is eleventh: work done at the order of Csar Samuel when he established his capital here. In the rough 'park' somewhat south of the fortress, going towards the lake, are the roofless remains of a mosque which was built by the Turks on the ruins of a ninth-century monastic church.[1]

Sooner or later in your strolling west along the edge of the old town and below the castle you will come across a tiny church on a ledge above the lake: the fisherman's church of **Sv Jovan Bogoslov** (the Baptist) near the village of Kaneo. This was built in Csar Dušan's time and, though there is little to see within, outwardly, and by virtue of its position, it is an object of delicate beauty.

As I have suggested Ohrid makes a very good base for excursions: for example, to the monastery of Sv Erazma (about five kilometres to the north-west) where fairly recent digging has revealed cyclopean fortifications dating from the Illyrian period. They were probably erected in the third century B.C. against Roman invasion. Another possible objective is Leskoec, about the same distance in a north-easterly direction. The church here, Sv Vaznesenja (the Ascension), possesses some quite good fifteenth-century frescoes. On the northern border of the lake, hidden in dense vegetation, lies the monastery and church of the Holy Virgin of Zahum, founded by a son of Vuk Branković, the fourteenth-century warrior who was unfairly accused of treachery in the battle of Kosovo. Among the frescoes is a portrait of King Uroš I. (For directions to these places ask in the Tourist Office at the bus station.)

However, the excursion that nearly everyone makes is to the monastery of **Sv Naum**, the other end of the lake and very near the

[1]They have recently excavated an important Byzantine basilica nearby. The mosaic floors are particularly beautiful.

Albanian frontier. A daily boat goes there and back and the one-way trip takes about ninety minutes. The rustic buildings of the monastery sit on a rocky promontory above the lake. The original foundations were probably laid by Sv Naum, a disciple of St Clement, in the tenth century; and there are still a few monks there.

The paddock, which is spacious and well-walled, has round its sides some handsome and very old farm buildings with wide, tiled roofs propped on wooden pillars and loggias. Fowl, peacocks and beasts wander at will. The Turks used to hold fairs here and the Christians sometimes used it for markets. The church is tiny, secret, dark as a dungeon. Through the murk little candles burning before the icons throw a fitful light. In one of the gloomiest recesses is the marble tomb of Sv Naum, an object greatly revered by the peasants of the region. Unfortunately nearly all the frescoes in the church are nineteenth century and rather poor at that.

A short way down the road the Crni Drim, which rises in the springs on the side of the mountain that divides Prespa from Ohrid, jets into the lake in a long, horizontal pale plume and is partly unified with it for its whole length until it re-emerges at Struga and begins its winding, furious marathon through the mountains to the north of Albania and then across through Lješ (also in Albania) and into the sea about forty kilometres south-east of Ulcinj. A remarkable river.[1]

The whole area round Sv Naum is voluptuously green and luxuriant (ideal for picnicking) and the best thing to do is to combine a boat trip one way with a journey by road along the eastern shores of the lake. There are several pretty fishing villages on the way, especially Peštani,

To the north of Ohrid are a number of hill villages worth exploring if you have the time and inclination for long walks. The people are most hospitable and you can get an idea of traditional rural life in Macedonia. During July and August you may be fortunate enough to witness a wedding ceremony accompanied by many ancient customs. A not untypical sequence of events is roughly as follows:

Early in the day the music of drums and pipes announces the start of festivities. In the morning there is much sociability and entertainment with fare like *rakija*, olives and goat's milk cheese. Meanwhile the indefatigable bands circulate briskly along the stony paths. Early in the afternoon the bridegroom, probably in modern dress but riding a caparisoned horse and accompanied by two

[1]Near the river source is an open-air restaurant.

mounted best men, is led through the village. Outside the bride's house, from within which sounds of exuberant revelry will be coming, the retinue halts. A formal request is made for the bride's hand—which, as formally, is declined. The party goes on—inside and outside. Many of the men outside now dance the *kolo*, or *oro* as it is called in Macedonia. Later, a second formal request is made and declined. More music and dancing. Later still a third request, followed by acceptance.

The women of the bride's family then bring out the dowry: sheets, blankets, towels, clothes, pillow slips—a complete equipment for a household; and everything, of course, has been made in the home. All is mounded on to the waiting horses. Finally a great marriage chest is brought forth, also full. More music. *Kolo* after *kolo* is danced. Still the groom waits.

The guests and family come out of the house and at last, in costume and heavily veiled, the bride appears, perhaps two or three hours after the arrival of the groom. A procession is formed and moves up the village. The bride comes after the horsemen and carries a kerchief which is held by a relative who leads her to her new home. The dancing and the music, the feasting and the drinking, go on for the rest of the day and far into the night. Sometimes a hundred or more people will form one *kolo*, which will expand into double and triple *kolos*. Usually the threshing floors are used for these dances.

As in many other parts of the world many wives in Macedonia used to be bought like any creature in the market, and you can still buy a wife in the Balkans. Prices fluctuate in this as in other commerce but you could probably get one cheaply for about thirty-five pounds. Lest this shocks anyone it is as well to remember that a century or so ago you could buy a wife for a fiver in England (witness the opening scene of *The Mayor of Casterbridge*, which was based on fact) and in the remoter country districts before the First World War you could get one for ten or fifteen pounds. A few years ago a man died in Surrey who had bought a wife at the beginning of the century for seven and six—in Guildford.

Such a ceremony of the kind I have briefly described is a regular feature of rural life in Serbia and Macedonia and it is on such occasions that one has the chance of watching the traditional dances.

These dances, especially the *kolos*, are an immense subject in themselves. They are very old and many of them tell some kind of story at several different levels so these various planes of meaning turn them into a particularly rich and sophisticated form of stylised drama in which dozens of subtle variations are possible. Music, song, movement, gesture, posture, the general and the individual effect, all contribute. (See p. 432.)

From Ohrid to Bitola a good up-and-down road passes through rugged and fertile country and on the way there are several distractions. The first town of any note is **Resen** which straggles in a basin surrounded by hills and produces, surprisingly enough for such a torrid climate, a very decent apple. Many Macedonians from this area have affiliations in the States and you may well be momentarily startled to hear a resonant twang coming from a man in a *kalpak* and homespun breeches.

From Resen you turn off for **Lake Prespa**, some sixteen kilometres distant, which is shared by Jugoslavia, Greece and Albania. It is a big shallow lake, getting on for three thousand feet above sea level. It freezes over completely in the winter and, like Ohrid, has a great reputation for its fish: carp as well as trout. It is supposed to be connected with Ohrid by underground channels. Ornithologists find it especially interesting because it has always been a great sanctuary for wild birds, including the pelican.

The deserted shores are unspoilt except at Oteševo which will become a kind of holiday village with some small hotels and sporting facilities: a putative hybrid of Butlin's and the Club Mediterranée. A good spot for a languid week.

On the eastern side, near Asamati, in the village of Kurbinovo, you find the tiny church of Sv Djordje: a twelfth-century foundation with some vivid frescoes by the same school of painters who worked at Nerezi. On the lake, just within Jugoslav territory and where the three frontiers have a watery union, is a small granite island—Veliki Gradon—on which stand the remnants of the old town of Prespa and the remnants of Sv Petar's monastery. There is

---

PAINTING III. *Above left*, Gračanica. A fourteenth-century fresco portrait of Queen Simonida, the child wife of King Milutin: one of many royal portraits in the churches. She is usually depicted with the large ear-rings. The disfigurements of the eyes may have been done by iconoclastic Muslims—or devout Christians (see page 247). *Right*, Monastery of Manasija: this warrior saint is a typical painting of the Morava School, late fourteenth century. *Below*, Lesnovo: a portrait of the fourteenth-century Despot Oliver holding a model of the church he founded. The inscription records that he is the Despot—a great warrior and ruler, who founded this church.

PEĆ, the weekly market. Men wearing white skull caps are Šiptars (Albanians);
others are Serbs or Montenegrins. The veiled women are Muslim

another small island, Mali Grad (in Albanian territory) whose sole adornment is a fourteenth-century monastery plus a chapel in a grotto dedicated to St Paul. Yet another island, Ahil (in Greek waters) is littered with the ruins of palaces, citadels and at least a dozen churches.

This is a very superficial summary of a district that might divert one for weeks. From the point of view of casual sight-seeing the two lakes take a good deal of beating. You might come across anything in these parts . . . Fading frescoes in some half-buried church; a Greek beauty queen in a bikini; mountain tribesmen dancing an *oro* in a village square; or even one of those brown bears guzzling ripened figs and grapes.

It is not far from Resen to Bitola and the road continues good. In spring the country is extremely beautiful. Jonquil and the wild white narcissi bloom in myriads, heavy, voluptuous peonies fill the air with an exotic fragrance, and the forests leaf into a sharp, almost painful, green.

Bitola, or Monastir as it used to be called, one of the fairest cities in the Balkans and the second in Macedonia, spills into the valley at the foot of Mt Perister. It is more like a garden with houses in it than a town and reminds one of Peć and Prizren; a placid, leisurely place of balmy air through which the River Dragov burbles: a sort of Macedonian Worcester with a blue sky and guaranteed sun for two-thirds of the year. The principal hotel, the Makedonija, is in the main street (opposite the People's Theatre) and the Tourist Office is next door. A few yards down from it, on the left, is a small museum.

In the centre of the town the Orthodox church of Sv Dimitrije is worth looking at. It has a fine iconostasis and a number of icons from the sixteenth to the nineteenth centuries. The best of several mosques is the Hajdargazi Džamija, hung with crystal lustres and laid with sumptuous carpets. Near this is the old Bezistan or covered market: a *very* miniature replica of the one in Istanbul. This stands at the edge of the Čaršija quarter which is nothing like so interesting and animated as those at Skopje and Sarajevo, but it is spacious and worth visiting on Tuesday for the weekly market. Otherwise it has a rather wan and deserted air and you won't see much in the way of costumes, except, possibly, vestigial signs of the yards and yards of thick black braid the women used to wind round their waists as a protection against the kicks of the Turks. The women were even reduced to stuffing wool and other padding under their clothes to pretend they were pregnant because they believed the Turks would not molest expectant mothers.

Bitola gives the appearance of having been a wealthy and comfortable town and many of the houses are palatial. This is explained by the fact that several thousand rich Greeks and Jews used to live here and under the Turkish régime the richer Turks built ample *konaks* in broad gardens. Even today the city contains a high proportion of Turks and Albanians. One old man to whom I spoke in a café once remembered (or said he remembered) Kemal Ataturk who trained here as a young man in the Military Academy.

A short walk out of the town (south and just off the road to Greece) you find the ruins of the **Roman Heraclea,** a site which is still being excavated. Heraclea used to be the capital of one of the four districts into which the Romans divided Macedonia. The amateur and the expert archaeologist will find a lot here to interest them. For those who are neither it makes an objective for an agreeable stroll.

Outside the town at the other end is another very large French cemetery. The whole of this area is closely linked with First World War campaigns in which the French armies fought. It was at **Kajmakčalan** ('the Buttertub'), sixty kilometres away on the Greek frontier, that one of the biggest and most decisive battles was waged and the Serbians dislodged the Germans and Bulgarians from an apparently impregnable position seven thousand feet up in the mountains. A trip to Kajmakčalan is a memorable experience and so is a journey round Mt Perister which is now part of a huge national park.

East of Bitola lies a wild and primitive upland region—the Mariovo—where the peasant women wear particularly gay and elaborate costumes. Red, black and yellow embroideries on white are common styles. Shifts, shirts and bodices are intricately woven with geometrical patterns—rhomboid, octagonal and triangular. The traditional Arab symbolism is very obvious.

The road to Prilep runs first alongside vineyards which produce a tawny, almost *rosé*, white wine which I find excellent, and then crosses the Blato plain where, appropriately enough, water buffalo wallow in the muddy shallows. The land is patterned with bright green mosaics of rice fields, and in drier parts acres of white and purple opium poppies drowse languorously under the steeping sun.

Prilep, another tobacco town, sprawls across the prairie and is more or less surrounded by crenellated hills, so arid and bare they seem a proof of the old Macedonian proverb that where the Turk treads no grass grows. At a distance they look more like veined, rucked parchment. There is a pleasant hotel (the Skopje) in the centre of the town near the bus depot; and I think it is worth spending a complete day in Prilep, especially Saturday, the market day. The tiny museum a few yards from the hotel has been devoted to a record of local Partisan activity. In fact, it was at Prilep that the Macedonian Resistance made their first attack in October '41.

The town, now prospering, is a most congenial place with rather the same character as Tetovo. There are a number of mosques and handsome houses, several Orthodox churches, a market and Čaršija area and a lot of quite interesting modern building. High above it juts an imposing rocky hill on which are the massive and haunting ruins of the castle of Marko Kraljević, son of King Vukašin (*kraljević* means 'king's son') of the fourteenth century, the central heroic figure of one of the most famous cycles of epic legends and songs in existence.

There are two accounts of **Prince Marko.** He was a historical figure and he became a legendary hero of the Serbs. He was a man of enormous strength (his mace alone weighed 186 lbs.) and of considerable cunning and he had an inexhaustible capacity for liquor. He was chivalrous, fearless and passionate. He was also capable of acts of the most ruthless brutality, even to women. Hector, Beowulf and Roland were not more heroic. Robin Hood, Tarzan and James Bond were mere neophytes by comparison.

He was also in league with the supernatural powers, more particularly the *vile*—the mountain fairies; no doubt relations of the Greek oreads. Marko also owned a horse, Šarac (Piebald), which was the fastest in the world and had the gift of speech. Šarac also had a considerable capacity for liquor and Marko always shared his wine with him.

Marko is quite often described in the ballads in the repetitive way characteristic of the genre. He is very big, with dark eyes and a black moustache as large as a six months' old lamb. He wears a *kalpak* (a fur hat) and a cloak made of wolf-pelts. Across his back is slung a spear and from his girdle hangs a damascened sword. From his saddle hang his mace and the big wineskin. Periodically you may meet somebody in much the same rig-out these days, though without the weapons.

In poetry and the popular imagination Marko was identified with the resistance against the Turks, the exemplar of heroic valour and the embodiment of the spirit of independence. In historical fact he became (like a good many other Serbs and Macedonians) a vassal of the Turks and died fighting for the Sultan *against* the Christians at the Battle of Rovine in Rumania in 1394. Before that conflict he is supposed to have prayed to God to give victory to the Christians even if it cost him his own life.

Legend and a ballad report that he died in this fashion: one morning he was riding Šarac along the road when the horse stumbled and wept, omens that Marko immediately recognised as evil. Whereupon a *vila* appeared and spoke to him thus: 'Brother-in-God, Marko Kraljević, it is true that no one can take Šarac from you nor can you be killed by strength, sword, spear or mace. You are not afraid of any earthly knight. But you shall die, Marko. By the hand of God—that old slayer!'

Marko was then three hundred years old and Šarac had attained a hundred and sixty years. Marko accepted that his time had come. He killed his horse so that it should not fall into the hands of the Turks and gave it an elaborate burial. He then broke his sword and spear, threw his mace over the mountains into the sea and lay down and died.

One legend says that a priest found his corpse and took it to Mt Athos and buried it there. Others say he never died but, like King Arthur, sleeps—to rise again in time of need. A Bulgarian version records that he lies asleep in a great cave with his beard wound round and round him.

This is a very simplified account of a complex character about whom any Serb or Macedonian is prepared to talk at length, but it seems fairly clear that somewhere along the centuries the lines have gradually crossed and history and poetry have synthesised to produce one story or a series of stories for what seem to have been two quite different characters: brigand and patriot.

The stronghold of **Markov Grad** is about seven hundred feet up and encompasses approximately the same area as Chichester Castle. Some walls built on rock and some cracked and eroded towers are all that remains of a once massive castle probably first established early in the eleventh century. In summer the only occupants one is likely to find are lizards, soldier ants, butterflies and the odd donkey browsing on the dense brambles. However, it does command a fine view over the red-roofed Prilep, the rice fields and the lines of poplar which stretch away into the huge plain.

On the southern side of this hill, and tucked up against it, is the important **Monastery of St Michael the Archangel** (known as Sv Arhangel). Substantial walls protect the conventual buildings and monastic church, which is a combination of two churches built at different times. The older part, a one-aisled basilica, lies to the east. The western portion, added later, is rectangular. By it is a porch with a bell tower. This monastery was almost certainly founded by King Vukašin, father of Marko. The original frescoes have been much damaged and covered by nineteenth-century restoration. However, one can still see portraits of Vukašin and Marko on either side of the entrance on the western facade. They are dressed in the robes of Byzantine emperors, and were probably painted in the fourteenth century. Another painting of note is the *Betrayal of Christ* in the upper zone of the south wall of the second church. One of the monks here will take you round and show you a carving of a cheerfully villainous character riding a large horse. This is believed to represent a pagan deity: Rhesus, the Thracian rider, who was worshipped by the Roman soldiers. There may be some connection between this god and the personality in the Marko legend. But then the carving of the Horseman of Madara in Bulgaria is also believed, by some, to represent the Thracian Rider.

This monastery belongs to a group of six that have survived in part in this suburb of Prilep and which is referred to as the *varoš*, or 'the suburb' (it can also mean a 'village'). Looking due south over the scattered modern suburb you can clearly see the ruins of the Church of St Athanasius (the saint was a monk in the tenth century of Mt Athos) which is a fourteenth century foundation. A little beyond is Sv Dimitrije, a conglomeration of several buildings from several periods. It was probably built early in the fourteenth century (Csar Dušan refers to it in 1335). Unfortunately most of the frescoes have rotted away.

If, on leaving Sv Arhangel, you walk eastwards along the base of the hill you soon see a little below you two other churches isolated on bare ground. The nearest is St Peter's, a single-aisled rough little church (more like a barn) from the fourteenth century. Within are frescoes in four zones. Those on the west and north walls are tolerably well preserved; the rest are more or less destroyed.

A little below St Peter's is the much more interesting **Church of Sv Nikola.** Again it is a one-sided aisled church in bright brick and mortar. Somehow it manages to be both natty and venerable and it is difficult to believe that it was very probably built in 1299.

Apart from its exaggerated height in proportion to its length and breadth an outstanding feature is the ceramic decoration on the façades. The interior has frescoes in three horizontal bands. In the first are impressive full length pictures of the *Warrior Saints* and other worthies. In the second the sequence of *The Passion*. In the third scenes from the *Life of Christ*. Nearly all the paintings have warm, intense colours and there are quite a number of attempts at realistic narrative and at achieving perspective, especially in the *Last Supper* and the *Prayer on Mt Olivet*. This suggests that they were done in the fourteenth century and they may be compared with the frescoes at Staro Nagoričino, Markov Monastery and Sv Andrija.

Thirty kilometres west of Prilep, four thousand feet up in a very wild and mountainous part of the country is **Kruševo**. For the republic of Macedonia this place has a special significance because it was here, in August 1903, that one Nicholas Karef organised the first rebellion against the Turks and proclaimed the first Macedonian republic. Though it lasted only twelve days it was a great incentive to the others.

Kruševo has a number of unusual features, more particularly several houses whose walls are decorated with paintings and which have quoit-shaped stone roofs. Surprisingly enough for such a back of beyond place it has a cinema and an art gallery. An ethnic curiosity are several families who speak Rumanian and keep up Rumanian customs. In this area and in much of central Macedonia the *hajduks*, (the *hajduci*), used the mountains and the forests for hideouts. These men were wild brigands who played havoc with the Turkish occupying powers. Their tradition spread throughout Serbia and they were obviously the prototype Partisans and guerrilla troops. The Marko Kraljević of legend was one of the greatest *hajduks*.

North of Prilep the road follows the plain and then rises steadily towards the forested mountains of Babuna. *En route* there is a possible but not essential diversion to the monastery of Treskavac. By virtue of its site it is one of the most beautiful of the Serbian and Macedonian monasteries. From it, on a fine evening, you view the whole of Pelagonia and the towns of Bitola, Prilep and Kruševo. It is a thirteenth century foundation (some of the monks' quarters are later) and was probably restored in the reign of Milutin. Its church is one-aisled with a triple apse and the frescoes belong to several periods. The patrons are painted on the east wall of the narthex.

These are fourteenth-century. The frescoes in the nave are mostly late fifteenth-century. Among the best here are those of the warrior saints clad as rich nobles and without the traditional armour and weapons. In frescoes of these subjects in the post-Kosovo period you would expect an absence of militancy (see p. 286). The conventual buildings round the church were still inhabited by a few monks the last time I visited it. With typical hospitality they will offer their *slatko*, their excellent apples and their well water whose merits are praised far afield.

It was not only the *hajduks* and the *komitadži* who sheltered in these inaccessible regions. It seems more or less certain now that the original home of the heretical **Bogomil** sect was Macedonia and, more especially, this particular area, as well as that between Kičevo and Tetovo.

A certain amount of evidence is supplied by place-names which still retain roots derived from names by which the Bogomils were known in the Middle Ages. The commonest is *babun*, derived from *baba*, meaning 'an old woman'. The Bogomils were probably called *Babuni* because their faith was associated with superstition and magic and so they were said to believe in old wives' tales. The Babuna mountains and the Babuna river probably got their names from Babuni who are frequently mentioned in this region in the Middle Ages. One of the most famous of the *hajduks* was called Babunski and a small village called Bogomila lies in the heart of the Babuna mountains.

They had other names which are associated with existing place-names: *Kudugeri*, for instance, which survives in two Macedonian villages—Kutugertsi and Kotugeri. They were also called *Torbeši*, from the Serbian and Bulgarian word *torba*, 'a bag'. The Bogomils were supposed to carry a bag on their shoulders which contained a book of the Gospels and the alms they received. The name *Torbeši* is still applied today to Muslim Bulgarians living in central Macedonia.

They were called Bogomils after the founder of their heresy. Bogomil ('beloved of God') was a tenth-century Bulgarian priest about whom virtually nothing is known except that he was the greatest heresiarch of the Middle Ages and gave his name to a schismatic and heretical church that lasted for centuries and whose influence spread all over Europe, even as far as England. The last survivors of this church are believed to have died in Sarajevo as recently as 1878.

The key source for evidence about the heresy is a sermon composed by a priest called Cosmas in the second half of the tenth century. In it he describes the behaviour and beliefs of the Bogomils and lays special emphasis on the fact that it was a dualistic heresy according to which the Devil was the creator of the world:

'They say that everything belongs to the Devil: the sky, the sun, the stars, the air, man, churches, crosses; all that comes from God they ascribe to the Devil; in general, they consider all that is on earth, animate and inanimate, to be of the Devil.'

It naturally followed that in order to escape from this diabolic creation and be united with God all contact with Matter (and therefore with flesh) should be shunned. Hence they condemned activities like marriage, eating meat, drinking wine. Such beliefs were bound to bring an anti-sacramental view and gradually they rejected the sacraments and symbols. They condemned the use of icons and the veneration of relics, in fact anything which impeded the liberation of their spirit and a more direct relationship with God. They even rejected churches because they were material creations. The iconoclastic aspects of their convictions obviously foreshadow forms of Protestantism.

Bogomil doctrines are related to all the other big heretical movements—particularly the Manichee, the Paulicians, the Paterines and the Cathars. The idea of the demiurge was, of course, very ancient and the fundamental dualistic theory almost certainly stems from the teaching of the Persian philosopher Zoroaster. Nearly all dualistic theories were an attempt to justify or explain away evil in the world.

On the vast and intricate subject of Bogomilism and related heresies—a subject which has exercised some of the best scholars in Europe for a very long time—one can hardly do better by way of introduction than read two classic works: Sir Steven Runciman's *The Medieval Manichee*, and Obolensky's *The Bogomils*.

Beyond the Babuna mountains you cross a lovely valley, golden with sun-flowers, luxuriantly green with fruit trees and acacias; then a great, torrid rolling plateau strongly reminiscent of the tawny and desiccated prairies of central Sardinia. You climb, climb, and then fall, steadily, twisting, to the cup and valley of the Vardar and Titov Veles—also a Bogomil stronghold.

CHAPTER 15

Eastern Macedonia

Titov Veles—Gradsko—the ruins of Stobi—Lake Dojran—Strumica—Vodoča—Štip—Monastery of Lesnovo—Kratovo—Staro Nagoričino—Kumanovo—Monastery of Matejić

The main road south from Skopje is the *autoput*. It goes to Greece and for much of the time follows the railway and the valleys of the River Vardar: the old caravan route. On the way, a mere three kilometres from Skopje, you pass the ruins of the old Roman town Skupi, but there is little to see.

After an exciting drive through the hills you come to **Titov Veles,** an agricultural and industrial centre. It is a small Turkish town rising in terraces round the bowls and slopes of the hills each side of the river and looks especially beautiful in the late afternoon of a summer's day. There is not much here in the way of antiquities, despite the fact that it is a very ancient site. In 216 B.C. it was called Bylazora and then, like Skopje, came under the rule of the Byzantines—who were followed by the Serbs, the Bulgarians and the Turks. Like many other places in the Vardar valley it was a key town in the First World War during the advance of the Franco-Serbian army. There is an agreeable modern hotel in the main street.

From Titov Veles onwards the scenery becomes even more interesting and varied. Narrow gorges give way to rolling plains, then the land folds in upon you again and you squeeze through another aperture in the mountains. The plains are tawny, very torrid in summer. People I have met say they are reminiscent of parts of Australia and the mid-West of America, and it is not uncommon to see two hundred or more head of cattle moving in a long veil of dust across them, one or two mounted herdsmen and some dogs in control.

Incidentally there are a lot of dogs in Macedonia and Serbia,

233

lean, shaggy, ferocious beasts which are used for protection and warning as well as flocks. Unfortunately these animals are unused to motor traffic and when they see a vehicle they no doubt think it is a runaway beast or possible prey. The result is that large numbers of them are killed on the *autoput*. I have seen half a dozen corpses in an hour's driving before now. Quite apart from imperilling themselves they can easily cause serious accidents. So be prepared for a sudden attack.

There isn't a great deal to pause for until, a little south of Gradsko, you come to the ruins of Stobi in the valley of the Crna Reka. **Gradsko** itself is of limited interest except that its station has platforms and a subway which, until quite recently, were unique amenities in this country. Not surprisingly it was the Germans who built them, a detail in their grand strategic plan to build a railway on the ancient Roman Via Egnatia from this point to Drač on the Albanian coast.

The ruins of **Stobi** lie just off the main road to your right and you have to look out fairly carefully for the battered signpost to a track that winds over a hill. I shouldn't turn here but go on a few hundred yards until you find a few buildings, some trees, a well, and another woebegone signpost. Park your car here and then it is only a few minutes' walk to the site.

This has been described as the 'Macedonian Pompeii', a grandiose and misleading title. It does not compare with Pompeii or half a dozen other Roman towns in Europe and there are fewer excavated ruins here than there are, for example, at Salona. Nevertheless, in a great expanse of undulating, sunbaked arid country bounded by the jagged crests of distant mountains, Stobi is an ancient and important place.

It was not discovered until 1861 and then digging did not begin till the mid-twenties. Excavations are still far from complete though intermittent work has been going on recently. What you can see are a Greek theatre, later transformed into an amphitheatre, the remains of basilicas and remnants of three palaces where the excavators found a lot of Greek and Roman objects, including two splendid bronze satyrs now in the National Museum at Belgrade. There are also the ruins of two small churches, baths and a large number of houses. Several streets are quite clearly defined, as are walls and fortifications. Everywhere the mounded contours of the ground suggest the shape of various structures. Long before the site was opened up what the peasants had always described as a *porta*

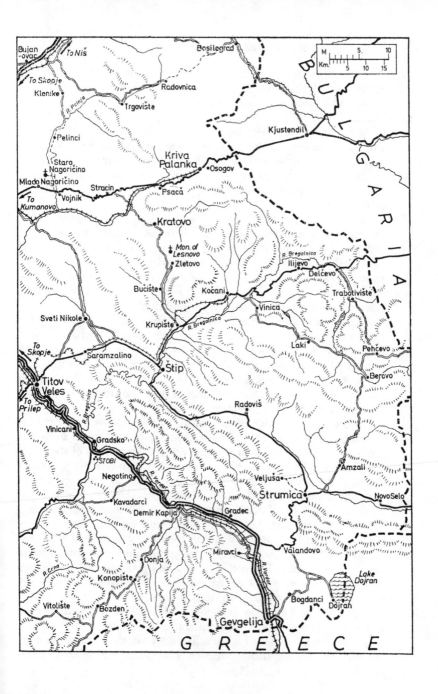

was found in fact to be the city's north-east gate. Macedonia has many buried cities like this and anyone with a million or two to spare and an interest in archaeology could spend a lifetime revealing them.

As at Salona one definitely needs a guide here but so far they are not available. In the absence of one, cast about for the double gate (in the south-west quarter) from which the main street leads to the centre of the town and a square. Near the square you will soon see the remains of the bishop's church whose atrium still has some columns.

Directions through this overgrown wreckage are impossible but you may be able to distinguish the three main secular buildings, all palaces: Parthenius, Peristerea and Polyharmos. The first, erected in the fifth century, is a very large one with a swimming pool. The bronze satyrs I mentioned above were found here, plus a number of mosaics and sculpture in marble and bronze. There is no doubt that this was once a princely and lavish building.

The Peristerea palace is misleadingly known as the 'palace with the double doors' because of its two apses placed alongside each other. It, also, had a wide courtyard with a swimming pool. On a street next to this palace stands the town fountain, and very near this the town baths. Adjoining the baths are the ruins of the Polyharmos palace whose peristyle had colonnades on three sides round which were grouped the palatial guest rooms.

On the southern edge of the town you will discover the remains of the large theatre, still being excavated. As one gazes from the 'upper circle' across the barren mounds and declivities of the city's precincts, which, sporadically, are mottled with patches of bright green, it becomes easier to understand why the 'romantic' poets found mourning and valedictory odes difficult to resist. For nearly a thousand years Stobi has been crumbling into Macedonian dust, deserted, overgrown, habitat of insect and reptile, and brilliant butterflies that flit and swoop across the rotting stone and marble.

Thirteen kilometres beyond Stobi you come to a turn on your right to Kavadarci. The oenophil will find this irresistible because it leads to Tikveš, the biggest vineyard in Jugoslavia (over six thousand acres producing ten million litres of wine per year).

If you are in the area you should sample the Kavardaka, a product of the *starušina* grape—the oldest of its kind in the region. It is a very dark wine, almost black, full-bodied, as the catalogues say, but with certain lingering subtleties. Then there are Belan and the local Smederevka (much sweeter than the Smederevska of the Danube vineyards) and Prokupac, one of the most popular wines in Jugoslavia and which is also plentiful in England. Try, also, the Kavadarci Žilavka, a rather astringent white wine which you will come across again in Hercegovina; though there the climate and soil give it a very different flavour.

When you are sober enough it is advisable to return from Tikveš to the *autoput*.

About twenty kilometres on you pass what is known as Demir Kapija, the Iron Gate, through which the River Vardar rushes on south. In the forests that surround this wild defile there are bear and wild boar. The plain beyond is one of the loveliest in Macedonia.

After about half an hour's driving you pass near the village of Miravci which is one of the best places to see some traditional ceremonials (descended from fertility rites) called *rusalije*. These used to be observed throughout southern Macedonia and are now performed in a few places between January 8th-19th (see p. 436).

At Gevgelija, the frontier town for Greece, I suggest you turn off to visit Lake Dojran from where a most interesting trip can be made back north to Kumanovo. The road, except for one or two patches, is surprisingly good. You go through the village of Bogdanci and eleven kilometres beyond turn off to Dojran, a small village straggling along the lake shores.

Lake Dojran (part of which belongs to Greece) is not so beautiful as Prespa or Ohrid but it is well worth seeing. According to legend it was once a field (more accurately a plain) with a deep well in the middle which was safeguarded by thirteen locks. A local girl called Dojrana was deeply in love with a young man from nearby. Unfortunately, the Turkish Janissaries also had their eye on her. Preferring death to concubinage she ran to the middle of the field and jumped down the well. The locks never closed again and the water gushed forth for days until it had flooded the whole field.

Science, more prosaically, tells us that the lake is tectonic; that is, formed by those forces and pressures that crack, bend and warp the earth's crust, as distinct from those forces which level its surface. The tectonic movements here have produced a very shallow lake which contains an unusual variety and quantity of fish.

Herodotus was round these parts in the course of his many travels some time during the fifth century B.C., at which time the lake (so much for legends!) was called Prasias. He describes the houses of the lake-dwellers which were actually in the water and stood on platforms supported on long piles and were approached from the land by a single narrow bridge. 'Originally,' says Herodotus, 'the labour of driving the piles was undertaken by the tribe as a whole, but later they adopted a different method. . . . Every man drives in three for each wife he marries—and they all have a great many wives. Each member of the tribe has his own hut on one of the platforms, with a trapdoor opening on to the water underneath. To prevent their babies tumbling in they tie a string to their feet. Their horses and other pack animals they feed on fish, which are so abundant in the lake that, when they open the trapdoor and let down an empty basket on a rope, they have only a minute to wait before they pull it up again, full.'

This is a particularly interesting description because when you reach the densely sedged shores of the lake one of the first things you will notice is a number of small huts on stilted platforms well out into the lake. Near them, fixed to piles, are stockades made of reed fencing. All this is part of the apparatus used for catching fish.

The Chinese still catch fish with birds as, I believe, some people do on parts of the Pacific coast. The fishermen of Lake Dojran use cormorants and have done for centuries. The season begins when large flocks of marsh birds migrate south. The fish, alarmed, flee from the middle of the lake to the shelter of the rushy shallows. Here the men have built reed enclosures called *mandre* (fish pens) which are open on the side facing the lake. However, the fish won't enter these traps voluntarily and this is where the cormorants are useful.

When catching cormorants the fishermen make a rough fence in the mud and then cover the area with a net which has holes in it. Under the net are placed a lot of dead fish. The ravenous cormorants come, are trapped under the net, are caught and then their wings are clipped. The cormorants drive the fish into the *mandre* which are so constructed in partitions that the fish can escape through apertures too small for the cormorants into another enclosure. Because their wings are clipped they cannot fly into these either.

The fishermen then make another compartment and leave an aperture for the fish. The cormorants are released again and the fish escape. This process is continued until all the fish are in the smallest compartment of the *mandra*, namely the *moma*. Once there they are netted and one haul may amount to several tons. The cormorants are still used for the driving but the gathering is more usually done by electrocuting the fish with electrodes in the water.

Temporarily stunned, they float to the surface and can be easily taken.

From Dojran to Strumica a tolerably good unmade-up road loops through some very wild country where there are few villages and little sign of any kind of life except butterflies and snakes and the magpies which are ubiquitous in Macedonia and Serbia. Though it is only forty-odd kilometres away it will probably take you an hour and a half to reach Strumica, but there is no point in over-taxing your car in these remote parts. If anything goes wrong you may have a lot of walking to do.

Strumica has much the same position as Bitola at the very foot of wooded hills and overlooking a luxuriant and fertile plain covered with wide orchards, cotton and rice fields. Very few tourists come here but there is a pleasant new hotel in the middle of the town and a number of ruins in the neighbourhood, including several castles on the hills above; all very inaccessible except on foot. There are also two nearby monasteries: the Vodoča and the Veljuša.

In a gorge near the Vodoča monastery one of the more horrifying acts of fastidious cruelty was performed nearly a thousand years ago when the Byzantine Emperor Basil II defeated the armies of the Bulgarian Csar, Samuel. Fifteen thousand Bulgarians were taken prisoner and, by order of the Emperor, blinded. However, one in every hundred was left with one eye so that they might guide the others home to their Csar. The name Vodoča comes from the Serbian words *vadi oči* which means 'to put out the eyes'.

The whole of eastern Macedonia consists of remote mountain fastnesses and plateaux which stretch far on into Bulgaria and north-wards to the Danube. In its austereness and aridity it is similar to the mountainous areas of Turkey. The people are Greek, Slav and Bulgar and live much the same kind of primitive rural life as those in central and western Macedonia. There are no towns and few villages, with only one or two simple inns and cafés. The roads are very rough and you can travel for miles without seeing a soul.[1] In fact it is one of the most primitive parts of Europe. I wouldn't risk a car in these parts but if you have time you can make an exciting journey on foot, bicycle or mule on the few roads and tracks there are. A good semicircular tour is via Berovo, Pehčevo, Trabotivište to Delčevo, where you can get on to a much better road via Kočani to Štip. You need have no fear about your reception. The people are hospitable and courteous and, of course, completely unused to foreigners. Travellers with a taste for the simple and the back-of-

[1] Roads and facilities are now much improved.

beyond will be in their element. But I think you must know a little Serbian or Macedonian to enjoy it fully.

For the less adventurous there is a good road north of Strumica to Štip, firstly up a broad plain and then through mountains: scenery which always reminds me of Turkey and parts of Greece. Under the vast canopies of the sky, silence and solitude extend like something palpable. The whirr of crickets, the cackle of a magpie, the horrisonous braying of a Macedonian ass . . . there are few other sounds unless it is the noise of your own feet crunching the stems of parched grass. You can walk all day and see perhaps a few men riding donkeys (sitting sideways, the usual mode in these parts) a shepherd or two with their flocks, a hooded woman carrying a double yoke from a well. And, of course, those lovable creatures, the tortoises, heaving their leathery bodies and armoured carapaces ponderously over the seamed earth: not by any means a symbol of Macedonia, for its people are volatile, progressive and capable of great physical urgency, but a symbol rather of the slow turning of the centuries, of the inexorable natural cycles that can never be hastened and which here are a stern reminder of the forces against which man contends.

At **Štip** the authorities (or the Americans) have indulged in one of those extravagant gestures which are so often the father of white elephants. A big hotel with marble floors and sumptuous fittings has been erected in the middle of the town. I hoped that Jugoslavia had grown out of the need to make prestige gestures of this kind but it seems that the immediate post-war tradition is still alive. Then it was found necessary to put up huge post offices and office blocks and stations when many of the population were living in shacks or the open air.

The last time I visited Štip there was a notice hanging inside the main door saying *Otvoreno* (open). In fact it was firmly shut. There was not a living thing in it except for trapped flies. However, a little farther up the main street there is a smaller hotel, the Makedonija, where you can put up and have a simple meal. Once when I came here there was a notice in the door saying *Zatvoreno* (shut). But it was open.

There is not all that much to see in Štip, which is a predominantly Turkish town whose centre, like Tetovo's, has been razed in order to put up new blocks. But there are several churches (the nineteenth-century Sveta Bogorodica has a lovely iconostasis) the remains of a mosque that was a church (Sv Ilija), some small mosques and a large Turkish *konak*, formerly a pasha's house, which has been turned into a good little museum. On the ground floor you find some Roman remains; upstairs a small ethnographical section which includes eight interesting costumes from nearby villages, a room mocked up as a Turkish apartment (with sofas, ottoman, decorations, etc.) and another room devoted to frescoes from the Vodoča monastery. There is one particularly arresting painting of a medieval saint with large dark eyes and a haircut exactly like the Beatle Paul.

Near the Makedonija, in the main street beside the River Bregalnica, there is a daily fruit and vegetable market; and on Fridays the weekly market day, the town fills with local villagers: an occasion worth seeing. To the south-west, on the big hill which shadows the town, you can see the remains of a medieval castle (it's worth climbing up for the view) and, half-way up, on what is little more than a ledge, the small fourteenth-century church of Sv Arhangel. Apart from the fact that some of the best rice and tobacco in Jugoslavia is grown round Štip the town has another claim to fame. It was here that, in the early thirties, the last pair of working camels in Europe died.[1]

Štip can be superficially assimilated by the busy tourist in a morning or an afternoon, but you need a whole day to visit the **Monastery of Lesnovo**—and this is not to be missed. Before going you should make inquiries from the police about a permit. Not long ago you needed permits for all sorts of places and in the remoter parts of Macedonia the permit habit hasn't been shed. This is not only a relic of the police state; it is also a reminder of wretched times when every activity was suspicious. If you do get into difficulties over things like this, patience and determination are your best equipment.

However, let us assume that all is well and you take the main road west from Štip towards Titov Veles. After three kilometres, opposite the petrol station, turn off to Krupište. You run along a shallow, green valley of rice fields where you will see long lines of women in white scarves and red dresses working from dawn. The water buffalo wallow in the river and the mud.

At Krupište you turn left. It is thirteen kilometres to the next village, Bučište. A little way beyond it is an unsignposted turn to

[1]Not quite the last, because in September, 1966, I found the two best fed, best groomed, least supercilious dromedaries in business anywhere on the beach at Slančev Briag, on the Bulgariad coast.

the right (it runs back at a sharp angle at the foot of a hill) and this takes you along one of the worst roads in Macedonia for six kilometres to Zletovo: a strange and rambling little village. From now on you must rely on your feet and local assistance. Your arrival is bound to arouse a good deal of curiosity and somebody is sure to offer help. The chances are that someone from Lesnovo will be in town, as it were, and will be prepared to guide you to their village on their way back. Whatever the time of day, your age and fitness, you should allow a minimum of ninety minutes for the climb which takes you up to three thousand feet. I walked up once with two village girls and a man of seventy who had been making the trip all his life and it took us eighty minutes.

At the top you find a typical Macedonian hill village: the ancient threshing floor round which the horse or mule patiently plods to separate grain from ear; the pig and fowl wandering in and out of the houses; home-made furniture and utensils. But the twentieth century encroaches. One or two people have radios. A lot of the children and some of the young men and women wear factory-made clothes and shoes. A new school has been built. I remember one old woman here who had probably been a village beauty when the Sultan's rule was in the final death throes. She was boiling water in a cauldron on a wood fire outside her house. With a gourd she ladled the water into a copper bowl full of laundry. On to this she sprinkled a packet of Jugoslavian Daz.

In the middle of a paddock, surrounded by big, balconied *konaks*, is the church of the now monkless monastery. It was built in 1341 by the Despot Oliver, a powerful feudal lord who ruled over a very large region and who was married, curiously enough, to the stepmother of the Csar Dušan six years after the murder of her husband. With her Stefan Dušan gave a large dowry which included the town of Titov Veles and what was called the Sheep's Field—the big plateau that lies between Štip and Veles.

It is a most elegant church of brick and stone in the form of a Greek cross with a narthex and two cupolas. By it stands a venerable mulberry tree which the locals say was giving fruit before the church was built. The frescoes in the church were done round about 1350 by a local artist called Michael of Lesnovo, and they are particularly interesting because they include motifs not very often depicted in Orthodox churches.

The narthex contains a large painting of Dušan, a powerful and forbidding figure. If it is at all lifelike, and it looks realistic enough, here is Dušan as history shows him to be: a ruthless, able and ambitious politician and soldier. With him is his wife. Below are Oliver and his wife; unfortunately Oliver's face is disfigured. The other two figures are his sons but they are almost indecipherable. Also in the narthex are portraits of Constantine and Helena, again in the rich attire of playing card king and queen. Opposite them is a magnificent angel.

Scattered about the narthex is a fascinating series of paintings of animals, birds, fish, the Calendar and musical instruments. Most interesting of all is a group of figures dancing the *oro*: nine men in short tunics accompanied by two musicians. One of the latter has a familiar-looking drum, the other plucks a rather odd stringed instrument. They are dancing a kind of closed circle *oro* with arms interlaced.

On the north wall of the naos there is a splendid *portrait of the Despot Oliver* holding a model of the church. A handsome and rather sinister figure he looks, for whom the title Despot is apt. In the naos you should also have a look at other scenes which show the death of the hermit Sv Gavrilo Lesnovski who is buried here, the cycle of the *Miracles of St Michael*, and the scenes from the *Life of Christ*—especially *The Passion*. The carved iconostasis is another masterpiece comparable with those at Sv Spas in Skopje and Sv Jovan Bigorski.

After Lesnovo you can either return to Štip and take the road across the plateau to Titov Veles, or continue north to Kratovo and thence to Kumanovo.

The journey over the plateau is memorable. It is more like crossing an upland tract of Mongolia. The undulating grasslands unfold, unroll, merge imperceptibly into hills. Hawks hover. Groups of horses graze. An occasional lone horseman passes. Up a long, tawny field a team of six buffalo draw a plough, patiently, laboriously, plod by plod, through the stubborn earth. Behind them treads the ploughman, a slow somnambulist.

The main road on the north to Kratovo from where you turn off for Zletovo has been much improved recently and it runs through delightful scenery.

I suggest you pause at **Kratovo** (a pleasant new hotel here) once a miners' settlement in an extinct crater. It is a medieval town, with five towers, built round the meeting place of two rivers crossed by high-arched bridges. The Romans knew it as Cratiscara and the population was more or less exclusively involved in silver and gold mining. So it continued. When the Arab geographer Edrizi visited the town in 1153 it was still an important trading centre. Naturally enough the Turks were interested in its wealth and by the middle of the seventeenth century, as Evlija Čelebija (see p. 344) records, it was a very prosperous town with some hundreds of shops, twenty mosques, baths, fountains and schools. The work of its coppersmiths was famous throughout the Balkans. Unfortunately the town was devastated during the Austro-Turkish war of 1689-90 and the mines were sealed. When they were opened again early in the nineteenth century Kratovo enjoyed a boom. In 1836, another Arab travel writer tells us, there were over fifty thousand inhabitants. But the Turks exploited them so ruthlessly that they emigrated en masse. Fifty years later there were two thousand Macedonians left. Today, apart from the towers and some imposing balconied houses, it has little to show for its past. Veiled women shuffle through the dusty streets, ageing Muslims squat at booth and *chibouk* and the River Tabačka trickles indolently under the massive grey bridges.

From here, on a good road and through very beautiful fruitful valleys you go to Stračin, and then turn due west for Vojnik, Nagoričino and Kumanovo. If you want to cover the ground thoroughly there is a possible diversion in the opposite direction here to Kriva Palanka, a small town in the kind of scenery which by now will be becoming almost commonplace to you. Near Kriva Palanka are two monasteries: Sv Nikola, near the village of Psača; and Sv Jovan Osogovski, three kilometres from Kriva. Sv Nikola was founded in 1358 by a man called Vlatko and a prince Paskac. The portraits of the founders' families are among the best of the period. You should also have a look at the *Assumption of the Virgin* on the west wall, and the scenes illustrating the *Life of St Nicholas*. The paintings on the western façade were done at the turn of this century.

Five kilometres beyond Vojnik, twelve short of Kumanovo, you will find a turning off to the right for **Staro Nagoričino** and one of the loveliest small churches in the country. It has no monastery now and you might almost mistake it momentarily, largely because of its situation, for a parish church in an English village You have to inquire at nearby houses for the key because the church is rigorously guarded. In fact I have even found a policeman on duty while a Belgrade artist was making copies of the frescoes. If you can't get anyone to let you in then you must seek the help of the authorities in Kumanovo.

The monastery and church of Staro Nagoričino were founded in 1314 by King Milutin. The church, dedicated to St George, was built on an eleventh-century foundation of which you can still see signs. It is mostly composed of stone and brick and has five modest cupolas of exceptionally graceful proportions. The decoration of the façade which looks as if it was once part of an exonarthex (see p. 171) is a particularly pleasing mixture of brickwork patterns and inlaid ceramic. The designs are often in the form of a cross and may have filled in arcades and windows.

The frescoes inside are splendid; vital and vigorous work, again largely the achievement of Mihajlo and Eutihije; you can see their signatures on the robes of the warrior saints on the north wall and on a pillar on the right hand side. The narthex has an interesting cycle of paintings which illustrate the Calendar of the year, and portraits of King Milutin and his child wife Simonida. The queen looks rather demure and wears the huge ear-rings with which she is often represented. The king holds a model of the church.

In the naos there is a very fine sequence portraying the *Legends of St George*, and another depicting scenes of *The Passion*. The most outstanding in the latter group is *The Flagellation*: an intricate and almost theatrical composition. One of the things you will notice about nearly all the paintings in this church is how detailed the decoration is. There are elaborate architectural compositions and there is every effort to make a full narrative. Lastly, do not miss the *Virgin and Child* on the iconostasis.

If you happen to be in rural districts like this on August 28th, which day, in the Orthodox Church, is the feast of the Assumption of the Virgin, you may well witness traditional festivities and *sabori*. Hundreds of villagers congregate on a hallowed site, perhaps a field, and there drink, dance *kolos* and make merry. It is one of the great social events of the year, their equivalent of a garden party, a May ball and Ascot rolled into one. The origins of such gatherings are often fertility rites adapted to Christian beliefs and rituals in the ninth century and thereafter.

When you return to the main road turn right. Clearly visible some distance to the south is the small village of **Mlado Nagoričino** (Young Nagoričino). This was a Bulgarian village, whereas Staro was Serb. The frontier between Turkey and Serbia once ran through the valley below. There are still a lot of predominantly Bulgarian villages in east and north Macedonia and in the past there has been considerable friction between the Serbs and the Bulgars. The nearest analogy I can think of, but a by no means accurate one, is to imagine relics of German occupation in the shape of village enclaves scattered about Kent and Hertfordshire. High on a rocky bluff beyond is a monument to those who fell in the Battle of Kumanovo in September 1918 when the French troops defeated the Bulgarians.

Just up the road towards Kumanovo you come to another church on the right, also dedicated to **St George**. Alongside it are a large number of weathered gravestones and stone sarcophagi without bottoms and a hole at one end for a cross to be set in them. Most of them are quite old but there is one grave of a young man killed in the Skopje earthquake. Strewn among them are remnants of offerings for the dead: broken pots of the kind you see in the local markets, fragments of food, and burnt offerings which include candles stuck to the gravestones. Beside the church there are also long triple rows of stones so arranged that trestle tops can be laid on them for a funeral feast or wake, or for days like All Saints when friends and relatives come out and eat for their dead. As the saying is: *Mrtvom za duša a živom u gušu.* ('Food for the souls of the dead is found in the mouths of the living.') Considerable ceremonial precedes these feasts, which begin early in the day and become quite a social occasion. They are common all over Serbia and Macedonia: I once saw at this place an almost macabre scene of twilit lamentation confused with bonhomie as black-clad women knelt keening at the graves of their loved ones and others still ate and drank at the trestles. Amongst them little candle flames guttered and wobbled fitfully through the encroaching dusk.

The church itself is very old and the frescoes are nearly all covered with chalk and whitewash—not by the Turks but by the Christians: either because they didn't want them defaced or because they were already spoilt, as may well have been the case because of the peasant habit of fixing burning candles to the walls. In the narthex, especially round harvest time and on the days of great feasts, you will find offerings of wool, corn, flowers, maize and other objects.

Just down the hill the other side of the main road stand the ruins of the **Church of Sv Petka** (the *čuvar* for both churches lives nearby). Sv Petka (literally 'St Friday') is one of those odd embodiments which represent a meeting of a primitive cult and Christian belief. It is a form of symbiosis. It has always been customary to personify and deify natural forces and this anthropomorphic process extends to abstract notions and even days of the week. So, in this part of the world, Sunday is also a saint (the mother of Friday and Saturday) and Sv Petka has a daughter called Koga (the Plague) still represented as a diabolical looking woman who sometimes acts as a succubus and is in fact a kind of disease goddess who has to be placated.

There are some lovely little frescoes in the church but, unhappily, there has been no roof for years and they are very faded. There is a particularly vivid painting of Sv Petka; another of a woman riding two fish, with an octopus above her. Some of the eyes of the figures have been gouged out—not only by the Turks and by Communists from the locality but also by devout peasants. Here we have a perverse overlap of superstitions. Many frescoes were damaged by the Turks because they feared the Evil Eye. Fanatical Communists have disfigured the paintings because they thought them barbarous relics of superstitious and outmoded beliefs. Zealous peasant women have scraped away portions of the holy figures because they believe this dust will protect them and make them fertile. These observations apply to many damaged frescoes in this country.

Ruined and exposed to the elements the church may be but it is still often used by the locals and any time you visit it you are likely to find offerings: food, flowers, burnt flowers, burnt maize and so forth. Outside there are more rows of stones for wakes. There is no doubt that in these regions one comes very close to ancient forms of ritual: pagan, Muslim and Christian. The sacrifice of animals like goats and lambs still occurs. On the Sheep's Field that I mentioned earlier there used to be a sacrificial stone which was used regularly. However, if anyone is inclined to think that this is barbarous (which it is) it must be remembered that the country people in these parts of Europe were, until only thirty or forty years ago, little more advanced than their counterparts in England in the fourteenth century. In the wilder parts of the British Isles the sacrifice of animals was still going on a century ago.

This little church of Sv Petka as well as its surrounding buildings was denuded of much of its materials by Turks who wanted to build a mosque at Mlado Nagoričino which you can see the other side of the valley. However, the locals say they lost two dozen oxen in the effort of transporting the stone and then gave up the idea. It sounds like one of those tales that needs more explanation.

Kumanovo (its Hotel Kristal is comfortable and lively) is quite a large, pleasant place with a considerable Muslim population and an interesting gipsy quarter. There is not much in the way of antiquities but there are several mosques and it makes a convenient centre for getting to the Nagoričino churches if you have come from

Skopje; and also for paying a visit to the Rotunda Church near the neighbouring village of Konjuh (ask for directions in the Kumanovo Tourist office), a church which was discovered by local peasants in 1919. This is a remarkable site. The church probably dates from the sixth century AD and is an unusual one for this part of the world. The rectangular foundation is within a circle, the whole being surrounded by a horse-shoe passage with an entrance at the west. The rotunda finishes in an apse. The altar was separated from the main body of the church by a barrier of six ornamented columns. The centre of the church was formed by four columns and six shafts in a circle from which extended colonnades. Of the many stone carvings only fragments have survived.

Kumanovo is also a springboard for reaching Matejić, the other side of the valley and high on the forested eastern slopes of the Skopjska Crna Gora. You must make very careful inquiries about how to reach the **Monastery of Matejić.** There is an extremely roundabout route which approaches it from the north-east (on no account let anyone persuade you to take the road via the station the other side of the *autoput*) and once you have set off from Kumanovo the only thing to do is to ask at regular intervals. Unfortunately this is a case where maps are unobtainable and detailed instructions would run into pages. I must confess I have only been to Matejić once and I lost my way and went up hill and down dale and through forests for three hours. If you happen to be in Kumanovo on market day (Thursday) you might easily find someone who wants a lift back to one of the nearby villages.

The church and what is left of the monastery has a magnificent position on very high ground in the midst of dense forest. Until fairly recently it was well-fortified (to keep out wild animals as well as human enemies) but it has been allowed to fall into disrepair and when I went there was only a villainous old drunken *čuvar* in charge; though, of course, the local villagers go up there on feast days, especially those connected with the Virgin.

The church of the Holy Virgin was built at the command of Helena and her son Uroš V in 1356, a year after the death of Csar Dušan, though there are records of a monastery here fifty years earlier. It is a solid building of brick and stone with five cupolas and we are fortunate that it exists at all. The big fissure down the north-west wall is a relic of the Skopje quake. In addition, there was no roof for many years and so the frescoes are much faded. On the south wall are the figures of the founders Uroš and his

mother Helena. On the other walls one can still discern scenes from
the life of the Virgin and Christ, the Legends of the Virgin, the Acts
of the Apostles, The Miracles of St Michael, the Legends of St John
the Baptist and the hermit St Anthony. On the west wall, very disfigured, is the genealogical tree of the Byzantine emperors.

It is not at all easy to plot a journey round Serbia. Much of it is
mountainous and many of the roads are bad or dreadful. However,
in the next chapter I propose to cover what can loosely be described
as south-western Serbia (one of the most interesting parts of Jugoslavia) and go up as far as Kraljevo. In the chapter after that I shall
cover eastern and central Serbia south of the Danube.

Assuming that you do not wish to retrace ground from Skopje to
Kačanik the best plan is to go up the *autoput* from Kumanovo and
turn off left across country at Bujanovac. The road from Bujanovac
is poor for much of the way but it is a most interesting ride and takes
you through the village of Gnjilane. A little to the north of it are the
ruins of Novo Brdo (New Hill), a fortified medieval mining town
occupied by the Turks in 1441. In the middle of it you can see the
remains of the pentagonal fort, flanked by six towers, which was
built early in King Milutin's reign. Early in the fourteenth century,
by virtue of its gold and silver mines, it had strong commercial links
with Dubrovnik.

From here you take the road to Uroševac, a thriving town with
several mosques, and then turn north towards the plain of Kosovo to
Štimlje and Lipljan. There used to be a Roman settlement at Lipljan
and then a Byzantine town in Justinian's time. At last we are on that
piece of ground which is more sacred than any other region in Jugoslavia and whose name has become something of a refrain in this
book: Kosovo Polje.

CHAPTER 16

Western Serbia

Kosovo Polje—Priština—Monastery of Gračanica—Vučitrn—Kosovska Mitrovica—Zvečan Castle—the Sandžak—Novi Pazar—Djurdjevi Stubovi —Ras—Monastery of Sopočani—Gradac—Monastery of Studenica— Maglić Castle—Kraljevo—Monastery of Žiča

Uranila Kosovka devojka,	Early rose the maiden of Kosovo,
Uranila rano u nedelju,	She rose early on a Sunday morning,
U nedelju prije jarka sunca,	On a Sunday before the sun had risen.
Zasukala bijele rukave,	She rolled up her white sleeves,
Zaskula do belih lakata,	Rolled them up to her white elbows,
Na plećima nosi hleba bela,	On her shoulders she carries white bread,
U rukama dva kondira zlatna,	In her hands two golden goblets,
U jednome ladjane vodice,	In one she has poured fresh water,
U drugome rumenoga vina . . .	In the other red wine . . .

Thus begins one of the most beautiful ballads in the epic cycles of Jugoslav literature: *The Maiden of Kosovo*. At once one can see typical features of ballad literature in the oral tradition: the simple language, the broad detail, the repetition.

She goes down to the plain of Kosovo which is littered with shattered weapons and strewn with the bodies of horses and soldiers dead and still dying. She finds one warrior, the prince's standard bearer, bleeding to death. She gives him wine and water and white bread, obviously symbolic of the last sacraments. Then a curious dialogue follows, not relevant here.

Kosovo Polje, the field of the blackbirds. A haunting name for holy ground and it was on this plain, on 28th June 1389, that the Serbians were finally vanquished by the Turks. Every spring blood-red peonies flower over it and legend says they blossom from the blood shed by the *élite* of Serbian chivalry. They not only do that: they symbolise and commemorate it. Five hundred and twenty-four years later, when the first victorious Serbian units

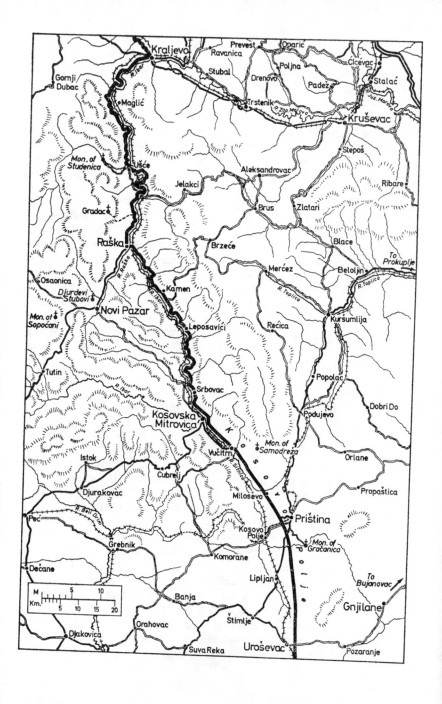

reached it in the Balkan War, the soldiers fell on their knees, kissed the ground and gave thanksgiving to God for its liberation. When they rose again they marched on tiptoe lest they should disturb the sleep of the dead.

For us Kosovo is one of those vaguely recollected names linked with some event of long ago, the kind of name that sticks from a superficial perusal of an *Outline of European History*. Indeed, as the train lumbers stertorously north, comes up across the plain and finally wheezes to a stop there is nothing to evoke or suggest the momentous past. Kosovo Polje is a small, shabby station, a mere halt of a few buildings. A doss house stands beyond the yard. In all probability there will be a group of peasant women, chickens in their laps, crouched by their bundles against the railings, and a mous-tached Serb or two in black *kalpaks* gazing contemplatively into the distance. It might be a wayside scene in *War and Peace*.

I recall a particular incongruity on one occasion. In the dusty yard outside the station there was drawn up an old Green Line Southdown bus which, according to its destination winder, was going to Chalk Farm It was partially appropriate for, though the plain of Kosovo is not like Sussex, it is very like areas of Hampshire and Wiltshire, and more especially Salisbury plain. The existence of a large barracks outside the nearby town of Priština helps the impression.

But the sky seems higher, more broadly arched, and curves beauti-fully like the inside of some blue and as yet unadorned Byzantine cupola from mountains to mountains. On a summer noon little fleecy clouds like the doodles of fresco painters for plump cherubs swan it ephemerally across the lofty spaces. Beneath them—the plain: a succession of easily undulating contours across which the almost luminous winds smooth, ruffle and brisk the acres of corn and maize and the pale prone amplitudes of grass. I doubt if the *polje* has changed much since June 1389.

The events which led up to the conflict are fairly well documented but there is much disagreement about the details, as there is about the details of the actual battle. After the death of Csar Dušan and while his son was still nominally king a number of nobles (*vojvode*) like Vukašin and Marko Kraljević began to fashion for themselves small kingdoms out of what was left of the Serbian empire. When it became clear that the colossal and very efficient might of the Turkish military machine had to be confronted once and for all a number of them combined their armies under the leadership of

Prince Lazar, whose main stronghold was very probably at Kruševac in central Serbia. The Turkish Sultan, Murad, was at the head of his own army.

On Vidovdan (the feast of St Vitus) or more probably a day or two before, the Serbs went down to Kosovo. The Turks were probably about seventy thousand strong and the Serbians had not much more than half that number. A good many Christian allies and vassals of Prince Lazar did not come in time. The *vojvode* might well have waited for the full complement and it looks suspiciously like a case of Slav impulsiveness.

There is a story that the Serbs lost because of treachery in their own ranks by Vuk Branković, one of the greater nobles, who was alleged to be jealous of Lazar and his brother-in-law Miloš Obilić. One theory is that at a crucial point in the battle Vuk Branković, who was supposed to have been bribed by the Sultan, defected with twelve thousand cavalry. I suspect this treachery hypothesis derives from a distortion of the facts and desire to whitewash the Serbs. In epic poetry there are several examples of characters involved in grand betrayal: for example, Ganelon in *The Song of Roland*, and, in a different way and to a lesser extent, Unferth in *Beowulf*. There is also a tale that Miloš had been slandered by Branković and, in order to prove his loyalty, gained entrance to the Sultan's tent before the battle (ostensibly as a deserter) and there stabbed 'the shadow of god' to death. The Sultan certainly died at Kosovo and if this was how it happened it supports the theory that Miloš's deed began the conflict too soon and before the Serbs were ready.

Whatever the truth the Serbs were defeated and the stigma of defeat has influenced them like an ineradicable stain ever since. It is as if we had never forgiven the Normans for our defeat at Hastings or the French had never forgiven the English for their defeat at Agincourt. And even today, more than fifty years after their revenge, the mention of the battle of Kosovo will bring a frown to the face of a Serb.

At the time it was thought that the Serbs had won and the news that they had spread across Europe. It is more likely that it was a 'drawn' battle, and as there were at least three more battles of Kosovo after it which never received any publicity it looks as if legend and speculation, as well as mere lack of reliable evidence, have obscured the true facts for ever.

The main interest of the battle for us now lies in the epic cycle of lays and ballads which grew out of it, which are very familiar to all

Serbians and have been sung ever since the event. In fact, they know many of them by heart and the *guslari* (the blind itinerant minstrels who used to travel the country and recite them) knew many thousands of lines, perhaps sixty or seventy thousand. But there are very few *guslari* left.

The poems belong to the genre of traditional popular narrative poetry based on historical events and created mainly by individual members of an illiterate or semi-illiterate society and preserved by oral tradition. We possess them in print now because a great nineteenth-century Serbian scholar, Vuk Karadžić, spent much of his life collecting them from the *guslari* while there were still plenty of them about who had capacious repertoires of word-hoards. In addition to the Kosovo ballads there are three other main epic cycles: the Marko Kraljević group which I have already mentioned; the pre-Kosovo group which treats of myth and legend; and a third (the most recent) that comprises all the poems dealing with the struggles against the Turks during the nineteenth century.[1] The metre common to most of them is a decasyllabic trochaic (—u) with a caesura after the fourth syllable—thus:

> *Póletio* ‖ *sóko tica siva*
> *Ód svetinje,* ‖ *ód Jerúsalíma.*

The recitation is extremely formal and stylised because there is an enforced stress and this, to the accompaniment of the monotonous note of the one-stringed *gusle*, produces a strange and wild tension. You can hear the tradition perpetuated in a lot of popular songs. It is exciting and, despite the monotony, capable of considerable subtlety. Quite a lot of half rhyming occurs because the lines tend to end in vowels but there is no regular pattern and the irregularities help to disperse the strict rhythms and forced stresses.

In all four cycles fact and reality have been both confused and enhanced by reality, and ultimately I think that the ballad accounts of Kosovo are a good deal more interesting than the historical details. The poetic version of Prince Lazar's decision to fight is very

[1] These songs or ballads are known as *narodne pesme* ('national songs', or 'peoples' songs') a term which covers a wide variety of forms. *Pesma* is also the word for 'poem'. There are nine epic cycles. The other five deal with (a) the Serbian nobles and their conflicts after the battle of Kosovo until towards the end of the fifteenth century, (b) the exploits of the *hajduks* against the Turks, (c, d and e) Montenegrin, Bosnian and Dalmatian struggles against invading powers. There is no tradition of ballad literature in Slovenia. There the lyric has flourished.

interesting in itself and provides a good example of how poetry can transcend reality by extreme simplification. It begins:

Poletio soko tica siva,	There flew a falcon, a grey bird,
Od svetinje, od Jerusalima,	From the holy city, from Jerusalem,
I on nosi ticu pastavicu.	And carried in its beak a swallow.
To ne bio soko tica siva,	But that was not a grey falcon,
Veće bio svetitelj Ilija:	It was the holy man Elijah:
On ne nosi tice lastavice,	And he does not carry a swallow,
Veće knjigu od Bogorodice . . .	But a letter from the Mother of God . . .

The letter offers Prince Lazar the choice of a heavenly kingdom or an earthly kingdom. If he chooses an earthly kingdom he must gather an army and he will defeat the Turks. If he desires a heavenly kingdom then he must build a church on Kosovo, not of marble but of samite and scarlet (*svile i skerleta*). The letter also says that his army will perish anyway. So he chooses the kingdom of God and begins the church. The rest of the ballad gives a very brief account of the battle, and concludes:

> *Sve je sveto i vestito bilo,*
> *I milome Bogu pristupvano.*

Everything was done honourably, all was holy. The will of God was fulfilled at Kosovo.

The Serbs could have compromised with the Turks. They could also have given up their faith. The Greek Church did compromise. It even collaborated with the Sultans. The Serbian Church did not. As the Serbian proverb says: 'It is better to die honest than to live in disgrace.'

Another ballad, one of the most moving, describes how the wife of Jug Bogdan, a Serbian lord, goes to the field of Kosovo and there finds her dead husband and her dead sons—the nine Jugovići. She steels her heart and returns dry-eyed to her white castle and her nine widowed daughters-in-law. The next morning two ravens drop a severed hand into her lap. On it a golden ring shines. It is the hand of Damian, one of her sons. This is too cruel a stroke for the old lady. Her heart swells in anguish:

> *Za svojijeh devet Jugovići,*
> *I desetim star-Jugom Bogdanom.*

It breaks in grief for the nine dead Jugovići and the tenth, Jug Bogdan, their father.

Priština, a few kilometres away, is a very amiable market town, now quite large, which spreads across the slopes above the *polje*. It is very informally planned, like so many southern Serbian towns, and usually only receives a perfunctory mention from travellers. But I rather like it. It is conveniently near the monastery of Gračanica and it has an excellent new hotel, the Kosovski Božur (*božur* is the word for peony), which is quite one of the most successful pieces of modern architecture in Serbia. The mosaic of mounted warriors on the outer walls is splendid. Now the hotel has become the focal point of town life in the evenings.

Priština used to be the capital of the Serbian kings, whose court was itinerant in order to deal with their vast country. No relics of royal occupation survive but there are a lot of interesting new buildings and the old 'Turkish' quarter, though rather squalid and poverty-stricken, is fascinating. Apart from the *konaks* you should look at the fifteenth-century Imperial mosque, the *hammam* of the same period and the clock tower (*sahat kula*) which is nineteenth century. On market day (Tuesday) you can see plenty of costumes (you'll see quite a lot anyway because of the gipsies) and there is also a small museum, well signposted, in the more prosperous part of the old town. I have never been able to get into it because it has always been shut for 'restorations'. 'Tomorrow is wiser than today,' says a Serbian proverb and when you are confronted with delay, the insolence of office, prevarication and contumely, it is just as well to remember it.

Nine kilometres south (take the main road and turn off at the signpost to Gnjilane) is one of the greater masterpieces of Serbian art: the **Church of Gračanica**. There is not much left of the monastery but the church is more or less intact: the supreme example of the 'Central School'.

Pink and tawny, of highly polished stone, with a most elaborate superstructure of pepper-pot cupolas and wavy roofs which contrast vividly with the almost bare walls, it seems to sit neat and demure and say: Look at me. Am I not perfect, or nearly so? Almost every inch of its walls is covered with frescoes and they may well have been painted by Mihajlo and Eutihije. Certainly by their style they belong to the genre you have already seen at Staro Nagoričino, for example, and Sv Nikita, and will see again at Studenica, in the King's Church.

The church was founded by King Milutin in 1321 and in the narthex there is a gallery of royal portraits which includes one of Milutin and his wife Simonida. Handsome and sinister he looks in

CASTLES. *Above* Maglić: after Smederevo the most splendid and romantic of the Serbian medieval strongholds. *Below*, Nehaj, near Senj on the Croatian coast: built by a General Lenković in 1558

TETOVO. *Left*, the 'Painted Mosque'. The tiled and grilled wall is very typical of many mosque surrounds. *Below*, the *Tekija* or Whirling Dervish 'monastery'. The open pavilion, in whose centre ran a fountain, was used by the Dervishes for recreation

his stiff tunic studded with jewels. Most paintings of Serbian monarchs emphasise their status, their material magnificence. Nowadays Milutin, like Csar Dušan, would have been a tycoon or possibly a dictator. Other portraits here show Helen of Anjou, wife of Uroš I, and other Serb royalty. There is also a Nemanjić family tree, the first to be painted. Above the narthex you find a small gallery, really a kind of royal box, which the sovereign occupied while remaining invisible to the congregation. The secret door and stairway to this is in one of the south-westerly pillars.

The naos contains numerous paintings which illustrate the life of Christ and the Calendar. In the apse are some incidents from the life of the Virgin. The little chapel on the north side contains some scenes from the *Life of St. Nicholas* and a magnificent painting of *St John the Baptist*, generally regarded as one of the finest of all portraits in Serbian art. The features reveal a profound dignity and strength; the stern, uncompromising eyes are enough to make one quail. Some kind of refractive magic, as well as the painter's art, gives all these frescoes a pinkish, luminous glow which, quite apart from enhancing them, makes them easier to see in this very dark church. There are several other notable works: especially the *Dormition of the Virgin* on the west wall and the *Last Judgment* in the narthex. Some of the quainter details in the latter are reminiscent of Bosch.

Near Priština (ask for directions at the Tourist office) is a *turbeh* claimed to be that of Sultan Murad. It is rather a shabby tomb and hardly worth visiting unless one is a connoisseur of the necropolitan. Apart from that there is only one other visible remnant of that momentous conflict—a tomb supposed to have belonged to a Turkish standard bearer. Spring fertility rites are still performed at these shrines each year. They include the sacrifice of cocks and lambs and are an odd amalgam of Muslim and Christian tradition.

At Gračanica itself, however, there is a much more easily identifiable ritual. The church is dedicated to the Mother of God and has its festival on the Assumption. A large number of peasants celebrate it in the monastery grounds with feasting and dancing. Such an occasion is called a *slava* or *krsna slava*, which is the feast of the patron saint of the home or village or monastery or region and is celebrated by Serbs wherever they are. According to peasants in Serbia the Christian missionary who first converted a family *ipso facto* converted their household god into a Christian saint and most families keep the *slava* on the chief day of the saint. It is essentially the festival of the home and is celebrated by the *domaćin* or head of the household. Not to keep it is a sin.

A *slava* used to go on for a week at least, but now it lasts only a day or so and is accompanied by much visiting, feasting, drinking and dancing. On the first day everyone togs up in their best and the *domaćin* lights the *slava* candle and, if there is no priest present, blesses the *slava* cake of bread or *kolać*. This cake is the focus of a complicated ceremonial. It is a home-made loaf as a rule, unleavened and decorated with holy symbols and patterns of birds and ears of corn. The priest may bless it in a church (I have only seen this happen a couple of times—once in Belgrade) or in the home. The priest then repeats prayers and blessings over it and makes four cuts on its underside in the shape of a cross. Into the arms of the cross he pours red wine. There are many other rituals involved in the preliminaries. The *kolać* is eventually eaten by the guests. Sometimes, when a complete village or an individual monastery is involved, every family has its *slava* on the same day.

From Priština you take the main road up the plain towards Vučitrn and Kosovska Mitrovica. A little short of Vučitrn there is a turn off to the monastery of Samodreža which is mentioned several times in the Kosovo ballads and is traditionally the place where Prince Lazar and his army (or part of it) took communion before the débâcle.

Vučitrn is a large Muslim village founded on the site of a Roman settlement and at one time belonged to Vuk Branković. It possesses several antiquities, including a tower and a medieval bridge over the dried up bed of a river that has changed its course.

Kosovska Mitrovica is also Muslim and is quite a sizeable town, swelteringly hot and dusty in the summer, cruelly cold in winter. It has a musty and simple hotel, the Jadran, of much character and relatively little comfort. You should have a look at the small museum, in whose garden is what looks very like a pagan sacrificial stone, and also the small Čaršija full of booths and workshops. Market day is a Saturday and is very colourful. The men wear much the same garb you will have seen at Peć and Prizren and the women still wear striped aprons and purple basques over their chemise dresses. Instead of *jeleci* they have broad, brightly coloured bands.

On a nearby hill (about half an hour's walk) stands the ruined castle of Zvečan, originally a Roman fortification that was rebuilt in the twelfth century. It is rich in the history of Serbia because for a time Stefan Nemanja occupied it and it contains the remnants of a cistern and a church built at his command. It was here also that Csar Dušan's father was strangled in 1331. When the Turks captured it it became a powerful stronghold.

Quite near here post-war excavations have revealed a neolithic settlement, the first to be discovered in the region. Six kilometres north-west is the Banjska monastery, yet another of King Milutin's foundations in 1312. The original was virtually destroyed by the Turks and later it was rebuilt. There are no frescoes.

To the west of Kosovska Mitrovica stretches a range of almost uninhabited and extremely wild mountains and the only way north lies up the Ibar valley on a poor road. There are a few small villages *en route* but nothing of any note until you reach Raška where you have to turn south down the Raška valley to Novi Pazar. Again the road is very poor but for a long time they have been building a new asphalt road from Kraljevo to Novi Pazar which should certainly be finished by 1968.

I think that **Novi Pazar** (new bazaar) is one of the most interesting towns in Serbia. It is remote, primitive and Muslim, and I recommend a full day here, preferably two. It lies in the region known as the **Sandžak**, a term that needs some explanation. When the Turks overran the country they divided it for administrative purposes into *sandžaks* which were later grouped into regions called *pašaliks* ruled over by a *beg* or a pasha. Each pasha had his own council the *divan* (the Sultan had a *divan* in the Seraglio in Istanbul and our word comes from it) and his chief justice, a *kadi*. The basis of Turkish rule was the Koran and Muslim law deriving from it. Slavs who refused to become Muslims (and the majority of Serbs *did* refuse) became *rayah*—that is, serfs of the Turkish empire. This abolished the class system and explains why there were very few class distinctions amongst Serbs when they regained their freedom. Land was assigned in fiefs to Muslim knights on condition of military service, and these knights, known as spahis, were obliged to give personal service to and provide troops for the Sultan. Taxes were levied on the *rayah* and they had to pay tithes. The Turks also introduced the much hated system of an annual seizure of healthy young men between the ages of ten and twenty who were taken to Istanbul and trained for the crack corps of Janissaries.

It seems that at first relationships with the overlords were not too bad but gradually the enforcement of the privileges of a ruling class produced and nourished a deep resentment and hatred. Serbs were

[1]There is now a good road all the way.

forbidden to carry arms or ride a horse in the presence of Turks and the *rayah* were forced to perform the most degrading jobs, all of which helps to explain why you sometimes come across a churlish and almost brutish behaviour among the South Slavs. Turkish justice was rough, punishment rapid and severe: usually beheading or impalement.

There was no economic or political development in Serbia during the occupation and as the Turkish Government became inefficient and corrupt so the country became more and more retarded. It was only the Church and a deep nationalistic spirit which brought the Serbs through. Of course, as in any other occupied country, there were quite a large number of Serbs who compromised and collaborated and by so doing they were able to remain alive and prosper.

If you stay at Novi Pazar use the Hotel Beograd, a simple but quite comfortable establishment just off the main square. The more interesting part of the town lies away to your right when you come out of the hotel. After crossing the little river you enter a long main street flanked by many little shops and booths and bakeries. Immediately the other side of the bridge are the remains of a Turkish fort. Farther on you find the main mosque, the Altum Alem, in a lovely courtyard with a big *konak*.

Novi Pazar used to be the main capital of the early Nemanjić dynasty and later it became the principal town of the Turkish *sandžak*. Nothing remains from the days of royalty, but to make up for that there is an exciting weekly market on a Tuesday. To reach it you turn left down by the river (on this side of the bridge) and it's only a few minutes' walk. The mountain tribesmen look like Crusaders and Saracens and the *hajduks* of old. Some wear turbans; white, green, checked, and red. Their wide cummerbunds are striped green and red, their trousers or baggy breeches are tucked into embroidered stockings. Some wear skins and *kalpaks*, others are Albanians. Often the women are half veiled and many wear hybrid costumes with golden or yellow scarves. Their skirts are usually dark and are worn with white blouses and dark *jeleci* which are sometimes embroidered with gold. They all have a dignity and nobility of mien that makes them look superb even when they are wearing rags.

An hour's walk west of Novi Pazar, on a high hill above the town (you can actually see it from outside the hotel) are the lonely ruins of **Djurdjevi Stubovi** (St George's Pillars). Surrounded by trees and scrub, it is a melancholy, windswept relic of the twelfth century and was originally created by Stefan Nemanja. Amazingly enough some of the frescoes survive, especially a faded picture of St George himself on a galloping white charger. Most of them, however, have been removed completely (there weren't many) and can be seen in the National Museum in Belgrade. On the hills below, a little to the north of Novi Pazar, are three unexcavated iron-age forts with very clearly defined fortifications and deep ditches. I am rather proud of having found these because nobody seemed to know about them.

A little below and beyond these (within a few yards of the main road into Novi Pazar and on the right as you approach the town) you see a little circular church with a cupolaed tower rising from the middle of it. This, the oldest church in Serbia, was built early in the tenth century and is vaguely reminiscent of Sv Nikola outside Nin and very nearly as old as Sv Kriz. On one side lies a cemetery with many lichened gravestones of primitive design.

It was in this **Church of Sv Petar** that Stefan Nemanja was converted to Christianity and it was here also that he held a council about the Bogomil heresy, the results of which helped to disperse and suppress Bogomilism in Serbia. In fact the Nemanjić kings persecuted the Bogomils very ruthlessly. This led them to spread and may be an additional reason for the absence of tombs in Serbia and Macedonia.

Inside, the church is dark and mysterious and possesses a most potent atmosphere of antiquity. The frescoes have been ruined by heavy chipping, but you can make out a number of them (including a St George). Very unusually, they are nearly all in red and black. The combination of these sombre colours with the old stone is overwhelming. The feeling of reverence that one experiences here is heightened by the knowledge that underneath the church there was buried an Illyrian prince. During restoration in 1958 his grave was found below the flags of the floor and about the royal skeleton were a girdle of gold, golden rings and ear-rings, amber masks, statuettes, and pots decorated with black figures in the Greek tradition. It has been deduced that this prince died in the fifth century. All the treasure can be seen in the National Museum in Belgrade.

From Novi Pazar an essential visit is Sopoćani. You take the road west and at Pobrde bear left. About six kilometres on you turn off the main road near where the ancient city of Ras once stood. This was a Serbian city in the ninth century and became the capital of the early Serbian kingdom known as Raška. Half way through the twelfth century it was severely damaged in conflicts between the Serbs and Byzantines, but remained a capital of Nemanjić kings until 1314. After that it began to lose its importance and Novi Pazar developed. Now there is virtually nothing of Ras to be seen and it takes some fairly conscientious searching to discover even fragments of battlements.

However, a few kilometres up the valley, near the source of the Raška river which springs from a deep gash in the rocks, lie the **Monastery** and **Church of Sopoćani,** one of the masterpieces (thought by some to be *the* masterpiece) of the Raška School. Outwardly it is not unlike Dečani and Studenica. It was founded at the command of King Uroš I in the middle of the thirteenth century and, despite numerous depredations and prolonged exposure to the elements, many of its frescoes survive. Fifty years ago it was a ruin, roofless and overgrown; but restoration has saved some of the finest paintings in European art. The compositions are monumentally large and the figures majestic—almost god-like: their emotions sublimated in expressions of serene gravity and solemn joy. It is 'visionary' painting, bright, tranquil and combining the subtlest harmonies of colour and shape. Over a great diversity of figures and scenes Christ in glory is dominant. Most of the paintings here show close kinship in style and quality with the best work of Giotto and Duccio.

The Dormition of the Virgin is the most monumental of all and I think is the best of the Serbian treatments of this subject. The reflective compassion in the face of the Christ who is holding the swaddled soul of the Virgin, the attentive and inquiring expressions of the attendant angels and holy men, and the graceful and serene features and figure of the sleeping Madonna, make a composition of solemn splendour.

There are many other paintings of the same quality, particularly the *Birth of Christ,* the *Descent into Limbo* and the *Transfiguration* on the north wall. On the south wall you find the *Crucifixion,* the *Presentation of Jesus* in the temple and Christ among the learned men. Near the altar the subjects are the *Fathers of the Church,* the *Communion of the Apostles* and the *Incredulity of Thomas.* There is also an outstanding fresco of the resurrected Christ appearing before some women. In the little chapel on the south side of the narthex you find some scenes illustrating the life of Stefan Nemanja. The frescoes in the narthex were not done by the men responsible for the naos and the main body of the church. Their subjects include the mother of Uroš I and the legend of St Joseph. There is a great deal more one might say about Sopoćani and I think you need at least two or three hours to look at the paintings.

From Sopoćani one has to return to Raška and go on up the **Ibar valley.** About ten kilometres north of Raška there is a signposted turn to the left to Gradac and the remains of the monastery founded at the end of the twelfth century and restored in 1270 by the wife of Uroš I. You will notice that it has several Gothic features, especially in the pillars and doorways, and it may be that craftsmen familiar with Western religious architecture had some hand here—as they did at Dečani and Studenica. The church has been severely damaged but in 1948 a roof was put over it and some frescoes have survived. The most notable paintings are the *Crucifixion* on the west wall, the *Dormition of the Virgin* on the north wall and several scenes in the narthex which illustrate the life of the Virgin.

You have to return to the main road again and continue to Ušće where you take a signposted road through very fine scenery to **Studenica.** This is the richest and most magnificent of all the Serbian monasteries and still owns a good deal of land. It used to have vast estates. However, there are still a number of monks here and one feels immediately that it is a prosperous and progressive place: the focus of much if not all local activity.

There are three churches and spacious monastic buildings within its powerful walls. The big church is dedicated to the Virgin; one of the smaller ones to St Nicholas; the third is known as the King's Church (Kraljeva Crkva). The **Church of Sv Bogorodica** was founded by Stefan Nemanja himself and finished in 1191 and it belongs, of course, to the Raška School. Its most obvious features, apart from the beautifully polished marble exterior, are the towers and the great cupola in the Byzantine tradition, and the doorways and windows in the Romanesque tradition—as at Dečani. The external decorations of sculpted figures, animals, gryphons, birds, centaurs and so forth, and the capitals with carved acanthus leaves, are as good as anything done on the cathedrals of places like Trogir, Šibenik and Korčula. In the tympanum of the west door there is a magnificent carving of the Virgin between two angels.

The frescoes inside were done in 1209 (there is an inscription in the cupola recording the event). Chronologically speaking the monumental style of painting in Serbia began with the fresco at Djurdjevi Stubovi but the first genuine originality in style is to be found at Studenica. All the fundamental elements of the thirteenth-century

263

painting in Serbia are already apparent here: the epic quality, the emphasis on the physical strength of the human body, and the clearly defined character in the rendering of features.

Most of the frescoes were restored late in the sixteenth century when the whole monastery was restored. The main picture to look at is the monumental Christ in *The Crucifixion* on the west wall. This, one of the earliest paintings, is a masterpiece of tremendous power and gravity. When you look at art of this quality you realise why the discovery of Serbian frescoes has made such an impact and why there may have been some connection between the early Italian painters and those working in Serbia.

In the apse are frescoes of the Virgin, St John the Baptist and St Stephen the martyr. The *Dormition of the Virgin* on the north wall is a later work. In the south chapel of the exonarthex you find a number of royal portraits and here also the monastery treasure is (or was) on display.

Stefan Nemanja abdicated at Studenica and passed the throne to his second son before retiring to Athos. When he died his son brought him back. You can see his tomb by the south wall and above it a portrait of him holding a model of the church. His feast day is May 24th and there is a considerable pilgrimage here to celebrate the event.

The small white church nearby is **The King's Church,** (founded by King Milutin in 1314) and it contains a portrait of the king between his wife Simonida and St Anne. The main theme of most of the frescoes is the life of the Virgin—a sequence pervaded by a solemn gaiety celebrating the spring of life and beauty. The *Birth of the Virgin*, the *Presentation in the Temple* and the *Dormition* are particularly rich and animated. A feature is the amount of detail: in the Birth scene, for instance, little houses, arches and terraces, porticoes with capitals; in the *Dormition*, any number of rural scenes with lambs, kids and other creatures.

St Nicholas's, built about the end of the thirteenth century, also reminds one of architecture on the coast. Unfortunately only fragments of fresco survive.

When you grow weary you may need some refreshment, and a little way beyond the monastery you will find a small hotel which serves simple meals.

From here it is back to the main road and on up the Ibar valley through wild and romantic scenery. You pass through several small villages but there is little to detain you until you reach the **Maglić Castle,** distainfully remote and inaccessible on a hill above a wide

Above, a Macedonian *oro*. The dancers are in traditional costume. The musicians are wearing a type of Šiptar costume. *Below*, a festive scene in Peć. Most of the men are Šiptars

Above, Novi Pazar, the main town of the *Sandžak*. On the left, characteristic Turkish houses. *Below*, River Vrbas, near Jajce. A traditional method of travelling on Bosnian rivers

curve in the river. It was built in the thirteenth century and once belonged to an Orthodox archbishop and is, I think, the grandest of the hilltop fortresses in Jugoslavia. It is worth clambering up to look at its battlements, within which are the ruins of a palace and a church. The main obstacle is the river. There is a ferry—but there may not be a ferryman. Failing this, you can use the railway bridge two kilometres farther up the road and walk back. I have tried to wade the river but it is too swift and dangerous.

There is not much for the tourist in **Kraljevo** itself, but it is a large market-town beginning, I suspect, to acquire a *petit bourgeois* atmosphere. It has an average hotel (the Turist) and a rather inefficient Tourist office next door in the main square. However, a few kilometres south-east is the important **Monastery of Žiča.** It is easy to reach. You take the Kruševac road and turn right shortly after the bridge over the Ibar. Soon you see its three cupolas and dark tomato-red walls half hidden among the trees. It was here, you remember, that Sv Sava first established the patriarchate and it was founded by Sv Sava and his brother Stefan. Local tradition, sustained by the 'nuns', holds that it is called Žiča (*žiča* is a 'thread' or 'cord') because Stefan was led to the future site of the monastery by a golden thread. It belongs to the Raška School though the narthex and bell-tower were added a good deal later. The church has been much restored (especially since the last war) and is now in excellent condition. Resident monks still use it. The frescoes vary a good deal in quality and period. Most of those in the north and south of the transept date from the thirteenth century. The *Dormition of the Virgin* is later and there is a theory held by some experts that Astrapas worked here round about 1310. At any rate, some of the frescoes show a combination of the monumental and the narrative styles.

A few kilometres beyond lies one of the many spas in Serbia whose brochure offers cures for any virulent and hideous diseases. This one even offers to cure you of women!

CHAPTER 17

Central and Eastern Serbia

*Serbia—Vranje—Leskovac—Caričin Grad—Prokuplje—Kuršumlija—Niš
—Tvrdjava—the Tower of Skulls—Zaječar—Gamzigrad—Ravanica
Monastery—Manasija Monastery—Kruševac—Prince Lazar's Castle—
Monastery of Ljubostinja—Monastery of Kalenić—the Šumadija—Kragu-
ievac—Karadjordje—Miloš Obrenović—Topola—Požarevac—the Castle of
Smederevo*

'If vinegar is free it is sweeter than honey.' It is a Serbian proverb and
it summarises Serbian pride and independence. On the whole they
have chosen vinegar, a choice which has brought them enormous
suffering but has at last (and, let us hope, for ever) brought them a
considerable measure of freedom which, because they are such uncompromising people, may well increase.

Of course they love their land deeply and as you travel up through
Serbia it is easy to see, on the more superficial count, why they do.
It is a country of great beauty and variety: not as grandiose as
Montenegro and the Croatian littoral, not as austerely magnificent
as Macedonia, but it is still very hilly and mountainous in the south
and there are big forests. And then much of it is quite gentle,
reminiscent at times of counties like Derbyshire and parts of central
Wales. Sometimes it is as green as Ireland, as meticulously cultivated as Tuscany. North of Belgrade, by contrast, lies the great
Danube plain which has hardly a bump on it for hundreds of square
miles.

The *autoput* runs very levelly from Skopje to Belgrade, keeping to
the river valleys, and if you want to see eastern Serbia (a part that
few people visit) the most sensible plan is to go up the *autoput* and
digress from time to time while making use of the best roads available. It involves retracing ground several times but I believe this is
preferable to risking a car on very bad roads in remote districts

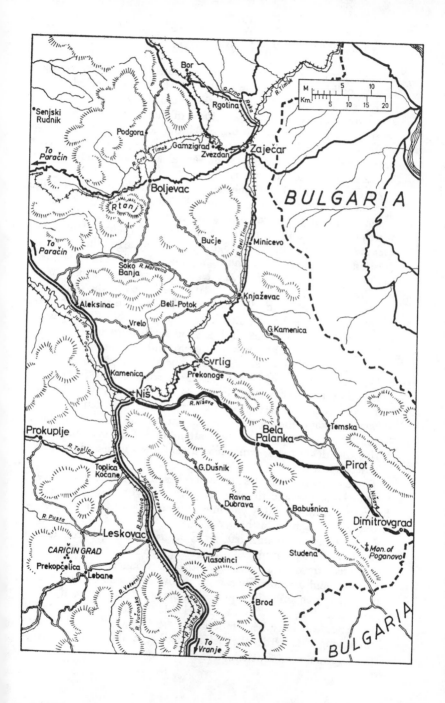

where, if anything goes wrong, you may easily lose two or three days of your holiday. Some of the roads in Serbia are unspeakably bad.

Going north there is little to detain you until you reach **Vranje**, a small town off the main road (most of the towns have been by-passed by the *autoput*) which has much the same position as Tetovo and was captured by the Turks in 1454, sixty-five years after the battle of Kosovo: which gives one an idea of how gradually the Turks consolidated their gains.

At the top end of the main street you find the only hotel: the Evropa, a very simple establishment.[1] There is not a great deal to see in Vranje but it makes a pleasant halt for a couple of hours, in which time you can wander in the old 'Turkish' quarter, look at the *hammam* and the Turkish bridge and visit a large blue building (just off the main street on the right going up) which belonged to a pasha and was built late in the eighteenth century. Behind is an equally large pink house which used to be joined to the other by a closed-in 'bridge'. The pink house harboured the pasha's harem, which must have been quite a substantial stable. The pasha's quarters have been turned into a good small museum.

To the north of the town is a grim and well-preserved castle called Markov Grad—one of the old *hajduk's* strongholds.

'The Manchester of Serbia' is the nickname that Serbs have given to **Leskovac**, but the comparison ends abruptly at its import-ant textile factories. Leskovac is a very old Serb settlement and I strongly recommend a day there, which, ideally, should be a Saturday for this is when you can attend one of the best markets in Serbia. Besides this the town is near a most interesting and accessible archaeological site.

There are two hotels close to each other in the centre of the town: the old Dubočica and the new Beograd. I advise you to eat at the Beograd. On Market day you must rise early—not later than six—to get the full benefit of the occasion.

From the Beograd turn left, go as far as the bridge, cross it and turn right. Fifteen minutes' walk brings you to the markets. As usual one is devoted to stock, the other to produce. They are both very large and attended by several thousand people every week. I have never seen anything quite like the stock market and, as at Prizren and Peć, you find a remarkable variety of people. Some such scene must have been familiar to the Crusaders in the course of their long ride across the Balkans and it is almost as if a con-

[1] There is now a motel in Vranje.

course of people in flight or migration, moving lock, stock and barrel with chattels and flocks, have come briefly to rest. Wagons and carts of every kind are parked amidst hundreds of kine, swine and horses. Many of the carts are carved and painted, a fitting accompaniment to the costumed men and women.

You find numberless pigs all over Serbia, for they are and have long been one of the main bases of Serbian economy. In all these markets you will see porkers of every conceivable shape, colour and temperament, from tiny little furiously squealing piglets to somnolent and mammoth sows.

In the town centre, just off the main street (7 Juli Ulica) there are two churches and a small museum worth visiting. The church of Sv Nikola was built during Turkish rule and is therefore below ground level. When I last saw it the complete roof had fallen in owing to an enormous weight of snow—an extraordinary thing to happen anywhere. Sv Troica nearby is quite modern and the museum has the kind of small collection you would expect in a provincial town. In the Leskovac region the people still celebrate a number of traditional rites, especially the *Lazarice* procession on the Saturday before Palm Sunday (*Vrbica* or willow Sunday) which is known as Lazar's Saturday and also as Lazarus's Day. This looks like another case of symbiosis.

The Lazar songs are sung by groups of girls (six, eight or a dozen) who, decked with flowers and arm-in-arm, are led by the Lazar and the Lazarica—two who represent Prince Lazar and his sister. The rest of the group are called *prednjarke* and the last two, the *krošnjarke*, carry a basket into which are put little gifts offered to the prince and his sister. The group processes from house to house and the songs they sing concern the occupants and past of each building. Such customs, once again, are very probably spring fertility rites in origin. Easter is celebrated with tremendous pomp and ceremony in the Orthodox Church and Holy Week is a very good time to be in Serbia if you are interested in traditional ritual.

By contrast to the *Lazarice* there are the *koledari* processions—a joyously comic performance by men which normally takes place between January 2nd and January 6th in many parts of Serbia.

Two dancers are dressed as hunchbacked monsters with horned masks representing sheeps' heads. (The masks and other items are on show in the Leskovac museum.) Four singers accompany the dancers and a figure called *snaška*: a man dressed as a woman carrying a distaff. To the music of bagpipes they proceed through their

269

village, stopping in front of each house. They then perform a ritual game of jumping on to wooden sawhorses and balancing for as long as possible. They then enter each house waving swords and ringing bells.

There are any number of explanations for the details of these rites, but their traditional purpose is to banish the evil spirits of winter. The South Slavs have always been an extremely superstitious people ever since they populated their world with good and evil spirits in the sombre and forested wildernesses of the Pripet marshes.

What you should certainly do from Leskovac is to visit **Caričin Grad.** You take the road south-west to Lebane (not a bad road) twenty kilometres away. Go through Lebane, which is a small village of little interest, and take a signposted fork right to Prekopčelica. Eight kilometres beyond, just after rounding a small cemetery on a wooded knoll[1], you will see up on a hill to your left part of the eastern fortifications of the sixth-century Byzantine town which some experts think may have been Justinian's capital in these parts. Judging by its extent it was destined to be an important place and they built an aqueduct twenty kilometres long to supply it. Excavations began in 1913 and have gone on intermittently since. A lot has been revealed but there is very much more to dig up.

As you come up to it from the road (about fifteen minutes' walk) you are confronted with the remains of the fortified east gate. Beyond, a broad well-defined main street leads up to a large circular space and cross-roads: obviously the Circus of Caričin Grad. To your right are the foundations of a large basilica and away to your left, behind the quite substantial remains of some houses, the foundations of what was probably the governor's palace. All the main buildings and areas have signposts.

There are at least seven basilicas here (the main one, next to a mausoleum, is triple-naved and about sixty yards long) and it is thought there are several more waiting to be unearthed. As you wander you will find extensive fortifications, five of the city gates, the baths, a number of mosaics and the remains of many houses flanking broad streets down which local cattle graze. The city's main axis was the north-south road running through the circus and its general shape was uneven, with a considerable bulge on the west side. The main area of the city was about two hundred and eight yards wide and three hundred and fifty long. At its largest it was probably not above a quarter of a mile in length. It is not

[1] On June 3rd a *pomane* ceremony takes place here. See p. 279.

thought to have lasted long and was probably evacuated early in the seventh century.

In lay-out it is fairly typical of early Byzantine towns. When you stand in the middle of the circus and take your bearings you see clearly, away to the north-east, the remains of the crypt basilica. Reconstruction has shown that it had a nave and two aisles separated by twin rows of four columns. It had a single apse, no narthex, and three doorways leading directly from the atrium into the nave and aisles. Beneath all this was an unusually large crypt, probably devoted to the burial of important clerics, and perhaps some secular dignitaries.

In the north-west quarter from the circus are the ruins of substantial houses, and almost immediately west the remains of the most important ecclesiastical buildings: the *episcopal basilica and baptistery*. The bishop's church was a very large triple-naved, triple-apsed basilica with a narthex and atrium. Some mosaic flooring was uncovered in the nave: a series of squares containing a bird, or an embroidered sack. The motifs are still common in Macedonian folk art. What survives of the baptistery lies on the southern flank of the basilica: a quatrefoil inscribed in a square. One can still get an idea of what an elegant building it was.

Having clambered about here the wisest thing to do is to return to the circus and then set off down the main street southwards. About seventy yards along you find on your left what is known as the cruciform church (the atrium fronts on to the street) which has points of resemblance with the crypt of the crypt basilica, a fact which has led scholars to the theory that it may have been erected as a private chapel and memorial to a military governor some time towards the end of the sixth century. This type of cruciform church may have originated as far away as eastern Anatolia.

The other side of the street (almost exactly opposite but behind and beyond the ruins of private dwellings) is the south-west basilica —not discovered until 1957. It had a nave and two aisles and a single apse. This is a church of modest size and is thought to have been used for worship by tradesmen and artisans who lived in the immediate neighbourhood.

If you continue down the main street you soon arrive at the imposing southern gate in the city walls. A little beyond it, on your left, lie the ruins of what is called the south church: a transept basilica with a nave, two aisles, narthex, atrium and apse. Here a considerable portion of the flooring has survived—part brick, part mosaic. The best preserved mosaics are to be found in the narthex, nave and sanctuary. In the narthex and south-west area of the nave the tessellations depict a variety of birds, and objects like chalices, goblets, dishes and baskets of fruit. At the eastern end of the nave a peasant represents the Good Shepherd with his flock, a very rare subject for the period. Apart from the tunic his dress is not dissimilar to that worn by the upland Serb and Macedonian shepherds today. Next to him a hunter is spearing a lion. In the northern half of the nave there are some magnificent mounted Amazons and centaurs, and another scene of the chase with a hunter in pursuit of a wounded bear, while a smaller bear is escaping in the foreground. To the Slavs the bear, lord of the woods, stood as much the same kind of symbol as the lion to other Christians: a source of danger and evil, to be guarded against and propitiated. There are numerous interpretations of the symbolism in mosaic decoration. Everything that survives in this church is finely executed work, footnotes, as it were, to the 'monuments of unageing intellect'.

Next to the basilica are the baths and, scattered about in the area, the remains of a large number of unexcavated buildings whose broken bones, so to speak, protrude through the arid soil.

You have to return to Leskovac from here and pursue the *autoput* towards Niš. A little short of Niš, at Toplica Kočane, there is a worth-while excursion on quite a good road up the River Toplica valley to Prokuplje and Kuršumlija. Prokuplje is an ancient settlement on the old Dubrovnik-Constantinople route and the centre of a well-known wine producing region. The red wines are especially good. The town is interesting and has many medieval remains and fortifications. The castle on the rock above it was a Byzantine stronghold. Kuršumlija has a splendid situation, where the Banjska and Toplica rivers meet, surrounded by very high mountains. There are the remains of a church here built by Stefan Nemanja about 1170.

Niš is a large, dull and dirty town for which I have never been able to develop much affection. But it is an important place and there are a number of interesting antiquities in it. You may want to spend a night here and if so I suggest you put up at the Hotel Park, right in the centre of the town, near the river and just off the main Trg Oslobodenja; or at the hotel Niš. I cannot recommend the motel on the Dimitrovgrad road.

The other side of the bridge which crosses the River Nišava from the *trg* is an immense fortification (the **Tvrdjava**) which was mostly built by the Turks at the end of the seventeenth century, though it is more than likely that there was a Byzantine citadel here in the first place. The main gateway is very fine, and within the polygonal ramparts, which are very nearly as massive as those round Dubrovnik (in fact, Dubrovnik would just about fit inside them), there are now public gardens and an open-air cinema. There are several remains scattered about including a Turkish arsenal and a mosque.

If you retrace your steps to the *trg* and turn right down the main street you will find a small Art Gallery (Umetnička Galerija) two blocks down and, a little farther, the Museum of the People's Revolution. There was severe fighting here in the last war and because of its strategic position on the main route to the Aegean Niš has been fought over many times. The Emperor Claudius defeated the Goths here in 269, and the Huns, in their turn, took and sacked the city. It was then rebuilt by Justinian and became an important town during the Nemanjić régime. It remained in Serbian hands until the Turks captured it and since then it has been a target in several other campaigns.

Return from here to the *trg* and turn south down Ulica Pobede and carry on till you reach Trg 14 Octobar. From here, a little away to your left, you find two nineteenth-century Orthodox churches with fine iconostases. The bigger of the two, Sv Troica, has a rather remarkable balcony with curving staircases and an immensely high pulpit. Most of the decorations are poor and reveal a great disparity between them and what had been done in the late Middle Ages. Architecturally the buildings are also disappointing, in rather the same way that nineteenth-century neo-Gothic is.

Dimitrija Ulica runs out of the south-east corner of the Trg 14 Octobar and a short way down on the left you will discover the Archaeological Museum which I have never been able to get into because of the infuriating Serbian habit of closing museums and galleries for reconstruction or re-arrangement at the very time of the year when visitors are most likely to want to see them. One has to remember that their conceptions of standards of efficiency are many years behind ours, but it is by no means all their fault. 'Remember Kosovo!' as a Serb is reputed to have said to a Turk recently when the latter expressed some displeasure over Jugoslav organisation. A very double-edged riposte.

From the Trg Oslobodenja take the Vožda Karadjordja which becomes the Braće Taskovića: this is the main road east for Dimitrograd. About three kilometres from the town centre you will see signs saying **Ćele Kula** (Tower of Skulls) which is a very odd *memento mori* indeed. It is covered over and lies behind an imposing entrance on your right.

This macabre relic exists because in May 1809 the Serbs mustered an army to attack a weak Turkish garrison at Niš. Instead of getting on with it and using their undoubted numerical superiority they foolishly wasted time digging themselves in on a nearby hill called Čega. The Turks gathered reinforcements and attacked them. Soon the Serbs were encircled and their leader Sindjelić, preferring death before dishonour in the true Serbian tradition, ignited a large quantity of gunpowder barrels. The explosion blew to smithereens a large number of Turks and all the Serbians.

The Turkish pasha decided to teach the Serbs a lesson. A herald went round Niš offering money for each Serbian head and the collection was sent first to the local leather-workers who stuffed the skins and scalps with cotton and sent the trophies to Constantinople. The remaining skulls of nearly a thousand Serbs were embedded in the stone tower. There are only a few dozen left now because for many years the tower (which was much higher and stood isolated on the plain) was exposed to the elements and also to the predatory hands of relic mongers (no doubt some of them were kin of the dead) who not only removed the teeth but prised out complete crania.

Lamartine on the way back from his oriental tour in the 1830's was one of the first to give a description of it: not a bad description for him: 'The sun beat down. About a mile from the town I perceived a white tower rising in the middle of the plain and gleaming like marble. A path led to it. I drew close and let a Turkish child following me hold my horse while I dismounted and sat in the shade of the tower to rest. Raising my eyes to the monument in whose shade I was sitting I saw that it was made not of marble but of even rows of human skulls. The skulls, bleached by sun and rain . . . completely covered the victory monument. Some of the skulls still had some hair on them which fluttered in the wind like leaves on trees . . .'

He goes on to explain that a stiff breeze blowing off the mountains whistled through the skulls and made them emit a mournful sound. Extremely unlikely I think, even though the tower is hollow inside. But Lamartine (who calculated there were over fifteen thousand skulls!) wouldn't have missed a chance like that.

A possible excursion from Niš is to continue on the Dimitrovgrad road up the Nišava valley. The surface is quite good and there are some interesting places *en route*. Bela Palanka has a lot of medieval remains and the ruins of a Turkish castle. **Pirot** (with a modest hotel, the Nacional) is quite a large town (once a Roman settlement) set in a big plain. Its main interest for the traveller is that for at least seven centuries it has been a centre of carpet-making. In fact, the bright *kilims* of Pirot, which greatly appealed to the Turks, still find their way round the world. Carpet-weaving remains an important cottage industry there and the traditional motifs are still worked from the wool of sheep reared on the nearby Stara Planina.

Beyond Pirot, road, river and railway are squeezed between the jagged walls of a lofty canyon—fourth in grandeur after the Tara, Drina and Neretva gorges. It is Wild West country inhabited by wolf and bear.

There is little to see at Dimitrovgrad, the frontier town for Bulgaria, but ten kilometres south-east of this, in unexplored regions of mountain and forest, and very difficult to get at, is the **Monastery of Poganovo,** built towards the end of the fourteenth century by the Serbian nobleman Dejanović. The frescoes are well-preserved. From the artistic point of view this is not an 'essential' journey; from every other point of view it is one of the most exciting excursions to be made in this part of Jugoslavia.

Whether you decide on the trip up the Nišava valley or not do not miss the little museum on the left hand side a little farther up the Dimitrovgrad road from the Čele Kula. There is a signpost on the left to a track across the fields. The museum consists of part of a Roman villa with mosaic floors (the whole of the district is littered with Roman remains) which has been roofed over. There are a number of objects in cases the most interesting of which is a copy of a head of Constantine the Great who was born at Niš (the original is in Belgrade). The Greek Byzantine eyes and brows of the bust are unmistakable. A tape-recorded commentary in four languages (including English) will be switched on for you by the *čuvar*.

There is virtually nothing to detain you on or near the *autoput* between Niš and Ćuprija, a hundred kilometres on, which is where you turn off for two of the best monasteries of the Morava School. So I suggest you digress from Niš via Knjaževac to Zaječar and then return on the cross-country route through Boljevac to Paraćin and Ćuprija. They are building a new road between Zaječar and Paraćin and with any luck it will be finished by the time you read this.

They are also making a new road between Niš and Zaječar and this was already well advanced in 1966.[1] To reach it you turn right from the Trg Sindjelića when you come back into the town centre and take the Filipa Kljajića Ulica up to the river. On the other side bear away past the triangle and take the farthest road on your right. Just over to the left of the shabby triangle are the foundations of a Byzantine basilica, and a Byzantine crypt which is in a remarkable state of repair considering it was built at the end of the fifth century.

Once you have left the drab suburbs of Niš the countryside is very impressive: big tawny hills, thickly wooded in parts, and quite reminiscent of the central massif of the Gennargentu in Sardinia. At Svrlig there is a large medieval castle and near the neighbouring village of Prekonoge some extensive caves. The biggest grotto is about four hundred yards long. Knjaževac isn't particularly interesting but the whole area round it is covered with Roman and Byzantine remains many of which have been incorporated into villages built by the Serbs.

At **Zaječar** I recommend a day. There is a very agreeable hotel here, the Putnik, where they serve good food and the wines of the district: an astringent dry white wine; and a very purply, almost black, red. Farther north, round Negotin, they produce two good red wines: Prokupac and Negotin.

By now you will have noticed that the urban and rural architecture has been changing gradually. There is less specifically 'Turkish' influence. The roofs are different. Thatched and wooden roofs are quite common. More stone and brick are used. Nevertheless, all over Serbia south of Belgrade a large proportion of houses are made of mud bricks and everywhere you will find groups of people making them. Most of the towns are developments of villages and are informal and irregular. However, the flatter the ground the more regular they become, and the villages and towns of northern Serbia are utterly different from those in the south. There are, of course, fewer mosques the farther north you go and fewer of those green, spacious, walled gardens. Public gardens, however, are common and the streets are often lined with trees.

In the countryside a good many interesting customs and superstitions are still attached to the selection of a site and the building of a house. For example, some peasants still put four stones in a field over night and next day the site is decided by the stone that hides an insect. If there is no insect the process is repeated. An old ballad,

[1] This road is now more or less completed.

The Building of Skadar, describes how a girl was deceived into being immured in a building and it was commonly believed that a bridge or a house or a town could only be strong if something had been sacrificed in it and to it; not necessarily a human being. To this day animals and insects are immured in buildings before their completion to ensure their safety. Sometimes a lamb or kid is sacrificed on the foundations of a house and its blood scattered on to the stones. Sometimes a cock is killed and its head buried in the foundations. There are many variants. They are probably survivals of heathen traditions when people believed that jealous gods only allowed people to build in return for the sacrifice of human beings.

The Hotel Putnik lies on your left as you reach the centre of Zaječar and just before the main *trg*. From the far northern side of the *trg* a street leads down to the fruit and vegetable markets which are worth visiting, especially the dairy section. A little way down on the right is a good small museum which dates from when excavations began in Gamzigrad (see below) in 1953. There are several unremarkable pictures by artists of the locality but the archaeological and ethnographical departments are most interesting. Look particularly at the Roman objects and the very complete section devoted to a Roman farrier's equipment. Elsewhere there is a superb carved wooden table and an instructive section on weaving which, of course, is done in nearly all peasant homes all over the country. There are also some examples of pleated skirts which are pressed when wet and then left for three months to set between weights.

The part devoted to **Gamzigrad** gives you a good idea of this Roman *castrum* in the depths of the countryside twelve kilometres away: a discovery to which I strongly recommend a visit. You take the road to Boljevac, branch right a little way out of Zaječar and drive up the shallow valley of the Black River. The first village you come to is Zvezdan (ruins of a twelfth-century church here) and not far beyond you see a big sign saying: '*Posetite Rimsko Grad*' etc. (Visit the Roman Castle.) Turn up and drive along the track. After half a mile bear left and quite soon you come to the ruined west gate of a large Roman fort.

Its shape is trapezoid and most of the ramparts, which had six towers on each side, are overgrown so that from a distance the area looks like a small wood. You can clamber round and over the ramparts and work out the general formation. The interior is now mostly grass with a few modern buildings (in one of which an amiable old Serbian *čuvar* lives) and several mounds under which are Roman buildings. There are some pavements visible, mosaics and the remains of baths. Part of the vestibule to the bath is intact, an octagonal chamber with a large room over the hypocaust and a larger room with an apse. All the building is believed to belong to the early Constantinian period. The mosaics are particularly beautiful: *venatori* and wild beasts fighting, a sylvan scene of a hunter with his dog, surrounded by carpet patterns. They are probably third century.

This strongpoint which lay on the main route from the Danube to Niš was probably built in the fourth or fifth century and was an important commercial centre. When the Slav tribes arrived they occupied and reinforced it and during the Byzantine period it continued to be important.

From here you have to return to the main road to Boljevac. I omit the whole of the north-eastern region of this part of Serbia, not because it is dull but because there is much more of interest to be seen elsewhere. If you do venture into it you will find that it is wild, mountainous and wooded, with fertile valleys. There are a few small towns and a large number of villages but communications are poor; and there are no antiquities of much importance. The only town of any note is Negotin, near the Danube and the junction of the Rumanian and Bulgarian frontiers. It has two simple hotels: the Beograd and the Obilić. From Negotin there is a splendid drive to Kučevo and on to Belgrade. I now follow the other route, west.

It is a fairly up and down road from Zaječar to Paraćin and you pass through several small villages. Beyond Boljevac a big mountain range rises to nearly five thousand feet away to the south, culminating in the Rtanj peak: very wild and beautiful country. On the return to the *autoput* you go due north to Ćuprija and at the flyover for Ćuprija turn right for Ravanica. I shouldn't bother to visit Ćuprija or Paraćin (see map on p. 281).

The **Monastery of Ravanica** is about twenty kilometres up the valley and beyond a pretty village. The road is not too good and becomes progressively worse. Surprisingly enough a railway line runs apparently nowhere into the hills. At last you come to the long, white outer wall with its tiled roof and high-peaked gate, so oriental that for a moment you might again think you are visiting a Tibetan monastery. It was very heavily fortified, like Manasija a few miles away, but most of the ramparts are now destroyed. Beyond the walls is a lovely paddock in which fowl strut and peacocks dander. It is the same idyllic rural scene you have found at Mileševa and Dečani and half a dozen other places.

There are a few monks here and a great many sisters, over thirty in all. It is sad there are not more monks because, quite apart from anything else, they are a perfect accompaniment aesthetically to these surroundings. If the monks of Ravanica are scholars and mystics—and as they stroll in the orchard in their long cassocks and high black hats they look very unworldly—then the sisters are the farmers and workers. Busy, skilled and friendly women they are. They make and grow everything. They even have their own carpenter's shop: a disused railway freight truck outside the monastery walls. One of them will show you round the church.

It belongs to the Morava School and like most churches in that school its exterior is highly ornamented in an intricate brickwork design, especially the cupolas, the doorways, the vaulting and the windows. A particularly good example is the rosette above the window on the west façade. If you reflect for a moment on the appearance of, say Sopoćani (p. 262) and Lesnovo (p. 242), the differences are at once apparent. Another characteristic of this school is the apse on the north and south arms. These, in conjunction with the traditional eastern apse, produce a trefoil.

The churches and therefore the paintings of this school represent the last expression of Serbian medieval art. The artists didn't create anything new but they tended to eliminate certain elements. The monumental and the narrative aspects have now gone and we are left with the decorative and the 'sentimental': a very refined, graceful and much quieter painting, what has been described as 'the art of consolation'. It must be remembered that these churches were built during the decline and disintegration of the Serbian empire, and most of them (Ravanica is an exception) *after* the battle of Kosovo.

The frescoes at Ravanica were done by a man called Constantine whose inscription you can see in the northern lateral apse. I think the best ones are on the left hand wall immediately you enter the church. They represent Prince Lazar and his wife and their two sons, Stefan and Vuk. There are a great many others, including warrior saints, the great feasts, the life of Christ and His miracles. The *Entry into Jerusalem* is a particularly good scene.

We are very lucky so much survives, because this church was devastated several times by the Turks and not restored until the eighteenth century and it was some time then that the present narthex was built and painted. In the first place it was founded by command of Prince Lazar in either 1377 or 1381 and it was here that the prince was buried after the battle of Kosovo. One of the ballads describes how it came about.

A Turkish boy found the decapitated body on the battlefield, wrapped it in a mantle and carried it to a fountain where it lay for forty years: '*Lepo vreme četrdeset leta.*' The body remained on Kosovo Polje, uncorrupted. One day some young men travelling from Skopje to Niš slaked their thirst at the fountain and found the head. They took it out but it vanished and flew to rejoin its body. Then a vast procession of ecclesiastical dignitaries came to the plain and to the accompaniment of many rituals asked Prince Lazar where he wished to be buried. They made various suggestions, all of which he rejected. Then:

> *Već on hoće svojoj zadužbini,*
> *Au svoju krasnu Ravanicu*
> *Pod visokom pod Kučaj-planinom*
> *Što je laza sagradio crkvu*

Which means roughly that he preferred his own splendid Ravanica at the foot of the high mountain Kučaj where he had built a temple to God.

However, in 1683 his remains were transferred to the monastery of Vrdnik in the Fruška Gora to the north-west of Belgrade and there they remained until the last war when they were again moved for safekeeping to Belgrade because it was feared that the Ustaše Fascist group under Pavelić might desecrate them. They now lie in the Orthodox church in the capital.

From Ravanica the best thing to do is return to the village and then go on via Senjski Rudnik to the **Monastery of Manasija** near Despotovac. The road is not good but it runs through attractive countryside and it is only about thirty kilometres. The monastery is a little beyond Despotovac and as you come to it it looks more like a Byzantine castle. In fact, the fortifications at Ravanica were probably quite similar to these. It used to be known as Resava from the stream that runs past it and it was under that name that it was founded by Stefan, Prince Lazar's eldest son, and built between 1408 and 1418.

The high defensive walls and the eleven colossal towers are very like the land walls of Constantinople but this stern exterior conceals a calm and rural paddock and a lovely church which is itself un-

Carvings of the Morava
and Raška Schools.
Above, detail of a
window in the south
façade of Kalenić monas-
tery church (see plate
on page 280). *Below*,
a church window at
Dečani, with the typical
floral and animal motifs
of the Raška School

THE DANUBE. *Above*, a quiet beach near Belgrade. *Below*, Golubac Castle, built over 600 years ago to guard a great sweep of the river. The other bank is Rumania

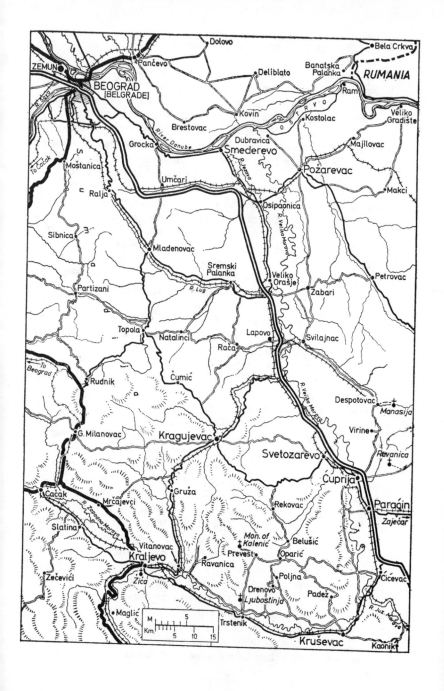

usual because, unlike most examples of the Morava School, it is largely composed of ashlar with an arched 'frill' running round below the eaves. The narthex was built in the eighteenth century because the original was destroyed by an explosion (no doubt it was used as an arsenal). The frescoes, similar in style to those at Ravanica and Kalenić (near Kraljevo), have been very badly damaged. Among the best are a big portrait of the founder on the west wall; and, in the lower part of the northern lateral apse, some impressive figures of fighting warriors. Above are compositions illustrating the life of Christ. On the whole all the figures here are large, bold and well-spaced and in this respect they are closer to the Raška School.

In the fifteenth century, under the rule of Stefan Lazarević, Manasija became one of the main shelters of artists and writers who fled from subjugated provinces and, as a distinguished Serbian scholar, Radojčić, has put it, 'Out of impotence and resignation arose an elegiac and contemplative style, which expressed itself strongly in the whole spiritual culture of society.' It looks, in fact, as if the creative forces of the Serbian artists had been used up, at any rate temporarily, by the time the Turks arrived: certainly by the middle of the fifteenth century. It seems a case of a natural conclusion to a series of developments and styles. Nevertheless, if it had not been for the Turkish occupation Serbia might have experienced the equivalent of an Italian renaissance.

From Despotovac one can return easily along quite a good road to the *autoput* via the small village of Virine. You emerge on the *autoput* just north of Ćuprija, and now there is a difficult choice to be made. You can either go back down the *autoput* as far as Deligrad and then turn off for Kruševac or go up to Svetozarevo and turn off for Kragujevac and from thence to Kraljevo, Trstenik, Ljubostinja and Kalenić—and after that back by a choice of three roads from Belušić to the *autoput*. Of course, if you have omitted the trip from Skopje to Niš and Zaječar the business is simplified when leaving from Kraljevo; and if you are coming from the north it is also somewhat simplified. The main problem in this area is that all roads leading to Kalenić are bad—but Kalenić is the most important monastery in the Morava School and therefore should not be missed.

The truth is that if you do not go to Svetozarevo you don't miss much, but if you do go there is a pleasant new hotel (the Palace), a picturesque gipsy quarter and a number of Turkish houses. So I think the best plan is to return to Deligrad (it is well under an hour's run) and then take a poor road across country to **Kruše-**

vac: a small and interesting town (the Hotel Evropa is adequate) which was founded in the 1370's and which Prince Lazar made his capital. It was not finally subdued by the Turks until long after the battle of Kosovo (in fact probably not until 1455) by which time most of the population had fled north to Hungary. For the next four hundred years it remained in Turkish hands and was ultimately liberated by the Serbs in 1833. Many other battles have been fought round it since.

The most interesting part is right in the centre where there are the remains of Prince Lazar's palace and castle and from where, according to the ballads, the armies set off for Kosovo. One of the ballads gives a most moving description of Lazar's wife trying to persuade him to leave one of her nine brothers (one of the nine Jugovići) behind when they go. There is also a vivid account of the great cavalcade leaving the gates of the city.

The castle is still being excavated and the most outstanding vestiges are a big tower and a complete church—one of the best of the Morava School. The strange part about this building is that it looks as if it might have been built in the last twenty years or so, and was in fact erected at the command of Prince Lazar in 1380 or thereabouts. This brand new appearance is not the result of excessive restoration; even the carvings, that have been untouched, are only slightly worn. The intricate stitched patterns of bright red brick and white mortar are almost gaudy. The brickwork of the windows and doorways, exquisite in its detail, is unblemished. Since the eve of Kosovo only the frescoes have been lost—destroyed very thoroughly by the Turks. But if we apply the stricter canons which govern the balance of form and decoration I think we are bound to come to the conclusion that the church is not satisfactory. There are too many arches and mouldings, too much braiding of 'petit-point' brickwork, too many scrolled pink embroideries, rosy plaits and wreathes and meticulous decussations. And all this is over-balanced by two ponderous cupolas and an excess of fussy roofs.

South-west of Kruševac, near Mrmoš and Aleksandrovac, are four more churches of the Morava school but only the most intrepid and conscientious traveller will visit them.

From Kruševac a good road runs due west to Trstenik. You must turn off for the town (it is signposted) and then drive through it and over the Zapada Morava river. (There are several signposts for the monastery.) You then take a narrow lane for about four kilometres beside a river that is usually dried up in summer and up which you

283

can drive a car. At the end of the lane is the **Monastery of Ljubo-stinja,** in a delightful setting of forested hills. It consists of a spacious walled paddock with a church, and a large number of conventual buildings, including a magnificent black and white timbered *konak*: a princely residence. Ljubostinja is quite a busy and prosperous monastery, or rather a convent now because there are only two aged monks and no fewer than fifty sisters as diligent and creative as nuns everywhere. They even have a little shop in the monastery.

One of them will show you the church which, externally, is an outstanding specimen of the Morava group; especially the upper half. Some of the sculpted work round the slit windows is masterly in its detail and delicacy. The rosette windows, similar to those at Kruševac and Kalenić, are like a fretwork of pale red lace. Only fragments of painting survive, of which the best are in the narthex. On the west wall on the north side of the door are portraits of Prince Lazar and his wife Milica; on the other side, Stefan and Vuk.

This church was founded by Princess Milica after Kosovo and built between 1402 and 1404 by a man called Rade Borović whose inscription is to be found on the face of the step below the door leading from the narthex to the naos. In the north-east corner of the narthex a secret door leads to a narrow staircase used as a hide-out and for treasure. In the naos lies Princess Milica's tomb and also the tomb of Stefan, son of another Serbian noble called Uglješu who is mentioned several times in the epic ballads. Princess Milica retired here and became a sister in company with many other noblewomen widowed by the Kosovo disaster.

From here there is nothing for it but to return to the Zapada Morava, turn left and take a series of very poor roads (forty kilometres in all) via Drenovo and Oparić to Kalenić (the road from Oparić is not too bad now). Kalenić is always something of a challenge. I have approached it from three different points and the most enjoyable, though the most arduous, was the westerly and this involves a long walk. For anyone with plenty of time I recommend it.

You take the main road from Kraljevo to Kragujevac. At Vitanovac you turn off and cross the railway and the small River Gruža. Thereafter the village to aim for and ask for regularly is another Ravanica. Amazingly enough the roads are good and about twelve kilometres from Vitanovac you turn back to the right (there is a house on the corner at the turn) and follow a narrow track. After about three kilometres you have to abandon your car at a ford and start walking. You follow the river the whole way to the head of the valley, where the stream more or less vanishes, and then cut up across the hills to the right and over the saddle. There are plenty of people about so you can ask your way regularly. Beyond the saddle you go down a valley dense with beech and finally arrive at the very beautiful **Monastery of Kalenić**. If you decide on this excursion you should allow three hours each way between Ravanica and the monastery.

Kalenić, a well-ordered and affluent place run by a large number of 'nuns', was founded round about 1415 by a Serbian nobleman called Bogdan and the church is the culmination of the development of the Morava School. Much of the exterior is adorned with polychromatic stonework and minutely carved decorations on the frames of the portals, the windows, the arches and in the marvellously intricate rosettes. A quantity of varied figures are involved with the geometrical patterns: gryphons, for example, birds, huntsmen, Samson fighting the lion, the centaur Chiron, dragons, and a splendid relief of the Virgin on the south façade of the narthex. Many of the designs are adaptations of miniature work and wood carving. Rich and complex though they are, these embellishments are perfectly subordinated to the main shape of the church.

Within, the frescoes are also subject to a strict logic and the proportions of the compositions and their figures are carefully judged to combine with the dimensions of the building in the most balanced concord possible.

On the north wall of the narthex you find a portrait of Bogdan himself with his wife Milica and his brother Peter. In front of them stands the despot Stefan Lazarević. Other scenes in this part depict the life of the Virgin. All the scenes and the sizes of the figures in the naos and apses are subtly graded (for example, they become larger and larger the nearer they reach the summit of the cupola) and there is the same delicacy and ethereal refinement in feature, posture and drapery that you have seen at Manasija and Ravanica. This is especially noticeable in what is probably the best of the paintings: the *Marriage Feast at Cana* in the southern apse. This is a most carefully constructed narrative composition. The Virgin is speaking to Christ about the wine, the two old men are in fact tasting it, three young servants are in attendance and the bride and bridegroom are performing a ritual ceremony. The groom is about to prick the finger of his bride. This signifies the preliminary to the very ancient custom of mixing blood and wine and pledging each other. It was an old Serbian custom and the primitive blood myth has survived until recently in Montenegrin rites. This apart, the outstanding features of the group are the graceful gestures and clothes, the austere elegance of every line.

The beautifully painted *warrior saints* in the naos reveal the same refinement and decorum. So do the scenes depicting the life of Christ. The significance of the warrior saints, figures of heroic proportions in armour, with swords, spears and bucklers, has been stressed by several scholars. They are in sharp contrast to the various orders of the church, especially the martyrs, eremites and apostles. They represent the secular power and they coincide with a time of peril. Their tranquillity also suggests how ineffectual they were. Some of them could be sheathing their weapons, as well they might for the Turks had been using gun-powder for some time. The honour and glory of proficiency with the sword was over. The post-Kosovo warriors look resigned.

It has been more or less established that there is a definite connection and similarity between the paintings at Kalenić and the mosaics in the Karieh in Istanbul. Always there is the emphasis on inner, spiritual values as well as on good manners.

A biography of the despot Stefan Lazarević mentions the graceful behaviour at his court. 'All were like angels and behaved with great decorum and modesty. Noise or tapping of feet or laughter or clumsy clothes might not even be mentioned and everyone was dressed in light-coloured robes which he himself (the despot) gave them.' It is an interesting footnote to the evolution of the Morava School. If the paintings of this period (and the comments of its writers) are truly representative of a new sensibility then the cultivation of polite behaviour and general refinement seem to anticipate those very influential ideas later to originate in Italy and spread across Europe which laid so much emphasis on courtly manners, on *virtù*, on doing things gracefully—ideas which produced a spate of courtesy books and etiquette books (by people like Castiglione and della Casa) which has never ceased.

However you reached Kalenić the next place to aim for is **Kragujevac**—not in fact very interesting for the casual traveller though it is a big commercial town and the most important centre in the Šumadija ('a forest land'). It was here that in 1941 the Germans executed the entire male population over fifteen as a reprisal: seven thousand in all. Schoolboys were marched out of their classrooms with their masters. The German passion for order and symmetry obliged them to bring the figures up to seven thousand by shooting a number who were not even fifteen. One of the more successful funeral monuments (by a man called Gržetić) commemorates the dead and this dreadful deed. Kragujevac always depresses me slightly, as if the atmosphere were still tainted by the crime.

Until the seventeenth century it was no more than a village but in the nineteenth it became the capital of Miloš Obrenović whose name brings us into contact with a most important phase of Serbian history. In 1804 there was a rebellion against the Turks in the Šumadija and its leaders were the local heads of families (*kneževi*). They were supported by most of the peasant population and their elected 'general' was Djordje Petrović (known as Karadjordje—Black George) a wealthy pig farmer and a man of great courage and determination. The rebellion began at the small village of Orašac and within four years the *pašalik* (an area administered by a Pasha) of Belgrade, had been regained from the Turks. At this time the Turks had their hands full with Russian designs on the Balkan empire and potential aid for the Serbs, their fellow Slavs. But when Napoleon attacked Russia all Russian troops were withdrawn from the Balkans and Turkish rule was renewed with great severity in the Šumadija. The leaders were killed and Karadjordje fled to Austria. One of the best of the main cycles of Jugoslav epic poetry is concerned with the struggles against the Turks in this period. Some ballads describe the battles very vividly, particularly the capture of Užice and Belgrade. Rebel leaders like Karadjordje were celebrated as heroes by the poets in their own time. Miloš Obrenović, a village headman, raised another revolt in 1815 and the following year Serbia, though still a province of Turkey, became more or less independent. When Karadjordje returned in 1818 he was murdered with Obrenović's connivance. This act began a bitter rivalry and a blood feud between the Karadjordjević and Obrenović families which lasted nearly a century—a typical Balkan situation. However, Obrenović was recognised as Prince of Serbia by the Treaty of Adrianople in 1829 and he decided to give back to the Serbian peasants all land surrendered (Turkish garrisons remained in towns and fortresses).

Obrenović advanced and enriched himself and his family by a great deal of bribery and unscrupulous trading and his methods established a tradition of government corruption which lasted until the Second World War. Progress was made but it was always being jeopardised by the rival families. Both claimed the right to rule and both provided rulers. There were a large number of assassinations and the Obrenović family was finally eliminated by the murder of King Alexander in 1903. Thereafter the Karadjordjević line ruled until the beginning of the last war. This is a very terse summary of a very complex period. In detail it makes fascinating if rather sombre reading.

From Kragujevac the best thing to do is to go up to **Topola,** where the Karadjordjević family lived. There are still remains of their house and its fortifications in the small town and up on the wooded hill above (called Oplenac) lies a large white marble church dedicated to St George. This curious building was founded by King Peter I (he followed Alexander Obrenović) and consecrated in 1912. The design is a mixture of Serbian and Byzantine styles and the inside is covered with mosaics done in the 1920's. They all reproduce frescoes from the famous Serbian monasteries. This is an interesting idea and there is no doubt that though it is only a kind of copying it has been consummately well done by talented craftsmen. The church is really a mausoleum for members of the Karadjordjević family. Black George himself lies in a massive marble tomb by the royal throne and near him is the tomb of King Peter I. In the crypt are several more, including King Alexander's and his mother's. This was the Alexander assassinated at Marseilles in 1934: yet another murder in the long Balkan tradition of trying to solve things by violence. Near the church you find a comfortable hotel, the Oplenac.

From Topola I suggest you go north to Mladenovac, cut across to the *autoput* at Sremski Palanka and go up the *autoput* until you find a turn to Osipaonica and **Požarevac.** The latter is a most agreeable small town on the rim of the Danube plain. It has a hotel (the Avala), a place of some character and very animated in the evenings. Near it is a good small museum which possesses a number of Illyrian and Roman remains. Its lapidarium has several sarcophagi and one enchanting little primitive Christian tombstone bearing a crudely cut cross. It was at Požarevac that an important treaty was signed in 1718 between the Austrians and the Turks. Prince Eugène of Savoy had beaten the Turks and taken Belgrade the previous year, and by the treaty the Turks ceded large areas of south-east Hungary, Serbia and Bosnia. Unhappily, the Serbs weren't very much better off under the Austrians. Local military government was harsh and inefficient and when war broke out again in 1738 the Serbs gave little support to the Austrians. The Turks recaptured Belgrade and the Morava valley, and the Danube again became the frontier of the Austrian and Turkish empires.

Above, the Neretva Gorge, on the way to Mostar. This is one of the wildest regions of the *karst* land. *Below*, Mostar, capital of Hercegovina. Hajrudin's sixteenth-century Turkish bridge spans the emerald Neretva

TOMBS. *Above*, Bogomil tombs: at Radimlje (*left*), near Stolac — one of the most important Bogomil necropolises. These coffer-shaped *stećaks* are to be found in many parts of Hercegovina. At Brotnice (right), the figures seem to be performing a *kolo*. A predatory bird is attacking some animal, and a wolf is devouring a victim. *Below left*, a typical Turkish tomb, in the Mostar region. *Right*, a *krajputaši* (peasant wayside tomb), near Karan in Serbia. The Serbian soldier, with fez, dagger and umbrella, "Miloš Jovančićević who lived 28 years"

North of Požarevac, close to the Danube, are two very ancient sites: Dubravica and Kostolac. Round **Dubravica** lie the remnants of several prehistoric and Roman settlements; and at Kostolac a big Roman camp and town known as Viminacium, probably of the first century A.D. It was the barracks of the VIIth Legion. Most of the excavated objects (like those from Dubravica) are now in the National Museum in Belgrade. At **Kostolac** you can still see the general plan of the town and fortifications but they lie on much cultivated ground. Drains running off the hill go through the village and were used as hide-outs during the war. They are large enough to negotiate by crouch and crawl and I once went about fifty yards up one. It gave one an idea of what life in the burrow is like. The entrance was covered over by a woodpile in the yard of one of the villagers' houses.

The church on the hill is a small copy of Dečani, a curious and interesting example of a modern *zadužbina*. The *ktitor* or donor, Todić, was a rich shipowner and a captain of steamers sailing the Danube. Amidst the traditional frescoes of the medieval genre are portraits of Captain Todić and his wife holding a model of the church they have founded. The worthy captain is in naval uniform and they stand against a background of the great river. After so many gorgeously caparisoned kings and queens they make an incongruous but touching pair. (The priest who lives nearby will very willingly show you the church.)

In the district of Zvižd beyond Požarevac (as in several parts of eastern Serbia) we again meet the survival of pagan rites connected with death. On All Souls' Day (in the Orthodox Church a moveable feast that falls a month and a half after Easter and usually in June) a special ritual called the *pomane* is observed for the repose of the souls of the dead. Funeral meats—food, fruit and wine—are laid on tables in the cemeteries. The mourners, in bright costume, hang long white scarves decorated with flowers down their backs and carry lighted candles stuck into small bouquets. Thus decked they perform their commemorative *kolos* round the laden tables and invite the dead to share their feast. This is a fairly merry occasion, but there is nothing macabre about it once one has dismissed the Gothic, northern and Protestant idea that it is irreverent to enjoy oneself in a graveyard.

From Požarevac you have to return to Osipaonica and then take a good main road to **Smederevo**, formerly a Roman settlement *en route* from Belgrade to Viminacium. In 1427 it became the capital of Serbia and it is to that event that we owe one of the most magnificent castles in Europe: a vast ruin on the very banks of the Danube. It is triangular in shape, with five gates, an elaborate system of moats joining the Danube and the Jezeva (it was surrounded by water), and twenty-five huge towers—as big as those on the Constantinople land walls, which they resemble. At one end is a smaller stronghold—within the greater—a palace and citadel. This nucleus has its own moat and four bastions one of which bears an inscription and the date of building: 6938; that number of years in the Orthodox reckoning from the beginning of the world; 1430 on the Roman calendar. At the apex of the inner fortress is the keep, whose walls are fifteen feet thick and in part of which a minute apsidal chapel was made, a kind of bubble in the stone. From the apex round the perimeter and back is nearly a mile and each of the three walls is approximately five hundred yards long.

From the windows of the palace hall (little survives of this) you look out over the Danube towards Hungary. The brimming river, open drain to half a continent, swirls turbidly past towards the Iron gates, the plains of Bulgaria and the blue glitter of the Black Sea. Into its depths plunge the reflections of the colossal towers, cracked, split, eroded, part of the greatest fortification of the time and, ironically enough, already obsolete as a defence when they were erected.

The castle was built with amazing rapidity in one year, in 1429-30 (a feat which rivals the effort of the Turks in building Rumeli Hisar on the Bosphorus in three months). Every piece of available stone in the neighbourhood, including a lot from Dubravica and Viminacium, was brought to its construction by order of Djuradj Branković (son of Vuk Branković) who was the Despot at the time. It was hoped that this castle would prove an invincible barrier against the Turkish advance into Europe and it was the product of what must have verged on despair. Legend has it that the peasants who built it (most of them were in an extreme state of poverty and malnutrition) had to supply thousands of eggs to mix with the mortar in order to cement the stones more securely. A strong tradition ascribes the order for the building of the castle to Branković's wife Jerina; 'the accursed Jerina' as she is referred to in epic poems and legends. She is always depicted as a tyrant who became a symbol of evil, largely because of the forced labour levied to build the fortress. A number of proverbial sayings survive from those desperate times.

In fact it took the Turks at least twenty years to subdue it and when it finally succumbed in 1459 (probably through treachery rather than assault) the surrender marked the final victory of the Turks over the whole of Serbia. They made it the headquarters of their *pašalik* in this region and it remained so (apart from a period of Austrian occupation) until 1805. In that year Karadjordje formally received its keys. Near the centre of the town an immensely old mulberry tree propped up by stonework has a plaque by it recording the event. The Cyrillic says: 'On Nov. 8th 1805 Karadjordje received the keys of the citadel.' Traditionally, the exchange was made beneath the tree. The plaque was put up in 1951.

Now the great castle contains a football ground and has become one of the main tourist sights of Jugoslavia. All that mars the enjoyment of its monumental splendour is the memory of the hardship that went to its creation.

If you want to stay in Smederevo there are two pleasant hotels—the Park and the Smederevo. They serve good food and the local wines which are renowned for their excellence—as they were in Roman times. The red and the *rosé* (Smederevska Ružica) are delicious. The white is even better. If you can manage to get some sterlet (*kečiga*), which abound in the Danube, the white wine goes uncommonly well with it.

There is nothing to detain you between here and the capital and the only village of note is Grocka where there used to be a big *han* because it was on the main route to Constantinople.

CHAPTER 18

Belgrade, the Danube and N. Serbia

*Belgrade—the Danube—Golubac Castle—Tablet of Trajan—the Iron Gates
—Sremska Mitrovica—Ruma—the Fruška Gora—Vrdnik Monastery—
Hopovo Monastery—Krušedol Monastery—Sremski Karlovci—Novi Sad
—Galerija Matice Srpske—Sombor—Subotica—Pančevo—Vršac*

Probably the most remarkable thing about **Belgrade** is that it
exists at all. In its long history it has been devastated more than
twenty times and the reason people have gone on living there is that
it occupies a vital strategic position at the confluence of the great
natural obstacles and frontiers of the Sava and Danube rivers, and
lies on a cross-roads between east and west, commanding the plains
and the entrances to the principal passes through the hills.

The Celts were among the first to fortify the site and later the
Romans built a city there. The Huns, the Goths and the Avars all
possessed it and in due course it was settled by the Slavs and
remained, with interruptions, one of the chief cities of the Serbian
state until the Turks took it from the Hungarians in 1521. Numerous
battles have been fought for it, in and round it. It is not surprising
therefore that very few antiquities survive, though there would have
been many more but for the violent German bombardment in 1941.

As late as 1918 it was not much more than a quiet and fairly
small country town, so most of what you see today is quite modern,
much of it post-war. I don't think its most chauvinistic zealot would
pretend that it is beautiful. Much of its architecture verges on the
nondescript. There are few old buildings and most of the new ones
are mediocre or ugly. Some are impressive but the majority are
typical of the packing-case geometry which has tended to disfigure
many large towns in Europe since the war. But its people are delightful: vivacious and energetic, hospitable and extremely independent
and they atone for what is really one of the drabbest of capitals. It

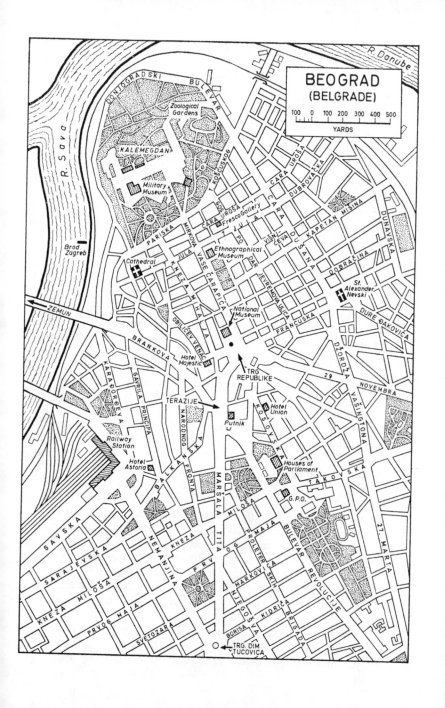

BEOGRAD
(BELGRADE)

100 0 100 200 300 400 500
YARDS

R. Danube

R. Sava

DONJOGRADSKI BULEVAR

Zoological Gardens

KALEMEGDAN

Military Museum

Brod Zagreb

ZEMUN

PARISKA

Cathedral

Fresco Gallery

Ethnographical Museum

National Museum

Hotel Majestic

BRANKOVA

KARAĐORĐEVA

GAVRILA PRINCIPA

Railway Station

Hotel Astoria

SAVSKA

SARAJEVSKA

KNEZA MILOŠA

PRVOG MAJA

SVETOZARA

NEMANJINA

KNEZA

BALKANSKA

NARODNOG FRONTA

TERAZIJE

Putnik

TRG REPUBLIKE

Hotel Union

Houses of Parliament

G.P.O.

MARŠALA TITA

MILOŠA

PROLETERSKIH

MAJA

NJEGOŠEVA

MARKOVIĆA

BORISA KIDRIČA

BULEVAR REVOLUCIJE

BRIGADA

TRG. DIM. TUCOVIĆA

CARA UROŠA

9 JULA

MIRKOVA

VASE ČARAPIĆA

JULA

KNEZ MIHAILA

OBILIĆEV VENAC

CARA UROŠA

CARA DUŠANA

DUBROVAČKA

VIŠNJIĆEVA

JEVREMOVA

ULICA

FRANCUSKA

KAPETAN MIŠINA

ĐURE ĐAKOVIĆA

St. Alexander Nevski

DOBRAČINA

DUNAVSKA

ĐORĐA VAŠINGTONA

29 NOVEMBRA

TAKOVSKA

27. MARTA

is not a place visitors wish to stay in for long, and I should think the average traveller with a three week holiday would find three days sufficient. However, it is an admirable centre for excursion and exploration.

When coming from Smederevo you enter on the long, broad Boulevar Revolucije which takes you straight to the heart of the city: the **Terazije** and **Trg Republike,** the Times Square or Piccadilly of Belgrade (*I* call it by its familiar name, though in Serbian it is Beograd—'White City'). There is, of course, a pretty good selection of hotels: grand, average and simple. The 'A' category hotels are palatial and fairly expensive and, like most of their kind, rather dull. The best of them is the Majestic, in Oblićev Venac just west of the Trg Republike. The best among the 'B' categories are the Beograd, the Astorija and the Union. I suggest that when you arrive you call at the Tourist Office in the Terazije and get all the information. In the high season Belgrade is often very crowded so you may have to take a private room which the Tourist Office will arrange. If they are shut you will have to traipse round. As a last resort (I had to use it once) there is the *Brod Zagreb,* a very old Danube paddle-steamer which is moored just north of the main bridge to Zemun. You can get a dingy cabin there for a pound. It is a squalid and insanitary old tub but it has a passable restaurant and any amount of 'atmosphere'. It is the nearest, I think, that you are likely to come to the Edwardian nostalgia of a Danube cruise.

The Trg Republike is the obvious place from which to make a tour of the city, and the most important port of call is the Narodni Muzej on the northern side of it. The big equestrian statue represents Prince Michael Obrenović who reigned from 1839 to 1868. With his right hand he is gesturing towards all those territories which at that time were still under Turkish domination. The relief-work depicts various episodes in the long struggle against the Turks.

The **National Museum** is one of the greater museums of Europe. It was founded in 1844 and consists basically of six main departments. With characteristic impulsiveness the authorities decided to shut the whole place recently for eighteen months in order to repair the roof and refurbish it. It may be therefore, despite careful verification, that some of the lay-out I mention has undergone slight modifications.

The presentation in the museum is extremely good and so it seems pointless to give a detailed account room by room. Indeed, as there are two hundred thousand exhibits even a summary treatment would run to a complete chapter. However, some indication of the contents will give you an idea of what to expect, and unless you possess unusual powers of stamina and concentration I think you should pay two or three separate visits: the first to get a general idea, the others to dwell on things which interest you particularly.

Hall I on the ground floor houses the prehistoric remains, of which the most outstanding have come from Staričevo and Vinča. The Staričevo section is the earlier and brings us down to about 2600 B.C. The Vinča period runs from then to round about 1900 B.C. They are both represented by a large number of utensils, implements and figurines of animals and human beings. It is now clear that in the late Stone Age the region of what is now Serbia was densely populated with prosperous settlements. From the Starčevo period three types of pottery survive: the first a crude form with ornaments worked by slapping wet earth on to the surface of the vessel; the second is monochromatic from light brown to black; the third type is the most sophisticated both in shape and colouring. There are a few idols, usually female seated figures. From the Vinča periods there survive bowls, amphorae and urns, and vessels shaped to the likeness of human faces and figures. Numerous idols have been left to us from this age: rather sinister robot figures with masks or images of animal heads hiding their faces. Usually the female figure is represented and animal shapes were often worked into vases. Almost certainly these crude, toy-like objects were associated with religious cult.

In Hall II you find the Graeco-Illyrian and Roman collections which include everything they found at Trebenište, Stobi and Radovište, as well as items excavated on sites in Vis and near Budva. The outstanding pieces (apart from the Trebenište vase) are some magnificent masks from Smederevo and Trstenik, a marble figure of Athene found near Bitola, a collection of bronze and silver objects, jewellery and pectorals and other treasure from St Peter's church at Novi Pazar, as well as what are the two most beautiful and precious exhibits—the bronze of Constantine and the fragment of cameo which represents a mounted Roman (possibly an emperor) of the fourth century.

Halls I and II on the first floor are devoted to the Middle Ages and this section, taken in conjunction with the Gallery of Frescoes (see below), helps to consolidate a general and comprehensive picture of Serbian art. Apart from fragments and copies you should look at some of the smaller objects: particularly the Miroslav gospel

(Miroslav was a twelfth-century prince of Hum), the Prizren transcript of Csar Dušan's Code, a double icon of Our Lady and the Annunciation from Ohrid, an icon of Sava and Nemanja, the Nativity Icon and Queen Theodora's gold ring.

The third hall on this floor is devoted to Serbian art through the seventeenth, eighteenth and nineteenth centuries. Many of the artists worked in northern Serbia and in the Vojvodina monastries in the Fruška Gora region when it was a part of the Austro-Hungarian empire. The principal members of the most distinguished earlier groups are Kračun, Češljar and Orfelin. In their work you can see the influence of the Byzantine tradition mingling with the influence of Baroque and Western art.

The so-called classical or neo-classical period is best represented by Teodorović, Djurković, Avramović and, most accomplished of all, Daniel. These artists are loosely associated with what has been called the *Biedermeierstil*, a name deriving from two fictitious characters—Biedermann and Bummelmeier—who were supposed to represent actual German philistines. The term now covers painting, sculpture, furniture and so forth which is reckoned to be representative of early nineteenth-century German art.

Next we have the so-called 'Romantic' period (which overlaps with the neo-classic) principally represented in Jugoslavia by two women: Catherine Ivanović and Mina Vukomanović; and two men: Jakšić and Teodorović. The outstanding painter from the 'Realist' school (not to be confused with the 'naturalistic') was Krstić. I recommend also a look at the so-called Serbian primitives, particularly Konstantin Arsenović, Vasilije Božić, Georgije Bakalović, Dimitrije Petrović, Živko Petrović and Arsenije Petrović. They were all working in the nineteenth century and are well represented in this museum.

In the first hall on the second floor there hangs a large collection of paintings by twentieth-century Jugoslav artists, and several works by Meštrović and Rosandić. In the second hall, a very valuable collection of pictures by painters mostly from France, England, Germany and the Low Countries. The French section is easily the richest and nearly all the main nineteenth- and twentieth-century artists are represented. The principal Englishmen are Steer, Sickert, John and Nash.

When you have recovered from this marathon in one of the popular open-air cafés in the *trg* go up Vase Čarapića which runs along the eastern side of the Museum. Some way up on the right, just beyond some public gardens, you come to the **Ethnographical Museum** which is also excellent. It shelters a comprehensive collection of costumes, weapons, ornaments, boats, utensils and maquettes of characteristic Serbian houses—indeed everything you might expect.

On leaving here take the Ulica Mirkova, a continuation of the Čarapića, and turn down Cara Uroša Ulica a short way along on the right. A minute's walk brings you to the **Fresco Gallery.** The copies here (they are very accomplished) are continually being added to and the assembly is now most impressive. You will recognise many of them at once and they are all clearly labelled so there is no point in going round item by item. The great advantage of this gallery is that in an hour or two one can see some of the best examples of each school and period and, because they are so near each other, compare and contrast without effort and note the main features of change and development.

From here go on down the street and turn right into Gospodar Jevremova Ulica. Almost in front of you is the sole survivor of the original thirty mosques (which gives one an idea of the destruction to which the city has been subjected) a seventeenth-century building named the Bajrakli Džamija (it means 'the flag mosque') because the signal for the hours of prayer was given from here by waving a flag.

Go on down this street and at no. 19 (it may have been altered) you find a large Balkan-type house which is now a theatre museum and has quite an interesting collection of old programmes, photographs, sketches of sets, models and so forth which give one some idea of developments in the Serbian theatre. The Serbian theatre didn't really become established until early in the nineteenth century and then largely as the result of the efforts of one man: an ambitious and hardheaded writer called Joakim Vujić who founded a theatre at Kragujevac. Later Vujić organised a company at Novi Sad and in Belgrade. Jovan Popović and Anastasije Nikolić were the leading native authors, and Popović was a kind of Serb Molière. A tradition was established (and just maintained) through a most disrupted period. By the end of the nineteenth century a large number of Serbian dramatists, none of whom is known outside the Balkans, were writing comedy and chronicles in verse and prose. Since the upheavals of the World Wars the Serb theatre has slowly re-established itself.

Immediately beyond is a big house that was formerly occupied by a pasha and his harem. It has been restored but retains the *haremlik* and *selamlik* divisions. Now it is devoted to the memory of the Serbian scholar Vuk Karadžić (see p. 254), whom I mentioned in connection with the epic ballads, and contains a lot of his letters, books, pictures, furniture and personal belongings.

Karadžić, an extraordinary and fascinating man, was the creator of the modern Serbian language and orthography. He was born in the small village of Tršić in west Serbia in 1787 and to his life's work applied the motto of a schoolmaster: 'Write as you speak, read as you write.' He laid the foundations of the modern literary language and grammar of the Serbs based on the speech of the people. After a long struggle this replaced the archaic, official literary language derived from Old Slavonic which was unintelligible to most people. Very few Serbs in his time were literate, and he had to contend with the most deeply rooted prejudice and philistinism of those who were against any kind of reform. He was much hated and persecuted by most civil and religious institutions from the Prince downwards.

He taught himself to read and write and though there was scarcely a book in his village he did it so well that he couldn't even remember the time when he was illiterate. His first teacher, a relative, told him to mix some gunpowder with water (how symbolic that is of Jugoslav history!) and copy some letters on to a sheet of paper. Laboriously he learnt. Then he acquired a primer with pictures in it and carried it with him wherever he went. Whenever he saw someone who looked as if he might be literate he would ask whether or not he was reading particular words correctly. By the time he was sixteen he was the best-educated person in his region.

In his life he achieved virtually single-handed what in other countries it has taken numerous institutions and generations of scholars to attain. Apart from his major works, his Serbian dictionary, grammar and orthography, he published many volumes of folk poems, tales, proverbs and historical studies.

He was an invalid most of his life and all this was done not only against hatred and persecution but for much of the time in poverty approaching destitution. Eleven of his thirteen children died before he did. But he had a fine wife and his most talented daughter, a beautiful girl and one of the few cultured Jugoslav women of those times, became a painter. She was Mina Vukomanović, whose work you have already seen in the National Museum.

In his way Karadžić is the intellectual and literary counterpart of those national heroes whose weapon was the sword rather than the pen. Like them he showed indomitable valour and tenacity. Like them he would have died rather than yield to his enemies, and towards the end of his life his efforts were rewarded by international recognition and the membership of numerous academies and learned societies.

Go on from here and then turn right up Višnjćeva. A short way along you find one of the few relics of Turkish occupation in the shape of a *turbeh* built about 1873. It is a rather pathetic remnant, with its broken windows and dusty furnishings, yet, judging by the number of dinar pieces scattered on the floor, it still has power to move the hearts of some faithful.

You can get back to the 7 Jula Ulica from here via the Ethnographical Museum and having struck this street again turn left and continue for several hundred yards west. You will eventually see on your right the Orthodox Cathedral and, the far side of the street, the ugly Patriarchy inhabited by a large number of those bearded priests who always look much too urbane and sinister for their calling.

The neo-Baroque **Cathedral** was built during Prince Miloš's reign about 1845 and contains a number of interesting objects. The fine iconostasis was made by Dimitrije Petrović. The icons and paintings are by Avramović. There are several tombs, including those of Karadžić, Prince Miloš, Uroš V and Prince Lazar.

There is a side entrance to the Patriarchy Museum a little farther along 7 Jula Ulica. The collection here, as you might expect, is largely religious. There are many icons, MSS. and vestments. One of the more precious objects is a robe that belonged to Prince Lazar.

Shortly before you arrive at the cathedral you may have noticed a rather handsome Balkan-type house with tables and chairs outside it. This is the **Cafe?**, a quondam focus of Bohemian life and much frequented by artists, writers and actors. It is one of several interesting cafés in Belgrade. The others you should try are the Three Hats (Tri Šešira) and the Skadarlija.

The Café? was first built in the 1820's by a man called Naum Ičko and afterwards bought by Prince Miloš who made a present of it to a man who had healed him of serious wounds. This man, Hećim Tomi, decided on the cumbersome name of Café by the Church of the Holy Synod. The clergy over the way were offended by this and orders were sent to have the blasphemous sign removed. The sign-painter replaced it with a question mark—which remains.

This is a good spot at which to refresh yourself before the final assault on the Kalemegdan fortress, a complex of park, gardens and fortifications that occupies many acres on the bluff immediately above the junction of the Sava and the Danube. Its higher points afford the most magnificent views across the great river and the green luxuriant plain that merges imperceptibly with the sky in the dusty haze on the rim of the horizon and stretches for hundreds of miles up into central Europe. The ideal time to be up here is early in the morning or towards sunset. The watershed of the Danube is immense. It drains half Europe before it runs into the Black Sea, and when you gaze across the broad, swift waters of the river you feel the authentic movement of fear and respect that great rivers always inspire: a feeling well conveyed by Eliot at the beginning of *The Dry Salvages*. And the Danube is never blue. It is brown, sullen and implacable.

The **Kalemegdan** is one of the biggest fortified networks in existence and it is almost impossible to provide accurate directions for getting about it. However, an hour's stroll will give you the lay-out and a vivid impression of an area that contains a large number of interesting items—including a zoo, two small churches, some deep Roman wells, an art pavilion where they have regular exhibitions of contemporary work, several busts of famous Serbs, a huge monument in honour of France by Meštrović, and the moated Citadel itself where originally there stood a Roman fort and then a medieval fort. Nothing of the forts remains and what we see today was put up by the Austrians early in the eighteenth century.

Outside it, in the moats and elsewhere, are a number of tanks and guns which are part of the collection belonging to the **Military Museum of the Jugoslav People's Army.** The bulk of this museum is housed within the formidable ramparts of the citadel. It is a brilliantly imaginative and comprehensive piece of work; in fact, a work of genius, though obviously the result of the combined efforts of a large number of people of exceptional ability. As a military museum I doubt if it has an equal; regarded just as a museum it must be among the best anywhere. The historical sequence is presented in the most masterly narrative exhibition I have ever seen, and though its theme is war it is in effect a history of Jugoslavia. A tour of it requires a considerable effort of concentration and you should allow at least three hours for a general impression. Then you can return and look at sections that interest you particularly. Let me stress also that it is not just of interest to men. I have seen women somewhat apprehensive of such a masculine theme, but soon, like most children over, say, thirteen, they are spell-bound and remain so.

I have been round it several times and each time have come out wiser, weary and, strangely enough, deeply moved. Not the usual reactions of a veteran museum campaigner. The point is, I think, that the exhibition combines the range and momentum of epic narrative and the relentless logic of tragedy in such a way that the senses and emotions of the spectator, all the faculties, are brought to a state of the keenest expectation and total absorption. It is the *last* room that is the culminating stroke of inspiration. It might spoil it to give away the end of the plot, so to speak, and thus I merely say it is an unerring gesture of pride which is consistent with everything that has preceded it.

After this one definitely needs a drink and from here I suggest you make your way to the north-eastern point of the outer fortifications where you find an agreeable open-air café. From such a point the Roman sentries first saw the gathering multitudes of the bar-barians on the far side of the river, just as, fifteen hundred years later, their Slav successors saw Hitler's Stukas screaming down out of the sky.

Near here, below the fortifications (accurate directions are almost impossible) there are two small churches: the Ružica, once a Turkish arsenal and then transformed into a church in 1830 (not the usual order of things); and Sv Petka, formerly a place of pilgrimage because of its miraculous reputation. If you continue round to the right from here you soon discover a rather impressive Baroque gate-way named after Prince Eugène of Savoy and erected in 1717 to commemorate an important victory against the Turks. From here the best thing to do is to go down the Cara Dušana. If you walk south along this for about five hundred yards you arrive at the modern Byzantine church of St Alexander Nevski. Its white marble iconostasis is worth looking at.

After this cut back up the Francuska Ulica which brings you to the Trg Republike, which in turn gives on to the Terazije: the main shopping centre. The Bulevar Revolucije forks left from this very soon. On the left you see the Houses of Parliament (more or less opposite the former palace), the G.P.O. and a garden on the farther rim of which is a curiosity in the shape of a modern church, Sv Marko, designed like Gračanica. The rest of the southern part of the city is not likely to be of much interest to the average visitor.

There is one excursion from Belgrade which you should not fail to make, and that is a trip down the Danube. A fast hydroplane (it turns in a steady thirty knots) leaves from near the Brod Zagreb most days of the week at six in the morning, goes all the way down to the famous Iron Gates and brings you back about six in the evening. You must book a seat for this well in advance at the Tourist office.

You used to be able to go as far as Prahovo, well beyond the gorge, but now, unfortunately from the tourist's point of view, they have built a dam in the gorge and so the trip is curtailed[1]; nevertheless it is still an exciting trip. I retain the bulk of my original description for what it is worth.

The river has always, of course, been a vital line of communication and commerce and you still pass a variety of barges and paddle-steamers of several nationalities: Bulgarian, Rumanian, Jugoslav and even Russian. This is the true cloak-and-dagger country of the Balkans. It is easy to imagine Richard Hannay hiding in one of the timber barges or one of Smersh's men drawing a bead on an escaping diplomat.

At Smederevo you get a magnificent view of the castle (it looks even better from the river) and not long after that the river becomes very wide (sometimes it is well over a mile broad) and there are several large islands. Ostrvo, for example (it means an 'island') is about twelve miles long! On the southern banks here you may spot the ruins of a sixteenth-century castle called Ram. After Banatska Palanka the river becomes the frontier between Jugoslavia and Rumania and soon the plains are left behind. The hills become higher, wilder and very, very gradually, over a distance of about sixty miles, the river narrows. (For map see p. 303.)

After Veliko Gradište there is another big island, the Moldava, and then you come to **Golubac** (it means 'a dove'), a superb ruin of medieval Serbia. High on a rocky point above the dun, swift river its nine ruined towers and crumbling machicolated ramparts rise in lonely splendour. It is the most haunting of all Jugoslav feudal strongholds. The Romans first built here and there are numerous legends attached to it. It belonged to Serbian noblemen and was inhabited until the Turks were finally ousted.

Not far beyond the castle, but scarcely visible from the boat, there are big grottoes, known as the mosquito caverns, which are a kind of hatchery for these creatures. From this damp womb they hum forth every spring in millions.

[1] You now disembark near the dam and take bus to Kladovo.

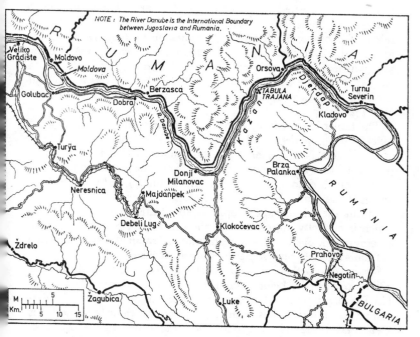

NOTE : The River Danube is the International Boundary between Jugoslavia and Rumania.

After two small ports, Dobra and Donji Milanovac,[1] the river narrows increasingly and you enter the great defile of Kazan ('the cauldron'). The mountains rise to nearly two thousand feet and the yellow-brown waters swirl faster and more sinister. The whole defile is extremely dangerous because of the rapid currents, and whirlpools whose murky depths are inhabited by the famous sturgeon which weigh anything up to five or six hundred pounds.

From now on keep a sharp eye open for the **Tablet of Trajan,** low down on the right. This has been raised high up the mountain

[1]Fourteen kilometres north-west of Donji Milanovac, in a recess on the river bank, at Lepenski Vir, archaeologists some years ago discovered a very important neolithic settlement. It dates from 4500 BC to 5100. Examination of eight different layers of settlement suggests that it was inhabited by a well-established fishing and hunting community. There was no evidence of agriculture or stock-breeding. A large number of trapeze-shaped houses were discovered. In the floors were solidly constructed hearths. There were also a number of skeletons and fifty-four curiously sculpted boulders. Some were sculpted into animal forms, some were merely linear; the majority were human heads. This remarkable site has now been submerged by the dam.

303

side.) It was erected by order of the Emperor Trajan in 102 to mark the completion of a Roman road that was begun in the reign of Tiberius in 28 and to commemorate Trajan's campaign against the Dacians. The road was a great feat of engineering and you used to be able to see the holes in the rock into which were driven huge beams to support it. In effect it was a road cut from the lower faces of the mountain and in parts actually hung out over the water.

The tablet is beautifully carved but unfortunately one passes too quickly to see the details. What it says is: 'The Emperor Caesar, son of the divine Nerva, Nerva Trajan Augustus Germanicus, great pontiff, tribune for the fourth time, father of the country and consul for the fourth time, has conquered the mountain and the river and opened this road.'

I think there is a grand simplicity about this imperial inscription which is perfectly appropriate to the surroundings and to the task accomplished. Farther down, at Kladovo, Trajan also built a bridge but unfortunately only some piles of this survive.

Some way farther on you reach the **Iron Gates** themselves (Djerdap) shortly before the river re-emerges into the plains. The Djerdap is a most dangerous rapid, impassable to boats. Therefore part of the river has been canalled on the right bank and this stretch takes the shipping. However, the water rushes down so violently that the boats have to be towed up the canal by locomotives on the rails alongside.

Kladovo (which has a renowned caviare factory) is just beyond Djerdap and the best thing to do is to disembark here. The journey down to Prahovo is rather dull, so you can have a meal in Kladovo and pick up the boat on its return trip. Prahovo itself used to be important and was probably the site of Trajan's town Decelbalum.

The immediate surroundings of Belgrade are worth exploring. **Topčider Park,** to the south, can easily be reached by tram and is a good picnic spot. Other objectives for the excursion are provided by the former residence of Prince Miloš, now converted into an interesting museum; and in the eastern part of the park there is a pretty church once used as a royal chapel. Outside it stands a fountain known as Miloševa Česma.

Beyond Topčider is another park, the Košutnjak. The fountain near the entrance is called the Hajdučka Česma, once an assembly point for rebellion. The monument farther on marks the spot where Prince Miloš Obrenović was assassinated in June 1868. The wooded heights to the east of here belong to the suburb of Dedinje, a region of handsome residences in spacious gardens. On the highest point is Marshal Tito's home—the **Beli Dvor** or white palace, well guarded by smart soldiers.

About eight kilometres south-east of Topčider (the tram takes you all the way) is the eighteenth-century monastery of Rakovica which was destroyed by the Turks and has been much restored. One of the 'nuns' will show you round and in all probability offer some *slatko*. The tomb in the church belongs to one of the more celebrated *vojvode*, Vasa Čarapić who died in the 1806 rebellions against the Turks.

Farther south-east still is the wooded hill called Mt Avala, a popular pilgrimage and picnic spot among the Belgrade people. There used to be a Turkish fortress on the summit and in its place there now stands Meštrović's **Monument to The Unknown Soldier.** The black marble caryatids that support the mausoleum represent provinces of Jugoslavia. It is regarded by many Jugoslavs as one of Meštrović's greatest works.

The other side of the dun-coloured Sava, a river that appears to be full of the city's ullage, lies **Zemun**—which I find rather dull. Originally a Roman settlement and then a fortified medieval town it is now almost a suburb of the capital, a very big suburb of well over 100,000 people. It possesses two comfortable hotels (the Grand and the Central) which are useful in the emergency of an over-crowded Belgrade. The most interesting buildings date from the eighteenth and nineteenth centuries and there are two churches worth looking at: Nikolajevska, erected in the late 1720's, with an iconostasis by Bačević which reveals a tolerably successful blend of traditional Serbian painting with a decorative Baroque; the little church of Our Lady is late eighteenth century and has an iconostasis by Teodorović.

On the way to Zemun, away to your right, on low-lying, swampy ground, in the angle made by the junction of the Sava with the Danube, stand high rusting skeletons of steel—an abandoned project and the result of an imprudently calculated post-war prestige gesture. When the edifices had reached their present stage it was discovered that their foundations were of sand. A Belgrade wit labelled them the 'Temples of Bureaucracy', and by this name they are known. Ozymandias would have appreciated their futility.

From Belgrade one can make a most interesting trip round northern Serbia, the Vojvodina and the Pannonian Plain and see all the main sights in about four days. It is very flat here and very fertile and most of the main roads are good. The autonomous **Vojvodina** (the 'dukedom') is a very mixed land ethnically, composed of Serbs, Croats, Slovaks, Ruthenes, Rumanians, and large numbers of Hungarians for at one time a considerable part of the plain belonged to Hungary. In fact the Vojvodina is almost a microcosm of Central Europe.

I suggest your best plan is to go straight up the *autoput* towards Zagreb and turn off for **Sremska Mitrovica,** known in Pliny's time as Sirmium and formerly one of the main cities in the Roman Empire. Several Roman Emperors lived here and no fewer than four were born here. The Avars did their work particularly efficiently but laborious excavation (which is still going on) has revealed a great many Roman remains, many of which are in the archaeological museum in Zagreb. On the spot in the centre of the town —which is an untidy, dusty place of considerable character—are the remnants of Roman baths and an early Byzantine basilica. Sremska is a rewarding place to wander round for an hour or two.

Farther south of Sremska, on the Sava, in the midst of very fertile countryside, lies Šabac: a medieval town in origin where Mehmed II built a big fortress in 1470 which was to be a base for his advance into Croatia. A good deal of it survives despite several battles for it between the Turks and the Serbs. Like Sremska, Šabac is a pleasant town in which to pass a morning or so.

From here you return and recross the *autoput* and go up to **Ruma,** a very typical Serbian town of the plains. None of these towns and villages makes any attempt to compete with or assert itself against the vast expanses in which they lie. Space being no object many of them are laid out on a rather monotonous grid pattern of straight, intersecting roads and have spread and spread until the main street of a village may be as much as three miles long. The modest single-and two-storied houses are often built end on to the streets and lie in big gardens. The colour schemes of pale Wedgwood blue, beige, yellow and green are subtly varied and the walls, doorways and windows are very often decorated with traditional patterns in white. The spaciousness typical of the towns and villages is echoed in the patterns of the countryside, in the immense fields (sometimes hundreds of acres in extent) of maize, corn and sunflowers which ripple and undulate for miles beneath the vast, over-arching canopies of sky. In proportion, too, are the herds and flocks. Herds of horses a hundred and fifty strong are not uncommon. Equally big are the flocks of sheep. Flocks of geese run into thousands. And the pigs are uncountable: rank after rank of chop and rasher, sounders of gammon in black, pink and grey. It is worth being in one of these villages towards sundown when the livestock is brought back for the night.

Ruma, like Sremska Mitrovica, was the site of one of the earliest prehistoric settlements and nearby there was another large Roman town called Bassiana. Thanks to the Huns virtually nothing remains. Just east of the main cross-roads in Ruma (which has an agreeable hotel called the Srem) and on the road to Novi Sad there is an entertaining little village museum illustrating the Celtic and Roman periods, local crafts and the Partisan revolution. As so often in these country museums there are numerous photographs of local men and women who were executed by the Germans or the Ustaše.

To the north, clearly visible from Ruma, stretches the **Fruška Gora:** a long, fairly low range of hills, covered with thick forest, that runs east-west for about seventy kilometres. The forest harbours many deer, wild boar and wild cat, and the lower fertile slopes, that dwindle into the plain, produce large quantities of excellent wines. It is one of the loveliest parts of Serbia: a fact the Orthodox Church was early to appreciate, for on it and round it are twenty or more monasteries—the main concentration being on the southern slopes. There is little point in trying to see more than a few of these and among the more interesting are Vrdnik, Remeta, Hopovo and Krušedol.

From Ruma you take a dusty road across the plains west towards Radinci and after eight kilometres turn north to Jazak, running parallel to the railway which goes up to Vrdnik and stops. At Jazak there is a monastery with two churches, one in ruins. The survivor that dates from 1736 has a fine iconostasis by the eighteenth-century artist Bačević. Six kilometres farther north on a poor road you reach **Vrdnik,** built some time in the sixteenth century and then restored by monks from Ravanica in 1687. It was to here they brought Prince Lazar's body. The monastic buildings have now been turned over to an asylum and hospital (this has happened to several north Serbian foundations) but there is still one charming old priest called *pop* (very aptly to English ears, though *pop* is the

Serb for 'priest') who will show you the church built about 1801 to 1811. Its iconostasis was made by Avramović who also did some paintings in the cupola.

From here there is a short trip on a poor road to Irig (marvellous views over the plains from this vantage point) a small and pretty village on the main road from Ruma to Novi Sad. Turn left here and quite soon you find a signpost on your right to Novo Hopovo.

In 1541 Sremski Karlovci became part of a Turkish *pašalik* and the Serbs who had fled began to resettle in the region. With the restoration of the Patriarchate of Peć in 1557 the Orthodox Church began to consolidate its position as best it could. A number of monasteries in and round Srem were restored and rebuilt and one of these was **Hopovo,** whose church reminds one of the Morava School. The twelve-sided dome encircled by colonettes is a beauty and there is much rich decoration on the exterior of the rest of the church. Most of the paintings that survive were done in the first half of the seventeenth century, very probably by Greek artists from Mt Athos and Crete. The best frescoes are in the narthex.

From here return to the main road and then to Irig. Take the road to **Krušedol** and the big monastery founded in the sixteenth century by a nephew of Djuradj Branković who ruled Serbia for about ten years and later became an archbishop. The church, surrounded by spacious monastic quarters, contains the tombs of a number of princes and Serbian patriarchs, and the paintings, considerably under the influence of Baroque, were mostly done in the eighteenth century. Some of them are interesting but few are comparable with the medieval art.

Remeta, about three kilometres north of Krušedol, is a much earlier foundation and tradition ascribes it to King Dragutin at the end of the thirteenth century. Unhappily most of its paintings were ruined during the last war. The road on joins the main road to Novi Sad which brings you to **Sremski Karlovci** on the banks of the Danube, one of the most attractive small towns in Serbia. It used to be the seat of feudal lords but there was little more than a village here until late in the sixteenth century. In the eighteenth it became the cultural capital of the Serbs and of the Vojvodina. A number of nineteenth-century painters were born here and worked in the region and the town has never quite lost an air of modest sophistication.

When you arrive in the centre which consists of a tree-shaded

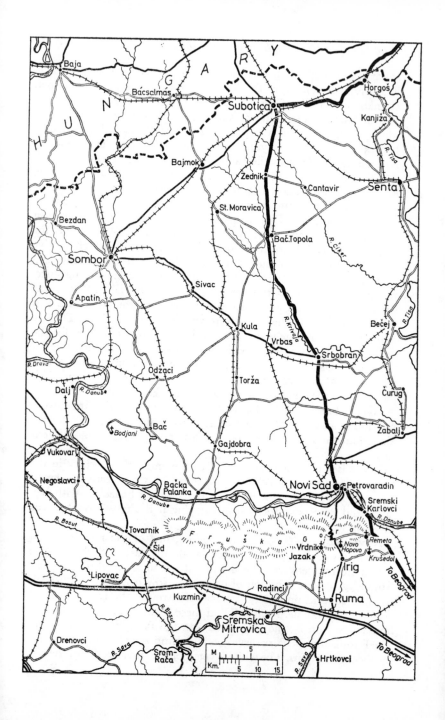

square, you might well be in a small university town in Provence. The irregular oblong of the *trg* (named after a famous Serb poet, Branko Radičević, of the 'Romantic' period) is adorned by a red marble baroque fountain and surrounded by a series of very handsome Baroque buildings: a palace, a cathedral, several magnificent houses and the neo-Byzantine patriarchate. The iconostasis by Kračun and Orfelin in the cathedral is well worth looking at, and so is the museum (in the patriarchal palace) which has an interesting ethnographical section devoted to the neighbourhood. There is another small museum devoted to Radičević just off the square.

This region of the Danube plain was the site of some of the most ancient human settlements in Europe; partly because of this the Vojvodina has folklore traditions of great antiquity which survive vestigially in certain customs. Many of these, as in most rural communities, are associated with the main natural cycles. For instance, in the Bačka area (at the north-western end of the Fruška Gora) the harvest festivals are accompanied by numerous dances and a procession whose leader wears a crown made of ears of corn. The *kolo* dancers used to pour water over each other to ensure rain for the next sowing. Other rain invocations include a dance when there is a drought. Usually a group of girls dance from house to house and while doing so sing songs which are also prayers for rain. This particular ritual had one very interesting feature (now, I believe, no longer done). The Dodola, the chief performer in the ritual, wore no clothes but was clad in leaves, flowers and grass. She danced alone and the householders poured water over her; a kind of libation.

There is a curious part parallel to this in England—Jack in the Green, a feature of the chimneysweepers' May-day festival, when a figure is covered with a frame of basket-work bedecked with ivy, holly and flowers so the person carrying it is almost invisible (see p. 354).

Novi Sad, capital of the Vojvodina, one of the most civilized Serbian towns, has played a very important part in Serb life since the eighteenth century. The fact that it was nicknamed the 'Serbian Athens' gives one a notion of its status. Now it is a big industrial, commercial and university city scattered round the Danube and if you want to stay here you will find three friendly and quite efficient hotels: the Putnik, the Vojvodina and the Park, all in the centre. The Putnik and the Park serve good food and wine and I recommend the local *vins du pays*. The white is very golden and refreshing; the red strong and metallic, excellent with grills. The region also produces a sweet sparkling wine called Biser, and several dessert wines.

As you come in, and before you cross the river, you pass a huge castle up on your left: **Petrovaradin.** It is part of a separate township of the same name and has a network of fortifications which rival the Kalemegdan and the Tvrdjava at Niš for size. It is nicknamed the 'Gibraltar of the Danube.' The Romans had a fortress here and various additions have been made since the Middle Ages but most of what you see now is early eighteenth century. Its dungeons have held some distinguished prisoners, among them Karadjordje and Marshal Tito. Part of its buildings are being converted into museums and there is already a terraced café and restaurant high above the Danube; an ideal spot to dine on a summer's evening.

Petrovaradin is an important place in the history of the wars against the Turks for it was here that Prince Eugène of Savoy trounced a Turkish army in 1716. Even the Janissaries were outclassed and great spoils fell to the victors. They included the Grand Vizier's tent, a canvas so vast it would have accommodated Bertram Mills and needed five hundred men to pitch it.

Some of the more successful modern building and town planning is to be seen in the centre of Novi Sad, and in addition to several churches there are two first-class museums: the Muzej Vojvodina and the Galerija Matice Srpske. The first has an instructive archaeological collection, sections devoted to the history of the town and a natural science department. The **Galerija** is one of the most important in Jugoslavia and contains an excellent representative selection of the Vojvodina artists.

The ground floor is devoted to copies of frescoes, mostly from the monastery of Bodjani, a fifteenth-century foundation beyond Bačka Palanka towards the north-western end of the Fruška Gora and worth visiting if you have plenty of time. The paintings here were done in 1737 by a prolific and successful itinerant artist called Žefarović, and are interesting because they illustrate some of the coarser and more decadent features of a stylised tradition. In many ways they are almost a form of commercial art, but they are also an attempt to modernise the traditional. The influence of Baroque is at once obvious and the emphasis is secular, as, for instance, in his pneumatic and *decolletée* ladies who look very like Turkish odalisques. Žefarović, who made a lot of money, would have made even more as a paperback cover designer.

On the first floor most of the pictures are by eighteenth-century artists. On the left hand side of the long landing there is a fine seventeenth-century *John the Baptist*, and on the right an *Annunciation* reminiscent of that in Sv Kliment. In the long room parallel to the landing (Room I) you find a number of paintings by Teneski. The self-portrait, third on the left, is outstanding. Turn right out of the long room (Room II) and here you find an interesting *Christ* and *St John the Baptist*. In Room III there is little of note, but in the next room the anonymous *Crucifixion* on the left wall, primitive and clumsy though it be, is a powerful work. There is nothing to detain you in the fifth room.

From here return, re-cross the landing and at the end of the corridor on the left you will notice a copper engraving of Dečani done in 1746. In Room VI, off this corridor, I recommend you to look at the *Annunciation* immediately on your left and the *Virgin and Child* on the main long wall. The seventh room is rather dull, but the eighth has two good Virgin and Child pictures. In Room IX there is a wonderfully bad painting of a prince on a pink horse killing what might be a Turk.

The second floor is devoted to the nineteenth-century artists. Room I contains some accomplished portraits by Radonić, especially three on the left hand wall, and a number of rather poor paintings by Jakšić. Room II is mostly Simić. The portrait of his mother on the right hand wall is the best work. There is nothing much in the next room but in the fourth there is a curiosity in the shape of a melodramatic *Calvary* by Aleksić. The fifth room has nothing of note.

From here re-cross the landing again to Room VI where there is a good portrait of a girl by Djurković in the far right corner. The seventh room has an admirable group of portraits by Aleksić and the eighth is devoted to Daniel. The painting of a young woman (second on your right on entry) is one of the best portraits in the gallery. In the next room there is a self-portrait by Katarina Ivanović.

After Novi Sad I suggest you make a quick tour of the northernmost part of Serbia by going first to **Srbobran** and **Sombor**. The former is a small town with a pleasant Orthodox church and a rich iconostasis by Radonić. The latter is a delightful place: a green and prosperous country town and once an important centre under the Turkish régime. There are a lot of Hungarians here (the biggest minority in Serbia) and you will notice that Serbian and Hungarian are used in all notices. The hotel Sloboda lies near the centre and you can eat quite well here with the excellent white and *rosé* wines of the district.

Round the main square you will find as handsome a group of public buildings as you are likely to come across in a provincial town. They include a palatial town hall, a big *konak* that was the summer residence of the Belgrade Pasha, a museum with an ethnographical section and a picture gallery, and a big *turbeh* transformed into a Catholic church; not to mention a large number of lovely houses round and about the *trg*. It is well worth spending half a day or so in Sombor. Or even a day if you want to potter in the locality. Given luck there may be a horse fair going on somewhere nearby, for this is a very horse-conscious part of Jugoslavia, and such an event is not to be missed. Covered wagons, *fiacres*, gigs, buggies, traps— every conceivable kind of horse transport is driven in and the whole scene is like some extraordinary mixture of point-to-point, Tattersalls and a rodeo which needs the Faulkner of *Yoknapatawpha County* to do justice to it.

From here there is quite a good road across the steppe-like plains to **Subotica,** one of the largest towns in Jugoslavia, where the Hungarian element and influence are even more apparent. Apart from the ornate and bizarre town hall with its coloured tiles and a good archaeological and ethnographical museum (it is difficult to believe that Gaudí did not design this) there is not a great deal of outstanding interest. If you are inclined to stay here put up at the Palić hotel, named after the nearby park and lake (which form part of a popular spa in the parkland) or at the spa itself in the Jezero or the Park, the kind of sombrely grand *fin de siècle* establishment in which secret agents take cyanide or conceal the microfilm in a stuffed paprika. The food here is good, and try a local speciality: *erdeljski drveni tanjir*—numerous meats served on a wooden dish. Sample also the local red wine, Skadarka, and a strong white called Cigani Baro.

After this make for Horgoš and Kanjiža. South from Kanjiža you pass through an area that used to consist of hundreds of square miles of marshland. From Senta there is a rather poor road to Kikinda, another quite large town which possesses an interesting small museum. It was close to here that they discovered the ancient Slav town of Gradište. The road on to Melenci and Zrenjanin is good. Mile after mile the plain repeats itself: vast, hypnotic, monotonous; yet never dull. Five hundred golden hectares of wheat succeed a

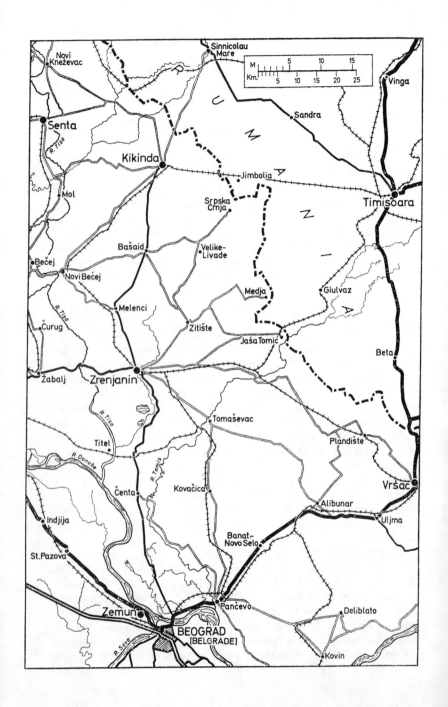

miniature steppe of rustling maize. Savannas of sunflowers incline to their orb. Vine, vegetable and fruit multiply the pied tessellations of an enormous mosaic veined and flecked with blue.

Zrenjanin is worth stopping at for a few hours. It has several fine nineteenth-century buildings and a good ethnographical museum. The main road west from Zrenjanin crosses the River Tisa and some of the most desolate marshlands of the Pannonian plain. Should you go this way look out on your right for a war memorial not far beyond Aradac. From the midst of a wild lacustrine reach three spectral figures rise in gaunt silhouette against the sky. They symbolise death yet also imply the possibility of life. It is one of the most successful monuments in the country.

Another possible trip from Belgrade (this can be encompassed within two days) is round the region immediately to the north and east of the capital. You cross the Danube and take the road to **Pančevo,** twenty kilometres away, an important commercial town. The Hotel Sloboda in the main *trg* is a congenial place which serves adequate food and good red *vins du pays*. The local white wines tend to be rather etiolate.

The original town was medieval. During the Turkish occupation, it became an important centre of Serbian culture and two of the more famous Serbian artists, Teodorović and Arsenović, were born here. In the eighteenth century it was occupied by the Germans and in the following century by the Hungarians. It still possesses a number of distinguished buildings, particularly the Narodna Pivara (The People's Brewery). The town museum was (they were threatening to move it recently) almost immediately opposite the Sloboda, the other side of the square. It is worth visiting for its archaeological and ethnographical sections.

A mere seven kilometres away (ask for directions at the hotel) is the monastery of **Vojlovica,** built at the end of the fourteenth century. This is the oldest monastery of the Banat, as this region is called. The icons and pictures are mostly by eighteenth- and nine-teenth-century artists.

From Pančevo I suggest you take the quite decent road south-east to Kovin: a small pretty town inhabited by a mixture of Serbs, Hungarians and Rumanians; a very ancient site. From here you can drive on poor roads over the Danube plain to Bela Crkva (White Church) founded by the Germans in the eighteenth century.

After Bela Crkva strike north to **Vršac** which possesses a good hotel (the Srbija) and two churches worth looking at: the Uspenska and the Saborna with iconostases by, respectively, Teodorović and Djurković. Among the secular monuments the main item is the building known as the Kuća kod Dva Pištolja (House of the Two Pistols). The story behind this bizarre name is that Karadjordje took refuge here in 1804. He had no money to pay for his lodging so he settled his account with two pistols. These are still to be seen in the museum which has modest ethnographical and archaeological sections.

High to the east of the town is a volcanic hill—one of the peripheral knobs of the Carpathians—topped by the ruins of a late medieval fortress. From this vantage point one gets a magnificent 'aerial' view over the Danube plain. In winter, the locals tell me, the wolves come down from the Carpathians to raid the flocks, and even cross the frozen Danube to prey farther south.

From Vršac there is a well-surfaced road back to Belgrade. On the way you pass near the town of Alibunar and then through Vladimirovac which is the starting point for Deliblatska Peščara, a vast area covered with fine humified sand, the most unusual range of dunelands: in parts they rise to a height of seven or eight hundred feet. The region is rich in flora and is well known for its game. In fact the whole of Banat has a great variety of fauna.

There is nothing to detain you between Alibunar and the capital though you may be lucky, as I was once, and see a gipsy cavalcade with covered wagons, horses, wild dogs, droves of irrepressible children, and performing bears. There were several of these. Two snoozed comfortably amidst the pots and pans and bed-rolls on the carts; two others, huge and woolly, padded amiably along behind their masters.

CHAPTER 19

Central Jugoslavia

Slavonski Brod—Djakovo—Osijek—Čačak—Ovčar-Kablar Gorge— Požega—Arilje—Titovo Užice—Višegrad—Drina Canyon—Ivo Andrić —Goražde—Foča—Rogatica—Sarajevo—Ilidža—Neretva Gorge—Mostar —Radimlje—Počitelj

On the whole I think one wants to avoid the Danube plain west of Belgrade. The region has many interesting villages and small towns but the roads are usually rather poor and the trip up the *autoput* is most monotonous unless you are in a hurry to reach home. However, if you *do* go straight up the *autoput*, **Slavonski Brod**, just under half-way to Zagreb, provides a useful stopping place. The Park Hotel is adequate but there is nothing much to interest you in the town —whose site was once a Roman settlement. Almost nothing survives.

North-east of here, the other side of the *autoput*, is the town of **Djakovo**: the former episcopal seat of Bishop Strossmayer—of whom more in the next chapter (see p. 360). There used to be a Roman town here on the route between Sisak and Sremska Mitrovica. Bosnian bishops controlled it in the thirteenth century and they remained until 1526 when the Turks captured it. When Djakovo was liberated from the Turks in 1687 only thirteen houses were inhabited. When the town recovered it again became a diocesan seat and eventually, in 1882, a cathedral was designed and built by Baron Schmidt, the greatest of the nineteenth-century neo-Gothic architects. It is a colossus of red brick with three apses, a cupola and two steeples, and seems to me more harmonious internally. The frescoes, by a father and son called Seitz, are lavish examples of their genre. The most interesting is the picture of SS Peter and Paul in the main apse. This also shows Bishop Strossmayer kneeling and holding his foundation: the cathedral. In the garden nearby are the remains of a Turkish fortress and a mosque now transformed into a church.

Thirty-five kilometres north-east of Djakovo you come to the only other town of importance in the region—**Osijek**. Though a pre-historic site and subsequently a Roman town founded by Augustus it has few antiquities. However, it has been the seat of a bishop since the second century and it possesses a number of palatial buildings, a Gothic cathedral and an impressive castle in a park. Anyone interested in the manufacture of matches should definitely visit Osijek for here are the main factories.

Some way to the north-west of Slavonski Brod is Slavonski Požega, a pretty market town with a thirteenth-century Franciscan mona-stery and small museum. Apart from this there is little to divert you as you go on up the *autoput*.

As no visit to Jugoslavia would be complete without seeing some-thing of Bosnia (and especially Sarajevo) it is much better to take the road south from Belgrade to Čačak, via Lazarevac and Rudnik (see map on p. 325). Once again you pass through the Šumadija, where the mountainous and forested region of **Rudnik** is particu-larly beautiful. The outward fairness hides a deep wealth: this has been one of the main mining areas since the Middle Ages.

The Rudnik region is ideal for walking and you can give yourself various objectives: for instance, in the village of Ramača, the church of Sv Nikola built by a priest and his son in the fourteenth century. The frescoes have only been restored very recently and there is a good sequence of scenes illustrating the life of the saint. The Veliki Stura peak, about three thousand feet high, makes another goal. There is a big castle on it, as there is on Mt Ostrovica. The latter is in a much better condition.

Čačak lies on the Zapada Morava river (western Morava) and it was round here that Miloš Obrenović and his men fought some of their fiercest battles against the Turks. In Čačak itself there is an interesting small museum in a house that belonged to the Obrenović family. As you come into the centre of the town you find a church on your right and two streets beyond the triangle. Take Csar Dušan street and very soon you will see a handsome Serbian style *konak* with a coat-of-arms on the wall. Within are furniture, pictures, costumes and so forth.

In the Šumadija region (especially round Čačak) and on the Zlatibor massif south of Titovo Užice you will see a large number of peasant tombstones, known as **krajputaši,** a form of folk art

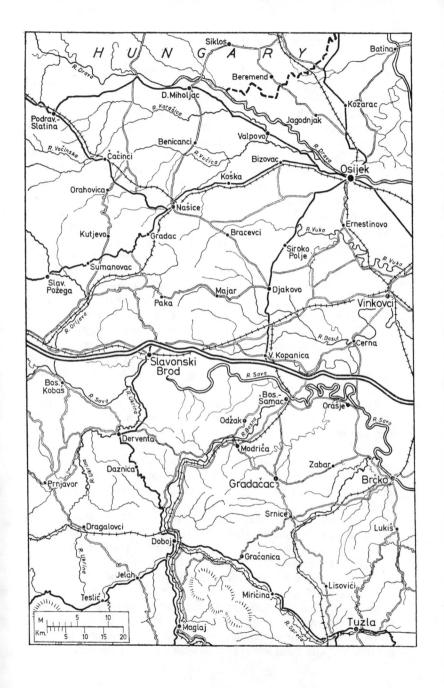

peculiar to these areas. Many of the villages have cemeteries of them, but solitary monuments are to be found in fields and on the roadside—hence the name *krajputaš* which means 'a waysider'.

Sandstone is the material commonly used because it is easy to cut and takes paint well. Many of the stones are gaily adorned in blues, reds, greens and yellows. The craftsmanship of the stone-cutters is as vivid in its crude and naïve way. The stiffly hieratic postures of the figures are at times reminiscent of Byzantine mosaic and medieval fresco. In some cases they are closer to the traditional figures on Bogomil tombstones.

Very often a complete human figure is carved, and there are numerous subsidiary details of decoration: grapes, leaves, cattle, wheat, flowers, birds and so forth. Large numbers depict soldiers killed in the many rebellions and wars the Serbs have waged. Soldiers usually have a rifle and other weapons. An artisan is shown with a hammer or some appropriate tool; a schoolmaster with a book; a publican with tankards; a woman with a distaff . . . I have seen one of a woman with an umbrella, and another near Čačak beautifully carved, with, among other items, a playing card showing the ace of clubs, scissors, a tape-measure and a ponderous Singer sewing-machine. Singer, in bold Cyrillic (СИНГЕР) inscribed on the apparatus. Somebody should sing a song of tribute to the ubiquity of this machinery.

The tombstones nearly always bear epitaphs in prose or verse which reflect a wide variety of sentiments and views on life: from the gay to the sardonic, from the grief-stricken to the optimistic. They often include quite lengthy accounts of the person's life and the manner of their death. Here are some examples:

1. 'Mileta Maričić . . . fell for Serbian freedom in his 26th year at the Krstac position, killed by the Austro-Germans in 1914. May God rest his soul . . .'

2. 'She was met by that devil Milan who with scythe in hand killed her here in cold blood. May God rest her soul. The memorial to her is erected by her sorrowing son Marko, daughters Stojanka and Dušanka in 1954.'

3. 'Here I lie while you read. But it would be better if you lay here while I did the reading . . .'

In the hill country south of Čačak (an area known as Dragačevo) there are several interesting villages with a long tradition of weaving and knitting, a cottage industry for which a surprising range of ma terials(apart from wool) is used—corn silk, for instance, hemp,

Above, near Otočac (Croatia, near Plitvice). These black crones are Croats, but women spinning like this are common throughout the country. *Below*, harvesting in the Bela Krajina (the White Borderland), the only part of Slovenia where traditional costume is still in normal use

A typical Slovene mountain valley, in the north-west near the frontier. The peak is Jalovec, 8,670 feet

wild vines, creeper and forms of grass—to make anything from hats to bedspreads. The motifs of the *krajputaši* re-appear on cloth, rafia and wicker-work.

From Čačak there is a good road to Požega (not to be confused with Slavonski Požega) and Titovo Užice. On the way you go through the rugged **Ovčar-Kablar** gorge cut by the Morava. Here another constellation of a dozen or more monasteries shelters under the precipitous rock faces. Small, hidden, remote, they date from post-Kosovo times when the monks chose the most inaccessible regions in order to elude the Turks. In this cœnobitic retreat one understands the loneliness and austerity of the truly ascetic life.

The monastic churches are a mixture of the three main styles already established because the monks built according to the designs they already knew. They formed a little religious power house which now has an imposing profane counterpart in the gorge in the shape of a huge hydro-electric installation.

The most accessible of the churches is Blagoveštenje above the Ovčar spa. You can also reach Sv Nikola and Baznesenje where they once found the beheaded skeleton of a monk who still clutched a key in one hand. It had belonged to the church which he had founded and which the Turks destroyed when they executed him.

You won't find much to occupy you in Požega, though it has a good market on Saturday, but I recommend you digress here to **Arilje,** a village with a very pretty, pink, cupolaed church in the Raška tradition founded by King Dragutin in 1292. You will notice that it has elaborate frilled arcading of small arches within other arches, another sign that we are nearer to the Romanesque style. The exonarthex was added later but nearly all the paintings are thirteenth-century and are particularly interesting historically. Astrapas is believed to have worked here in 1296. The narthex has an excellent portrait of King Dragutin holding a model of the church. Beside him are Milutin and his wife Katelina. These figures, larger than life, have a particular place in the development of Serbian portraiture. You will notice that founder and ruler are almost oblivious of Christ. The glorification of the head of state, richly and royally attired, is more important. Near Dragutin are his two sons: Urošić and Vladislav, both unlucky youths. The former died very young; the latter attempted unsuccessfully to take the throne from his cousin Stefan Dečanski. There is also a big composition showing the council of Stefan Nemanja, and a number of portraits of the Nemanjić dynasty. But easily the best composition to my mind is *The Annunciation* on the pillars of the naos: the angel on the left hand, the Virgin on the right.

Arilje is seldom visited so if you do go there (and it will be more accessible in the future because of a new road) you may as well see the place thoroughly. There are several other paintings worthy of scrutiny: for example, the *Sacrifice of Abraham* on the east wall of the narthex, and the monumental *Tree of Jesse* on the west wall. It is one of the earlier examples of this theme in Byzantine art. The motifs in the naos are traditional. In the lowest zone the place of honour is given to St Achilleus (a Roman soldier who became a Christian and was martyred with his companion Nereus) the patron saint of the church, beside Christ. You should also look at the *Adoration of the Sacrament* and, above it, the *Communion of the Apostles*. One interesting detail in the latter is that Judas appears as the leader. Usually it is St Paul. The diaconicon contains paintings showing the life and miracles of St Nicholas.

In many of these frescoes you will easily be able to distinguish the 'naturalistic' elements combined with the monumental style typical of the Raška School. Some scholars think there is a definite connection here between the tradition of the Comnenes and the later Palaeologue era. The layman can see for himself that the architectural detail and background is much more naturalistic. So, in some cases, is the treatment of the figures. This is more noticeable in the Communion of the Apostles, the Betrayal and the Transfiguration.

It is very probable that the fresco painters employed by King Dragutin were faithful to the older and more stylised tradition of the late twelfth-century and early thirteenth-century Comnene period, but at the same time were trying to experiment and make their own laws. It must always be remembered that this art was oriental in its hieratic arrangement: God goes there, the Virgin there, the apostles here, their hands and clothes thus . . . It was all as elaborate as the ceremony and protocol of eastern potentates and, I should think, without a parallel in the culture of Western Europe. Indeed, apart from cricket (Asian in its devious subtleties) the nearest analogies I can think of are the *Nō* Theatre and Chinese Classical drama whose presentation has been established and remained more or less unchanged for centuries. As in iconography, position, gesture and expression are prescribed by rules of great antiquity.

From here return to Požega and press on with a good road to

Titovo Užice, a large and quite prosperous town in splendid mountainous scenery. It has an obvious importance strategically, as it had during Roman times. During the battles against the Turks in the last century it was virtually destroyed but now it has been rebuilt and the town centre provides a most rewarding example of modern Jugoslav planning at its best. On a Saturday you will find an entertaining market.

It was in this town that Tito set up an H.Q. in 1941 and it was from here that the Partisans made a famous withdrawal across the Zlatibor Planina in the winter of the same year. A massive statue of the eponymous hero of that particular epic adorns the main *trg*. When you see the rough, shaggy hill-men with their indestructible women riding in on their all-wooden bullock carts (even the very chocks are made of wood, as they were a thousand years ago) you get an idea of the calibre and strength of the Partisans. After all, for a long time many of them had only their bare hands and farm implements to fight against the best-equipped military machine the world had ever known. And those were the weapons they used. Their deeds, like those of the *hajduks*, are celebrated in epic lays which, if you are fortunate, you may still hear recited by *guslari*.

Beyond Titovo there is a hair-raising and memorable journey to be made on a bad road across the Zlatibor mountains, a trip which provides marvellous views over Bosnia and Montenegro before you wind down into the Drina valley and come to Višegrad.

Višegrad is more or less famous because of its bridge, immortalised by the Bosnian writer Ivo Andrić in his novel *Bridge on the Drina*, in my view one of the outstanding works of fiction of this century. Višegrad itself is an attractive village with two small mosques, one with a wooden 'lighthouse' minaret. Its **bridge** is one of the noblest spans you are likely to see. It is not perfectly symmetrical for it has four and a half arches one side and five and a half the other and so the parapet or *kapija* is slightly off-centre, but its honey-coloured stone, its massive piers and graceful arches combine an elegance and strength which it is worth going a long way to see.

It was begun about half-way through the sixteenth century (there is a masterly account of its foundation and growth by Andrić) and finished in 1571. On the *kapija* there is a plaque saying: 'Bridge built by Mehmed Paša Sokolović in 1571. Severely damaged by the Germans in 1943. Restored between 1949-52.' Mehmed Paša was the Turkish Vizier. There are numerous stories associated with it and legend says that during its construction twins were immured in its central pier to ensure its safety. But the master mason had pity on them and their mother and left slits in the pier so that she could feed them. In memory of the mason's compassion a thin, white, milky stream has flowed from the slits for many years. Men used to scrape off the traces and sell it as medicinal powder to women who could not give milk after they had borne a child.

From Višegrad, or much farther up at Foča, it is possible to make an exciting excursion by raft and canoe. The lumbermen have been using rafts on the Drina for centuries and a good deal of logging still goes on. Now they have properly organised raft trips for tourists. The full trip to Zvornik takes two days. There is a certain amount of danger involved but the navigators are very skilled men. Between Višegrad and Boljević you pass through a terrain of canyons and wooded mountains that is grandiose and wild. Eagles pern across the lofty precipices; bear rove in the forest.

Between Višegrad and Goražde the **Drina Canyon** becomes even more like part of the Canadian Rockies. Road and railway, toy-like encroachments, twist and loop from one side of the green glitter of the river to the other. Sun-shafts split the forest crests and fall in long criss-crossing beams to the depths of gladed colonnades. The river narrows. The defiles become steeper. Little disturbs the profound silences except the burble of water in a shallow or the plonk of an axe on trunk.

The elegant minarets of Goražde rise from stone and wooden houses near a site that was once Roman; and in the nearby village of Sopotnica there is a fifteenth-century Orthodox church that was actually built on the foundations of a Roman house which in the Middle Ages had become a necropolis.

Thirty kilometres south of Goražde, still following the Drina, you reach **Foča,** an important trading centre in the Turkish régime and now becoming a modern town. But it still has several mosques, a *han*, a clock tower and an impressive Muslim cemetery. You should certainly have a look at the arabesqued Aladža mosque, one of the most graceful and urbane creations of the best period of Bosnian Muslim architecture.

South of Foča lie the Zelengora Mountains and the Sutjeska Gorge. East of the gorge rise the peaks of Maglić, Studenci and Vlasulja—all nearly eight thousand feet high. It was in this region that another epic legend was created by the Partisans. There were twenty thousand of them against five divisions of fully-equipped

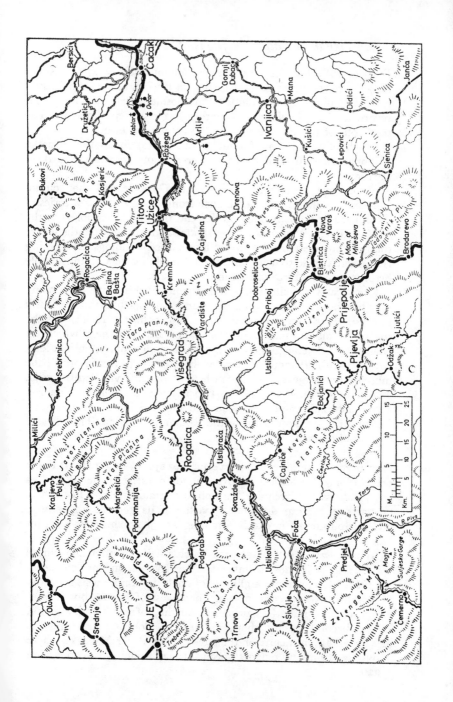

Fascists with full air-cover. They fought their way across the Sutjeska to the north and escaped with the loss of nearly half their men. Tito himself was wounded. The Bosnian poets have long since recorded their exploits in another cycle of epic poems. The traditions of the Homeric bards are as alive as ever.

Much of this region (about 40,000 acres) forms the Sutjeska National Park, in which are scattered many memorials to dead Partisans.

From Foča I suggest you return to Goražde and then climb, spiralling, to Jabuka: an eminence from which one has a series of incomparable views. Then you descend through beech forest to the Prača valley, a chasm of amber shades and sun-shot depths where the grey boulders are the size of four-storied buildings. Everything is on such a scale that it seems a land made for acts of improbable heroism and the birth of legends.

Rogatica was quite important during Turkish rule and many *Begs* had houses there. It has deteriorated somewhat, though it still possesses several mosques and an Orthodox church. It occupies the site of an old Roman settlement called Bisinium near which, at Glasinac, archaeologists found a prehistoric necropolis with at least twenty thousand tombs. Many of the objects recovered are in the museum in Sarajevo, which can best be reached via Podromanija. The most exciting part of the trip is from this village. You rise across a broad wooded plateau and higher still to five thousand feet and the topmost point of the Romanija Planina. Then begins a gradual descent.

One needs something in reserve for **Sarajevo,** but really it defies description. The answer is to see it for oneself. In detail it does not please as the irregular harmonies of smaller places like Ohrid or parts of Prizren do, but, by virtue of its general appearance and surroundings, it excels anything you have hitherto seen inland.

'Where East meets West' is a much used and often inaccurate epithet but it is most suitable for Sarajevo—it means 'palace in the fields.' One catches a glimpse of one's first minaret as far away as Bosanski Novi in the distant north-west of Bosnia but it is at Sarajevo that you find an authentic mingling of orient and occident. It has become a city about as large as Bournemouth and lies in a broad amphitheatre on the banks of the River Miljačka where it bubbles from the narrow gorge through which you come from

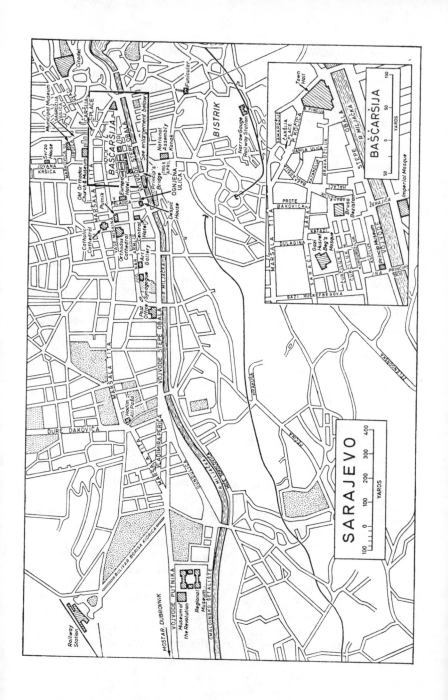

Goražde. East to west the river runs shallowly and sometimes red under a series of elegant bridges and thence into a wide valley along which modern Sarajevo is gradually spreading. Round and above hills rise to five thousand feet. If you climb some way up one of these and look down it becomes clear why Sarajevo has been described as the fairest city in the Balkans. It is a vision of a suburb of Xanadu. From amidst the gardens and orchards, the parks and medleyed rooftops of old Turkish houses, rise the minarets of nearly eighty mosques. A more careful scrutiny reveals the odd sky-scraper and factory chimney, and other symbols of that policy of westernisation the state has pursued so vigorously: for example, London double-decker red buses and Green Line coaches.

You need at least two days for Sarajevo and you have a good choice of hotels. I usually stay at the Central or the Evropa; preferably the latter, in Jugoslovenske Narodne Armije Ulica. To reach it you turn right just beyond the third bridge as you drive along the Vojvode Stepe Obala beside the river. It is a comfortable place, a little expensive, but the food is good and it has a terrace and garden which are one of the main centres of social life in the evenings. It is pleasant to sit here for an hour or two with Turkish coffee and *šlivovica*, listen to the band and singers and watch the youth of Sarajevo twist, creep, madison, mash-potato, or whatever the current craze may be. The singing, like the songs, will probably have variety, but you are more likely to hear national songs and music in remoter parts. The Bosnian love-songs, the *sevdalinke* (the word is Serbian, based on the Turkish *sev*—meaning 'love') are like the songs of Moorish Spain and are especially beautiful and haunting. They evoke a vanishing, if not a vanished, age and the singing of them was an intimate art a world away from pop and crooning. They were composed to be sung in the old houses of the *Begs* and if you saunter late among the antique Turkish houses and spacious gardens thick with plum and lime you may still hear some fatalistic voice lamenting the pangs of unrequited or disprized love.

East of the Evropa's garden and the old city walls which are illuminated at night, the minaret of **Gazi Husref Beg's Mosque** rises with ethereal grace, and next to it a rather remarkable seventeenth-century Turkish clock tower: one of the best preserved in Jugoslavia. The characters on the clock-face are in Arabic letters. This is very rare now and probably unique in Europe.

Gazi Husref, one of many enlightened and civilised *Begs*, was governor of Bosnia in the sixteenth century and it was he who ordered the building of the mosque in 1530. The architect was Sinan, the greatest of the Muslim architects. The courtyard in front of it is planted with trees which shade a fountain; nearby are two *turbehs*: one contains the founder, his secretary and adopted son; the other the first administrator of the mosque, Murad Beg Tardić.

The mosque itself, the finest in Sarajevo, is a square, monumental mass crowned by a flattened dome which rests on an octagonal drum. Two smaller cupolas adorn the portico whose ogival arches are supported by slim marble columns. The whole structure gives a completely satisfying effect of grace and strength. Within there is the same austere beauty relieved by sumptuous rose-coloured carpets.

If you stay in the Evropa or nearby you may well be woken at dawn as the *muezzin's* sinuous invocation winds its way into your sleepy brain . . . 'God is great . . . There is no God but Allah.' It seems that nowadays only the larger mosques give the five daily calls to prayer.

Gazi Husref was responsible for several other buildings, more especially the *medresa* (a religious school) next to the mosque and built in the style of the *medresas* in Istanbul during the reign of the great Sultan Mehmed II. Its roof and many squat cupolas are made of lead, hence its name Kuršumlija; like the ruined *han* in Skopje.

The only other mosque of special note is the Imperial Mosque which stands almost opposite, just the other side of the Miljačka. This was founded in 1450 by another governor, Isa Beg, burnt in 1480 and rebuilt about 1565. In front of it is a building which contains Husrefs Beg's library, and behind it stands the old *Konak*—former palace of the Turkish governors and now the seat of the National Assembly of Bosnia-Hercegovina.

Before we discuss any more sights I think it is essential to say a few words about the formation of the **State of Bosnia,** for its history is very different from Serbia's.

The Sarajevo district, like the rest of Bosnia, has a record of human activity dating from prehistoric times when there were scattered settlements of which many traces survive. It was touched by civilisation when it formed part of the Roman Empire under Tiberius and was subsequently settled by Serbs and Croats. Out of barbarism, in what is still a wild and impenetrable land covered by over five million acres of forest, feudalism grew. In the fourteenth century the site of the citadel to the east of the city was topped by a castle, Vrh Bosna, belonging to Bosnian lords. Below it a litter of houses developed. When the Turks invaded they founded the town of Sarajevo beneath the fortress—though its name is not mentioned before early in the sixteenth century.

Much earlier than this the Catholic and Orthodox churches had collided in their attempts to convert people and establish their respective faiths. The antagonism was unresolved well over eleven hundred years later. In the last war members of the two faiths murdered each other in thousands. Many Jews were murdered by Fascists.

While the faiths conflicted in the late Middle Ages **Bogomilism** spread and it seems that a strong desire for an independent Bosnian Church developed some time during the twelfth century. It was hoped that such a church would rid them of both Catholic and Orthodox factions. Bosnia first became an independent state under King Kulin (1180–1203) himself a supporter of an independent church and possibly a Bogomil. Bosnia continued to be more or less independent for well over a century and a half but it never became properly unified because of continual civil war between rival lords. During this period Bogomilism established itself thoroughly and became the Bosnian Church. In fact, early in the thirteenth century the only priests in Bosnia were Bogomils. The Bogomils were attacked and persecuted by the Catholic and Orthodox Churches but one group of Bosnians, under the leadership of a nobleman called Stefan, decided to set themselves up in a separate kingdom in the mountains to the south. Stefan made himself *Herceg* or duke and this explains the existence of Hercegovina.

When the Turks invaded Bosnia round about 1400 they were welcomed by many Bosnians and the Turks offered protection to the Bogomils and full liberty to practise their religion provided they regarded themselves as Muslims and not Christians. Thus the Bosnian feudal lords became Bosnian *Begs* (or *Beys*) primarily as a means of keeping their estates. Many of the peasantry followed their example; but not all. A minority of Catholic and Orthodox Christians survived and became *rayah*. As a result of all this the Slav tradition of Bosnia has evolved along two broad lines: one Christian, peasant and rural; the other Muslim, aristocratic and urban.

By 1482 most of Bosnia and Hercegovina had become a Turkish province with a feudal system. From 1451 to 1553 Sarajevo was the residence of the Turkish Viziers and its central situation at the crossroads of the main routes through Bosnia ensured that it would prosper. From it ran the old military road, the Stambul Djol, all the way to Constantinople. Under the Muslim *Begs* it became a luxurious city with a reputation for civilised hedonism, and a spirit of gaiety which is still alive. But it was the Slavs converted to Islam who remained largely in control. The Pasha of Bosnia himself was not allowed to stay more than one night in the city and the province was governed from Travnik, fifty miles away. Even the Janissaries, the Sultan's Praetorian Guard, were Slavs and a law unto themselves. When Selim III and Murad II tried to disband them they survived in Sarajevo and were not dealt with till 1828.

During the seventeenth and eighteenth centuries the feudal system in Bosnia became more and more corrupt and inefficient. The ruthless exploitation of the peasants led to repeated revolts against Turkish and Slav officials and against the Janissaries who had acquired estates. By 1875 South Slav nationalism was well developed in the Balkans and Serbia was anxious to liberate Bosnia and Hercegovina. But Serbia needed the help of Russia. However, Russia decided that Serbian rule in Bosnia-Hercegovina would not help her intentions. The Russians fought the Turks in 1877 and beat them but at the 1878 Treaty of Berlin Bosnia was assigned to Austria. It is not difficult to imagine what the Bosnians felt about that.

Though Austrian rule was better than Turkish, hatred against it increased steadily and was promoted by the nationalistic fervour of the South Slav peoples. On June 28th 1914 (the feast of St Vitus (Vidovdan) and the five hundred and twenty-fifth anniversary of Kosovo) a young Bosnian called Princip took up his position in the crowd in the street and shot dead the Austrian Archduke Franz Ferdinand and his morganatic wife.

One of my earliest recollections of Sarajevo is seeing three men taking photographs of a section of pavement in this street which leads to Principov Most (Princip's Bridge). Closer examination revealed that the subject was a pair of artificial footprints in the stone: in short, the spot where Gavrilo Princip is believed to have stood when he fired the shot that precipitated the First World War. A few paces from here are the plaque and small modern museum— The Princip Museum—which commemorate the assassination of Franz Ferdinand and the movement of the Young Bosnians against Austrian domination. It is a slightly *macabre* room which contains, among other gloomy relics, the assassin's waistcoat and photographs of hanged men. To the Jugoslavs Princip was a patriot whose action led to the downfall of the Habsburg empire and to the

331

eventual liberation of the Jugoslavs. He and his companions are still venerated and on 28th June each year there is a considerable ceremony at their tombs in the old Orthodox cemetery.

From all vicissitudes and alien dominions the people of Sarajevo, like the Bosnians in general, have emerged pretty well undaunted. But Bosnians, like their neighbours the Montenegrins, have always been a particularly proud and independent people and they are among the best fighters in the world. Bosnia itself, which is about the size of Wales, is a natural home of resistance and during the last war was the centre of guerrilla activities. In Sarajevo there was an extremely efficient underground organisation. You might say, in fact, that Princip's gesture of defiance was symbolic of an established tradition.

At the angle where Ognjena Ulica joins the Vojvode Stepe Obala stands the **Despić House** (no. 2), an important piece of domestic architecture and the kind of house that affluent merchants would have lived in. The oldest part is seventeenth-century but most of it is and looks nineteenth-century as a result of restoration. Its furnishings and decorations give one some idea of the taste and culture of bourgeois Serbs.

A little east of Husref Beg's mosque you find the **Baščaršija,** the most typically oriental part of the city. Here, in an agglomerated maze of narrow streets and alleys, of tiny tumbledown shops and rickety wooden booths, an ancient and traditional way of life and commerce is maintained. One may easily while away whole mornings sauntering round it, watching the copper-smiths and silver-smiths, the pastry-cooks and tailors, the cobblers and leather-workers and saddle-makers and a dozen other kinds of craftsmen. Many of the items made by the metal-workers are in traditional designs of which you will see variations in the museums, like the brass Turkish coffee pots (the *džeže*), the broad copper pans (*tepsije* and *sahani*) and the bulging, lidded ewers called *djugumi*. There are many other items which you can buy—and they are quite cheap. You can also see carpets bought and fezzes being ironed, filigree worked and *opanci* made, and sit for hours drinking Turkish coffee. It is a bright gay place that swarms with a variety of people. There is everything from superb hillmen in red and striped turbans, braided belts and gusseted homespun breeches, to young men in mass-produced suits and shoes very like winkle-pickers. Some of the townsmen are already beginning to acquire the etiolate appearance and slouchy posture of Western corner boys. But, of course, they can read and write. Clerk's blood runs in their veins. Yet most of them are a pleasure to look at. Like the Hercegovinians and Montenegrins they are very tall and handsome. So are many of the women, who wear a greater variety of costume. There are Muslim women in bloomers worn, so legend has it, lest a male descendant of the Prophet should touch the soil at birth; Catholic peasant women in voluminous black trousers and boleros; Orthodox women in the black robes of a Sophoclean chorus. The Muslim women have been deprived of the veil (*zar*) by government order but here, as in so many other places, they retain the kerchief which they draw across their mouths. Many villages round Sarajevo have distinctive female costumes. Some wear breeches like the men's, others, bloomers and chemise dresses with hip-length sleeveless coats of blue or black embroidered with symbolic designs. They often wear wine-red or dark blue scarves and their belts are also interesting. Sometimes they are of gold and filigree with buckles and rosettes, or velvet with leaves and crescents of silver filigree worked on them. After a few hours one begins to sort them out. . . . In short, the Baščaršija is a place of endless interest and diversity where you may even hear Spanish spoken by descendants of Jews who fled from Spain during the Inquisition. And I am assured by experts that if you are fluent in Tamil the gipsies here will understand you.

In this congestion is the **Brusa Bezistan,** a covered market and one of the most graceful examples of Turkish architecture. It was built by command of the Grand Vizier Rustem Paša (a relation of Sultan Suleiman I) in 1561. It used to be the market for silks and brocades brought from Brusa in Asia Minor at the foot of the Turkish Olympus. Now it is used for less exotic purposes like the sale of cheese and butter. Apropos of that, I am told that by local custom, on Ascension Day, in many villages round Sarajevo, the milkman scatters milk at the morning milking to increase the yield from his beasts.

Just on the north side of the Baščaršija is the old Orthodox church which the Turks allowed provided it was invisible to the eyes of the faithful. This church of the Holy Archangels was therefore surrounded by a high wall, one side of which still stands. It is a tiny, dingy, sixteenth-century building whose woodwork and numerous icons are smoke darkened, but it possesses an extraordinary atmosphere of peace and spirituality. On his feast day the patron saint's hand is shown to the congregation after the morning service. Lying on cotton-wool on a copper tray it is carried in by the sacristan and laid on a table beside a huge vessel of water. The reliquary is then dipped in the water. The people fill cups, glasses, bottles, mugs and what not with the now holy liquid and either take it away or drink some of it on the spot.

At No. 6 in the Jovana Kršiča (you can reach it via the Sagrdžija Ulica and the Markovica Ulica from the north of the Čaršija place) stands the **Svrzo House,** an outstanding example of Turkish domestic architecture from the second half of the sixteenth century. Now a museum, its rooms are furnished much as they used to be and give a memorable idea of the ease and good taste of the affluent under the old régime. They also show the organisation of a Turkish household with the various divisions between the *selamlik* and the *harem,* the receptions room, etc. There is a guide if you want one.

On the way back from here it is worth spending an hour in the **Municipal Museum** which is conspicuous in the Sagrdžija Ulica. It is an unmistakably Moorish-type building of the very late nineteenth century. The atrium and ground floor contain an exhibition which depicts the economic and cultural history of Sarajevo from neolithic times to the end of the Turkish occupation. The Municipal Museum taken in conjunction with the Regional Museum the other end of the town give one a comprehensive survey of the past.

East of the Baščaršija quarter the Museum of the Revolution and the National Library are housed in the Town Hall, a large, ugly and ostentatious building by Wittek in Spanish-Moorish style. It was here that Franz Ferdinand received an address of welcome on his last day. It came shortly after a bomb had been thrown at him and shortly before Princip squeezed the trigger. The Archduke stood no chance that day. There were several other assassins waiting to nail him.

There are two other interesting parts at this end of the city. High above the Baščaršija rises the **Citadel** which has Turkish gates and ramparts and has now been converted into a barracks. The whole quarter round and beneath it is very largely Muslim and possesses the most beautiful of the Muslim houses, in luxuriant gardens. The main street here used to have a mountain stream running down the middle of it which powered a dozen small water-mills. At the top of it, near the Yellow Bastion, you will find a pleasant tree-shaded *kafana* which affords a splendid view of the whole city and valley. One can cool off here with a raspberry drink or a fresh lemonade, attempt once again to count the minarets which rise like some improbable assembly of moon rockets, or merely do what the

Muslims have always been so good at—namely sit and enjoy being.

Opposite, on the far side of the River Miljačka, **Mt Trebević** soars to over five thousand feet. It takes a couple of hours to climb to the top and the best alternative is to take the funicular whose boxes crawl like bugs up the pine-furred flanks. (The station is a little behind the National Assembly *Konak.*) At the top is quite a good restaurant where you can sometimes get roast boar and roast kid with the local red wine. Unfortunately a combination of unsuitable climate and soil and strong Muslim influence have prevented much wine production in Bosnia, but some of it is good.

At the foot of Mt Trebević are the suburb of Bistrik and the gipsy quarter of **Dajanli Osmanbeg.** In Bistrik there is a station for the narrow gauge railway that runs all the way down to Dubrovnik in one direction and up to Belgrade in the other. Intrepid connoisseurs of railway travel should not miss this trip, but allow about three days! In Dajanli the steep winding streets dribble away into lanes and paths. Shacks and wooden houses lean and cling on the slopes at precarious angles. Among them crouch tiny mosques with wooden minarets. Little streams are diverted through gardens and down the 'streets'. They are all Muslims in Dajanli and many are gipsies. Swarthy, bloomered women squat at their doors sewing and mending, or stride barefoot with loads upon their heads. The children swarm, and almost as numerous as the children are the cats; these are greatly revered by the Muslim for the marks of the Prophet's hand can still be seen on their heads. There is a legend that Mahomet cut off a portion of his robe rather than disturb a cat sleeping on it.

There is poverty here but not depression. A plank or a packet of nails may represent a day's wage and you won't have gone very far before you see numerous examples of that thrift and improvisation at which the Jugoslavs are expert. This part makes an interesting contrast to the town centre with its opera house and its banks, its university and its theatre. But slowly the changes come. As Ivo Andrić, himself a Bosnian, puts it, 'this is a town which is decaying and dying and at the same time is being reborn and transformed.'

As you move from east to west the town becomes, appropriately enough, more occidental. If you take the Vase Miskina from behind the Evropa and stroll westwards—and there are few pleasanter places than Sarajevo for strolling—you discover the principal sights with little difficulty. A little way down on the left is the Tourist office (this may have changed its site) and almost opposite is the

Catholic Cathedral. The Orthodox Cathedral is a little farther down on the left. Both cathedrals are minor curiosities in this part of the world. The Catholic one is a form of French Gothic. The Orthodox is a descendant of the Macedonian-Kosmet School with a main cupola, four corner 'cruet' cupolas, plain 'baroque' walls, a frill of tiny arches at eave height, and, centrally, above the main entrance, a rococo type, onion-topped steeple. Both these buildings were a product of the Austrian rule. The historian might classify the latter hybrid as typical of it. The architectural purist will find it frankly emetic. If you turn left beyond this and take the first on the right you find the Synagogue and near it a small art gallery with a collection of nineteenth- and twentieth-century paintings by Jugoslav artists.

The Vase Miskina runs into the **Maršala Tita Ulica,** much of whose northern side is flanked by bosky parks which are very desirable in the long hot days of a Bosnian summer. In one of them is a whole batch of tombs belonging to national heroes. In fact tombs, and more especially gravestones, are one of the more ubiquitous features of Sarajevo—as they are of so many Muslim towns. Muslim tradition forbids the disturbance of the dead and all over the city, and all over the slopes round it, as numerous as daisies, the white steles sprout, lean and sag higgledy-piggledy in bunches of a dozen and in fields of hundreds. Some are plain, some are topped by fezzes and turbans. A woman's stele may have a lotus leaf carved or painted on it. Most of them are anonymous though occasionally you will see a text from the Koran, or a sword to show that the dead man was a Janissary.

The principal mosque in Tito's street is the Hadim Ali Paša, a satisfying building which belongs to the late sixteenth century, the high and palmy period of Ottoman architecture. You find it on your left just beyond a very large executive block. The traditional story is that when the mosque was built after Ali Pasha's death as a memorial to him a friend asked the architect why he had chosen a site so far from the city centre. To which the architect replied: 'When we are dust this mosque will be at the very heart of Sarajevo'. A prediction which has turned out to be more than correct for the city has now spread a good deal. From here follow the Maršala Tita which soon debouches into a big irregular *trg*. On the far side take the Vojvode Putnika which is the beginning of the main road to Mostar and Dubrovnik. On the way you meet a harsh reminder of the cost of heroism and resistance: a plaque commemorating seventy-five men who were hanged from the branches of a nearby chestnut tree a few days before the liberation in 1945.

A few minutes' walk beyond is the **Regional Museum** where a couple of hours is more then well-spent. It is one of the oldest scientific institutions in the Balkans. The archaeological section contains a valuable and very well presented collection of palaeolithic and neolithic remains from the area and an equally impressive assembly of Roman relics. The ethnographical department, the best in the Balkans, gives one a comprehensive insight into the customs and way of life in Bosnia past and present. Among many other things it has an array of national costumes. There are also a number of Bogomil tombs and mouldings. One special curiosity is a long, silver tube formerly used to pour medicine down the throats of sick camels. In a way this relic is symbolic of Sarajevo's central position between east and west. Here the camel trains from the Near East and farther stopped and the merchandise was transferred to mules and horses. Beyond this point camels never enjoyed good health.

A worthwhile round trip north of Sarajevo can be made on a good road across the wilds of Zvijezdan and Konjuh to Tuzla. There are a few typical Bosnian villages on the way, at one of which, Olovo, there is a collection of Bogomil *stećaks*. Tuzla is a thriving township which was already a centre of activity in the Middle Ages because of the salt mines; hence its name, for *tuz* in Turkish means 'salt'.

From here there is a pleasant run on average roads down the River Spreča valley to Doboj, a small town of considerable charm in an amphitheatre of wooded hills. The main antiquity is the ruined castle which, by virtue of its position at the confluence of several roads and rivers, was of great strategic importance for centuries.

After Doboj turn south down the Bosna valley via Maglaj, Žepče and Zenica. Maglaj, a centre for big game hunting and fishing, is well worth a pause. The Kuršumli Džamija, with its polygonal minaret and clock tower, is a particularly splendid mosque. Round the town there are numerous ruined castles and Muslim cemeteries.

Beyond Žepče the Bosna shoots a defile which brings you to the extraordinary village and fortress of Vranduk perched high on a sharp rock completely dominating the gorge. The Turks occupied this for two and a half centuries and were responsible for the castle.

Zenica is quite a large industrial town (a comfortable hotel, the Metalurg, whose mines were early exploited by the Romans. There are a few Roman and medieval remains in the locality. From here you rejoin the trunk road from Sarajevo at Kaonik.

There is a first class new road from Sarajevo to Mostar (see map on p. 347) which runs through Ilidža, only ten kilometres south-west of Sarajevo, a large spa with several hotels. If you don't want the full treatment you can take a free dip with the locals in the boiling, therapeutic waters after they have passed through the spa chambers. The Romans exploited these hot springs and they have been in use on and off ever since. The main complex of buildings is Austrian and it was here that the luckless Franz Ferdinand spent his last night. Beyond is Vrelo Bosne, a large, shady park where the River Bosna begins its career to the Sava. It bubbles almost fully grown from the base of the Igman mountain and its fresh waters have been adapted for a big trout hatchery.

From here (and this is a drive or train journey that should not be missed) the road twists through many miles of hill and forest full of big game, until you reach the famous Neretva river at **Konjić**. Another noble bridge crosses the river here in five arches. The original one was built by the Turks in 1682 but it has been much damaged and restored since then. In the first place there was probably a Roman bridge. From Konjić, incidentally, you can make kayak trips down the river: a thrilling and alarming experience.

Beyond, the river has been dammed to make an artificial lake which ends near **Jablanica** with the big dam itself. Jablanica is a new town surrounded by a *zareba* of jagged six thousand foot peaks. From here the road and railway corkscrew down the Neretva gorge amidst a landscape of awe-inspiring austerity. The river, a turbulent and icy turquoise, hurls itself furiously through a wilderness of gashed and fissured white *karst* which, like other parts of Bosnia-Hercegovina, is inhabited by the *poskok*—a deadly snake of the viper breed (*Vipera ammodites*).[1] Also known as the Sand or Long-nosed viper, the *poskok* (like many of the viper breed) is a good-looking if somewhat sinister snake which grows to a length of two and a half feet or more and is easily recognised by the upright scaly projection on the tip of the snout. It is thick-set with a triangular head and bears on its back a dark zig-zag stripe on a silver grey background. Its belly is blackish and the underside of its tail is often orange. If you meet one don't annoy it.

[1] I am indebted to Mr E. Arnold, of the British Natural History Museum, for an expert account of its habits. It prefers dry, rocky areas (the *karst* is therefore ideal

Mostar (it means 'old bridge') lies on a plateau in one of the hottest and most barren parts of Europe. It is an enchanted gesture of human defiance, a splendour of gold and white in a desert of skeletal stone, grouped about the now emerald Neretva. A couple of dozen slender minarets spike the irregular patterns of its roofs. In the gardens grow fig, apricots and lemons. An almost Persian fragrance of jasmine and roses hangs upon the torrid air. It is a kind of oasis and frontier town between the forest lands of Bosnia and the *karst* mountains of the coast, between the continental and the Mediterranean climates. Round it, thanks to the Neretva, spread vineyards, tobacco fields and orchards. Through it stroll the good-looking Hercegovinians with the air of people who owe nothing to nobody. They are a very proud people, and are reputed to speak the best Serbian. They have always been extremely independent and had an outstanding record of resistance during the last war.

You may be lucky enough to see some costumes here. Not long ago the women wore the *feredža*, a long enveloping garment of dark blue with loose sleeves which covered them from head to foot. Now this is only to be seen in museums. But quite a lot of Orthodox women wear long white dresses with fringed and striped aprons and white head-scarves which sometimes float down their backs like veils.

Most of the old town with its twenty-four mosques lies on the left bank of the Neretva. Once it was part of Tiberius's Roman Empire when it went under the name of Andetrium or Mandetrium. For a time also it was part of Csar Dušan's Serbian empire. Eventually the Turks took it and by 1469 it was the centre of a *sandžak* under the control of a *Beg*. Under Turkish rule it developed as a commercial centre. Later, large numbers of both Catholic and Orthodox peasants congregated there; but it has always been a predominantly Muslim town.

The northern end now contains a number of buildings in the worst of modern design but each side of the river by the main bridge are comfortable hotels: the Bristol and the Neretva. The food is quite good and the region produces two of the better known

---

for it) and is found up to 6,000 ft. It is quite a bold snake and is active by day and night, especially in warmer districts. For a viper it climbs a good deal and conveniently warns one of its presence by a prolonged and loud hiss. It lives off small mammals, birds and lizards. A curiosity is that mice and voles are bitten and then followed to where they have collapsed. Lizards and birds, on the other hand, are struck and immediately held. They die in less than a minute.

Jugoslav wines—Žilavka and Blatina. The Žilavka is a refreshing white wine (often better unbottled) and the Blatina is a strong red which should be drunk in small quantities.

The most interesting mosque is the **Karadjoz-begova Džamija,** in the centre of the old town, built late in the sixteenth century. Like the balcony of its minaret it is richly decorated. In front of it lies a small cemetery and the mausoleum of Djikić, a poet and national hero. If you come on the guided tour from Dubrovnik the coach contrives to arrive on the dot for the midday call to prayer which, prosaically, comes over the loudspeakers hung on the minaret. The 'group' is then hustled into the mosque to watch a few dozen of the faithful prostrating themselves towards Mecca.

From near here a street slopes down to a row of houses clustered on the steep banks of the Neretva. Their walls are painted different colours: originally, it is said, to distinguish them in lieu of numbers. You will notice that many of the older houses here (as in other parts of Bosnia-Hercegovina) still have quoit-shaped stone tiles, used, they say, because it is the best kind of roofing to withstand the winter gales that howl across these desolate mountains.

From the banks here (there is a well-sited café) one gets an incomparable view of the main attraction in Mostar—the Turkish **bridge** which crosses the gorge in one slender span between two massive towers. It was built by a man called Hajrudin (a pupil of the great architect Sinan) in 1566 and is thought to have replaced a Roman bridge. For a long time it was known as the 'Roman bridge', probably because the masons were Dalmatians who were called *Latini* by the local inhabitants.

There is a story about its creation. The first span collapsed and the Sultan, in a fury, sent for the architect and told him that the next one must stand or he would lose his head. He was given unlimited time—and he took his time. By doing so he could lengthen his life. At last it was finished and the supports were removed. The architect, certain that it would not hold, ran away in terror and hid himself. But the bridge stood and when the townspeople went to find the architect to acclaim him they found him in tears digging his own grave. He was duly borne to the Sultan and congratulated. The Stari Most has survived for, at the moment, exactly four centuries.

Farther up the left bank, at No. 13 Bišćevića Ulica (ask for directions) is a rather fine Turkish *konak* almost overhanging the river. It has been turned into a museum house where a fat and unctuous *čuvar* togged up as a Turk (his wife as a Turkish woman) scampers about offering you little cups of Turkish coffee. He will attempt to sell you carpets and Turkish clothes and other items. If you wish you can dress up in some Turkish garments and take pictures of each other. The whole routine is faintly ludicrous, but the house itself and its furnishings are well worth looking at.

While you are at Mostar I recommend a trip to **Blagaj** about ten kilometres south-east, on the River Buna. The *karst* is spectacular and remains so for several hours driving east and south of Mostar. Above Blagaj rise the splendid ruins of Herceg Stefan's castle. This was the duke who gave his name to the region. A short way from Blagaj the River Buna spouts in full gush from a precipitous cliff. Nearby you find the remains of a Dervish monastery and a ruined mosque built at the command of a nineteenth-century Vizier who had residence in Mostar and was governor of the district.

From Mostar (via Jablanica) there is a five star trip into the Bosnian hills. First, up the Rama valley to Prozor ('the window'), and well named for its stands at the slit which opens from the Rama gorge into the uplands. Here there survive things of war in the shape of burnt-out tanks, and slogans daubed on walls: *Viva Italia. Viva li Duce. Vinceremo.* Ironical epitaphs to a forlorn Italian venture. From Prozor the road loops and coils up to the Makljen Pass, somewhat over three thousand feet, where the Partisans were installed for some time (a simple monument commemorates them). A long descent through the wooded hills follows, to the Vrbas valley, passing through Gornju Vakuf, Donji Vakuf (it has a hotel, the Vrbas), Bugojno and on through forested valleys to Jajce (see p. 349).

From Mostar, again, on a well-signposted road in average condition, you can reach Stolac, a pretty village on a rocky bluff. Some Turkish houses and a *hammam* survive and it even boasts a small hotel, the Zelengora, a lively spot in the evenings. Very near Stolac is **Radimlje** and one of the most impressive of all the Bogomil necropolises: a large number of grey, carved tombs scattered like so many outsize crates and trunks on a deserted plateau. I have mentioned the Bogomils and their tombs a good many times in this book and it now seems an appropriate moment to say something in detail about this very unusual funerary art.

The main concentrations of **stećaks** are to be found near Zvornik and Vlasnica, near Glamoč and Bugojno and in a roughly triangular concentration whose apex is Konjić and whose base stretches from Lovreč (near Makarska) to Brotnice, south of Trebinje—a very large area indeed. We call them tombs, but they are monuments rather than tombs. (See map on p. 343.) Many legends and superstitions have gathered about them and they are widely believed by the peasants to possess magical powers. For instance, there is a popular belief that a storm will come up or lightning strike if anyone touches them. No doubt these beliefs have helped to prevent their use in the building of houses and walls.

As far as their shape goes they can be divided into two groups: the horizontal and the upright. The first consists of caskets, tablets and sarcophagi; the second of upright slabs, obelisks and crosses. Many of both kinds are decorated but the most detailed ornamentation occurs on the sarcophagi. In Hercegovina many of these have carved 'colonnades' on their sides; and many are gabled like huge old-fashioned trunks and coffers. On some the stylised arches and columns echo aspects of Romanesque architecture. Pointed arches suggest Gothic influence. They are often decorated with figures in low relief, sometimes single figures of men, animals and grotesque creatures. Hunting scenes are frequent, especially the stag hunt for which hounds and falcons were used. Huntsmen are shown armed with bows or spears. Occasionally there are hunting scenes with bear and wild boar. A common motif is the *kolo*. Sometimes a chivalric scene is depicted, a duel or a tournament. Family groups involve the father (or mother) with children.

Most of the work is crudely realistic. There is little sense of proportion and the main effect is naïve, childlike. A good deal of use is also made of symbols of which the most frequent are sun and moon signs. Sometimes these are alone or decorate shields. The cross often occurs and other decorations on Hercegovinian *stećaks* are friezes of foliage.

In east Bosnia, where most of the monuments are upright, (there is the occasional sarcophagus shape) we find imitations of houses, replicas of shingled roofs, corner posts and beams. This is understandable as it is a very wooded region and to this day the designs of houses are similar. The ornamentation of the east Bosnian *stećaks* is different. The dominant motifs here are floral: vines, leaves and flowers, for example. Human forms are rare.

About two hundred of the monuments bear inscriptions in an old type of Cyrillic script called *Bosančica* (Bosnian script). Most of them are curt and give a little information about the deceased. Here are

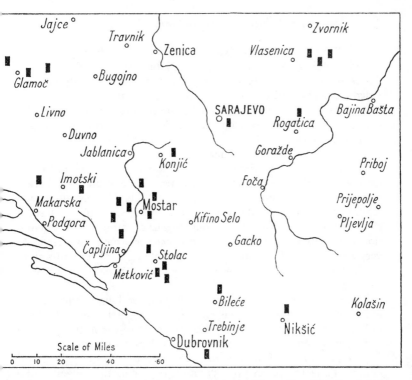

The symbols indicate the principal concentrations of Bogomil *stećaks*. But *stećaks* are to be found in and about all the places marked. This map is to be taken only as a *very* general guide.

a few of the more interesting examples:

1. Here lies Župan Juroje who died honourably in the service of his master. The prince has erected this monument to him.

2. On the eleventh day of March died Marija, servant of God, known as the maiden, wife of the priest Dabiživ, in the year 1231.

3. Here lies Pavko Radonić. I cut this stone in my lifetime. I beseech you, brethren and lords, touch not my bones.

4. Here lies Radivoj Draščić. I was a bold hero. I beseech you, touch me not. You will be as I am, but I cannot be as you are.

343

5. This is the cross of Radoje Mrkšić. I was praying to God and thinking no evil when lightning killed me.

There is something very touching about the terse dignity of these valedictory inscriptions, but my two favourites are:

1. Here lies Vlatko, who prayed to no man however powerful, and who knew many countries, dying in his own. He leaves neither son nor brother.

2. Here lies Dragac. When I wished to be I ceased to be.

Many of the inscriptions (they were usually only put on tombs for the 'upper classes') emphasise the transience of life, but there is also a concern for resurrection and eternal life. The monuments at Radimlje are a particularly interesting group and if you have a close look at them you can pick out various examples of ornamentation like: a battle scene; a *danse macabre* performed by women (a very unusual motif); a hunting scene involving a falcon and a stag; a tournament; and two *kolo* scenes, one with men, the other with women.

There is a legend that the Bogomils gazed so long at their navels for the inward light that their chins grew into their chests. Perhaps Othello was refering to them when he spoke of the anthropophagi and men 'whose heads do grow beneath their shoulders.'

Beyond Stolac is Ljubinje, in a beautiful and fertile valley, and Popovo Polje (maps on pp. 137 and 99): one of the biggest of the *karst* 'lakes' that produce fish for one half of the year and cereals and vegetables the other.

From Stolac in the other direction it is no distance to **Počitelj** (return to Rečice and take the road to Metković), a medieval and Turkish walled town straggling up a rocky slope above the Neretva[1]. This fortified settlement guarded the route to central Bosnia for five hundred years and the main fortress was probably erected by Tvrtko I towards the end of the fourteenth century. When the Turks advanced into Bosnia it became a stronghold of the utmost importance and men from Dubrovnik came to help strengthen it. However, it fell to the Turkish leader Hamza Beg in 1471 and most of the building that survives is Turkish.

That entertaining Turkish chronicler Evlija Čelebija passed through here in 1664 and gave some account of its principal features which have not changed much since. He remarks the main mosque built by Hadži Alija in 1563. 'There is a tall cypress in its courtyard,' he writes. 'This shining mosque was raised by a forebear of

[1] Now converted *en bloc* into an hotel complex.

our lord Ibrahim-aga. Alongside the town walls, beside the water, his honoured brother built a public kitchen (*imaret*) which distributes free bread and soup to the inhabitants day and night. On Thursday evenings it distributes spiced meat and savoury and sweet rice. The *imaret* will remain as long as God wills . . . In the town there is an elementary religious school (*mektab*). Later Lord Ibrahim built a secondary theological school (*medresa*) and also sent people to build public baths (*hammam*) and an inn (*han*) . . . The houses of the town are built one above the other, facing west towards the river. There are very many walnut trees here. Since the climate is mild fruit grows better here than in other towns.'

Evlija also mentions that Ibrahim built a clock tower whose bell 'heavier and clearer than any other in Bosnia and Hercegovina' was, according to legend, brought from Crete. For many years the bell tolled the hours for Počitelj and in calm weather could be heard in Čapljina and Gabela, just as the voice of the muezzin from the Počitelj minaret 'resounded from the stone into the far distance.'

The bell still tolled until 1917 when the Austrians, who had occupied the town in 1878, melted it down for bullets. It seems the Montenegrins weren't the only people reduced to extremities for ammunition.

The other route west out of Sarajevo goes past Ilidža to Raskršće and then veers north-west for Kiseljak, a small spa on the River Lepenica. From Kiseljak there is a worthwhile short diversion on a minor road south to Kreševo, a small, unspoilt Bosnian settlement many of whose houses are wooden and are roofed with the dark wooden 'tiles' characteristic of this part of the world. Kreševo has a long tradition of crafts, especially in iron-work and carpet making. The main objects to look out for are the wooden mosque and the remains of the medieval fortifications above the township.

Not far on from Kiseljak there is a turn off on the left to Fojnica, another spa fourteen kilometres up in the hills. The principal antiquity here is a fourteenth-century Franciscan monastery which has a small museum and a good library.

Having returned to the main road one goes on to Busovača, a fairly typical Bosnian village, and then to Kaonik. It now has an adequate hotel, the Stari Grad.

CHAPTER 20

Bosnia and Inland Croatia

Travnik—Jajce—Banja Luka—Prijedor—Sisak—Ključ—Glamoč—Karlovac—Plitvice Lakes—Zagreb—Šestine and Gračani—Novo Mesto—Kočevje

From Kaonik the road winds through superb scenery until finally you round a bend in the fertile Lašva valley to Travnik, one of the most delightful small towns in Jugoslavia. It has a rambling, shabbily comfortable hotel of considerable character called the Park towards the western end, and this is the only place you can stay. I once paid for a night's lodging there with some packets of razor blades, a rare commodity in Jugoslavia until recently.

Travnik means 'green city.' The name is appropriate, for it is full of luxuriant gardens and orchards amidst which are many lovely buildings of the best period of Bosnian Muslim architecture and a dozen or more mosques. The most important of these are the Hadži Alibegova, with a clock tower, and the Suleimanja whose outer walls are decorated very unusually (and quite differently from the mosque at Tetovo) with vivid paintings. It looks more like a house than a mosque. There are also a number of palatial tombs sheltering some of the ninety viziers who governed from Travnik during the four hundred years of Turkish rule in Bosnia. Unfortunately the governor's *konak* no longer exists. However, the principal relic of the past is the castle, an imposing and heavily fortified structure built in the fifteenth century by the Bosnian king Tvrtko II.

The day to be in Travnik is a Tuesday. I have only managed it once and I remember it particularly because I was woken about 4.30 a.m. by the sound of many hooves. Then came the dawn summons of the *muezzin*. The hooves went on, accompanied by the rumble of carts and wagons. It seemed that hundreds of horses were

346

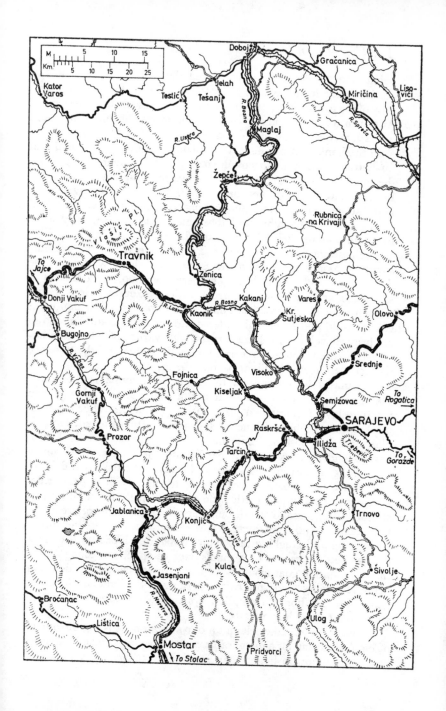

being ridden into town—and indeed there were. By six the two markets were in full swing: the stock market at the western extremity of the town; produce, clothes, utensils and so forth in the centre. At eleven o'clock I counted over two hundred and fifty horses and mules tethered in one of the compounds.

In the bank that morning were a couple of dozen turbaned and fur-hatted warriors in sheepskin coats paying in their takings from the market. I had been obliged to have some money cabled from London and as the dinars came over the counter there were congratulations on all sides for having conducted such successful business. Recalling how hard those men must have worked for a mere ten pounds I felt a little ashamed.

The costumes of the women in Travnik and its district are outstanding, as are the women themselves. The long white chemise dresses made of coarse linen are very common. Aprons vary a lot; some are dark, some narrow with horizontal stripes. Some women wear one in front and one behind and red is the dominant colour. Gold and silver embroidered *jeleci* are very common, and so are brightly coloured belts. There is a wide variety of coloured headscarves. When you see several hundred women in the produce market the effect is brilliant beyond description.

The massif which rises to the north of Travnik is the Vlašić Planina, magnificent countryside and a well-known ski-ing ground for Jugoslavs. I clambered up it with the villagers returning from market on a grilling afternoon. It was an arduous ascent for a fit man carrying nothing; but the women, bearing heavily loaded baskets and bundles on their heads, and the men and the young boys and girls carrying packages and sacks and chickens and furniture and cooking pans, an extraordinary variety of impedimenta, took it at a steady pace with little discomfort. By the time we had climbed two thousand feet through jagged, precipitous rocks covered with dense scrub and forest I was exhausted. Not so the locals. Chattering and laughing they sympathised and loped on. I can see now a chest of drawers on a man's back disappearing along a path that a mountain goat would have tackled with circumspection. Far below, for miles along the twisting tracks of the valleys, the cavalcades of mules, horses, oxen, donkeys and carts clopped and rattled away to far-flung homesteads.

Travnik has a further claim on our attention. It is the birthplace of Ivo Andrić and for a memorable evocation of a period of Travnik's past one cannot do better than read *Bosnian Story*. This book and

Bridge on the Drina give one a deep insight into the character and past of his homeland. I also strongly recommend that you read Sir Arthur Evans's remarkable account of his trip through these parts in the 1870's: *Through Bosnia and Herzegovina on foot during the Insurrection*, a vividly ebullient and stimulating travel book. It is also very learned.

The road from Travnik to Jajce (pronounced Ya-it-se) is bad[1] but it is not so very far and the scenery is still Bosnia at its best. Jajce is so famous as a beauty spot, mostly because of the many photographs of its waterfall, that I feel a little uneasy in never having thought *all that* much of it. But the traveller should not miss it, and it is a key junction town for several directions: eastwards to Travnik and Sarajevo, north to Banja Luka, south to Mostar and the coast. The journey west is an altogether special event. . . .

First **Jajce** itself: quite a small town surrounded by high forested hills infested with wolf and bear, at the confluence of the Vrbas and Pliva rivers. The renowned waterfall is the Pliva plunging into the Vrbas. (If you come to it from Travnik cross the bridge a little above the fall and branch left to find the comfortable new Turist hotel.)

Most of the town, which was for many years the capital of the Bosnian kings, is built round and on a small conical hill topped by a ruining castle built by Hrvoje Vukčić, a *Beg* and formerly one of King Tvrtko's generals, who came to Jajce from Split where he had made himself extremely unpopular, possibly because he was suspected of Bogomil sympathies.

The history of Jajce is closely linked with the history of Jugoslav resistance. In the fifteenth century it fought against the Turks for many years and was the very last stronghold of the Bosnian kingdom to succumb. It was here also that the last king of Bosnia lived, ruled and was executed: Stjepan Tomašević, who died in 1463.

During the last war Jajce played a vital part in the Partisan movement against the Germans and it changed hands several times. For a long period it was Marshal Tito's H.Q. and when Sir Fitzroy Maclean headed the British Military Mission from Churchill (he was parachuted into the hills near a village called Mrkonjić Grad, north-west of Jajce) he was taken to Jajce to make one of the early contacts with Marshal Tito. Other Allied officers had already been in the country for some time, more particularly Deakin, Stewart, Hunter and Jones—all intrepid and remarkable men.

It was here also that the National Parliament which contained

[1]This is now a good road.

the most prominent members of the National Liberation Movement (the AVNOJ for short) had its second session. On the eve of the meeting the town was bombed and Tito escaped narrowly.

The delegates came from all parts of Jugoslavia, armed, on foot and through enemy held territory. Some walked more than three hundred miles. Some had to fight their way through. The Montenegrins had to travel through two hundred miles of the roughest country in Europe. I doubt if any parliament has ever been assembled under such extraordinary circumstances.

The foundations of the new state were laid at this meeting on November 29th 1943 (now a national holiday in Jugoslavia) and it took place in the hall of the former gymnastic society which the Partisans had converted into a cultural centre. They even managed to perform plays there in the middle of the war. Now the hall is a museum and looks much the same as it did on that momentous night in 1943. As you come in from Travnik and approach the bridge you find it away to your left behind the bus station.

The Tourist office stands at the town end of the bridge over the Pliva (you can't miss it because it has a snarling bear in the window) and if you want to see the castle you will have to call there for a guide and a key. On the way up you pass the shell of a church dedicated to St Luke whom legend associates with these parts. The church is a fourteenth-century work and its campanile is intact.

The next item the guide will show you is rather extraordinary. You descend into the icy bowels of the earth, or rather into black rock, and find a kind of underground church which Hrvoje Vukčić is supposed to have had hewn out as a family crypt. The work is plainly unfinished, but you will notice the Vukčić coat-of-arms near the door and Bogomil symbols over the main altar. As I mentioned, Vukčić himself may have been a Bogomil; on the other hand this dank and sombre cavern may have been a Bogomil crypt that Vukčić decided to adapt for his own tomb. An odd choice for a man who obviously set store by ostentation.

Not far away are the remains of a **Mithraic temple,** one of many survivals in Europe of that strange and powerful cult that originated in Persia, was disseminated by the Roman legionaries and for a long time threatened to weaken greatly, if not supplant, Christianity.

The winged youth with the Phrygian helmet is in the act of executing the bull. The bull's blood and marrow are the source of earth and of life. From them, in the myth, came the wheat and the vine; and his seed was transformed by the magic of the moon into

350

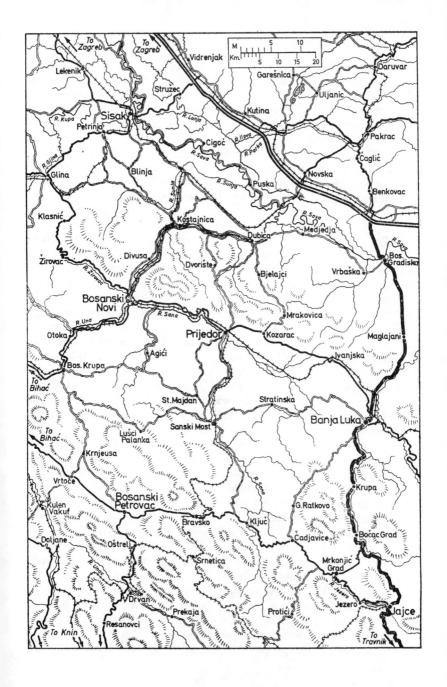

different kinds of animal. Life through death. The Christians abhorred the cult as an idolatrous mystery because it was a serious rival and because it parodied the Crucifixion. The cult has a potent appeal because Mithras was the god of Victory who sent success, and the conquest of the bull was symbolic of the power of mind and body combined over mere body.

The castle above is sombre. Thick grass and cypress trees grow in the sunken interior. Ruins crumble among them. Sheep owned by your guide pasture there. From the battlements there is a splendid view over the clustering, dark, tent-shaped roofs of Jajce and across the adjoining valleys.

Jajce's market day (on a Wednesday) is as impressive as Travnik's. There are plenty of costumes, hill-men in turbans and *kalpaks*, fezzed townsmen and merchants, and women in white robes embroidered black. The shepherds from this area have a long tradition of wood-carving, the results of which are available in the market. The objects to look out for are wooden mugs called *tasići*; two kinds of flute—the *ćurlik* and *dvojnice* (single and double piped); and little cases for curved razor blades called *britvenice*. They also fashion handsome boxes, named *vodjeri*, for whetstones, shepherd's crooks, spindles, distaffs and a multitude of other things. In fact many of the Bosnian villages keep up these rural 'industries': wood-carving round Jablanica; blanket-weaving and rag-rugs in Bugojno; metal-work at Mrkonjić Grad, and so on. The chances are that you will find many examples of wood-carving anywhere between Prijedor and Ohrid.

A few kilometres down the road towards Jezero (where there is a big lake) and Mrkonjić Grad you will discover a remarkable collection of small primitive **mills** on a gentle rapid of the River Pliva. They are no more than rickety cabins on stilts but the locals still ride down to them with a sack of grain for grinding. Such mills are not uncommon in Bosnia.

The adventurous traveller who has plenty of time and who relies on public transport can also make a most exciting journey by train from Jajce west to Prijedor. The narrow gauge railway runs through dense, evergreen forest, parts of which are completely unexplored. Wild animals abound here and the peasants who live in these remote retreats are among the most primitive in Europe. The only recent invention with which they would be familiar is an aeroplane, viewed from some forest glade.

However, most people will be going by road and there are

Above, part of the frieze of heads, by George the Dalmation, on Šibenik cathedral. *Below left*, detail of the silver reliquary of Sv Simun at Zadar. The saint is rescuing a storm-tossed boat, while the crew jettison cargo and a demon rocks the boat. *Right*, Kotor: a detail of the *pala* in the cathedral of St. Tryphon, by John of Basle

Above left, Ptjuska Gora: the Renaissance Virgin of Mercy above the high altar of the Gothic church. The portraits beneath the uplifted cloak (more than seventy in all) represent members of the family of the Counts of Celje. *Right,* the wooden iconostasis in the church of Sv Spas, Skopje, showing the delivery of the Baptist's head. Early nineteenth century. *Below,* twentieth century: *left,* a Meštrović portrait of his mother. *Right,* one of hundreds of Second World War memorials up and down the country

two main ways of getting to Zagreb, of which I will take the easier first.

The excellent northern road to Banja Luka runs for seventy kilometres along the Vrbas valley. The mountains are awe-inspiring and the forests impenetrable. Craggy summits are topped by derelict Bosnian castles and at every other curve in the road there is a new and wilder vista.

Banja Luka, somewhat less interesting than Jajce and Travnik, was a Roman watering place and military headquarters and has always been of strategic importance because it commands the entrance to the Vrbas valley. Hrvoje Vukčić ruled from here for some time and it has been the scene of numerous battles. The upper part of the town is the more interesting and a fine mosque survives from the late sixteenth century. It was built by Ferhad Pasha with the ransom for an Austrian general's son whom he had captured. The modern town has broad, tree-lined streets, a decent hotel (the Palas) and every Tuesday the whole place comes alive in a breezy, jostling market which approaches the scale of those at Peć and Leskovac. The shepherds here are unusually striking.

From here the good road continues to the *autoput*. The alternative is to stick to rather poor roads through superb scenery and go to Prijedor and Bosanski Novi. Prijedor, the most northerly of the 'oriental' towns, used to be an important commercial centre and was celebrated in one of the *sevdalinke*. It still has a stern fortress moated by the waters of the River Sana, and a number of mosques. There is little to detain you at Bosanski Novi and from here I suggest you cross country to Glina and then turn north to Sisak, an attractive small town seldom visited by tourists from where there is a good road straight to Zagreb.

Sisak was originally a Roman settlement called Siscia and it has always had some importance because it lies on the confluence of the Kupa and the Sava rivers. The Romans had foundries and smelting works here for coinage (there are some silver coins in the museum) and this tradition has been maintained. In the twelfth century it was a mining town and ever since the local resources of steel, iron and copper have ensured its life.

A little outside Sisak (turn right just before the bridge on the road to the *autoput* and follow the narrow track) is a triangular château which has been converted into a most interesting ethnographical museum. It used to belong to the bishops of Zagreb and in 1592–3 held out against the Pasha of Bosnia. There is a

C.G.J.—M

story that it was very competently defended by two Canons and a handful of men. A feature of the museum is a section devoted to fishing equipment used locally. Nearby is a row of wooden houses characteristic of the region. Much of the woodwork is carved and they have outside covered staircases. Another unusual detail is a kind of 'false' eave about half-way up the buildings. This, in conjunction with the roof eave proper, gives the effect of a double wooden frill.

Between here and Zagreb there are a number of villages full of houses of this type whose chimney-pots are favourite nesting places for the storks which come here in large numbers.

The village of Turopolje (about twenty kilometres from Sisak towards Zagreb) is quite well known for its annual festivities on St George's Day (April 24th), an anniversary celebrated in many parts of the country. The festivities are called *jurjaši* and the participants are usually boys, one of whom (called *zeleni Juraj* or 'green George') is covered with branches plaited in basket fashion so that they hide most of the upper half of his body. He is led in a procession which goes from house to house singing songs. At the end of each visit the boys are given small presents.

On the eve of this feast bonfires are lighted and there is a great deal of merrymaking, singing and dancing, as well as leaping over the fires: another traditional ploy to ward off evil spirits. There are obvious similarities between these customs and Serbian rites already described (see p. 310).

The other route (on poor roads) goes through even wilder forest lands to Bosanski Petrovac and thence to Bihać across ravaged *karst* plateaux. No wonder there is a South Slav demiurgic legend that the Devil created this part of the world. It is a wilderness fit for the wandering demon to cry his despair.

Ključ ('the key') is worth stopping at.[1] It's a very old town with several ruined castles in one of which, Blagaj, the unfortunate King Tomašević took refuge for a time. There is not a great deal to be seen at Bosanski Petrovac, though the ruin-addict will find several derelict castles in the neighbourhood. When you reach Vrtoče, twenty kilometres on, I suggest you turn off on a poor road to visit Kulen Vakuf, a small medieval town of great character dominated by the shell of a fortress—the Osječenica. Historians think that Kulin-Ban, the first Bosnian monarch, reigned here. You ought then to return to Vrtoče and continue to **Bihać,** another

[1] It has a new hotel, the Sana.

medieval town on the River Una. It has a Gothic church transformed into a mosque by the Turks, and the remains of a castle. Near the town lie the remnants of several other strongholds.

A further alternative after leaving Jajce is to strike south seven kilometres beyond Mrkonjić Grad and make for Glamoč. Again the country is almost frighteningly wild and desolate. Shepherds lead a semi-nomadic life in these parts and it will probably be half a century or more before civilization of our kind has much effect. Like the Montenegrin shepherds the Bosnians go in for rough-and-ready athletic competitions: running, heaving and throwing stones, horse racing and other trials of strength and agility.

Glamoč itself is a very old fortified town on a plain and gives its name to a traditional Bosnian dance: the *starobosanska* or *kolo iz Glamoča*, which has several interesting features, especially the different attitudes of the women. The women, restrained, are led by the men who dance with great zest. The restraint of the women clearly signifies their social inferiority, an undoubted fact in rural communities. The highlanders quite often beat their wives for laziness or incompetence, or even perhaps to show them who is master; though I doubt if that issue is often in doubt.

From Glamoč one can go on an adequate road to Livno and thence to the coast and Split—or across to Mostar. Incidentally, there is a magnificent ride (on appalling roads) to be made from Mostar to Split via Posušje, Imotski and Omiš—where the Cetina river emerges.

Alternatively there is another exciting route from Livno to Sinj and then back north-west to Vrlika, Knin and Obrovac. The road from Obrovac up the steepling flanks of the Velebit Mountains is nothing less than a hair-raising experience requiring the steadiest nerves. It was a feat of human courage to have built a road at all. When you have crossed the Velebit you go up the Lika valley to Gospić and thence to Plitvice. High plateaux, jagged bare mountains, remote villages and bone-shaking roads characterise all these routes, but to travel them is a most exhilarating adventure. One really does have the sensation of exploring unknown country.

The train journey from Split to Zagreb—especially between Strmica and Bihać—is an extraordinary event[1]. If you were stranded in some of these regions you could quite easily die of thirst in the summer and more easily freeze to death in winter. Even those who have trekked the great deserts and tundras of the world are not blasé about the *karst*.

[1] An excellent new *road* now also joins Zagreb and Split.

355

The veteran railway traveller can also go from Split to Prijedor. Near the source of the river Krka, in what is accurately described as the middle of nowhere, the line branches and the train drags its way laboriously, winding and hair-pinning, over mountains, through valleys and forests, for two days. The distance as the crow flies is barely a hundred miles.

Where the central Bosnian mountains meet the Velebit range the valleys used to mark the Turkish frontier, and in these parts (as well as farther north-east) the peasants have bull-fights. They are contests between two animals: the bovine counterpart of a wrestling match. The *corrida* is much simpler than the Spanish kind and also bloodless because the bull's horns are blunted and they only fight till one falls to its knees. Nevertheless, support is vociferous and rivalry between villages extremely keen.

If you decide to be unadventurous (or prudent) you will stick to the road from Jajce to Bihać via Bosanski Petrovac. Just beyond Bihać you enter Croatia and the road improves. When you reach Petrovo Selo I recommend that you turn off and visit the **Plitvice Lakes** in a national forested park. This is one of the most popular resorts among Jugoslavs, and the lakes, which lie at several different levels and run into each other down a series of increasingly steep falls, are extremely beautiful (see map on p. 44).

From here, north, via Slunj and Karlovac, the country alters considerably. It is much gentler and more heavily cultivated. The gardens and fields are greener, flowery. The houses are more Austrian, the people plumper and burlier, more sensual looking, with fine dark eyes and big, mobile mouths. After the macerations and famine of the *karst* this part of Croatia seems fertile and luscious to the point of self-indulgence. It is characteristic of Jugoslavia that in a hundred miles nearly every obvious aspect (and not a few of the less obvious) may change two or three times. This is especially true of Croatia which has more variety than any of the other republics.

Slunj is a straggling pretty village with an adequate hotel, the Slunjčica; **Karlovac** an expanding town which has played an important role in the history of Croatia.

It was founded by a sixteenth-century Styrian archduke called Charles when he built a fortress in an attempt to protect the area against the Turks. Once again one marvels at the tardy processes of military and tactical thinking. As usual the convenient course was

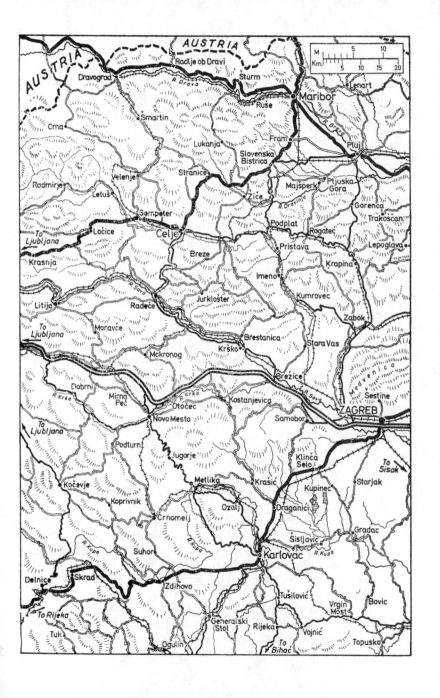

to occupy and devastate the region before concentrating on the castle. This, in the shape of a six-pointed star, was an enormous structure and we are unlucky that so little of it survives. Here and there you can see signs of its moats and walls.

By the end of the eighteenth century the Turks had withdrawn and the town became (as it has continued to be) an important commercial centre, especially as one of the main transit points for wheat from the Pannonian plain to the mountains. The grain was brought by boat up the rivers, and the dock installations on the Kupa are still used.

There is not a great deal to see in the town (which has several hotels: I recommend the Korana and the Central) but the municipal museum is worth visiting. This is contained in a house once belonging to the Frankopan family and used by them as a winter residence. Again we are in the country of the Zrinjski-Frankopan clans. Some miles south-west, at Dubovac, is another of their imposing fortresses.

Striking north from Karlovac you will find little to delay you until you reach the capital of Croatia.

If you approach **Zagreb** from Belgrade or Ljubljana follow the main road into the centre of the city until you reach the Trg Republike and then turn south down a broad boulevard of trees and gardens. This brings you to the station. If you come from Karlovac entry is also a simple operation. The main road runs into the Savska Cesta and the best thing to do is to take the second main turn on the right after you have passed over or under the third lot of railway lines. This turn is the Vodnikova Mihanovićeva which runs along by the botanical gardens and brings you to the station square.

You need at least two days for Zagreb so the first thing to do is to find a hotel. Very near the station you have the ornate Esplanade which is large, comfortable and fairly expensive, and the Central which is larger, as comfortable and less expensive. The latter also has a rather good restaurant and unless you demand a covey of waiters and attendants at the lift of an eyebrow the Central is the better bet. However, there are several other hotels all of which are very adequate or good.

It has become almost a commonplace to compare Zagreb (which suffered little by comparison with Belgrade in recent wars) with Dublin, and to compare the ancient Serbian-Croatian rivalries with Anglo-Irish rivalries. But the analogy does not go very far

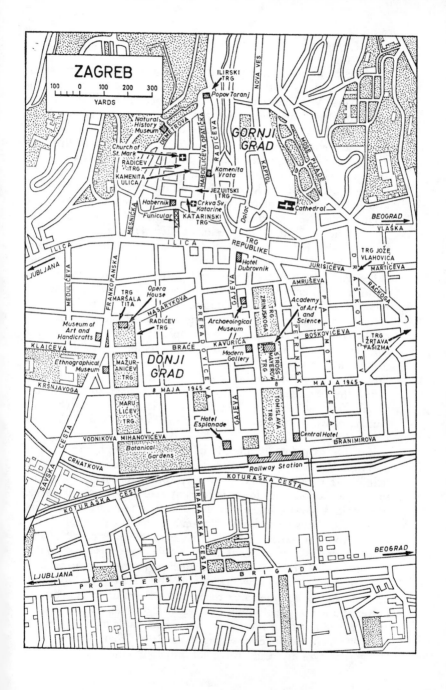

because the Serbs never exploited Croatia as the English shamefully exploited Ireland, and even Eire, though it chose to revolt in the First World War and remain more or less neutral in the second, was not capable of the general betrayal which the misguided Croats perpetrated against the Serbs in the 1940's.

Let us say there is a certain amount of misleading truth in the analogies. Zagreb is a city of many intellectuals, writers and poets. In fact it is the most cultured city in Jugoslavia and has been so for a long time. It is also clique-ridden and infested with snobberies. It also has a tradition of treachery and supine acquiescence which, even among the most depraved and pliable Balkan Greeks or the most decadent Irish, would be unequalled. During the last war it was the capital of a pro-Hitler Fascist state under the leadership of one of the most nauseating of twentieth-century despots: a man called Pavelić whose supporters and trained thugs murdered three hundred thousand Serbians largely because they were Serbs and members of the Orthodox Church. The Ustaše (Pavelić's crew) committed atrocities so appalling that even the Uskoks and *Hajduks* of old would have blenched. For example, they were in the habit of ripping out the eyes of their victims and bringing basketfuls of them to their leader as a kind of offering. . . . However, another forty or fifty years will dilute the bitter hatreds of these events and help to dispel the traditionally ambivalent and two-faced attitude of the Croats (largely brought about by their long affiliation with the Austrians) which is so much a part of their uncertainty about their national identity.

But one soon forgets all this in Zagreb, a handsome town of nostalgic Viennese charm where the people are most amiable and helpful. It is easy to find your way round, principally because most of what you want to see is concentrated in quite a small area. The main Boulevard bisects the city from south to north and forms a convenient axis poled by the station and the Trg Republike.

A thorough investigation can be begun in the lower part, the **Trg Tomislavov.** The monument in the middle represents King Tomislav, a notable tenth-century Croatian monarch, and near it is the Umjetnički Paviljon where they hold a variety of exhibitions. The next square is named after the nineteenth-century bishop Strossmayer and the statue of him is by Meštrović. Strossmayer, who died at the age of ninety in 1905, was a very remarkable man. For much of his life he championed the liberation of the Croats from Austro-Hungarian tyranny and strove for religious union between the

360

Croats and Serbs; that is, between the Catholics and the Orthodox. Unhappily he had little support from anyone. It is quite clear that he was a genius: brilliantly imaginative and intelligent, gay, urbane, formidably resolute, extremely shrewd and saintly. He was, in a way, the St Sava of his century, but even that great man would have met his match in Strossmayer. Zagreb and Croatia probably owe more to him than to any other person. Quite apart from everything else he was an exceptionally gifted linguist, speaking perfect Serbian, Russian, French, German, Italian, Czech, Greek and Latin. Latin was his best language.

North of this square, on the corner of the street called Braće Kavurića, is the Modern Gallery which has a good collection of contemporary Croatian paintings, some French impressionists and some works by, among others, Meštrović and Augustinić.

Opposite this, in the middle of another garden, you find **The Jugoslavian Academy of Science and Art** (Jugoslavenska Akademija Znanosti i Umjetnosti) which looks rather like a Renaissance palace but in fact was put up in 1867, originally a foundation by Strossmayer. It was he who financed the building, and a great proportion of the collection (256 works of art in all) were presented by him. The Italians are best represented from the trecento to the Venetian late settecento. Works particularly worthy of mention are a Giottesque fragment of a *Crucifixion* (ascribed to Daddi), *Madonna and Saints* by Caporali, *The Stigmata of St Francis and the Death of Peter the martyr* by Beato Angelico, a splendid Jacopo Bellini, *Christ with Donors*, and *St Nicholas and St Benedict* by Giovanni Bellini. V. Carpaccio is represented by a *St Sebastien*. There are two by Paolo Veronese: the *Allegory of Wisdom and Power* and *Christ and the Wife of Zebediah*. There is an interesting work by Andrea Medulić, a Slav, called the *Legend of Tobias. A Betrothal of St Catherine* is attributed to Tintoretto, and there are several paintings by the ever-prolific Palma the Younger, by Ribera, Tiepolo and Ghirlandaio. Among the Dutchmen look out for a fifteenth-century painting of the *Trinity* combined with the *Lamentation*, a *Worship of the Kings* by Jan Wellensz de Cook and several works by Nicolaes Maes, a pupil of Rembrandt. A small collection of French paintings include some by Lorrain and Rigaud and a really excellent portrait of *Madame Récamier* by Jean Antoine Gros.

On the left of the Trg Zrinskog (one of the main areas for the *korso*) stands the **Archaelogical Museum** which has an excellent prehistoric collection and also departments devoted to Egyptian and classical antiquities. Some of the Roman bronzes are especially worth looking at.

From here it is only a few paces to the **Trg Republike** dominated by the big, modern Hotel Dubrovnik and a skyscraper with a roof-top restaurant and café. In some ways this is about the most impressive modern civic square in the country and on market days you will still see a few costumed peasants from outlying villages. But in Croatia and Slovenia national costume tends to be worn only on festivals.

Fifteen minutes' walk away to the west (take the Ilica out of the *trg* and then turn down Frankopanska Ulica) you find **Maršala Tita Trg,** near which is a big group of important public buildings, including the University, the Opera House, the Museum of Art and Handicrafts (Muzej za Umjetnosti i Obri) and the Ethnographical Museum. In front of it is one of Meštrović's more satisfying works, a fountain called *The Source of Life.* The university was reorganised by Strossmayer in 1874 and owes much to him.

A few hours in the two museums are well spent. Both are so large and the objects are so well labelled that I see no point in giving lists. The **Ethnographical Museum** is particularly good because of its excellent folklore and costume sections (the costumes of nearly every region of Jugoslavia are represented), a good collection of musical instruments, and first-class reconstructions of peasant houses typical of four regions of Croatia: Prigorje, Zagorje, Podravina and Slavonia. A thorough visit to it will consolidate your general knowledge of Croatia very satisfactorily.

From here you have to return to the Trg Republike in order to explore the **Gornji Grad** (the upper city), quite the most interesting part of Zagreb. You can get up to it by the funicular, just west of the *trg* in the Ilica. This Gornji Grad is always distinguished from the Donji Grad, or lower city.

There was a Roman town here originally, of which next to nothing survives. Modern Zagreb dates from the end of the eleventh century when the King of Hungary established an archbishopric here. In 1102 the most influential families of the Croat nobility made an agreement (the Pacta Conventa) with the Hungarian king, by which he should rule Croatia on the understanding that the Croats retained their independent customs and so forth. This union lasted, through periods of acute strain and revolt, until 1918. Feudalism developed in the twelfth century and prevailed for a very long time. The land was divided among a number of extremely powerful aristocratic families (Hungarian as well as Croat) like the Frankopans and Zrinjskis. The partial subservience of the Croats to the Hungarian and then the Habsburg rulers helps to explain their traditional duality, and also the attitude of the more independent Serbs. The Tartar invasion obliged the inhabitants to build huge defences and it was behind these that the much pursued King Bela IV sheltered when the hordes swept across Europe. In memory of Zagreb's succour he gave it certain rights and privileges and named it a royal and free city. This fortified stronghold, called **Gradec,** was the seat of the Croatian *Bans* or vice-regents, and the kings of Croatia and Hungary built themselves a palace which does not survive—though a plaque on a house records the site. This was the secular city.

About the same time the clergy built themselves another fortified stronghold a little to the east and below Gradec. Each settlement maintained a separate and individual autonomy until the nineteenth century. Gradec was ruled by a council elected from the townspeople, whilst the Kaptol (which surrounded the Gothic cathedral) was ruled by the bishops and canons. It was an odd situation and the two factions quarrelled continually until well on in the sixteenth century when the common enemy of the Turk helped them to compose their frictions. The Turks made many attacks on the castles and the town below them but never succeeded in subduing them. Gradually the rival fortresses made peace.

Now, the **upper city,** which is tranquil and almost deserted, has a most substantial and aristocratic air. Indeed, most of its houses and palaces were built by and belonged to the Croat nobility in the eighteenth century. As a group of elegant and handsome buildings it has few equals in this part of Europe.

The first structure that confronts you is the fortified tower, called the Habernik, on the site of the old city gate. It has a bell known as the Lotršćak which has sounded the curfew at nine every evening since the Middle Ages and now sounds noon every day. It is also known as the tower of King Bela because that unhappy and fugitive monarch was obliged to put up here for a time.

It is almost impossible to give accurate directions for getting about the Gornji Grad, but if you bear right from the tower you soon come into **Katarinski Trg** on the right of which you find the old Jesuit Church—Crkva Sv Katerine, a seventeenth-century foundation with a Baroque interior. At No. 2. in the square is a small gallery which contains a number of paintings and some Roman relics from Sisak. Beyond is the Jezuitski Trg which has a fountain by Rosandić and on the right the buildings that formed the Jesuit seminary. On the left you find a small art gallery which exhibits contemporary work.

From the far side of the *trg* take the Jurja Habdelića Ulica and very soon you come to a magnificent old gateway, one of the most ancient parts of the original fortifications, called the **Kamenita Vrata** (The Stone Gate) which now shelters a small shrine hung with holy pictures. There is a continual traffic of people through the gate and they often pause to kneel, light a candle and say a prayer. Opposite there is a particularly venerable group of houses, and two more museums in Opatička Ulica away to your right.

Kamenita Ulica leads you to the main square, Radićev Trg. The glory of this heart of the old city is the **Church of St Mark** (Crkva Sv Marka) with its much photographed roof of brightly coloured tiles composed to represent the arms of Croatia, Slavonia, Dalmatia and Zagreb itself. The original church was built in King Bela's time and has suffered severely from earth-quakes and fires. Most of the main structure that survives is fourteenth and fifteenth century and the roof was done about a hundred years ago. Much of the restoration inside is even more recent. In 1937 the bishop commissioned Meštrović and the painter Kljaković, and the results of their work are successful even if they do not altogether blend with the Gothic. You should cer-tainly look at Meštrović's *Crucifix* (one of the maestro's best works) and the relief representing St Mark. Kljaković's *frescoes* illustrate the life of Christ and follow the Slav tradition of using contemporary peasant figures and types. You can see them again in the market. The stained glass windows were gifts from the leading families of Zagreb.

This square of St Mark's is traditionally associated with an out-standing event in Croatian history. Between the fourteenth and nineteenth centuries the Croat serfs rebelled many times against their oppressive feudal lords. *The* peasants' revolt occurred in 1573 and was led by a man called Matija Gubec. The principal enemy was a tyrannous count, Franjo Tahi, whose carved tomb, bearing lines that praise his heroism and nobility, still lies at Stubica. But the old peasants there say that the damp on the tombstone is the sweat of the suffering count in hell.

Gubec wanted to establish a democratic peasant government un-der the sovereignty of Maximilian II, and the rebellious movement spread rapidly. The sign of recognition worn by the rebels was a sprig of evergreen and the call to revolt was made by sending a cock's feather to each village. The local leaders then drew a large circle in the village square and those who wished to rebel would step inside, raise their right hand and swear an oath of loyalty.

The Establishment was so alarmed that they gathered a full-scale army and dispersed agents among the peasants to spread the rumour that the Turks were destroying their unprotected villages. Many peasants panicked and went home. The small and poorly armed remainder were no match for the professional soldiers. A typically Balkan massacre followed their defeat and Gubec was given a ceremonial execution in Zagreb during carnival time. Wearing an iron crown he was led into St Mark's square and there, according to tradition, formally enthroned. The iron crown was then made red hot and replaced on his head. After that he was dismembered. Another story is that he was burned in front of the cathedral in the Kaptol. Today, Gubec, unlike the count, has no tomb but he is a national hero: one in a long tradition of South Slav 'People's Heroes.'

If you bear north out of Radičev Trg and into Demetrova Ulica you will soon discover the **Natural History Museum** (Prirodoslovni Muzej). The zoological section is particularly well done and contains a complete collection of the fauna of the country. From here go on up the Demetrova Ulica until you come to the Popov Toranj (the priest's tower) part of the old fortifications and later turned into an observatory. Beyond this you can get into a street which returns you to the Trg Republike.

From here you can get up into the Dolac and the market place (don't miss the market) and thence to the **Kaptol**. Again, directions are almost impossible. It is a fascinating quarter of narrow streets and old houses dominated by the massive group of the cathedral and fortified bishop's palace and the remains of the medieval ramparts. The palace is an eighteenth-century structure. The twin-spired cathedral was begun early in the thirteenth century and has been restored several times since. Inside, the main things to look for are the stained glass window showing *The Assumption*, the choir stalls and a noble marble pulpit supported by an angel.

Behind and to the north of Zagreb (*za greb* means 'behind the cliff') stretches a big range of wooded hills and mountains called the Zagrebačka Gora (part of which is Medvednica or 'Bear Place') one of the most beautiful parts of Croatia and certainly the wildest interior region of the republic. I strongly recommend two excursions in particular into these parts to the delightful villages of Šestine and Gračani. Both are very near and you can reach them by tram (nos. 6, 13 and 14) or drive out on the Moše Pijade east of the Kaptol. Sunday morning is the time to go for then the local peasant women sally forth in their best costumes. These are very rich and gay and consist basically of white blouses with wide sleeves, vividly embroidered in red and other colours, full skirts, bright aprons and high white muslin caps that glitter with gold. Sometimes they wear big flowered head-dresses and necklaces of ducats and other ornaments. On special occasions you may see men in the traditional white, fringed and pleated trousers worn with red and orange waist-coats.

Another worthwhile excursion objective is Samobor, off the *autoput* to Ljubljana. It is a small, ancient town whose principal ruin is a thirteenth-century château. A couple of kilometres from here lies Mokrice, a spacious parkland with another château, this time of the fifteenth century, which has been transformed into a pleasant hotel and restaurant. All this area is ideal for walking and picnics.

From Zagreb the *autoput* by-passes all towns and villages as it runs through some rich and typically Croatian hill country to Ljubljana. One is not aware of crossing from Croatia to Slovenia any more than one is aware (as a rule) of a similar transition between any of the other republics (except, in some places, between Croatia and Bosnia) but not far out of Zagreb you have left Croatia and you may well notice fairly soon that the language sounds different. Gradually the details accumulate. The first menu you consult will look distinctly unfamiliar.

To put it to the test I recommend you to pause at **Otočec**, just off the *autoput* and about seventy kilometres out of Zagreb. Otočec is a castle built on an islet in the River Krka, a venerable stronghold with four towers that carries its seven centuries quite lightly. Within is a hotel and restaurant of excellence and style. I can't think of a better place to introduce yourself to Slovene food and wine. The castle is one of many fortifications in the Krka valley along the edge of what is known as the Bela Krajina, the White Border-land.

To the south and west there are several places of interest which can easily be reached by turning off the *autoput*. Firstly, **Novo Mesto** (New Place) one of the loveliest of the small Slovene towns with a fine town hall and parish church and several castles in the locality. Half an hour's ride due south is **Metlika,** so enchanting that most of it looks as if it was designed for a Mozart set. It was built on the site of a Roman town and has a good little archaeological and ethnographical museum. From here a poor road takes you to Črnomelj (again through richly fertile country), a large village also on a Roman site. Some Roman ruins survive. Thirty kilometres west of this lies **Kočevje,** a medieval town in wild, forested country which harbours a multitude of wolf, bear and wild boar. This is one of the best regions for walking that I know of, but you should avoid the thicker forests unless you are armed. After Kočevje I suggest you strike north to Žužemberk, a pretty village whose chief item of interest is the massive ruin of a medieval castle with six towers. You can easily get back on to the *autoput* from here.

CHAPTER 21

Ljubljana and N.E. Slovenia

Ljubljana—Kranj—Lake Bled—Lake Bohinj—Mt Trglav—Zlatorog—
Celje—Maribor—Ptuj—Ptjuska Gora—Varaždin—Trakošćan—Kumrovec

If you arrive in **Ljubljana** (the name means 'well-loved') on the *autoput* from Zagreb you enter the town rather abruptly because the city has never been spread out to the south owing to the marshlands, many of which have been converted into hop-fields. To avoid getting into difficulties cross the canal and river bridges, leaving the high wooded hill and castle on your right, and after the second bridge take the fourth turning to the right. This brings you into the main thoroughfare: Titovo Cesta (*cesta* is a 'street' or 'road'). If you are coming from the north (from Bled, for example) you run straight into the Titova at the main 'circus'. From Rijeka you will find yourself coming in down a broad road called Tržaška Ulica. Bear right at the big Trg Mladinskin and take the first main turn on the left at the lights and again you are in the Titova.

The centre of the city is compact and in it are all the main monuments, galleries and hotels. The Tourist offices and the agencies are in Titova Cesta. You have a wide choice of good hotels. I usually stay at the Union (in Miklošičeva Cesta, just off the Titova) or the Turist (two minutes' walk from here in Dalmatinova Ulica) or the Bellevue which is on a wooded hill half a mile from the town centre on the main Bled road (left hand side going out). All are comfortable and fairly inexpensive and the food is very good. The food at the Bellevue is excellent, partly because it is a high-powered and very efficiently run catering school. On the whole Slovenes organise their hotels well and there is a most agreeable atmosphere in them.

Most tourists don't spend more than a couple of days in Ljubljana —the townspeople concede it is a transit point—interesting though it is, and therefore I shall not deal with it in too much detail.

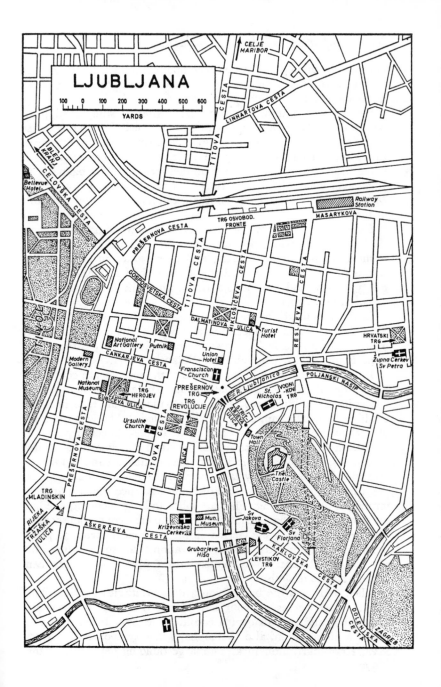

Happily the main sights can be encompassed in a few hours without undue exertion and the best spot to start is the **Prešernov Trg:** in the core of the old city by the river.

Here, as well as anywhere, you can see what a distinguished, prosperous town it is, a busy, clean, well-maintained place, much busier than Belgrade or Zagreb, in a style similar to many central European towns and much influenced by the Austrians. One might say without being too rude to the Bosnians or the Serbs that Ljubljana is to Jugoslavia what Milan is to Italy. It doesn't 'keep' Jugoslavia as Milan is said to 'keep' Italy—but you can see for yourself the truth of the analogy.

Its people, like most Slovenes, are hardworking, intelligent, thrifty, and somewhat withdrawn and grave. They are very adult, ironical, shrewd, great readers, and much gifted in organisation. But as soon as I have written this I have vivid memories of their gaiety, which can be exuberant. In our kingdom their nearest equivalent are the Scots.

In the middle of the *trg* is a statue of Prešern who was and is Slovenia's most famous poet. He was a lyricist who died in 1849 and is little known outside Jugoslavia. Overlooking the *trg* is the handsome **Fransciscan Church** (Frančiškanska Cerkev)—an example of Italian Baroque built in the middle of the seventeenth century. I have little affection for Baroque but the ornate and opulent excrecences in this building are less offensive to me than most, particularly the high altar by a minor Italian artist called Robba who did a lot of work in the city in the first half of the eighteenth century.

The whole area here each side of the River Ljubljanica has many fine houses, most of them products of the seventeenth and eighteenth centuries. They might very easily be part of Vienna and have about them that air of comfortable solidity and affluence which is at once impressive and deterring. They are sober and dignified and one has the uneasy feeling that their Austrian occupiers were perilously near complacence. Among the Germanic there is that tendency to prosperous philistinism and a certain enervation of the spirit induced by physical indulgence. Even dedication to work and money can become a form of sloth.

When you cross the bridge you are in **Stritarjeva Ulica.** The market place begins on your left (the seed market is especially interesting) and spreads over a considerable area. In front of you stands a big fountain, also by Robba, which symbolises the rivers Sava, Krka and Ljubljanica. The large building beyond with the clock tower is the Town Hall, rather an oppressive structure that was begun in the fifteenth century and transformed in the eighteenth. I think its most satisfying features are the porch, arcades and court-yard. There is another fountain inside by Robba: *Narcissus*.

Turn right coming from the Town Hall and you will soon find yourself on the flank of the ample **Cathedral of St Nicholas.** The original was burnt down by the Turks and the one you see was designed by the Italian Jesuit Pozzo whom I mentioned when writing of the Jesuit church in Dubrovnik. Inside, it is, as you expect, Baroque; so sumptuous that it almost induces a kind of aesthetic dyspepsia. Behind the cathedral is the palace of the old episcopal seminary (the caryatids are rather impressive) and beyond it is a broad square—**Vodnikov Trg**—named after a Slovene poet and philologist whose statue adorns it. Beyond Vodnikov Trg, along Poljanski Nasip and then over the river to Hrvatski Trg you reach **Župna Cerkev Sv Petra,** the oldest parish church in the city. A thirteenth-century foundation in origin, it was destroyed by the Turks and then rebuilt in 1730—which makes it, of course, Baroque. Inside there are a number of notable frescoes by Jelovšek, one of the better known eighteenth-century Slovene painters. The principal oil paintings are by Metzinger, also of the eighteenth century. Other work by both these artists is to be seen in the National Gallery.

On the right of Vodnikov Trg, almost opposite the statue (but ask your way here to be quite sure) a steep, old street, Studentovska Ulica, goes up to the castle. The **Castle** itself, reminiscent of a small forti-fied hill village, is the oldest building in Ljubljana: first erected early in the twelfth century but, of course, restored several times since.

There is no doubt that this is a very ancient site. Roman remains have been discovered here (there was a Roman town called Emona in the immediate neighbourhood) and it was very probably a pre-historic site also because the surrounding area has yielded many neolithic and Iron Age objects. In the late Middle Ages the castle belonged to feudal lords and has been used for a number of purposes since, including a barracks and a prison. Unfortunately there is hardly anything to see in the buildings, which are either closed or occupied by families, but you get a magnificent view of the whole city and the country round it. From this vantage point it is easy to see why Ljubljana has always been regarded as a strategic point (Churchill had a plan to capture it in a campaign against the Germans) and therefore why early settlers chose it.

I suggest you take the path on the far side from where you ascend and this will bring you down into an old part of the town where there are a couple of churches: Sv Florjana (St Florian) and Sv Jakova (St James). Both are Baroque but there isn't very much to see in them. The decorations in the latter seem to border on the artistically vulgar. If you scout near here you will find a very large house (called the Grubarjeva Hiša) which has a beautiful Baroque façade and a curious decorated staircase.

From **Levstikov Trg** you recross the river, take the second on the right and a short walk brings you to the Municipal Museum (not essential) near which is a small convent and church known as Križevniška Cerkev (Church of the Knights of the Cross). A few yards from this you enter Trg Francuske Revolucije in the middle of which is a large modern monument to *The Unknown French Soldier*: a belated tribute to French troops of the First World War. From here take Vegova Ulica, back towards the centre of the town, which opens into a huge square: the Trg Revolucije (the Peoples' Revolution this time). You may have time to look at a curiosity in the far left hand corner of the *trg*. It is the Ursuline church which has a lofty classical façade with Corinthian columns topped by a sort of Gothic pediment. It was built in 1713. The ornate high altar is by Robba; and there are some statues by Metzinger. If you haven't got time cross the *trg* diagonally and go over Titova Cesta and up Šubičeva Ulica. On your right you will find Herojev Trg and on one side of it a very large building which is the **National Museum.** This is one of the principal museums in Jugoslavia and has particularly good archaeological and ethnographical sections, plus an interesting natural history department. The best thing to do here is to buy a catalogue and you will need a full two hours to benefit from it.

When you come out turn left and take the first on the left and a minute's walk produces the Modern Gallery where they hold various exhibitions. Away to the north-west from this point, towards the wooded hills, stretches a luxuriant and spacious park, the Tivoli, surrounding a château near which they hold the Ljubljana Fair. From the Modern Gallery turn down Cankarjeva Cesta, as if you were going back into the town centre. The portentous building on your left is the **National Art Gallery,** another recommended stop. Round the landing or gallery over the staircase are copies of frescoes in Hrastov Pje in central Istria (an unusual one depicts the Dance of Death) about which I shall have more to say when I come to Beram in Istia. In show-cases on the landing there are a number of very pleasing small sketches and paintings by a little known Slovene artist called Šubić Janez. Three of the Italian scenes are excellent. Several of the large rooms on the west are devoted to landscape and portraits by Austrian and Slovene artists which are interesting but unimportant. The best part of the art collection is mostly lodged in one room off the main hall and consists largely of wood-carvings of the fourteenth and fifteenth centuries taken from small country churches. There are two very fine pietàs, a vivid *statue of St Oswald*, a rather amusing St George polishing off a dragon that looks like an alligator, a very sombre and haunting *Crucifix* of the early sixteenth century, and a fine, ungainly, primitive *Crucifix* of the very early thirteenth century. This last is almost certainly the oldest work of art in the gallery. There is also a good small relief of the *Death of the Virgin.*

Quite a lot of people arrive in Ljubljana by train and then want to hire a car, to tour Slovenia or other parts of the country. Fortunately communications in Slovenia are rather good and the roads are better than anywhere else in Jugoslavia. You should certainly try to spend some time exploring northern Slovenia and I especially recommend that you visit Kranj, Škofja Luka, Bled, Bohinj, Celje, Maribor and Ptuj. From Ptuj it is only a short journey back into Croatia to Varaždin which can be incorporated in a round trip and from where you could return to Zagreb either on the main road or, better, across country, via Kumrovec, Tito's birthplace.

First, **Kranj,** whose name comes from the Roman city Carnium and gives a title to the central region of Slovenia—Kranjska. This is a small, ancient city squatting high above the left bank of the Sava. It has a Gothic cathedral and a tiny ethnographical museum with a number of interesting utensils and implements which include a wooden sheath, rather like a small quiver, used for carrying a whetstone. Prešern died in Kranj so he has a couple of statues and his house has been turned into a museum. Near Kranj lies Škofja Luka, one of the oldest towns in Slovenia, whose castle adorns a green hill and shelters, incidentally, a good collection of wood-carvings and folk art. You should look particularly at the paintings on glass, mostly done by peasant women. The subjects tend to be biblical and rural and are characteristic of peasant life in many parts of central Europe.

If you continue on the main road towards Bled you should pause at **Radovljica**—also with its castle and Gothic church. In the Baroque palace there is a bee-keeper's museum and though you may have already seen the bee-keeping section in the National Museum in Ljubljana, I advise you to visit this one. The Slovenes have always been great apiarists and their bees are exported all over the world. It is characteristic of the Slovene's careful husbandry that wherever you go you will find clusters of beehives, many of them painted and carved—especially that part where the front door is cut. The workmanship is of the same crude and vivid kind that you may have noticed on Sicilian carts and also on the bullock wagons in Serbia and Macedonia.

Early beehives were decorated with stars and ornamental symbols. Later, the range widened to include illustrations of the Bible, seasonal events and everyday village life. So we have a sprightly, and, at times satirical chronicle from which, as with the frescoes, the *stećaks* and the *krajputaši*, we can learn a good deal. It combines the effects of a strip cartoon and the illustrations to a Book of Hours.

The size of individual figures usually depends on their importance. There are frequent tavern or domestic scenes where the drunkard, the braggadochio and the hen-pecked husband are ridiculed. The figures are stylised, as on the *krajputaši*.

Most bee-keepers had at least one picture of Job, their patron, on their hives. He is usually depicted sitting disconsolate and weary on a dung-heap, renouncing his worldly goods while his wife scolds him. The Fall is another popular theme, especially suitable for strip cartoon treatment. Guardian angels and saints are favourite subjects: particularly St Apollonia, the protectress of healthy teeth, St Lucian, the protector of good sight, and St Eustace, patron of the chase.

Notable political events are also recorded. For example, the French occupation of Slovenia is recalled by the scene of a Frenchman driving a cart drawn by cocks. The Turk is often shown in various comic situations, like marrying several wives simultaneously and not being able to decide which to take first. Anti-Reformation views were expressed by showing Luther with a woman in a cart drawn by goats—one of which is ridden by a devil hastening them straight to hell.

There are also numerous paintings of the fable genre, often involving a hunter with wild animals. Usually the hunter comes off worst and is made to look absurd. Some of the artists, especially from the seventeenth century onwards, have obviously based their

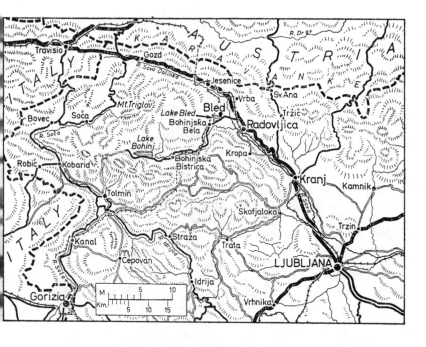

paintings on Baroque models and show a certain growing sophistication in their sense of perspective and dimension. In most cases the religious motifs are related to the Slovene peasant environment. Every genuinely original story lends itself to endless re-interpretation.

Recent inventions, like the train, the steam-ship and the bicycle, have also found a place in these simple pictorial annals. A caustic, self-protective humour gives the prevailing tone. Authority and misfortune are jeered at, death challenged with optimism.

Just south of Radovljica is the village of **Kropa,** the village of smiths, where doors, windows, fences, ceilings, staircases and hearths are decorated with wrought-iron. A swift stream runs through it and wooden conduits used to carry water to individual houses where were the forges for making nails, horseshoes and any number of wrought-iron objects. There was a tradition that you couldn't become a master smith until you could forge a horseshoe that would fit an egg without cracking or burning it. The tradition of craftsmanship—and Slovenia is the land *par excellence* of craftsmanship —has been kept alive and now there is a kind of co-operative depart-

375

ment which produces everything from chandeliers to ash-trays in many different materials.

Bled, very near Radovljica, is one of the most famous resorts in Europe and has been used as one since the eighteenth century. I don't like mountain resorts much but I must admit that Bled is delightful. The great Prešern eulogised it in one of his poems:

> *Tje na otok z valovami obadni,*
> *v današnjih dnevih božjo pot Marije;*
> *v dnu zad stoje snežnikov velikani . . .*

Here he evokes the lake, the pilgrims going to the church, the high, snow-capped mountains, and goes on to describe the castle and the green pastures beyond. There is not such a beautiful place in the country, he says. It is the image of Eden.

Indeed the lake *is* glorious and the church on the island (built on the site of a pagan temple) is a popular place of pilgrimage. The whole scene is encircled by mountains fissured with deep ravines and gorges and shaggy with forest. High on a rocky peak above the lake stands a castle which combines the fairyland of Grimm and the Ruritania of Anthony Hope. It has now been turned into a museum and I strongly recommend a visit there to see its tapestries, furniture and pictures.

There are about a dozen good hotels of the spa variety (some of Edwardian vintage) and in these the Slovene hoteliers dispense hospitality with considerable finesse. I can recommend the Park, the Toplice and the Jelovica.

In winter Lake Bled is frozen over, so everyone can skate, and the locals actually skate to church on the island. During summer the waters are smooth and warm for swimming, boating and regattas. When the high season is on there is a continual round of festivals, spectacles and tournaments. Even Marshal Tito goes from time to time and stays in his modern villa on the shores, thus emulating the former royalty and nobility who used Bled as a summer resort when Belgrade became too hot.

West, farther up in the mountains, are the villages of Bohinjska Bela and Bohinjska Bistrica—and **Lake Bohinj** which is larger and even more beautiful than Bled though not so frequented. If you are in this area towards the end of September do not miss the Kravlji Bal (literally 'Cow Dance') a vivid and convivial festival which celebrates the return of the cattle from the mountains. Dominating this area is Mt Triglav ('the three-headed'), the highest mountain in Jugoslavia and the Olympus of the Slavonic gods. Slovenes regard this peak with a certain mystical reverence and awe and there are a good many legends attached to it. One of the better known concerns a white chamois with golden horns. Once it was pursued by hunters who, naturally, wanted the gold. However, Zlatorog led them to an abyss and they all fell over bar one. This survivor managed to wound the chamois and out of the wound sprang a red flower. Zlatorog ate this and was immediately cured. Perhaps it was a carnation, for the red carnation is the emblem of Slovenia.

Not far north of Bled is the small village where Prešern was born: **Vrba,** at the foot of the Karavanke mountains, where his house has been turned into a museum. The poet wrote one of his best-known lyrics about this village, in a poem that apostrophises rather as Goldsmith addressed sweet Auburn:

> *O, Vrba Srečna, draga vas domača,*
> *Kjer hiša mojegu stoji očeta;*
> *Du b'uka žeja me iz tvoj'ga sveta,*
> *Speljala ne bila, golj'fiva Kača.*

Here he praises the village and then regrets bitterly having left it. What began as an ode continues through three more verses and concludes as a kind of personal elegy.

If you have gone thus far into the countryside you may have been struck by its resemblance to Austria and Switzerland. There are the same forested mountains climbing to snowy peaks: the same flowery valleys scooped with lakes and planed by long grassy slopes on which the flocks pasture; the same hay meticulously hung in long, roofed racks or carefully wound round poles. . . . The same Calvaries on the roadside, wrought-iron tavern signs, wooden chalets, orderly clean villages clustered round the square dovecot towers or bulbous onion steeples of the churches. . . . Even the people look different from other Jugoslavs, fairer, more Germanic. Everything conspires to persuade you that you are in the Tyrol, an impression intensified when you discover that many Slovenes speak excellent German (they are also very good at Italian) and were, until recently, quite often bi-lingual. Such an impression is both right and wrong.

The people are not at all like the Germans and Austrians. Their temperament, values and habits, even their vision of the meaning of existence, are different. They are Slav and their ancestors formed part of the Slav migration which began here some time in the sixth

377

century. In fact Slovenes are recognisably like other South Slavs. They have pronounced, well-rooted noses, firm jaws, a general strength and definiteness of feature, and highish cheek-bones. They tend to be fairer than, say, Serbs or Bosnians, and their complexions are lighter and their eyes greyer; but they possess what, in the final analysis, is an almost indefinable quality, not solely communicated by physical appearance, that indubitably marks them as Slav.

The past of Slovenia is really most unusual (the extraordinary thing is that it exists as an entity or nation at all) and helps to explain the ambivalent impact the country makes. In a sense it has no history. It has never been an independent state and, apparently, never wanted to be. It has been under German and Austrian domination almost from the very beginning, certainly from the tenth century, right up until the end of the First World War with the exception of six years of Napoleonic occupation between 1809–15. In short Slovenes have been subordinates for at least a thousand years.

You might suppose that such a rôle would render any people supine, unctuous and crafty. But it hasn't with the Slovenes, and so we have the probably unique anomaly of a small group of self-centred people of great individuality and determination who have always ignored frontiers and nourished within themselves a kind of secret, almost subversive, intellectual and cultural tradition of nationalism which has proved stronger than any of the political or military mights with which they have always been surrounded and which have preyed upon them for so long. Above all they developed and nourished their own language. In a way they have reversed the rôles of host and parasite.

The strength and resilience of their Slav nationalism was abundantly proved when it came to underground and guerrilla warfare against the Fascists. You might not expect a country of poets (there are more poets to the square mile in Slovenia than anywhere in the world) intellectuals, egg-heads and pedants to be expert in such activities, but their underground movement was the first and most efficient and deadly of all. Their record of sabotage was outstanding.

You cannot very easily travel from Bled across country to Celje and so the best thing to do is to return on the *autoput* to Ljubljana (it is only fifty kilometres) and take the main road north-east. An alternative is to turn off at Kranj and cut across to Kamnik which

378

you can reach anyway from Trzin if you elect to return to Ljubljana.

Kamnik lies in very beautiful countryside and has been a centre for Alpine sports since the seventeenth century. For that matter the whole of Slovenia has been highly organised for open-air sports for a long time: especially mountaineering, walking, hunting, fishing and ski-ing. Ski-ing is the national sport and most Slovenes are capable on skis. In fact they were pioneers of this and are the only people apart from the Scandinavians who have a word of their own for ski-ing—*smučka*. They have done it for centuries. One historian of the seventeenth century describes the peasants walking on the snow with the aid of planks and zooming down the slopes with the speed of demons.

At Kamnik there are some venerable castle ruins and a twelfth-century Gothic church. The whole area is ideal for walking or just doing almost nothing. One can spend weeks in Slovenia doing nothing without any notion of guilt and feel thoroughly refreshed at the end of it.

In country districts like this you may be lucky enough to see some costumes—not just the Tyrol knickerbocker suit plus hat with feather or claw, but more interesting regalia like odd fringed white trousers worn with a white tunic and drawn in by a coloured belt; above, a felt hat and a knotted handkerchief round the neck. The women's dress also tends to be white with strips of dark braid on the hem and the bolero. The head-dresses are most graceful and consist of a kind of veil which falls down the back and is rolled round the temples from where it spreads in starched wings.

The ideal occasion to see Slovene costumes is a country wedding, many of which take place near Easter on a Sunday morning and are sometimes accompanied by various traditional practices. Beforehand the engagement is announced by a crier who, decked with bells and carrying a scythe, goes from house to house inviting the guests. The wedding feast is held in the bride's home and when the groom's guests arrive the bride's remain in the house. Bargaining over the bride's price follows and a false bride (an old woman or a stuffed figure) is produced before the real bride appears. As the bride leaves her home her father anoints her bound hands with wine on the threshold. When the procession reaches the groom's house his mother awaits her daughter-in law with keys, wine and bread. The groom carries his bride in and then she lifts up a male child and walks round the hearth tasting various dishes as she does so. Needless to say there is a great deal of eating, drinking and dancing and

379

the festivities may go on for two or more days. Sometimes they are accompanied by improvised comic sketches.

Between Kamnik and Celje there is a broad extent of green, hilly country (at times reminiscent of Monmouthshire and Hertfordshire) bordered with pastures and dotted with farms and hamlets to all of which the Slovene has brought his ancestral thrift and innate sense of care and propriety. The ample houses are solid and well-made and scrupulously clean. Their steep red roofs slope to immense eaves, their walls are painted in subtle shades of buff, ochre and umber. Farms have magnificent wooden barns, in which the Slovene's craftsmanship is once again evident in the carving of beams.

Celje is only a small provincial town on a site first settled by the Romans, but it has an aristocratic air about it which is largely induced by many elegant buildings. High on the hill above stands yet another ruined castle which once belonged to powerful feudal lords whose last representative died (by assassination) as long ago as 1456. The buildings near the station recall eighteenth century Paris and London. Among them is a Gothic extravaganza for a town hall which should certainly be included complete in a Museum of Bad Art.

The focal point of the city is Tomišičev Trg (I do not call it the *korso* because you don't see this event so often in inland Slovenia) and a couple of minutes' walk east is the Gothic cathedral dedicated for some reason to St Daniel, presumably Daniel the Stylite. You should take a look at the high altar, the side chapel and the stained glass windows. On the external south-eastern wall are sunk a number of steles and plaques and a witty carving of St Daniel and the Virgin.

From here return to Tomišičev Trg and take the street that opens before you in the near left hand corner. Three minutes' walk and you arrive at the **Grofija,** a lovely early Baroque arcaded palace which has been converted into a most interesting museum. The proportions of the rooms are perfect and some of them have princely ceilings of carved wood. There are a Roman and Celtic section (the prize here is a bronze Bacchus) and a lot of paintings. One room has been devoted to a history of the noble families who ruled Celje and a great area round it. The objects include a number of their skulls. There is a more *macabre* relic than these in the shape of a long strip of dried skin, wound round a piece of wood, which at first I thought was a sloughed snake-skin. In fact it is human. In the old days it was the custom here to punish an idle peasant or disobedient slave by cutting a strip of skin one inch wide from his body. The executor began at the right thumb, went up the arm, across the body and all the way down to the left big toe.

The central room on the first floor has a remarkable *trompe l'oeil* painting on the ceiling which was done by a Venetian artist round about 1580. It was discovered quite recently underneath (or above, as it were) a false ceiling and shows two battle scenes, the four seasons of the year and four portraits of celebrities of that time. It is almost certainly done by one who knew Paolo Veronese's work and therefore he may have been a Venetian. As far as I know there is no record of Veronese having come up as far as this, but it employs the same technique of *sotto in sù* (from below upwards) as it is called and is a masterpiece.

The cellars of the Grofija are crammed with Roman stonework and in fact part of the Roman town stood where the palace now is on the edge of the river. It was a flood that swept it away and when they came to dig foundations much of it was revealed.

Between Celje and Maribor there isn't a great deal to delay you though there are many tempting vistas of valleys and glimpses of villages and castles to lure you off the main track. Nearly every village in Slovenia has its Gothic church and hilltop fortress encircled by houses: a typical scene compacted exactly by another prominent Slovene poet, Župančič, who died in 1949 and is generally regarded as the best Slovene translator of Shakespeare. In *Duma*, a kind of paean to his land, he describes the church in vigil above the surrounding cottages, watching the people in the fields, telling them the time, giving them the work.

Most of the villages and small towns have a *gostilna* or two. In fact there are getting on for three thousand of these inns in Slovenia altogether and they are friendly and inexpensive places to stay. The plumbing will be rather rudimentary but the rooms are comfortable and clean and you can usually eat and drink heartily—as the Slovenes do. Food is a little richer than in most parts of Jugoslavia. The soups are usually delicious. They cook ravioli well and some of the smoked and dried meats are most appetising. For drinks there are wines, of course, draught beer and any number of brandies. The Slovenes drink rather more than most Jugoslavs and when they do they become very convivial.

The southerly approach to **Maribor** is not very prepossessing and then suddenly you see this spired and towered city stacked irregularly each side of the River Drava, an ancient and mellowed town, the colour of yellow and red antirrhinums, which was founded in the twelfth century and is still a busy and important place.

Cross the bridge over the Drava and take the first on the left. This leads you to Glavni Trg a convenient spot to park and from which to explore. Probably the first thing you'll notice in this *trg* is the Baroque statue to the Virgin which commemorates the plague of 1680 and Her intercession. The building opposite to it is the Town Hall built in 1515. If you explore the narrow streets north of the *trg* you will soon find the Cathedral dedicated to St John the Baptist. Originally this was Romanesque (about 1150) but it has gradually been Gothicised and reconstructed and now forms an imposing hybrid of which the townspeople are very proud. Near the huge bell-tower are a pair of Roman lions salvaged from some excavation. The Slovenes have always been strict and devout Catholics and they bring their children up in the tradition. To this day the churches are well attended and the Slovenes' zeal is reflected in their good repair.

If you go due north from here you arrive in a long narrow street, Slovenska Ulica. Turn right and carry on till you reach another big square on the left of which is a rambling twelfth-century **castle and citadel**—now largely a museum. The archaeological and ethnographical sections are comprehensive. There is a lot of interesting furniture and a collection of portraits from the sixteenth century. You should also notice some examples of painting on glass, one of which is ascribed to Dürer. Near the Grad are the remains of fortifications which formerly surrounded the whole town.

Should you decide to stay in Maribor (the Orel and Slavija are two comfortable hotels) you will find it makes a good base for excursions especially into the Mariborski Pohorje in the west and north. Here, tucked amidst the rolling hills, lie numerous hamlets and villages of great charm whose homely, spacious inns seduce one to tankards of beer and copious meals. All about you spread fertile slopes patterned with streams, dotted with water mills and small, white, wine sheds. Over the vineyards the windwheels flutter and whirr like enormous butterflies. Prosperous grounds, tended by a kindly and hardworking peasantry.

Ptuj, a mere half an hour's run from Maribor, is my favourite town in Slovenia. It, also, lies on the banks of the swift deep Drava and is a very old site. It was founded by the Celts and captured in

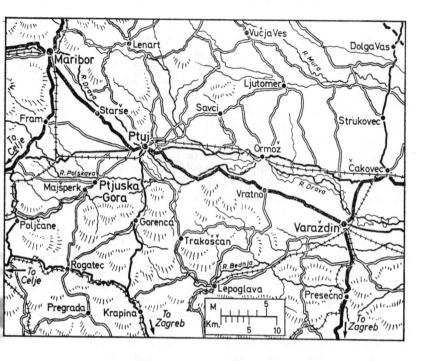

35 B.C. by Octavius. The Romans called it Poetovium and later, during the reign of Septimus Severus at the turn of the second century, it became a prosperous city with a palace, temples, baths and theatres. It has never quite lost its imperial look, despite a succession of disasters including fire and the Turks. Most of the buildings you see today date from the sixteenth to the eighteenth centuries and, apart from coastal towns like Piran, Rab, Korčula and Dubrovnik, you are unlikely to find many places where solidity and grace meet in such admirable concord.

Below the massive château on the knoll the weathered, terra-cotta roofs slope over spacious houses washed in umber, pink and sienna. Everywhere there is colour, elegance and gaiety, the sort of place that reminds you of Mozart and Haydn, even of Viennese waltzes which are supposed to have originated, like Haydn, in Slovenia. There is another theory that Haydn was a Croat but I believe that many pundits reject both notions.

There is not much in the way of hotels (I stay at the *gostilna* Beli

383

Križ and eat at the new Poetovio) but a certain amount of discomfort is easily supported in such surroundings.

The Gothic parish church of **St George** stands more or less in the centre and was built in the twelfth century. You should have a look at its high altar and the choir stalls. Separate from it is a very fine belfry, which had to be rebuilt after a fire in 1705; and if you examine the lower parts of it you will see incorporated quite a lot of Roman stonework, fragments of sculpture and inscription tablets. Next to it is a much more tangible relic of Roman times: a fifteen-foot-high marble funeral **monolith** erected by Severus in 194. It bears its centuries lightly and on it is a superb carving which shows Orpheus with his lute entrancing the birds and beasts. The best time to see it is mid-morning when it takes the sun full.

On the south-east edge of the town is the shell of the thirteenth-century church of the Minorites. It was burnt down recently but enough survives to show what a beauty it must have been. But Ptuj has been very unlucky with fires and in the main square there is a swirly rococo monument to St Florian (patron saint of firemen) erected as a 'protection' because of the many incendiary disasters of the previous century.

At the north-eastern rim of the town lie the Dominican monastery and church, now all a museum. It was a thirteenth-century foundation and the Dominicans were there until the end of the eighteenth. The church's façade is an example of hideous Baroque which wouldn't even qualify for the Museum of Bad Art. However, behind it there survives the now much-cut-about Gothic interior which shelters a collection of Roman remains and a mock-up of a Mithraic temple, three of which have been found in the immediate neighbourhood. In the monastic quarters and round the graceful glassed-in Gothic cloister there is a considerable collection of Roman and medieval objects which, the last time I was there, still awaited sorting and labelling. Whatever has happened to them by the time you arrive look out for a statue of the Virgin and Child, in black and gold, of the late fourteenth century and also (it was tucked away on top of a cupboard when I saw it) a sculpture of Romulus and Remus being suckled, a late Roman 'primitive' work which I would very much have liked to smuggle away.

There remains the **castle,** to which you can climb from quite near this monastery. As you reach the gateway look at the arms and motto. GRIP FAST, it says. Its presence here is explained by the fact that the Herberstein family, who owned and lived in this castle for

Lake Bled, with the church of St. Mary on the little island, a place of pilgrimage since the thirteenth century, and the chateâu on the far shore

Above and left, the Roman
Amphitheatre at Pula. O
of the greatest surviving
amphitheatres, it was ere
sometime between 30 BC
AD 14 and held over twe
thousand people

many years, had strong Scottish connections. They were a very wealthy and powerful clan who had huge estates all over northern Slovenia and whose survivors are now scattered round the world. Periodically they return to visit their family home.

The castle is fifteenth century and was a good deal restored in the seventeenth and has now been converted into an excellent museum which contains a collection of Baroque furniture, Flemish and Gobelin tapestries and a large number of portraits. There are paintings of several Scottish members of the family and you can easily detect the differences in the features. The ethnographical collection contains a large number of prehistoric finds and objects found in early Slav tombs. In one section there are some costumes consisting of sheepskins and rather grotesque painted masks (with a long nose and tongue, and teeth made of white beans) adorned by feathered, horned head-dresses. Towards the end of February every year in neighbouring villages, such costumes are donned for the *Kurenti* processions—ancient dance rituals to banish winter, the ghosts of winter and death.

Groups of men (usually four or five in each) move from house to house performing dances, the cow-bells on their belts jangling as they go. Each man carries a wooden stick called a *ježevka* to the end of which a hedgehog skin is tied (conceivably the survivor of some flagellant practice, or perhaps just a flail to ward off evil spirits). Each group leads a masker representing the devil who bears a pitchfork and is wrapped in a fishing net to signify that he has been captured, at any rate temporarily.

These men are then joined by the *orači* ('the ploughers') who, also masked, have a little wooden plough which they drag into each farmyard or courtyard they visit. At every stop one of the *orači* pretends to plough a furrow while another walks behind him and scatters sand to symbolise the planting of seed. This is one of the most fascinating rituals you are likely to see in Europe.

In Ptuj itself, these rituals are magnified into an historical pageant involving hundreds of people. To the accompaniment of a barbarous clamour of bells, clappers, rattles and clashing sticks a hundred or more *kurenti* in monstrous masks lead a long procession of people in a wide variety of costumes which represent traditional occupations and classes: shepherds, weavers, oxherds, dancing girls, mourners, monks, nuns and what not. Floats suggest different themes each year, dances and ceremonials symbolise important events in history. It is like an amalgam of the Lord Mayor's Show and a Spanish fiesta. Indeed, outside Spain I know of no spectacle of its kind which is noisier, more convivial or more colourful. Unfortunately such celebrations are likely to die out under the influence of a régime which regards them as a harmful survival of superstitious practice and religious belief. Many have already done so.

What is called the **Knights' Hall,** the baronial hall of the castle, is a lovely room. Round it are hung arms and a unique array of portraits of Turkish men and women at present being identified by scholars correlating evidence from archives in Istanbul where the Herberstein family had many diplomatic connections. In the middle of the hall is a four-sided ottoman sofa with a central backrest. The lid of this is removable and below there is sufficient space for a small man. They say that a dwarf used to be concealed in this compartment so that he might eavesdrop on the conversation of the knightly retainers and report anything subversive. Off this hall is the chapel which contains a painting of the martyrdom of St Peter ascribed, *very* dubiously, to Tintoretto.

Collectors of ' . . . slept here' souvenirs can add one to their album at Ptuj for there is a handsome bed in one of the rooms once used by Maria Teresa, a lady who seems to have shared with Queen Elizabeth that kind of ubiquity that attracts far too many claims for beds. In fact Maria Teresa *did* sleep here.

Down by the bridge stands a large round stone building, formerly a wine vault and now a viniculture museum. This is appropriate because the whole region is one of the principal vineyards in Slovenia and produces some of the best wines in Jugoslavia, as, apparently, it did in Pliny's time for he makes particular mention of them. A number are well known outside Jugoslavia, like Ljutomer Riesling and Jeruzalem (or Jeruzalemčan) both exhilarating white wines. The latter comes from a village called Jeruzalem which has a sister village called Bethlehem. An odd pair of names to find in this part of the world but the explanation is simple and fairly convincing: it is said they were founded by defectors from a crusading army, and one can well understand the temptation of this sunny and fertile land.

Other good Slovenian white wines are Pekrčan, Ritoznojčan and Haložan. The best red is Kraški Teran, and the standard *vin du pays* a *rosé* called Cviček. Many of the white wines are quite astringent. The answer is to experiment from region to region and you will find as in most other parts of Jugoslavia, that the *vins ordinaires* are often better than those with fancy labels prepared for shop windows.

If you can spare the time you should make a brief visit to a work of art at **Ptjuska Gora,** a tiny village on a wooded hill thirteen kilometres west of Ptuj (re-cross the Drava and then ask the way). The narrow, high, compact Gothic church (one of the best examples of Gothic in Slovenia) fits neatly on its hillock and though it is only a village church it has a most ducal approach of an ornate gateway and ample steps. Within, above the high altar, is a big relief in the centre of which stand the Virgin and Child. The Virgin's cloak or robe is held back and up by seven angels and beneath its pro-tecting folds is a dense crowd of kneeling and standing figures (well over seventy in all) who represent the family of the Counts of Celje. Each one is a tiny masterpiece of portraiture: the faces are vividly realistic, the costumes bright and varied. The artist is not known.

If you want to go to Varaždin you must return to Ptuj and con-tinue on the main road. On the way I recommend a diversion to the north-east (take the turn to Ormož and carry on towards Mursk Sobota via Ljutomer) where the River Mura irrigates the prettiest plain in Slovenia. The broad acres of maize and buck-wheat are laced by willowed and aldered brooks, and the low hills beyond thick with vineyards. Hidden among the acacia groves and plum orchards, village cottages cluster together in batches of bright green, red and blue. From the windows dangle garlands of paprikas and on the roofs the storks stand on their nests in aloof speculation. By tradition their presence confers good fortune. By a different tradition the nightingales celebrate it, autumn and summer, in 'full-throated ease'. Keats should have come here as an antidote to melancholy.

If you have gone as far as Murska Sobota I suggest you avoid re-tracing any ground and take the road east to Lendava from where you turn south to Čakovec and **Varaždin.** This is an aristocratic town of great antiquity (I advise the Istra hotel here).

It was founded by the early Slav settlers though its first reliable records date only from 1181 when it was ruled by a *župan* called Bela. Thirty-odd years later it fell to the swords of the Tartars and was then rebuilt by command of King Bela IV—he who took refuge from those same Tartars at Trogir. Later it was incorporated in the estates of the Counts of Celje who were to northern Slovenia and this part of Croatia roughly what the Frankopans and Zrinjskis were to the region round Rijeka and Senj.

Most of the buildings you see today are seventeenth-century.

There are several palaces and churches and dozens of distinguished houses. In fact its Baroque domestic architecture is delightful. Some of the fortifications from the original walled city survive. But the main thing to see is the fortress—which is very like a French château. Whereas Ptuj castle was quite definitely an establishment for noblemen the *grad* at Varaždin is more like a fortified manor house for landed gentry. Now, of course, it is a museum and its furnishings, portraits, implements and other possessions form an interesting collection though nothing like as valuable as that in Ptuj.

Opposite the château, the other side of the main road, is an unusual cemetery partitioned and surrounded by monolithic macracarpa hedges and crowded with elaborate Baroque monuments. It seems to be as much a public garden and a park as a graveyard and in the *korso* hour becomes a social rendezvous. There is nothing gloomy about it. As a modern Slovene poet wrote:

> Death is my old acquaintance.
> I am a tree whose leaves are scattered over tombs.
> I bear in my soul the gallows of my dreams.

From Varaždin I recommend the cross-country route to Kumrovec. The roads are poor and you will have to ask your way quite often but it is lovely, rolling, forested country with many fascinating little hamlets *en route*. At Lepoglava (the big monastery here has been converted into a prison!) I suggest you digress to Trakoščan, a much restored 'château' on the edge of a lake surrounded by woods, for which a great battle was fought in 1651: a good old-fashioned collision between noblemen who could command private armies at a moment's notice. At that time a Count Jaspar Drasković possessed the stronghold, but he held it quite illegally as he had filched it from his son-in-law, one of the Zrinjski family (who had actually bought it from him) while Nikola Zrinjski was contending against the Turks. After an exchange of verbal abuse (which ended by Drasković saying: 'I will defend Trakoščan to the last stone!') they got down to the serious business of fighting for it. As a result it was virtually burnt down. Having satisfied Honour, or whatever it was they were engaged with, they came to an agreement—and the gutted castle was left as a ruin. It was not restored until the nineteenth century and the new version is a museum rather like those I have already mentioned at Maribor and elsewhere.

Collectors of Baroque curiosities should not miss the church of Our Lady of the Snows in **Belec**, near Zlatar, in a region known as

Ivančiće and one of the loveliest parts of Croatia: a gentle and fecund land of wooded hills, flowery vales and hamlets, tiny lakes and meadows alive with the gossamer music of streams.

Belec, with its medieval castle, was given as a present by King Sigismund to Herman, one of the Counts of Celje, in 1339. It has a medieval church, but the later one, with its dapper belfry, towered cloisters and polygonal sanctuary, is more interesting. The outside is plain; the interior a banquet of gold and silver, of gilded sculpture and carving, swirling draperies and flamboyant ornament. There are also paintings and treasure. Most of the decoration was done about 1739.

Kumrovec, Marshal Tito's birthplace, is a small hamlet surrounded by woody hills on which are the remains of at least six castles. His home, a four-roomed cottage, has been turned into a small museum whose solid furniture was made by peasant craftsmen. One room is devoted to photographs, the others are much as they used to be.

Not many men have their birthplaces turned into pilgrimage sights in their own lifetime but Tito, after all, is a most extraordinary man, a person of invincible determination and courage who is still regarded with deep affection and respect by most of his countrymen. He is, in fact, a classic example of a man who, by sheer ability, has risen from the humblest beginnings to a position of wide power and influence. In his life he has done more than most people could achieve in a dozen. He is supposed to have got his nickname (his real name is Joseph Broz) from his habit of saying, when giving succinct orders, 'You—that'—'Ti-to'. He was born in Kumrovec in 1892, the son of a Slovene mother and a Croat father. This is hardly the place to attempt an account of the great warrior and statesman, and in any case there is already a copious literature about him.

CHAPTER 22

West Slovenia and the Istrian Peninsula

Western Slovenia—Postojna—Cerkniško Jezero—Koper—Portorož—Piran Buje—the Istrian Peninsula—Pazin—Beram—Poreč—Rovinj—Pula Labin—Opatija

There is a Balkan saying that behind every hero stands a traitor and, as I suggested in the first chapter, the history of the Balkans is a catalogue of heroism, violence, plotting and dreadful betrayals, most of which spring from extremes of nature. The north-west of Slovenia is no exception to the bloody catalogue or that tragic tradition which requires grand gestures of pride and defiance.

There is one village in the farthest Julian Alps, near the Italian frontier, which, up to a point, epitomises the history of the region (and, for that matter, many other parts). In 1943 a German general was killed here and as a reprisal the Germans massacred the male population completely. The women were forced to witness the slaughter. When it was over they were taken away. But they came back and rebuilt the village and from that day forbade any man to enter it. Like some stray and bizarre chorus of crones left over from a Greek tragedy the black-clad women live out their lives in solitude and desolation.

Not many tourists visit the remoter parts of the Julian Alps or their hinterland, except those who go to mountain resorts for climbing and ski-ing, but enormous numbers of them take the road or train from Ljubljana to Postojna and on from there to Trieste or Rijeka or round the Istrian Peninsula.

Between Ljubljana and Postojna the country, like that of the north and west, is green and woody and on every side there is the now familiar evidence of meticulous and loving husbandry. There are many enchanting villages of solid, stone-balconied houses, vine-trellised inns, cavernous barns, bowling alleys, courtyards gay with flowers which all Slovenes love.

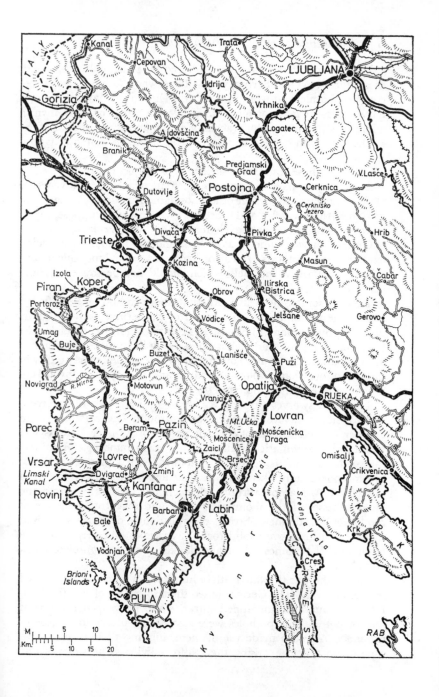

Fairly primitive methods are still used for much cultivation and, as in Macedonia and Serbia, you will find whole families, sometimes complete hamlets, at work in the fields. During the hay-cutting and harvest seasons it is not uncommon to see a dozen or more men in a long row moving easily, gracefully, in the ancestral rhythms of the scythers, a vision summarised for ever by Shakespeare in one hypnotic line:

'Those sunburned sicklemen of August weary.'

En route you pass through countryside which, for Slovenes, is closely associated with their other most famous author, Cankar, who died in 1918; a novelist and short story writer who, I suppose, might be roughly described as the Thomas Hardy of Slovenia.

Quite soon you come to **Postojna** and the famous caves which extend over a vast area of this northerly part of the limestone mountains. They are a spectacle which should not be missed on any account.

There is something a little infernal about the big gates into the side of the mountain but the crowd of chattering, excited visitors dispels apprehension. The big gates open. Uniformed officials take your ticket and you find yourself in a dimly lit 'station'. In it stands an open miniature train. You are on the lip of the biggest gullet in the world, one that swallows, astounds and regurgitates upwards of a quarter of a million tourists a year.

The train swerves through a narrow tunnel hewn out of rock, sweeps into a cavern, over the underground River Pivka, down another tunnel. Rollers of cold, damp air break over you. As you travel lights automatically illuminate the surroundings. A subterranean 'ballroom' is suddenly festooned with chandeliers. Bulbs bloom ephemerally like luminous fruit amidst the brittle fronds of stalactites. Arc-lamps abruptly slice chunks of darkness from the dingy recesses of the mountain's belly and reveal a landscape of rhodomontade dolmens. Strings of lights dangle over tripe-coloured fungi which in fact are solid rock. . . . Deeper and deeper into the mountain. It becomes colder and danker. You are completely disorientated.

During the war this labyrinth of hundreds of miles of caves served several purposes. The Germans used them to store fuel but the local Partisans found an unmapped entrance and blew up ten thousand tons of petrol. The potholes were also handy places to dispose of prisoners. All sides made use of them, binding their victims with rope or wire before tossing them into oblivion. The story of one young Slovene who managed to free himself and swim to the open joined the ballads of the locality long ago.

What makes the caves very strange is that the bizarre operations of nature here echo the creations of men. Here are dense phantoms of châteaux, solid mirages of cities, illusions of walls, of battlements, turrets and towers. In one glance there is a spire, in another a cluster of minarets, in a third a skyscraper. The foot of a bastion makes you look up for a crenellated wall. A buttress leads to a porch. Pillars make cloisters and colonnades. An aisle rises out of the mountain side and, as you look round, the ribbed and fluted walls invent some monstrous organ. Above, the formations are duplicated and multiplied by stalactites: fangs and prongs thrusting downwards. Some of the stalactites, and these growths are anything up to eighty million years old, are so fine, so delicate, they look like rapiers and poignards of glass. Amidst curtains of red cobweb, skin-coloured wings are furled, folded and spread, are tucked in and splayed over gaps and fissures. Draperies of rusty lace hang in immobile billows. Sails of buff muslin balloon in a silent gale. Orange membranes, like the pinions of giant pterodactyls, are stretched across clefts. In a clay-hued Gothic profusion lie the fossilised hulks of scaly Ichthyosauri and Plesiosauri and a museum of concrete phantoms which make the creations of Bosch, Piranesi and Doré seem like the illusions of a nursery escapade.

If you can you should lag behind and try to get a little time alone. Gradually you are besieged by an immense silence. Then sound re-establishes itself: the sound of water: minute sounds, the sibilance of softly falling moisture; in this windless catacomb the counterpart of dust lying lightly like a film or cataract.

After a mile or a mile and a half's walking (you are already three miles into the bowels of the mountain) you emerge into the gritty arena of a great cavern, 120 feet high. At one side there is a café, tables, chairs, big coloured umbrellas and a buffet bar tucked beneath the stalactites. Round the corner, the ultimate absurdity, an illuminated sign saying: w.c. The cavern is known as the 'Concert Hall' and can hold 1,000 people.

A little farther on you come to some pools in the rocks which contain the only living creatures in the caves: the eyeless *Proteus anguineus*. They are salamander-like creatures about eight inches to a foot in length and have limbs that curiously resemble human hands and feet on a miniature scale. They are palish white and pink, reptilian and oddly grotesque, like peeled lizards. They are alleged to be indigenous to the caves, and I suppose it is possible that they have been reproducing themselves for eighty million years. A sobering thought.

When you emerge from this fantasy it comes as a good deal of a surprise to find things like motor cars and policemen and daylight.

Quite near Postojna (ask for directions) is **Predjamski Grad**, a formidable castle built into the face of a cliff. The cave behind was occupied by prehistoric men and in the fifteenth century the first of two fortresses was built by a knight called Erasmus: a kind of Slovene Robin Hood who met one of the more bizarre of recorded deaths when he was blown apart by a cannon ball while sitting in the lavatory.

Some time later the castle fell into the hands of an Austrian named Kobenzl who built a new castle in front of the old one. This is well worth visiting. Corridors and rooms bulge and lean into odd shapes as they accommodate themselves to the rock faces. Walls drip. Lichen clings. It is a sombrely eerie place which, if it has no spectre, certainly ought to. (Erasmus himself, with jingling ball-cock and chain, would be a suitably anachronistic wraith.)

Some of the rooms contain portraits, relics of prehistoric men and a record of local Partisan activities. Behind the castle a stairway leads to the big cave out of which there is a narrow funnel and escape hole to the top of the mountain. In the valley far below runs the swift Lovka—a river in reverse, for it suddenly vanishes into a hole in the rocks.

A few kilometres to the east of Postojna is a large *karst* lake (Cerkniško Jezero) about seven miles long and several feet deep. Like many of these *karst* lakes it vanishes completely, together with its fish in the summer and then hay is grown. This is a haunted lake and from time to time skeletal cavalry, preceded by flocks of equally fleshless birds, prance and rattle round its shores. Slovenia has always been a land of trolls, spooks and clanking spectres.

From Postojna there is a good road to Rijeka and the Kvarner but the route I propose to follow runs across spectacular country via Divača and Kozina and down to Koper. The land is very wild here and once again you are in the *karst* proper which extends right down the Istrian peninsula. It is not nearly so bleak as the Dalmatian *karst* but, like that, it used to be covered with forest. In what remains of the ash, rowan and oak there are plenty of deer and wolf and some bears.

Koper, a small, compact town on a low hummock, was an island but has been joined to the mainland. The whole of this coast has been sinking for centuries so that many of the valleys have been turned into inlets and many of the outcrops into islands. A lot of rejoining has been done.

Mauve and red skyscrapers mingle with campaniles and old roofs and for a moment one thinks that by some atrocity of town planning these modern blocks have been erected in the original town. With relief one finds they are outside, on ground reclaimed from the sea, and are really quite pleasant—as are the two hotels by the little harbour: the **Galeb** and the **Triglav**, both quite lively in the high season.[1] There is even a Nočni Bar (night club) nearby, in the house that tradition maintains was the birthplace of Vittore Carpaccio.

You can saunter round Koper in a couple of hours but it is a pleasant place to pass a day or two and is a useful starting point for a tour of Istria since you can reach it easily by boat from Venice and Trieste as well as from inland.

Here we once more return to the history of Venice for Koper was captured by the Venetians in 1275 and held by them until 1797 after which it was briefly part of Napoleon's Illyrian province. The Congress of Vienna made it Austrian and in 1918 it was occupied by Italy. Like nearly every other place on the coast it had an Italian name as well as a Slav name and there has been a distressing tendency among foreigners to go on regarding this coast as Italian. At least one book recently written by an Englishman sticks to the Italian names and implies that Istria and Dalmatia are still Italian or ought to be. Such an attitude seems to me ignorant, and insulting. Neither the Italians nor the Venetians have ever had any right to this coast.

Long before its capture by the Venetians Koper was a considerable town which the Greeks and Romans had started and which the Slavs settled in the sixth century. It was once surrounded by walls and had twelve gates. The core of the modern town is Titov Trg, one of the most elegant squares on the whole coast. On one side of it is a graceful fifteenth-century Loggia and next to this a triple-naved **Cathedral:** a clear mixture of Gothic and Renaissance. The lower half was built about 1450 and the upper not finished until the end of the sixteenth century. Inside there is a sarcophagus surrounded by wrought-iron railings which is supposed to be that of St Nazarius, the patron saint of the town. Nazarius is believed to have been the son of a Roman officer and a Christian mother and is thought to have been executed with his disciple Celsus at Milan

[1]There is now also the new Zusterna.

where, in the fourth century, St Ambrose found what he thought were their relics. It is obviously one of those stories, like so many about the early saints, that is replete with speculation and next to no evidence. It is not certain why he is patron saint of Koper.

There are quite a number of good paintings in the town and some of them are or were in the cathedral, though they are apt to be changed around.

In the cathedral there are two interesting ones by Benedetto Carpaccio, a son of Vittore. One shows the *Madonna enthroned with St Nicholas and John the Baptist*: the other the *Presentation of the Virgin in the temple*. When you come out of the cathedral I suggest you climb the belfry which was begun much earlier than the cathedral, in the thirteenth century.

Opposite the loggia is what is called the **Praetorian House,** first begun in 1254 and restored a century later. Now this is fused with the Podestà, or mayor's house, a quaint building with pretty ogival windows, battlements in a fleur-de-lis design, and an outside staircase of white marble. On the walls are several coats-of-arms, plaques and busts of various governors of the town. The ensemble is rather operatic but the proportions are delightful.

A little way east off the *trg* is the **Civic Museum** (housed in a former palace) and a very good one it is. The lapidarium has an interesting collection of Roman and medieval stonework, bas-reliefs, sarcophagi and capitals. On the first floor is the main assembly of paintings: a *Madonna* by Giovanni Bellini; a *Madonna with SS Bartholomew and James* by B. Carpaccio; a painting by a follower of V. Carpaccio depicting *Christ on the road to Calvary*; and four pictures by V. Carpaccio himself: a *Podestà and Councillors*; a *Virgin with Six Saints*; *The Presentation in the Temple* and the *Massacre of the Innocents*. The last two *were* on the organ shutters in the cathedral. I believe they are all fairly late works. There is also a picture by Alvise Vivarini showing an enthroned *Madonna* with two musician angels. The rather fine painting of an old man was thought to have been by Paolo Veronese but it has now been more or less definitely ascribed to a later and less well-known artist—Bernardo Strozzi. Lastly there is a *Madonna* attributed to a follower of G. Bellini. While here do not fail to look at what was the door-knocker of the palace: an exquisite piece of work showing the birth of Venus.

The other main sight of interest is the church of **Sv Ana** which has several good pictures: one by B. Carpaccio showing *Four Saints adoring the Holy Name*; and four by Cima da Conegliamo. There is a

Deposition, two of *St Anne*, and a big *polyptych* depicting the Virgin with eight saints plus Christ and two more saints above them. This, I think, is the best work in Koper.

Quite a good road runs all the way down this coast but one has to turn off it fairly often to reach the coastal settlements, like, for example, Izola, a fishing town on a small island now joined to the mainland. There are several distinguished buildings here, including some palaces. The best pictures in the parish church are ascribed to Girolamo da Santa Croce and Palma the Younger.

Not far on, beyond the fertile Strunjan valley, where you will see a lot of salt and oyster beds, is **Portorož**—one of the best known Adriatic resorts, paradisally green and flowery. You can swim here all the year round and the whole establishment, geared for tourism, is quite sophisticated. There's no village here but a few kilometres west lies **Piran,** one of the most beautiful small towns on the whole coastline. It is built on a low point of land (the *rtič*) and like nearly every other littoral settlement belonged to the Venetians who sub-dued it in 1283. Once a buccaneer outpost, it rises in tiers to old ramparts; vaulted gateways join street to street and above the tumble of mossed brown and red roofs the crumbling church and campanile (a copy of St Mark's tower) rise like a manifesto of dignity.

The main square, which opens on to the small harbour, contains a *Statue of Tartini* (who was born a few yards away) and behind it rises a tall narrow house in exact Venetian red: the kind of building you see repeatedly in works by artists like Carpaccio. Near the edge of the harbour is the Museum. It shows some aspects of local develop-ment, has a room devoted to Tartini, another to the history of the town and a third to painting and sculpture.

On an isolated hill, a little farther on from Portorož, rises the medieval town of Buje whose basic circular plan is typical of the pre-Roman fortified townships in these regions. Now it is mostly a mixture of Venetian and Baroque buildings of which the most interesting are the church and bell-tower in the main square. Near them is a pillar recording standard measurements which served the same function as 'the elbow' in Dubrovnik. Round about Buje you find several antiquities: Monjan, for instance, with the remains of a medieval castle built on the rock face; and Grožnjan with its ram-parts and fortified gate.

From Buje it is easy to reach Umag on the coast: a small twelfth-century town on a slim tongue of land, and generally regarded as

one of the most agreeable bathing and camping sites on this coast.[1]
A little north-west of it lies the pretty and unspoilt fishing village
of Savudrija where the fishermen sling their boats in wooden davits
on the quay. It was here, according to legend, that Barbarossa was
captured. Scattered along the shore between these two places are
a number of secluded beaches overhung by pine woods.

It would be a great mistake to visit Istria without going inland,
but even if you don't it is useful to imagine the whole peninsula as a
triangular pyramid, with a mountainous apex, in three colours: red,
grey and white. The coastal regions and valleys are often covered
with a rertile red soil; the inland *karst* is grey and barren; and the
most desolate parts of the interior are the white limestone uplands.

You might not think that this rather poor piece of ground would
excite particularly strong covetous intentions but the fact is that
Istria has been a centre of bitter disagreement for centuries, and
until very recently. It has been conquered, laid waste and rebuilt on
countless times. It has been argued over, divided, separated, exploited, sold and given away.

The Slavs had it first, as it were—at any rate after the Illyrians
and Celts, the Romans and the Greeks—and now, in the shape of
the Croats and Slovenes, they have it again. There are still several
minorities of which the main is Italian. There are also Montenegrins and Serbs and, in the Ćićarija region, Rumanians who fled
from the Turks and who still speak a very odd dialect which is a
form of Rumanian.

The most harmful influences have undoubtedly been the Austrian
and Italian; that is to say, mostly over the last hundred and fifty
years. The Austrians do not like or understand the Slav temperament and they were merely exploiters. I don't think Italians understand it either, and Italian Fascism was especially disastrous here.
It showed the absolute lunacy and conceit of repression and conversion, and the depressing truth is that during the Italian, as well
as the Austrian domination, nearly every aspect of Istrian life went
into decline, a decline which reached a perigee between the World
Wars when the Italians tried to deracinate Slav culture, uproot its
language, destroy its traditions and alter its names—indeed everything—and Italianise the lot. It was one of the most wicked and
ignorant proselytising movements ever recorded.

Partly because of these wretched events Istria is sometimes de-

[1]Big new tourist complex consists of a number of hotels and annexes.

pressing. Still, occasionally, you get the feeling that people's allegiances are confused, their customs mixed, their past—as well as their vision of the present and the future—shadowed and infected by the memory of unease, the long malaria of dispossession, and the potential threat of its renewal. Only a gifted and detached minority can survive a lack of political and cultural identity and it will probably be quite a long time before the people of this peninsula feel they are properly integrated into the state of Jugoslavia. At least two generations must die, two come to maturity.

When you go inland (here, as much as anywhere, you realise what great differences there are between the seaboard and the interior) you find the well-established roots of a people and way of life that are indigenous and fairly invincible. The tenacity and ruggedness of the uplanders is symbolised by the many lonely and fortified medieval villages and small towns that cling to the windy crests of the *karst*. If you come up here in February or March when the *bora* is wailing across the peaks you get an idea of the fibre of the people, the will and resolution that can outlive even the schemes of megalomaniacs like Mussolini.

Many of the hill towns and villages are very old, like **Pazin** (this actually lies in an upland valley[1]) which was originally a Roman settlement and then a feudal enclave. Afterwards, of course, it came under the blight of the Austrian empire and for four hundred years ceased to develop. The parish church, with some fifteenth-century frescoes, is worth looking at; and so is the ducal castle on the edge of the chasm into which the River Fojba vanishes. The *ponor* or vanishing hole is a semicircular abyss four hundred feet deep and at the bottom of it the water plunges into an underground river which reappears in the Limski fiord thirty kilometres away. A tradition exists that it was this tremendous 'funnel' which inspired Dante's description of the entrance to the inferno. Very likely, I should think, if he ever came here. In the late Middle Ages, if not earlier, pits (and volcanoes) were popularly believed to be exits and entrances of hell for the very good reason that in those days the universe was thought to be geocentric and the lowest point in it, namely the centre of this globe, was deemed to be 'the pit of Sathanas' and the hub, linchpin and sump of that was the Devil himself, embedded in ice and fire. Numerous medieval 'visions' of the other world in European literature record the idea.

While at Pazin I advise a visit to the **ethnographical museum**

[1]It now has a motel, the Lovac.

in the castle. It contains traditional tools, wooden utensils and pottery of the kind you see in Istrian peasant homes and there is also a collection of costume of the sort you will still find from time to time in daily use. One can distinguish three basic forms. In the north plain fabrics and lines predominate, though the clothes of the herdsmen are brightly coloured. The costumes of central Istria tend to be white or beige. The women wear long white shifts (*stomanje*) with a white triangular head-scarf called a *facol*. In the south the colours are brighter, the embroidery more intricate. One of the commonest female garments is the *modrna*, a woollen dress with sleeves and beautifully embroidered borders. Naturally they vary from village to village. Some show distinctly urban influences. At Vodnjan, for example, not far from Pula, the women's costumes are of a Venetian cut. More jewellery is worn and the women put ornaments in their hair. At Peroj, also near Pula, where the descendants of immigrant Montenegrins have lived since the seventeenth century, the women's blouses show that they have come from the coast. Just as we used to be able to tell a person's class and income group from their clothes so the Jugoslav peasant can still say from what region or village another may have come.

If you go to Pazin you should make the short trip to **Beram,** a few kilometres away. There used to be a Bronze Age settlement on the hill and an Illyrian cemetery in the valley and Beram is a typically Istrian village which 'belongs' to its surroundings. The houses are plain, soundly made of stone, and in their midst is a hunk of Gothic church with a Baroque tower. This parish church of St Martin was completed in 1431 and contains some fragments of frescoes. Frescoes can be found all over Istria, and the late Middle Ages produced a whole 'school' of fresco painters much of whose work has luckily survived. The paintings were usually commissioned by villagers and parish priests from local artists who knew how to illustrate the Bible in simple, vivid terms for the benefit of the illiterate.

Those in St Martin's are quickly seen, but one kilometre away north-east is a tiny tree-shaded church called **Sv Marija na Škrilinah** (Virgin of the Rocks) which has a remarkable collection painted by a man called Vincent, of Kastav (a village near Opatija) in 1474.

On the west wall, either side of the door, are two symbolic scenes: a *kolo* and *The Fall*.[1] Above these is the *Dance of Death*. On the upper part of the north wall is the *Adoration of the Kings*, a huge painting.

[1] The same theme was treated by Ivan J. Kastav in Hrastorlje. See p. 372.

The scenes from the *Life of Mary* begin on the south wall where the birth is shown in the upper level at the eastern end. They go in a westerly direction and then pass on to a lower level of the same wall before returning in the opposite direction towards the sanctuary. *Christ's Life*, begun on the south wall, is continued on the lower level of this at the west end with the *Temptation in the Desert*. There is a gap of three pictures and then follows the *Entry into Jerusalem*. On the upper level is the *Last Supper*; then, on the lower again, the *Agony in the Garden* and *The Betrayal*. There follow the scenes of the *Passion* which are continued in the walls of the apse.

After a few minutes you will have grasped the sequence which makes a kind of strip cartoon constantly broken into by the figures of various saints and scenes from their lives. Of the smaller scenes I think that those of St Martin dividing his cloak with the beggar, and St George and the dragon are the best. In the background of the latter an apprehensive audience, looking like Gullivers in Lilliput, peer between the loopholed turrets of a fortress. There are pleasing details in other paintings, like the hill villages and castles in the *Wedding of Mary and Joseph*—an Istrian scene; and the spectators in the tree-tops in *Christ's entry into Jerusalem*, and all the details of the *Flight into Egypt*. These pictures, particularly, tell us a lot about attitudes, customs, scenery and costumes of that period. But the two finest paintings are the *Adoration of the Kings* and the *Dance of Death*.

The Adoration is a pageant, an encomium to the beauty and abundance of the world. Not only do we have a splendid cavalcade of gaily-attired knights and nobles pressing forward to visit the Virgin and Child who, if anything, form a rather subsidiary feature at one end, but below the hooves of the horses, in the style of Flemish tapestries, we have a wealth of fascinating detail; mountains, seas, galleys sailing, ploughed fields, hounds hunting a hare, peacocks, ducks, a bear cub frightened by a dog, Aesop's fable of the fox and the stork . . . a richly crowded scene full of exuberant life and gay solemnity. It is clearly the product of a fecund mind and, in its anachronistic mingling of secular and religious motifs, comparable with, for instance, Radovan's door at Trogir and some of the frescoes at Lesnovo and Staro Nagoričino.

In stern, but no less vivid, contrast is the pageant of the **Dance of Death**, or *Danse Macabre*, a favourite subject for fifteenth-century artists and writers. There is an early suggestion of the *Danse Macabre* in a twelfth-century poem, *Les Vers de la Mort*, written by a monk called Hélinant, in which death is encouraged to travel about visiting places and people in order to warn them that they must die. But the more immediate predecessors of the Dance of Death were the *Vado Mori* poems, the *Dit des Trois Mors et des Trois Vifs* and other controversial poems about the undiscovered country: for instance, the *Débat de l'Ame et du Corps*. The priority belongs to the tale of the three repulsive dead men who meet three noble living men and tell them of previous glory and future decay. The first use of the word *macabre* dates from 1376 when it appeared in a poem by Jehan Le Fèvre called *Respit de la Mort*.

The idea of death personified was firmly grasped by writers and artists and whereas before the fifteenth century the skeleton was seldom envisaged as the symbol of death (in classical times it was even a comic figure) now, as one writer put it, people came to regard skeletons 'as an integral part of the landscape.' From the literature artists took their cue. No doubt they were further stimulated by the terrible plagues of the fourteenth and fifteenth centuries, by the effects of wars and by the tradition of the *sabat* at which the famous dance or *ronde* always followed the banquet and led to unimaginable scenes of debauchery and corruption.

The two great works were the pictures and verses in the cloisters of the church of the Holy Innocents in Paris and Holbein's engravings. Death, as interpreted in the woodcuts of Holbein, is an individual who travels about and mingles with men like another human being. His clothing is varied to meet the occasion and he has a different treatment for each case. He is ubiquitous and inexorable. You see him strolling with a band of musicians, leering over the table of a monarch, running beside a ploughshare, spearing a knight and cackling over a miser. No one escapes and Holbein probably did more than any other person to popularise this dance. The themes of *macabre* and the dance have interested and influenced a quite extraordinary number of writers and painters (and some musicians) ever since.

In the Beram composition jaunty, almost skittish, skeletons prance amiably beside their victims and hasten their steps with the music of string, woodwind and bagpipe. The instruments look oddly familiar. The traditional implement of Death and Time, the scythe, occupies a prominent position and many of the main strata of medieval society are represented: Pope, cardinal, bishop, king, queen, innkeeper (a particularly vivid Chaucerian figure carrying a little barrel), soldier, merchant, beggar and so forth.

But in this apocalyptic jig of death the painter has omitted his own class: the Istrian peasant. Perhaps he did this out of superstition but more likely because he felt the peasant endured enough in his lifetime without being reminded when he went to church that he, too, must return to the very dust out of which he so painfully extracted a livelihood.

After the *memento mori*, the bracing air of the uplands and the prospect of life (for a time) will, I hope, encourage you to take the adequate road up to Motovun and Buzet, from where you can return to Pazin via Cerovlje, thus completing a circular tour of central Istria.

A man called Veli Jože (Big Joe) used to live at **Motovun**. He was a genuine giant and a valiant warrior about whom many legendary exploits have been recorded. One tale relates that in a spasm of fury against a despotic feudal lord he wrapped his Atlantean arms round the tower of Motovun and shook it. To this day it is cracked and leaning, but, like the rest of this prehistoric fortified settlement which the Croats have defended for a millenium, it stands as a kind of symbol for Slav independence.

Big Joe did not escape punishment. In the rock face of the Krvara canyon, a tributary of the nearby river Mirna, hang two iron rings. Legend has it that the upholder of the Peoples' Rights was manacled in those.

Motovun has other objects of interest: a double Gothic gateway through the ramparts; the castle; the loggia; the Baroque church and Romanesque campanile; a town hall first erected in the thirteenth century and, though much restored, one of the earliest buildings of its kind in the country.

Buzet, like Buje, sits on top of a lonely cone; again it is the site of a prehistoric fortified town. For the Romans it was Piquentum. Subsequently it became the property of the Byzantines, the Venetians and the Austrians, but for thirteen centuries the Croats have gone on living in it and they have shed a great deal of blood for it. In the last war alone, seven hundred of its men died.

Beyond the ramparts of this ancient stronghold stretch the central highlands of the Istrian *karst*.

You can return to the coast from Pazin on quite a good road direct to **Poreč**, and Poreč, I feel, is an essential stop. It lies on a low penisula on the edge of richly green and fertile land of orchards and vineyards. The grapes here produce a pleasant dessert wine called Malvasija. In fact the Istrian region yields quite a lot of wine, as it did when the Romans were here. The other white dessert wines worth sampling are Muškat and Semion. There are also the red Kabernet, pleasant with veal, and what they call Burgundac—a ruby-coloured red which varies a good deal. Traminac is another white you can try with your fish. Try, also, Kraški Teran, a mild red wine.

Poreč (the Slav name for Parenzo, the Parentium of the Romans) has other recommendations. It is ancient and beautiful, it is well-equipped for the visitor, and its basilica is one of the greater religious monuments of the Adriatic. The two best hotels are the Jadran and the Riviera; the latter is the focus of social life in the evenings. A lot of Jugoslavs come to Poreč on holiday.

The Illyrians were first on the scene here, five centuries before Christ; in the second after Him the Romans built a town whose ground plan and main streets are still clear, and whose buildings survive in fragments. The period of Byzantine influence ended in 1267 and after that its history was much the same as the rest of Istria. The principal minor buildings are a fifteenth-century Romanesque house with a balcony, a number of Gothic and Renaissance palaces with magnificent windows and open-work balconies, and the remains of two temples to Mars and Neptune. As you saunter you will recognise these easily.

But *the* object is the **Basilica of Euphrasius,** tucked away off a side street, hemmed in by buildings, quite inconspicuous. First, some details about its past. The earliest Christian structure here was called the Moor's Oratory, a hall in a Roman house used as a clandestine rendezvous by Christians during persecution. Some of its mosaic floor survives and it seems that another building was put up over this later, part of which may be the left aisle of the present basilica. The next stage consisted of two rectangular adjacent churches and then a triple-naved basilica with one apse above the original floor. Early in the sixth century, Euphrasius, bishop of Poreč, established the basilica more or less as we see it today, with an atrium, a baptistery and a palace. All the building of Euphrasius and the mosaics that survive were being accomplished in the same period as the great group of St Apollinare and San Vitale in Ravenna. Very probably some of the same architects and artists were involved.

Mosaic decoration was in constant use from very early times up to the thirteenth century, when frescoes became more popular and virtually replaced it—partly because it was cheaper, partly because it lent itself to greater realism. Mosaic is, of course, much more durable than fresco but it is also very much more laborious to execute. The most important mosaics that survive in Poreč are in the apse and on the triumphal arch. On the latter are Christ and the twelve Apostles and in the centre of the apse's conch is an enthroned Virgin with angels. It is thought that this was the first time in Christian art that the Virgin was sited in this position. The three figures on her right are, by tradition, guardians of the town. On her left is another group and their names are written: Maurus the martyr, Euphrasius, the patron, holding a model of the church, and the archdeacon Claudius accompanied by his son. Between the windows are an angel, St John the Baptist, Zacharius, The Annunciation and the Visitation. This last is especially vivid and naturalistic because of the young servant looking on inquisitively. The ensemble has a dignified and austere richness which is characteristic of the best mosaic art of the period though not, in my opinion, in the same class as the eleventh- and twelfth-century works to be found in places like Cefalu and Torcello.

I mentioned earlier that the Istrian coast has been sinking steadily for a long time and there is further evidence of this here because it has been necessary to raise the floor of the church at least twice. Through a trap-door you can still see older mosaic floors or pavements.

The next place of any note down the coast is **Vrsar,** once a Roman outpost and summer residence of the Poreč bishops. Here the bishop's castle survives and a thirteenth-century Romanesque basilica. The main road turns back inland from Vrsar and takes you near **Lovreč:** a fortified medieval town with a Gothic gateway and castle, a ninth-century church and many medieval houses. I recommend a pause here for an hour or two.

The main road from here to Pula runs across the topmost tip of a six mile fiord known as the **Limski Kanal.** They used this fiord some time ago to make a rather bad film called *The Long Ships.* The Viking settlement (known to Jugoslavs as the Wickings or Wikings), built on location has been preserved. It can hardly survive intact but pieces and implements may puzzle archaeologists a couple of thousand years hence.

There is another interesting item in the Limski. You may notice some steel apparatus from which ropes are suspended. On these are large bunches of oysters. In the breeding season they tip brushwood into the sea and the oysters cling on to it. They are then transferred

The Companion Guide to Jugoslavia

to the ropes which can be lowered at will into the sea until the oysters mature; a matter of three years or so.

Soon after crossing the railway you reach a cross-roads near the village of **Brajkovići** and I suggest you make a short detour east here to Kanfanar and Dvigrad. The latter is a small medieval town abandoned in the seventeenth century after a series of disastrous plagues and attacks by the Uskoks of Senj. In fact, by the end of the seventeenth century the whole peninsula had been severely depopulated by disease and invasion and the townships were falling into decay. The people had not properly recovered even fifty years ago.

The other arm of the cross-roads takes you to **Rovinj,** an amiable spot (nicknamed the Montmartre of Istria) with a history and appearance rather similar to Koper and Piran. It was originally on an island, now joined to the mainland to form a promontory. The Church of St Euphemia (a third/fourth century saint martyred near Byzantium) dominated the town. The present structure is baroque (1736) and the façade is nineteenth-century. The adjacent bell tower dates from 1677. Things to look for inside the church are: a marble relief of St Euphemia and the saint's sarcophagus. Down in the Trg Maršala Tita by the harbour are several buildings worth looking at, particularly the clock tower and the seventeenth-century town hall. The town also has a number of Gothic and Renaissance palaces.

Very nearly at the end of the peninsula, in a spacious, sheltered bay, is the large port of **Pula:** the economic and cultural centre of the region, as it probably was for the Romans who built here about a hundred and thirty years before Christ. It is not, I think, a place to stay in for long because the modern town is unattractive and there are few seaside amenities, but you need a full day for the Roman remains and if you *do* want to spend a night the Hotel Riviera is comfortable and possesses quite a good restaurant. There are two other sufficient restaurants in the main street.

The monument that everyone goes to see is the **amphitheatre** (down by the harbour): a magnificent golden shell whose triple-tiered arcades window the sky. It was probably erected between 30 B.C. and A.D. 14 and then enlarged (*c.* 67–72) during the reign of Vespasian. The two main entrances are at the ends of the oval. Between the arena and the tiers of seats is a passage for the gladiators which had high barriers to protect the audience from wild beasts. Below the seats lie store-houses and places for the caged animals. There was a large chamber below the centre of the arena

406

from which animals and gladiators could be lifted straight up. A network of passages connected various apartments. If you have seen the Colosseum you will have an idea of the lay-out and size.

We are lucky that so much remains because there have been a good many depredations for other buildings and a number of potential ones thwarted. At the end of the fifteenth century the Venetian Senate even decided that the whole thing should be dismantled and re-erected in Venice. Fortunately this foolish idea was balked by a Venetian senator, who is commemorated by a plaque on the arena. When the Austrians possessed Istria they cleaned the whole place out and now it is in very good order. It is not as large as the Colosseum but it holds well over twenty thousand spectators who nowadays watch the summer film festival there and see lust and blood on mere studio sand.

If you go south from the arena along the shore road you will find the cathedral, a blend of the original basilica, Baroque and Renaissance; but most of what you see dates from about 1640. The high altar is a third-century Roman sarcophagus.

Another building you should make a point of seeing is the **Temple of Augustus** (in a big open space off Rade Končar Ulica), a most harmonious building with six slender columns on steps and richly decorated capitals and friezes. The Byzantines turned it into a church and the Venetians used it as a theatre. At a later date it functioned as a granary. Now it has been restored to something very like its pristine elegance. Very near it is another temple (perhaps to Diana) semi-detached from the Town Hall built in the thirteenth century. The party wall, therefore, is the temple's. The hall, which has an elegant balcony and loggia, is still used for local government by the District People's Committee.

Go on down Rade Končar Ulica south-east and you come to a bombed site (it may now be built over) at one side of which stands a rather pathetic little Byzantine chapel, all that survives of a sixth-century basilica most of which was carted away by the Venetians and some of which was re-used in St Mark's.

On down the same street until you meet the big thoroughfare Boris Kidrič Boulevard (I advise you to start asking at this point). Turn left, cross the eastern side of the Trg Dante Alighieri and on the east side of the church Sv Milosrda runs Ulica Prvog Maja (May Day Street). In the courtyard of No. 16 are some Roman remains about ten feet below the surface. They include a magnificent mosaic floor which illustrates the legend of Antiope, who had an affair with Zeus and subsequently married Lycus, who left her and married Dirce. Dirce treated Antiope very badly (*menage à trois?*) but Antiope was revenged by her sons, Amphion and Zethus, whom Zeus had sired. The sons killed Lycus and Dirce and refortified Thebes. After that Amphion married Niobe, who produced a large number of sons and daughters (traditionally seven of each). It should have all ended happily here, but it ended, like Niobe, all tears. Apollo killed off all her children because Niobe thought herself superior to Apollo's mother and poor Amphion committed suicide.

At the eastern end of May Day Street stands the **Triumphal Arch** of Sergius, which was one of the several town gates. A very noble structure it is, richly ornamented with friezes. North of it is the main square of modern Pula, on the west side of which are the remnants of huge defensive walls. Beside these a street runs towards the sea via the Gate of Hercules (there's a bearded head of him on the top) and on to the Double Gate or Porta Gemina. Beyond this is the Archaeological Museum which is well worth visiting. It contains Bronze- and Iron-Age exhibits and a very big Roman collection. On the slopes behind the museum are the ruins of a Roman theatre.

There is much else to see in Pula, including the fortifications erected by the Austrians to protect the harbour (of particular interest to military engineers) and if you weary of the town you can cool off with a trip to the Brioni Islands, in the bay, which have become more or less famous because Marshal Tito has a summer residence there.

From Pula, if you intend to explore the Kvarner and go to Opatija, you are committed to a cross-country journey north-east via **Barban** and **Labin**. It makes an interesting trip through varied countryside, at times very wild, with stunted forests and thickets of hawthorn and oak. The vistas change. A campanile on a rocky crown. Three women in black carrying clay pots of water on their heads. A team of white oxen ploughing a dark red field. . . .

Between Barban and Labin you descend and then rise steeply near the head of another big fiord with precipitous sides.

The days of Labin are almost certainly numbered. The hill on which it stands has been honeycombed by coal miners (the Venetians were mining here early in the fifteenth century) and every few weeks fresh cracks appear in the walls of its buildings. Periodically a house collapses or a street slips a few more feet. In three or four years most of it will have been evacuated. A ghost town will probably survive for much longer while it gradually disintegrates. This is a great pity because it is a fine example of a medieval hill town with several churches and numerous palaces. The Labinese are being rehoused in the locality.

South of Labin you have a splendid view across the Kvarner Gulf where the stony humps of Cres and Krk are once again very clear. A little farther on you reach Plomin and its green creek sheltered by bare hills. Plomin is ruining slowly but it has a rustic Romanesque church which is worth looking at and which contains an important Glagolitic inscription: the *Plominski natpis*. In Serbian a *natpis* is an inscription, whereas a *potpis* is a signature. Beyond Plomin a glass and concrete drum turns out to be a motel. Both its food and view are memorable.

Soon you reach Brseč, a compact, fortified township perched on a cliff above the sea. Its houses are turned inwards on the mesh of narrow, interlocking streets and alleys through which Croat women weave like black wraiths. The Opatija Riviera begins here with a series of pretty villages lodged between the high Učka Mountains and the waters of the gulf. Mošćenice and Mošćenička Draga are especially attractive: the former aloft on a wooded pyramid; the latter far below on the white beaches.

I suggest you pause at **Lovran**: a very old town founded by the Slavs in the sixth century which has a history as a popular resort dating from late in the nineteenth. Above and round it hang opulent forests of chestnut and laurel (*lovran* means a 'laurel') and in the town you have a very wide choice of hotels, pensions and private apartments.

Lastly **Opatija** (Abbotsbury, formerly Abbazia) the Prestatyn or Torquay of Jugoslavia, though infinitely more beautiful. High mountains, sub-tropical vegetation, luxuriant gardens, golden beaches and a benign climate—for once the gaudy lure of the travel agent's poster almost comes true. Here are the Gardens of the Hesperides, the Happy Land of radiant faces, of mesomorphic females and tanned muscular men playing beach ball, that beckons to you at drab stations on the way to Camberley or Chelmsford. The sunbathing goes on for at least five months a year.

Opatija has been an international resort for a long time. A century ago it was a small fishing village clustering round the church of St James (Sv Jakov) built in 1506 and there was a Benedictine abbey here which gave the place its name. The first step towards making it a resort occurred in 1844 when a Rijeka business man called Scarpa built a large holiday villa. Then, in 1879, a Croatian doctor persuaded a Viennese colleague to encourage his patients to visit Opatija for their health. Three years later the railway company which had built the line to Rijeka bought the land round Scarpa's villa and built the Hotel Quarnero, now the Kvarner. In 1885 a medical congress in Opatija proclaimed the place a health resort. That was the imprimatur, so to speak. The *nihil obstat* has been provided by tens of thousands of satisfied customers who visit it every year.

There seems little point in recommending hotels because the whole place is one enormous hotel-pension-annexe-private apartment-chalet-hut-tent plexus and, with the exception of Dubrovnik, is the most highly organised resort of all. If you want to stay here you must book in advance. You will almost certainly be well looked after.

I come to it last in this book and, as it happens, it is one of the last places in Jugoslavia I would now bother to revisit. But that is a personal view, like so many of the opinions and tastes I have expressed.

Appendices

General Practical Information

THE TIME TO GO THERE

In the most popular resorts like Opatija and Dubrovnik there are three different hotel rates: the low season covers October-May; the season, June-September; the high season, July and August. May, June and September are the best months to go there. April is sometimes fine, but sometimes it is wetter and stormier than anything one experiences in the United Kingdom. The big resorts are very crowded in July and August. There is no problem about crowding anywhere inland but June, July and August can be pretty hot. Mostar, for example, is one of the hottest places in Europe in August. Serbia and Macedonia are always hot at this time but the heat is nearly always dry in Jugoslavia. October is a most delightful time, but few people go then.

HOW TO GET THERE

The best way by train is on the Simplon via Paris and Venice to Ljubljana and Rijeka. It takes about thirty-six hours.

It takes four or five days to drive there though it could be done in two and a half. Again the best route is via France and Italy.

There are many ways of getting there by air and the communications are improving steadily. All information can be obtained from the Jugoslav National Tourist Office, 143 Regent Street, W.1.

MOTORING

Only the larger towns have repair shops, and spare parts are difficult to get. The coastal repair shops are a good deal better equipped than those inland, and inland they are few and far between. It is almost essential to take a set of spare parts, including a fan belt, plugs, bulbs, fuses etc. You should also take a tyre pressure gauge, distilled water and brake fluid. The repair shops open at 6 a.m. or earlier and usually close for the day at 2 p.m.

Petrol is available at an ever-increasing number of petrol stations and I recommend that you use the Super Octane at 2·80 new dinars per litre. You can get petrol coupons from Anglo-Jugoslav Travel Service, 6 Rupert Street, W.1. and thus save yourself 5 per cent.

Only the main roads are well sign-posted and a map is essential. A good general map is the *IRO Strassen und Riesekarte: Jugoslavien* (published by Iro

413

Verlag, Munich). Turistička Stampa in Belgrade publish the *Roadmap Jugoslavia* and this contains detailed routes and information about them. Izdavački Zavod 'Jugoslavia', Belgrade, publish a Jugoslav guide called *By Car through Jugoslavia* which contains a good deal of information and detailed routes. There are a number of mistakes in this. A good map is produced by the Touring Club Italiano. The following maps also are good (published in Jugoslavia and apparently not available in the U.K.): (1) *The Yugoslav Coast: Guide Book and Atlas*, published by the Yugoslav Lexicographical Institute, Zagreb. This is available in English, contains a great deal of detailed information and has a large number of excellent maps. (2) The *Turistična Autokarta Slovenije*, published by Auto-Moto Slovenije. This covers the whole of Slovenia and parts of Croatia. (3) *Autokarta Jugoslavije*, published by Auto-Moto Zveza Slovenije. This covers the whole country. (4) *Autokarta Jugoslavije*, published by Mladinska Ljubljana. This comprises a series of maps designed to cover the whole country in four parts. Each year the Jugoslav Tourist Association issues a general map with a good deal of information on it about petrol stations, repair shops, camping sites etc. There are a lot of camping sites along the coast and an increasing number at the more popular places inland. Before going you should consult the R.A.C. or the A.A. and, when there, the Jugoslav Automobile Club, Auto-moto Savez Jugoslavia, Ruzeltova 18, Belgrade. Travellers who want to stay on the Dalmatian coast should get the Karta *Jugoslavenske Obale*, published by Ucila of Zagreb. The scale is about five miles to the inch, and it gives very detailed information on the coast.

CAR HIRE

This is expensive but worthwhile. The Volkswagen is one of the best types of car for the country though its clearance is not always adequate on the worst roads. Occasionally it is necessary to remove chunks of stone and small rocks and boulders by hand. The main agencies which deal with car hire are: *Kompas*, Miklošičeva 17, Ljubljana. The U.K. agents are: Hertz Rent-a-Car, 243 Knightsbridge, London S.W.7 *Putnik* Kneza Miloša 82, Belgrade. The London office is at: 223 Regent Street, London W.1. *Autotehna*, Braće Oreški 5, Zagreb. The U.K. agents are: Avis Rent-a-Car, 632-52 London Road, Isleworth, Middlesex. *Inex*, Trg Republike 5, Belgrade. These firms offer self-drive and chauffeur-driven cars. My own rather prejudiced view is that you should be careful in your dealings with all such agencies. They expect to be paid in pounds or dollars, and they calculate in terms of dollars whatever your nationality. But any money that has to be refunded (for example, from a deposit) will most probably be paid in dinars which you may have difficulty in changing into your own currency.

PUBLIC TRANSPORT

Air: J.A.T. (pronounced YAT) is the Jugoslav airline and its services are cheap and safe. In the summer months they are heavily booked but if you have planned your holiday carefully beforehand you can make the necessary reservations.

Ship: The boat services up and down the coast are *excellent* and inexpensive.

Train: Except on the main transcontinental lines train travel is slow or *very* slow, and even the transcontinental expresses are much slower than elsewhere. However, train travel anywhere in this country is always interesting. The trips from Split to Zagreb and Dubrovnik to Belgrade are spectacular. Fares are low and the trains are nearly always crowded. It is advisable to equip yourself with some food and drink before undertaking a long journey.

Bus: The services on the main routes are efficient and cheap, and the drivers and conductors are first class. Travel by more local services is extremely entertaining, but erratic and usually uncomfortable. NB Always book a seat the day before you travel and remember that if you are at a place between two depots which is not a starting point for a service your chances of getting a seat *en route* depend on the number of people leaving the bus and your ability to force your way on to it.

Taxis: You will find taxis only in the large towns and even there they are not plentiful. Some have meters, some don't. Jugoslav taxi drivers are honest by comparison with their counterparts elsewhere, but it is prudent to get some idea of the cost first. They tend to be rather dear.

Fiacre: There are a lot of these in Serbia and Macedonia and they provide a cheap and leisurely way of getting about. Quite long trips (for example, to churches and monasteries off the beaten track) can be made by arrangement. Always establish the price beforehand.

Horse, Mule and Donkey: these can be hired by private arrangement or through the local Tourist Office. Mules are very useful in the more inaccessible regions. Remember that the saddles will always be wooden.

(Note: a time-table for train and bus services throughout the country can be bought at most main depots and stations. It is called a *Red Vožnje* and is remarkably comprehensive. Details for travel by air and ship can be obtained from the relevant offices or the Tourist Office. As a general rule it is wise to check all information *at least* once).

USEFUL ITEMS OF CLOTHING AND EQUIPMENT

Something warm to wear in the evenings inland is useful; so is a travelling rug. You should take all the film you need. Most people find sun glasses very useful. An insect repellent is indispensable for many people inland. If your stomach is susceptible to a change of diet you should take some enterovioform or sulfaguanadin tablets. You should take your own soap, and pipe

415

tobacco. Tea is expensive in Jugoslavia and I find it useful to take a supply of tea and coffee. Fresh milk is often difficult to get and for emergencies I take a tube or two of Nestles Milk and a tin of powdered Marvel milk. For electric razors have an adjustable pin plug or an Edison screw adaptor.

HEALTH AND INSURANCE
If you are insured under the N.H.S. in the United Kingdom you are protected by a reciprocal agreement between the Jugoslav and British Governments. The necessary certificate can be obtained from the Jugoslav Embassy in London. If you do not take advantage of this you can always insure yourself before leaving.

WORKING HOURS
Government and business offices and so on work from 7 a.m. to 2 p.m. Banks are open to the public from 7 to 11 a.m. Travel agencies are open from 7 to any time between 11 and one o'clock; and again from 5 to 8 p.m. Restaurants are usually open from 6 a.m. until midnight. Government offices, banks, shops and travel agencies are shut on Sundays and national holidays: January 1 and 2, May 1 and 2, July 4, November 29 and 30. Each Republic also has its holiday: Serbia, July 7; Montenegro, July 13; Slovenia, July 22; Bosnia and Hercegovina and Croatia, July 27; Macedonia, August 2 and October 11.

Principal Coastal Resorts

A number of the larger resorts have bathing establishments and plages. For the sake of simplicity the term 'rock' below covers promenades, jetties, concreted and cemented emplacements and so forth. All the way down the coast (on the islands as well as the mainland) there are numerous unspoilt and deserted bays, coves and creeks. One warning: be careful of sea urchins. All the mainland resorts are well linked by buses and steamers from April to October.

Name of resort	*Nearest railway station*	*Types of beach in locality*
KOPER	Trieste or Kozina	*shingle, pebble and rock*
IZOLA	Trieste or Kozina	*shingle, pebble and rock*
PIRAN	Trieste or Kozina	*shingle, pebble and rock*
PORTOROŽ	Trieste or Kozina	*sand, shingle and rock*
POREČ	Rovinj	*pebble and rock*

Principal Coastal Resorts

Name of resort	Nearest railway station	Types of beach in locality
ROVINJ	Rovinj	sand and rock
PULA	Pula	pebble and rock
LOVRAN	Rijeka	rock
MLINI	Dubrovnik	sand and rock
OPATIJA	Rijeka	sand and rock
RIJEKA	Rijeka	sand, pebble and rock
CRIKVENICA	Rijeka	sand
KRK	—	rock and pebble
MALINSKA	—	sand
OMIŠALJ	—	rock and pebble
CRES	—	sand, pebble and rock
RAB	—	sand, pebble and rock
PAG	—	pebble and rock
ZADAR	(Railway from Šibenik still being built)	sand, pebble and rock
BIOGRAD-NA-MORU (Crvena Luka)	Šibenik	pebble and rock
ŠIBENIK	Šibenik	pebble and rock
TROGIR	Kaštel	pebble and rock
ČIOVO	Kaštel	sand and rock
SPLIT	Split	sand, pebble and rock
BRAČ	—	sand, pebble and rock
OMIŠ	Split	pebble and rock
BRELA	Split	sand and pebble
BAŠKA VODA	Split	sand and pebble
MAKARSKA	Split	sand and pebble
HVAR	—	pebble and rock
STARIGRAD	—	pebble and rock
JELSA	—	pebble and rock
KORČULA	—	sand, pebble and rock
OREBIĆ	Dubrovnik	rock
DUBROVNIK	Dubrovnik	sand, pebble and rock
LAPAD	Dubrovnik	rock
CAVTAT	Dubrovnik	rock
HERCEGNOVI	Hercegnovi	pebble and rock
KOTOR	Hercegnovi	pebble and rock
BUDVA	Bar	sand
SV STEFAN	Bar	sand
PETROVAC	Bar	sand and shingle
SUTOMORE	Bar	sand and shingle
ULCINJ	Bar	sand

Hotels

Nearly all information about hotels anywhere can date fairly rapidly. A new manager or a new chef may cause a hotel to deteriorate or improve in a matter of weeks. Information dates rather more quickly than usual in a country like Jugoslavia because new hotels are being built all the time and old ones are going out of commission.

However, the list below gives a selection of those which have been found to be good or satisfactory fairly recently. These data should be supplemented by the latest details from the Jugoslav National Tourist Office in London. Their hotel list is useful but their methods of categorising are often confusing. Therefore I give my own A, B, C rating. Quite often it corresponds with the official classification. I have not included details of the numerous chalet settlements, villas, holiday camps, bungalows and so forth which abound on the coast. One has to accept the fact that in many of the cheaper hotels the lavatory amenities are poor, but this is true of most of the Balkans and most people get used to it after a short time.

The main fault with many Jugoslav hotels is that the installations are not maintained regularly. Except in the very best hotels service is rather variable (for instance, you will seldom have your baggage carried to your room) but the reception offices are usually kind and helpful. Hot water is unpredictable. I recommend you always have a supply of lavatory paper and two wash-basin plugs: the very small size and the standard size. I never leave tips unless some especial service has been done. Tipping is not the custom in the country. If you particularly want to give something to a chambermaid or a porter then a small present would be deeply appreciated (for example, a pair of stockings, a few packets of cigarettes or a bottle of *šlivovica*). It has become too easy to discharge debts or cancel a feeling of obligation by merely handing out money, and in a country where human relationships always tend to come before mercenary interests I think some effort should be made to preserve such a sense of values.

ANDRIJEVICA		BAŠKA VODA		B	Balkan
C	Komovi	B	Dubravka	B	Astorija
BANJA LUKA		BELGRADE		B	Slavija
B	Bosna	A	Excelsior	B	Union
B	Palas	A	Majestic	C	Beograd
BAR		A	Metropol	C	Toplice
C	Rumija	A	Moskva	F	Brod Zagreb

418

BIHAĆ
B Park
BIOGRAD-NA-MORU
B Crvena Luka
C Ilirija
BITOLA
C Makedonjia
BLED
A Toplice
B Jelovica
B Park
C Triglav
BOHINJ
B Zlatorog
C Bellevue
BOSANSKI PETROVAC
D Grmeč
BRAČ (SUPETAR)
C Jadran
BRELA
B Maestral
B Tiha
BUDVA
C Avala
C Mogren
BUGOJNO
B Slavko Rodič
ČAČAK
C Morava
CAVTAT
B Cavtat
B Epidaurus
CELJE
B Celeia
C Evropa
CETINJE
B Park
C Grand
CRES
B Kimen
C Bristol
CRIKVENICA
B Therapia

B Miramare
C Crikvenica
ĆUPRIJA
D Sindjelić
DEČANI
B Dečani
DJAKOVO
D Sloboda
DOBOJ
B Bosna
DUBROVNIK
A Argentina
A Excelsior
A Imperial
B Adriatic
B Dubravka
B Neptun
C Lapad
FOČA
C Zelengora
GEVGELIJA
Motel Vardar
GORAŽDE
C Pobjeda
GOSPIĆ
C Lika
GOSTIVAR
C Makedonija
HERCEGNOVI
B Boka
B Topla
B Riviera
B Igalo
HVAR
B Dalmacija
B Palas
B Pharos
C Slavija
IGALO
B Igalo
ILIDŽA
B Srbija

IVANGRAD
C Beograd
IZOLA
B Belvedere
JABLANAC
C Jablanac
JAJCE
B Turist
JELSA (Hvar)
B Jadran
KAMNIK
D Planika
KARLOBAG
D Jadran
KARLOVAC
B Korana
C Central
KAŠTEL STARI
B Palace
KLJUČ
B Sana
KNIN
D Dinara
KOLAŠIN
C Bjelašica
KOPER
B Galeb
B Triglav
B Žusterna
KORČULA
C Korčula
C Marko Polo
B Park
KOSOVSKA MIT-
ROVICA
D Jadran
KOTOR
C Slavija
KRAGUJEVAC
C Dubrovnik
KRALJEVICA
D Almis

419

KRALJEVO
B Turist
KRANJ
B Creina
C Evropa
KRATOVO
D Breza
KRK
C Dražica
C Bor
KRUŠEVAC
D Evropa
KRUŠEVO
D Ilinden
KUMANOVO
B Kristal
KURŠUMLIJA
D Beograd
LASTOVO
C Solitudo
LESKOVAC
B Beograd
C Dubočica
LJUBLJANA
A Slon
B Bellevue
B Turist
B Union
LOPAR (Rab)
  Jadran
LOŠINJ (MALI)
B Alhambra
C Helios
LOŠINJ (VELI)
C Mignon
D Park
LOVRAN
B Beograd
B Miramare
B Primorka
MAKARSKA
B Park
C Beograd

C Biokovo
MARIBOR
B Orel
B Slavija
B Zamorec
MILOČER
B Miločer
MLINI
B Mlini
B Astarea
MLJET
C Melita
MOŠĆENIČKA DRAGA
B Miramare
MOSTAR
A Bristol
C Hercegovina
C Mostar
NEGOTIN
C Beograd
C Obilić
NIKŠIĆ
B Onogošt
NIŠ
B Park
B Niš
NOVIGRAD (nr.
  Zadar)
C Mediteran
NOVI PAZAR
C Beograd
NOVI SAD
A Park
B Putnik
C Vojvodina
NOVO MESTO
C Metropol
OHRID
A Palace
OMIŠ
C Plaza
OMIŠALJ (Krk)
B Adriatic

C Jadran
OPATIJA
A Kvarner
B Belvedere
B Brioni
B Dubrovnik
B Central
C Avala
OPLENAC
B Oplenac
OREBIĆ
C Bellevue
OSIJEK
B Central
PAG
D Dalmacija
PANČEVO
C Sloboda
PARAĆIN
D Makedonija
  Motel
PAZIN
C Partizan
PEĆ
B Metohija
PETROVAC
B Oliva
B Palas
PIRAN
B Metropol
PIROT
C Nacional
PLAV
C Plavsko Jezero
PLITVICE
A Plitvice
PLJEVLJA
C Tara
POČITELJ
B Starigrad
POREČ
B Jadran
B Riviera

PORTOROŽ
A Lucija
A Palas
B Central
POSTOJNA
B Kras
C Javornik
POŽAREVAC
C Avala
PRESPA
Oteševo holiday village
PRIJEDOR
C Balkan
PRILEP
C Jadran
PRIŠTINA
A Kosovski
   Božur
PRIZREN
B Theranda
PROKUPLJE
D Evropa
PTUJ
B Poetovio
PULA
B Riviera
B Ribarska
PUNAT (Krk)
C Park
RAB
B Imperial
B Istra
C Jadran
RADOVLJICA
C Grajski Dvor
RAŠKA
Motel Putnik
RIJEKA
B Bonavia
B Jadran
B Park
ROVINJ
B Jadran

B Crveni Otok
RUMA
D Srem
ŠABAC
D Zeleni Venac
SAMOBOR
D Lavica
SARAJEVO
A Evropa
B Beograd
B Central
SENJ
B Nehaj
ŠIBENIK
B Jadran
B Krka
SINJ
D Livno
SISAK
New hotel being
   built
SKOPJE
B Park
B Turist
SLAVONSKI BROD
B Park
SLUNJ
C Slunjčica
SMEDEREVO
B Park
B Smederevo
SOMBOR
C Sloboda
SOPOČANI
D Sopočani
SPLIT
A Marjan
B Bellevue
B Mosor
B Park
B Split
C Central
C Srebrena Vrata

SREMSKI KARLOVCI
C Turist
STARI GRAD (Hvar)
B Helios
ŠTIP
C Makedonija
STON
C Prapratno
STRUGA
C Grand
STRUMICA
B Esperanto
SUBOTICA
B Zagreb
B Palić
SUTOMORE
B Južno More
SVETI STEFAN
A Sveti Stefan
SVETOZAREVO
B Palace
TARA
B Tara
TETOVO
B New
TITOGRAD
B Crna Gora
TITOVO UŽICE
B Palas
TITOV VELES
B International
TRAVNIK
C Park
TREBINJE
B Leotar
TROGIR
C Radovan
TUČEPI
B Kastelet
B Jadran
TUZLA
C Beograd

421

ULCINJ	ŽABLJAK	ZAJEČAR
B Jadran	B Durmitor	B Putnik
B Galeb	ZADAR	ZENICA
VARAŽDIN	B Beograd	B Metalurg
B Istra	B Zagreb	ZEMUN
VIS	ZAGREB	B Central
C Borovik	A Palas	C Grand
VIŠEGRAD	B Beograd	ZLARIN
B Višegrad	B Central	B Koralj
VRANJE	B Dubrovnik	ZRENJANIN
C Evropa	B Esplanade	B Vojvodina
VRŠAC	C International	ZVORNIK
C Srbija	C Jadran	D Drina

Food

I sometimes meet English people who complain bitterly about Jugoslavian food. The truth is that if you take a little trouble over the matter you can eat very well. It is not, of course, in the same class as French cuisine but I should say that after the Turkish and Chinese, Jugoslavian food and cooking are among the best. If you go there expecting English food you are bound to be disappointed. The answer is to experiment.

Few Jugoslavs have breakfast. They content themselves with a cup of black coffee, usually Turkish, and perhaps a glass of *šlivovica*. However, you can have a kind of continental breakfast which consists of black or white coffee, bread, butter and jam. You *can* get tea but it is usually very anaemic. White coffee, except in the best hotels, is often foul. Tea with lemon is good and so is hot chocolate. I always make my own coffee and tea in the bedroom on a spirit stove. You can supplement the continental breakfast with a conventional English dish of ham and eggs which Jugoslavs cook well.

There is no such thing as afternoon tea and the two main meals of the day are lunch and dinner. There is a good deal of variety for these meals, the food is usually well cooked and helpings are copious. Soups, *hors d'oeuvres* and *entrées* are particularly well done. The principal dish will often consist basically of lamb, veal or mutton (good beef is very rare). They go in for a lot of stuffed tomatoes, paprikas and marrows. Fish on the coast is excellent (though few Mediterranean fish compare with what we get round the British Isles) and there is normally a wide variety. Cooked vegetables vary (and you seldom get them out of season) but the salads are delicious. They don't bother much about puddings, but there is usually plenty of fresh fruit, *gâteaux* and bottled fruits for compots. Cheeses are disappointing. One soon discovers that the main influences on cuisine have been Turkish, Austrian and Greek.

Below is a sample but by no means comprehensive menu. You will seldom get such a wide choice as this, except in the large restaurants; but in the best restaurants the choice may be greater. You will find that the names of some dishes vary in different parts of the country, and so does the spelling of the names. Many of the larger restaurants have menus in German, French and English but you cannot depend on this. In any case I think one should make some effort to discover things in the original. Fortunately the Jugoslavs have not yet introduced the despicable Italian habit of special menus with higher prices for tourists. Only rarely will you find the *table d'hôte* fixed price menu, though I dare say it will be introduced more and more.

Doručak
Doručak komplet

Bela kava
Crna kava
Turska kava
Čaj sa limunom
Čaj sa mlekom
Hleb or kruh
Puter or maslac
Džem
Šunka sa jajem (this also goes under the name of emendeks or hemendeks)

Breakfast
Continental breakfast with tea, coffee or chocolate, bread, butter and jam
White coffee
Black coffee
Turkish coffee
Tea with lemon
Tea with milk
Bread
Butter
Jam
Ham and eggs

Ručak i Večera
HLADNA PREDJELA
Pašteta
Mešani hordever
Hladne zakuske ⎱
Hladni narezak ⎰
Prešana šunka sa hrenom
Biftek tartar
Dalmatinski pršut
Jaja sa majonezom
Gavrilović salama
Ruska salata

Ruska jaja
Hladni odojak

Lunch and Dinner
COLD HORS D'OEUVRES
Pâté
Mixed hors d'oeuvre
Assorted cold meats, like salami, ham, smoked sausage, etc.
Ham with horseradish
This explains itself
Smoked Dalmatian ham
Eggs with mayonnaise
A kind of salami
Vegetables and strips of cold meat in mayonnaise
Hard-boiled eggs with ruska salata
Cold sucking pig

423

Sardine u ulju	*Sardines in oil*
Masline	*Olives*
JUHE–SUPE–ČORBE	SOUPS
Goveđa	*Consommé*
Bujon sa jajem ⎱ Buljon sa jajetom ⎰	*Bouillon with eggs*
Pasirana od povrća	*Vegetable soup*
Juha od rajčice ⎱ Juha od paradajza ⎰	*Tomato soup*
Jagnjeća čorba	*Lamb soup*
Goveđa supa sa prženim grškom	*Pea soup*
Riblja čorba	*Fish soup*
TOPLA PREDJELA	HOT ENTRÉES
Voloven	*Vol-au-vent*
Melančani sos tartar	*Aubergines with tartar sauce*
Pohani melančani sa tartarom	*Aubergines panée with tartar sauce*
Špageti na milanski način	*Spaghetti à la Milanaise*
Špageti na bolonjski	*Spaghetti à la Bolognaise*
Omlet sa sirom	*Cheese omelet*
Omlet sa povrćem	*Vegetable omelet*
Omlet sa šunkom	*Ham omelet*
Naravni omlet	*Plain omelet*
Cvetača na poljski	*Cauliflower à la Polonaise*
Pohani sir sa tartarom	*Fried cheese with tartar sauce*
Vrganji	*Mushrooms*
Punjene palačinke sa mozgom	*A kind of pancake stuffed with brains*
Srpska jaja	*An omelet with chopped peppers, tomatoes and cucumbers in it*
RIBE	FISH
Sufle od rakova	*Lobster in aspic*
Kečiga	*Sterlet*
Jesetra	*Sturgeon*
Pohani smuđ	*Fried perch*
Brodetto	*A fish ragout, a form of bouilla-baisse*
Pržena pastrva or pastrmka	*Fried trout*
Kesiga ⎱ Osliči ⎰ Bjelica ⎰	*Whiting*
Jastog	*Lobster*
Prženi šaran	*Fried carp*
Kalamari rizoto	*Fried squid served with their ink*
Cipalj, cipal, cipoli, bradeč	*Mullet*

Trlja, barbun	*Red Mullet*
Lokarda, skuša	*Mackerel*
Losos	*Salmon*
Letnica	*Salmon trout*
Oštrige	*Oysters*
Ploča	*Halibut*
Račići	*Shellfish*
Rah	*Crayfish*
Sledj	*Herring*
Mladica	*Char*
Tuna	*Tunny*
Bakalar	*Cod*
Srdjelica	*Whitebait*
Zubatac	*Gilthead bream*
Somovina	*Sheath fish*
Hobotnica	*Octopus*
Morski rak	*Crab*
List	*Plaice, sole*
Grgeč	*Bass*
GOTOVA JELA	PLATS DU JOUR (*literally 'ready food'*)
Teleći rizoto	*Veal risotto*
Kuhana govedina	*Boiled beef*
Pečena patka	*Roast duck*
Pečeno pile	*Roast chicken*
Svinjsko pečenje	*Roast pork*
Pečena divlja svinja	*Roast boar*
Teleće pečenje	*Roast veal*
Punjene paradajsi	*Stuffed tomatoes*
Punjene paprika	*Stuffed peppers*
Domaća sarma	*There are various forms of sarma* *Basically they consist of rolled leaf of* *pickled cabbage or vine leaves stuffed* *with mince meat and rice*
Punjene tikvice	*Stuffed marrows*
Teleći paprikaš	*Veal cooked in paprika sauce*
Kuhana kokoš	*Boiled chicken*
Pržolica sa lukom	*Entrecôte of beef or veal with onions*
Pilav	*There are various forms of pilaff*
Musaka	*This is international*
Sataraš	*Meat stewed with tomatoes and peppers*
Djuveč	*Meat stewed with rice, tomatoes,* *peppers, carrots and peas*

Kapama	*Lamb stewed with spinach and shallots and served with sour milk (kiselo mljeko*
Francuski krompir	*Potatoes and hard-boiled eggs in layers, baked in the oven*
Ćulbastija	*Boned beef, pork or veal, grilled and garnished with onions*
Gulaš	*Goulash*
Papazjanija	*Ragout of beef, pork or lamb with vegetables*
VARIVA	VEGETABLES
Pasulje	*Beans*
Špinat or spanač	*Spinach*
Kuhani krompir	*Boiled potatoes*
Prženi krompir	*Fried potatoes*
Grašak na maslacu	*Peas cooked with butter*
Mahune na maslacu	*Runner beans cooked with butter*
Riža	*Rice*
Kupus	*Cabbage*
Karfiol, cvetača	*Cauliflower*
Mrkva	*Carrots*
Repa	*Turnips*
Luk	*Onion*
SPECIJALITETI NA RAŽNU I ROŠTILJU	GRILLS AND ROASTS
Jetra na žaru	*Grilled liver*
Bubrezi na žaru	*Grilled kidneys*
Srce na žaru	*Grilled hearts*
Čevapčiči sa lukom	*Minced meat in sausage shapes served with onions*
Ražnici sa lukom	*A kind of kebab, slices of meat roasted on a skewer and served with onions*
Pleskavica sa lukom	*A similar dish*
Hajdučkî ćevap	*Pieces of pork and beef (or veal) roasted on a skewer*
Jagnjeći šašlik	*Pieces of lamb with potatoes and bay leaves roasted on a skewer*
JELA PO NARUDŽBI	MAIN DISHES (literally 'food to order')
Svinjski kotlet	*Pork cutlet*
Turnedos Rossini	*A veal or beef steak with a piquant sauce*
Lombarda pikato	*Fillet of veal with a piquant sauce*
Biftek obloženi sa jajem i povrćem	*A steak (usually veal) garnished with vegetables and served with an egg*

Ramstek	*Rump steak (usually veal)*
Zagrebački odrezak	*Escalope of veal stuffed with ham and cheese and garnished with vegetables*
Dubrovački Medaljon	*Veal stuffed with tomatoes, Hollandaise sauce*
Srpska plošča	*A massive mixed grill*
Nacionalj pladanj ⎫	
Mešano meso na žaru ⎭	*A mixed grill*
Šatobrian	*Double steaks with vegetables*
Pileći kotlet na kijevski način	*Chicken à la Kiev (but it varies)*
Pile na žaru	*Grilled chicken*
Pohano pile	*Fried chicken*
Teleći mozak	*Braised brains served with ham*
Teleća jetra na venecijanski	*Liver sautéed*
Bečka šnicla or šnicel ⎫	
Bečki odrezak ⎭	*Wiener schnitzel*
Naravni odrezak	*Plain escalope*
SALATE	SALADS
Cikla	*Beetroot*
Kupus	*Cabbage*
Krompir	*Potato*
Mešana	*Mixed salad*
Zelena	*Green salad*
Rajčica ili paprika	*Tomato or pepper*
Krastavac	*Cucumber*
Srpska	*Minced aubergines and peppers*
SIREVI	CHEESES
Trapist, ementaler, bel paese paški, gorgonzola	*The names are the same*
KOLAĆI	LITERALLY 'CAKES' (*but the term covers puddings, pastries, etc.*)
Savijača od jabuka	*Apple strudel*
Savijača od sira	*Cheese strudel*
Savijača od trešanja	*Cherry strudel*
Palačinke sa džemom	*Jam pancake*
Palačinke sa čokoladom	*Chocolate pancake*
Čokolada torta	*Chocolate gâteau*
Tufahija	*Poached apple stuffed with chopped nuts and cream*
Baklava	*The same*
Sladoled	*Ice-cream*

KOMPOTI	COMPOTS
Marelice }	*Apricots*
Kajsije }	
Breskve	*Peaches*
Trešnje	*Cherries*
Mešani	*Mixed compot*
Voćna salata	*Fruit salad*
VOĆE	FRESH FRUIT
Narandže	*Oranges*
Banane	*Bananas*
Kruške	*Pears*
Jabuke	*Apples*
Jagode	*Strawberries*
Breskve	*Peaches*
Groždje	*Grapes*
Trešnje	*Cherries*
Sljive	*Plums*
Kajsije	*Apricots*

Wines etc.

I have mentioned the principal wines of the country in the main text and the better restaurants often provide a wine list (*spisak vina*) which may include some or all of them as well as a number I have not mentioned. White wine is *belo vino*; red wine, *crno vino* (*crno* in fact means black); rosé wine, *ružica*. The *vins ordinaires* are served in jugs of various sizes and are known as *stolno vino* (table wine) or *obično vino* (ordinary wine) or *vino otvoreno* (wine already opened). Wine is measured by the litre. A half litre is *pola litra*, and the other commonest measures are *dva deci* (two-tenths of a litre) and *tri deci* (three-tenths). The safe thing to do is to start with *dva deci* and if you like it order some more. For references in the text to specific wines, see index entry: Wines.

Most of the apéritifs, liqueurs and cocktails have internationally recognisable names. Apart from these there are some home products like *šlivovica* and *maraschino* which I have mentioned, plus various kinds of *rakija* which means spirits in general. *Šlivovica* is plum-*rakija*. *Travarica* is herb-*rakija*. *Komovica* and *Lozovačka* are both grape-*rakijas*. *Prepečenica* is a particularly strong grape *rakija*. *Pelinkovac* is made from wood and tastes of wormwood. *Orahovac* is made from walnuts. *Kruškovac* is a form of perry. Many people acquire a taste for *šlivovica* and I have, but I find most of the others rather disgusting drinks.

Beer (*pivo*) is usually of the lager type and you can get it by the glass or the bottle.

There is a large variety of refreshing soft drinks, especially in Serbia and Macedonia, and every town has shops (usually called *slastičarne* and *aščinica*) and kiosks which sell these as well as ice-creams, cakes, pastries, etc. These establishments are more frequent in central, eastern and southern Jugoslavia.

Among the best of the soft drinks are what they called *voćni sokovi* ('fruit juices') which are all made from fresh fruit. In season you can get pure lemon and orange juice. The iced lemonades and iced barley water are delicious. And there are other fruit juices made from strawberry and raspberry to which water or soda are added. There are also various kinds of fizzy orangeade and lemonade, which I find revolting anywhere. A popular drink which varies from area to area and in quality is *cokta*: a relation of Coca-Cola. *Boza* or *bosa* (originally Albanian) is an iced milky drink made from maize and is available in most parts of the country. The whole country also produces large quantities of mineral waters. If you are really parched (in the summer thirst can be very acute here) you can hardly do better than drink milkless tea or just plain water (*pitka voda*). I know of no land where the ordinary drinking water is so excellent. Jugoslavs (like all peoples who live in very hot countries) are connoisseurs of this and discuss its merits as Frenchmen discuss wine. They are familiar with the quality of wells many miles apart. It is commonplace for them to recommend the water in a particular village or district.

Ice-cream (*sladoled*) is usually much better than anything you will get in England, or many parts of Europe. The water ices are first-class, so are the sorbets. Real cream is used for other ices, and I recommend the raspberry, strawberry, apricot and peach. Occasionally you can get chocolate, banana, coffee and vanilla.

In Muslim areas the bon-bons, biscuits, cakes and pastries are common and delicious. The *slastičarne* also sell Turkish delight (*rahat lokum, ratluk* or *lokumia*) and items like stuffed onions (*sogan dolma*). The answer is to explore these shops, ask for the names of things and experiment.

Two national 'dishes', as it were, are *slatko* (traditional offering to a guest) and *burek*. There are many forms of *slatko* (cherry, melon, strawberry, orange, blackberry, grape, plum, rose-leaf, green walnut and green fig) but the recipes are much the same. The fruit, to which a lot of sugar is added, goes through complicated processes of boiling, cooling and refining until the original fruit remains intact in its own syrup. A related conserve is *pekmez*, usually made from plums or rose-hips without sugar. *Burek* is a staple food in Serbia and Macedonia. You should certainly try it. It also goes under the name of *pita* and consists variously of meat with onions, or chopped spinach and pumpkin, or ewe's milk curds, or curds and eggs, or cheese and egg, set between very fine leaves of pastry and cooked in the broad shallow pans called *tepsije*.

Entertainment

Opera is very popular in the big cities and many of the smaller towns have theatres. Plays in translation are often performed, especially during festivals. There are numerous concerts, exhibitions and folk dancing performances—not to mention motor shows, fairs, chess congresses, sailing and rowing regattas, wine fairs, athletic meetings, ski-ing tournaments and so forth. Up-to-date information about most of these can be obtained from the Jugoslav National Tourist Office or from Generalturist.

Below is a selected list of particularly interesting events which occur every year. Many of them are not well known (not even at the Tourist Office) and most of them are concerned with traditional folklore celebrations and practices. I have mentioned and described some of them in the main text; others are dealt with in the appendix on music and dance. A few of the dates vary from year to year. The page references are to places in the text, and to the appendix on music and dance (see p. 432).

January 2-6 *Koledari*: in the Leskovac region (pp. 269-70)
January 8-19 *Rusalije* or *Rusalia*: in Macedonia (p. 436)
February (towards the end of the month; sometimes between Twelfth Night and Shrove Tuesday) *Kurenti* or *Kuranti*: in Ptuj and district (pp. 385-6)
April 23 *Kumpanija*: on island of Korčula (p. 113)
April 24 *Jurjaši*: celebrations in various parts of Slovenia and Croatia on St George's Day, especially at Turopolje between Sisak and Zagreb (p. 354)
April (Saturday before Easter) *Lazarice*: in the Leskovac region (p. 269) and also northern Serbia (p. 310)
April (Easter Day) *Velikonočno Valjanje*: a kind of skittle game practised in Slovenia. Girls and boys roll eggs (or oranges) down a board towards an egg or orange at the end. If the target is hit the person gets both eggs. This can be quite hilarious.
May 1-2 International Labour Day celebrations
May (first Sunday) *Ples pod Trešnjom*: island of Krk (p. 24)
May 6 *Sabor* celebrations: in the village of Banjani, north of Skopje. A costume event of music and dances of the Skopska Crna Gora (p. 206)

May (no definite date) *Grana*; celebration of the cherry harvest: in the neighbourhood of Jajce, Bugojno and Zenica; singing and dancing in which both Muslims and Christians take part.

June 21 Slavonski Brod Fair.

June 26 Traditional *Sabor* celebrations in village of Kučevište near Skopje (p. 206)

June All Souls' Day, (which normally falls a month and a half after Easter in the Orthodox Church) is usually celebrated by commemorative rituals (*pomane*) for the dead in many parts of Serbia (p. 289)

June 29 Bakarac *Ribarska Fešta*: fishermen's celebrations at Bakar, near Rijeka (p. 33)

August 1-15 (approx.) Split Summer Festival: drama, opera, ballet, concerts, Jugoslav folk songs and dances.

July 10-August 24 (approx.) Dubrovnik Summer Festival; similar to that at Split.

July-August Folk Song and Dance Festival in Sarajevo.

July-August Bullfighting in Bosnia (p. 356)

July 12 Wedding Day in Galičnik (p. 214)

July 13 Anniversary of the Montenegrin Uprising in 1941 (p. 151); an event celebrated in costume and dance.

July 17 Bohinj stages a traditional folklore event called the *Kmečka Ohcet*— a country wedding.

July 20-August 15 (approx.) Folk Song and Dance Festival at Ohrid.

July 22 The *Fašinada*; rituals at Perast (p. 141)

July 25 The *Dernek*: traditional celebrations at Vrlika (p. 434)

July 27 The *Moreška* Dance at Korčula (pp. 111-13)

August (on the Sunday closest to August 5) Krk Folklore Festival (p. 434)

August 2 Ilinjdan or St Elijah's Day: this is a most important feast widely celebrated in Orthodox regions. A good chance to see local dances, costume and custom.

August 7 Jezersko *Pastirski Bal*; dances and merrymaking to celebrate the return of the cattle from the mountains. Jezersko is near Kranj on the Slovene/Austrian border.

August 8 *Pastirski Bal* at Rateče Planica. This is also very near the Austrian border, a few kilometres from Podkoren.

August (usually on the Sunday closest to August 9) The *Sinjska Alka* at Sinj (pp. 93-5)

August (second Saturday) *Puntarska Noč*; 'Punat Night' at Punat, on the island of Krk (p. 24). A traditional event of songs, dances, firework displays etc.

August (usually on a Sunday) *Dužijanca*: a harvest festival in the north of the Bačka region (p. 308). A crown of wheat is borne by a young man and a girl in procession. They ride in a cart which is decorated with green branches and wheat sheafs, and at the village church the ears of the crown are distributed.

August 28 Celebration at the church of Our Lady of Škrpjela off Perast (p. 141)

August 28 Celebration at the Monastery of Savina (p. 138) near Hercegnovi. This is a pilgrimage spot and the Montenegrins wear their costumes and dance the *Skoke po Crnogorski* (p. 435)

September (first half) *Sabor* at Belgrade. A festival of folk songs and dances.

September (near the end of the month) *Kravlji Bal* (cow dance) at Bohinj (p. 376) to celebrate the return of the cattle from the mountains.

October 2 *Ribarsko Veče* (Fishermen's Evening), a celebration at Kraljevica (p. 33)

Music and Dance

As I have suggested in the main text many of the Jugoslav dances (and, up to a point, their musical accompaniment) stem from and are still associated with ancient fertility rites; and there are numerous ceremonial dances for the various festivals of the year: at Christmas, Epiphany, Easter, St George's Day, Whitsuntide, Midsummer, Harvest time, and so forth. They vary a good deal from region to region. Within regions there are still further variations according to costume, occupation and economic conditions. Many of them, of course (like, in some ways, the *Narodne Pesme*), are an expression of national consciousness, and it is no accident that the greatest number and variety of dances (and the most complex) occur in Serbia and Macedonia, which were under Turkish domination for so long. In Slovenia, by contrast, there are relatively few.

A further consideration is that until very recently they were one of the principal sources of entertainment for the majority of people in all rural areas, but especially in Serbia and Macedonia. In the absence of books, radio, cinema, newspapers, television, sport, circuses, theatre and indeed most forms of popular modern distraction, the onus was (and often still is) on the individual to provide his own entertainment. The need to do this will gradually diminish. I think it is more or less axiomatic that urban development brings about a decline in such culture. Spectating replaces participation. Traditional dancing and music of ancient origins is kept alive in countries like England by small, devoted groups of people who are fairly expert and who have probably *learnt* the dances 'a subject'. Among the South Slavs (and many Balkan peoples) children start imitating the steps very early. From the age of two or three they become familiar with dances that have been repeated in stylised forms for about eight hundred years and with the music of instruments that are equally old and traditional.

First a word about the instruments. These are relatively few but some of them go under different names in different regions. In **Istria** they have the *sopile* or *roženice*, a form of oboe; the *mišnica* (or *mih*), a bagpipe made out of goatskin or sheepskin (they are usually made from these in the Balkans); and the *vidalice* or *pastirski vidalice*, a wooden flute. This is to be seen in various forms all over the country and it is called *pastirski vidalice* because it is commonly the shepherds who make and play them.

In **Dalmatia** the wooden flute is called a *volarice*; and another form of flute is the *svirila*. The Dalmatians also use the *lijerica*, a pear-shaped instrument with three strings which is played with a bow.

In **Croatia** they have the *mišnica*, the *sopile* and the *tamburica*, a type of mandolin.

In **Serbia** the shepherd's flute is known as a *duduk*; and there are two other kinds of flute: the *kaval* and the *dvojnica*, a double flute. The bagpipe in Serbia is called a *gajde* and here they also use the bass drum—the *goč*. The traditional Serb instruments are those you commonly find in use in Montenegro and Bosnia, where the single flute is called a *ćurlik*.

In **Macedonia** the instruments are the bass drum, a *tupan*; a *daburka* which is similar to a mandolin; a *zurle*, a wind instrument like a clarinet; and the *šupeljka* which is a primitive type of flute.

The one-stringed *gusle* might be found in use in almost any district. Occasionally you may find a form of trumpet known as a *truba*. The guitar and the accordion are becoming increasingly popular in most areas. The more familiar and conventional pieces of a band or orchestra are not ones that Jugoslav musicians handle with much skill—as you will discover when you are staying in the hotels.

In **Slovenia** the western influence (especially the Austrian) has been so strong that the Slovenes have not developed the same traditions in music or dance to anything like the same extent.

This is a very rough general summary from which it can be seen that the range of sound possible is limited, but the average village three- or four-piece band is often very accomplished. To the inexpert or unaccustomed ear much of the music will at first seem monotonous but it is made for the dance, and the dance for the music, and when you find yourself actually participating rather than watching and listening the many subtleties and complexities become manifest.

Without lengthy jargoning and technicality, not here appropriate, I can only try to suggest what the effects are like. The reiterations of the bagpipe or the one-stringed fiddle (wild and exciting sounds) provide a kind of continuous theme and rhythm for a dance which are counterpointed by the more delicate and varied wind instruments which dictate the steps of the dance. The monotonous percussion of the bass drum gives a regular beat to contrast the very 'fast' fiddle and bagpipe music.

Some of the dances you are likely to see are as follows: In **Istria** (see chap. 22) and round the **Kvarner Gulf** (see chap. 1) one of the most popular is the *Balun*—a very energetic, whirling measure performed in pairs. This is nearly always put on at a festival. On the island of **Krk** (see pp. 21-4) they have a famous dance called the *Krčki tanac* which is executed by couples. Other traditional dances of the area are the *Bakarska*, the *Verec* and the *Šoto*. The music sometimes includes a melody called a *mantinjada*, which is believed to be of Roman origin and can be heard in Istria and many parts of the Croatian littoral. The playing of the *mantinjada* has a traditional importance at wedding ceremonies. By way of invitation members of the bridegroom's family 'serenade' putative guests a few days before the marriage. The melody is also played before the wedding procession sets out for the bride's home.

At **Pag** (see p. 40) a traditional dramatic pageant called *Robinja* (The Slavegirl) used to be performed and is likely to be revived. It has affinities with the *Moreška* Dance of Korčula (see pp. 111-13). Basically it consists of a very stylised musical drama in verse the climax of which is a battle with wooden hatchets for the ransomed slavegirl captured by the Turks. The rite may stem from a battle against the Turks in 1493. After the ransoming all the performers dance the *Paško Kolo* to the accompaniment of bagpipes.

At **Vrlika** near Knin (see p. 434) on holidays and Sundays and especially the Dernek festival on July 25th, the inhabitants dance the *Vrličko kolo*, a chain dance performed without music. The accompaniment is provided by the jingling percussion of the metal ornaments worn by the women This is a very exciting dance that becomes faster and faster and finishes very abruptly.

During the **Dubrovnik** (see chap. 8) summer festival there is an excellent opportunity of seeing many of the local dances, especially the *Lindjo*: a circular dance (to the accompaniment of the *lijerica*) with a leader in the centre who sings out verses at intervals. Other Croatian dances you may see on the coast or inland are *kolos* called the Poskočice and the *Kolo mista*. The latter is a very swift almost corybantic chain dance to the music of bagpipe and banjo. Other dances involving a shivering and vibratory movement of the whole body are called, appropriately, The Shaking (*drmeš*) and The Old Sieve (*velo šito*).

The *kolo* is the most popular dance in Montenegro and at **Kotor** (see pp. 142-44) usually on September 10th, the Bokelska Mornarica still maintain some old traditions. It is said that when Sv Trifun's relics were first brought the sailors danced a *kolo* round them. Thus was founded the *kolo*

Svetog Trifuna or the *kolo Bokeljske Mornarice* which consisted of twelve different figures in the fifth of which the dancers formed a large anchor.

On the whole the Montenegrins are not a very musical people and their *kolo* dances are usually performed without instrumental music. The beat for the song or dance is given by the thudding of feet. The dances tend to be very vigorous and free, often accompanied by high leaps. Two of the better known ones are the *Po Crnogorski* (a couple dance) and the *Skoke* (*skok* means a 'bound' or a 'leap') when the audience urges the participants to carry on for as long as possible. Women as well as men take part in these, but they dance with much more restraint than the men and repeat what the men sing. This is perfectly in keeping with the traditional subservience of the women.

The militant traditions of the Montenegrins are especially well illustrated in their sword dances: for instance, the *Borbena Rugovska Igra* (the Rugova war dance, named after the gorge) in which two dancers with swords fight for a girl. Many of the Montenegrin *kolos* are tests of strength and endurance.

In **Macedonia** the *kolo* is known as an *oro*. Basically there are two kinds: the *Lesnoto*, which is light and gay; and the *Teškoto*, which is slow and deliberate, even ponderous. Each *oro* usually has a leader, the *kolovodja*, who is usually a dancer of outstanding agility and skill. He has to be because the Macedonians are brilliant dancers.

Many of the *oros* are very complicated and the music has obviously been influenced by Turkish elements. Some of the more complex dances are performed in the Lazaropolje region (see p. 215). Round Skopje (see chap. 13) the dances are very gay and vigorous. People from backward and poor areas who had to go a long way to find work dance in a slow and melancholy fashion. Gradually the tempo quickens and culminates in a jubilant climax. The rhythms have almost certainly been affected by the Turkish occupation. A dance expressive of subservience and dejection would be lugubrious. Freedom, or the prospect of it, would encourage an optimistic and jocund conclusion.

An expecially good example is the style of dance in the **Kičevo** region, high in the mountains north of Ohrid (see p. 222). Here the peasants have expressed themselves in one tradition for a long time. Originally they worked on feudal estates and then under Turkish masters. Their dance, therefore, suggested a state of subjugation. But the *kolo* leader always held his fist clenched behind his back as a symbol of the continued spirit of resistance. After their liberation from Turkish rule the Kičevo dancers became more vivacious and danced more erectly to show that they were free. The clenched fist survives in some dances.

There are a large number of Macedonian *ritual dances*; for instance, those performed at weddings to protect the couple from evil spirits; and war dances where the men have very aggressive moves, and the women play a restrained, ancillary role.

Among the most interesting of all the Balkan ritual dances are the *Rusalije* or *Rusalia* which used to be done in front of every house in the village to ensure good health and good crops in the coming year. Now they are performed on that spot customarily used for village meetings. Southern Macedonia, especially the Gevgelja region (see p. 237), is one of the ideal places to see them.

The dancers, usually young men, perform in their own village and then visit others nearby. They wear dashing costumes of red and black stockings, flouncy white kilts and white shirts, red cummerbunds and black hats. Each dancer wields a wooden *yatagan* (it used to be steel) in his right hand, while the left is free for balancing if it is not actually on the hip. All the dances are very vigorous and intricate and accompanied by a good deal of brandishing of the *yatagans*. Each gesture is symbolic.

In contrast to these there are comic dances called *Džamalarska ora*. These are rarely performed now but when they are done it is on New Year's Day and during the harvest festival. The dancers wear old clothes (turned inside out) to which are attached bells that ring and tinkle to every movement. Improvisation is the key to success in these capers and each dancer tries to be as ludicrous as possible.

Another dance characteristic of the Gevgelja and Miravci region is the *Šareno oro* which takes place after sunset on the last day of the wedding festivities. It is begun by the parents of the bridegroom who are then joined by the groom and the men of his family. Then come the women with the with the bride. As they dance they interchange places until bride and groom are between their parents. Then, in order of seniority, all the other members of the families join. By this time there may be forty or fifty people involved.

The groom's father subsequently leads them all into the house and to the hearth—on which there must be a fire burning. The music and the dancing stop. The bride turns to the chimney, bows three times, and kisses the hands of her husband's parents. That is the end; one of the more remarkable marriage rituals in Europe.

At a Macedonian wedding another dance you may see is the *Svekrvino* ('the mother-in-law's') in which the bridegroom's mother leads the dancers. Tradition obliges her to balance a flower-sieve and some bread on her head. She also has to carry a pitcher of wine. After a time she gives way to the groom.

In **Serbia** chain dances predominate and, as in most *kolos*, the dancers are joined together by hand or clasped hand and arm, sometimes by scarves, strings of beads, kerchiefs and small towels. As in the Macedonian *kolo* the dancers sometimes grip each other by their belts or some other item of clothing.

436

One of the best known Serbian *kolos* is the *Tri Mlinara* (The Three Millers). This is a completely closed circle *kolo* in which men and women alternately are joined by hand. The *Župčanka* (The Cogwheel) is an open *kolo*, or semi-circular. Again the men and women are alternate. The *Zetsko* may be a closed *kolo*, or two closed *kolos* with one inside the other, in which men form one half of the circle and women the other. It may also be a double *kolo* consisting of men only.

The Serbian *slava* feast (see pp. 257-8) is always accompanied by dance and song to the music of bagpipe and flute and—more frequently nowadays —the accordion. Dances commonly associated with this event are: the *Kačerac*, *Žikino*, *Djurdjevka*, *Devojačko*, *Moravac* and *Čačak*. All are forms of *kolo*. The last two are obviously named after Morava and Čačak.

At Prizren (see p. 190) they still occasionally perform a famous dance called the *Kalač*, an intricate and stately measure in which the dancers joined together by crossed scarves complete five different figures.

If you happen to be in the Ušće area (see p. 263) on August 2nd. (the feast day of Sv Ilija) it is worth paying a visit to the traditional celebrations on the top of Mt Željin nearby. Separated friends and relatives make this an occasion for reunion. Naturally enough their news for each other may be sad and to mark their grief they dance the solemn *Žalosno kolo*: the *kolo* of sorrow.

In the Pirot region (see p. 275) there are two dances still done on special occasions. The first is the *Katanka*, a courtship dance performed by couples who go through a number of different figures: very lively formalised representations of flirting: pursuit, challenge, withdrawal, evasion and so forth. The second, named *Lilka*, is also very energetic and is accompanied by a traditional song which describes the behaviour of a Turk towards a Serbian girl.

Other dances you may witness in Serbia are the ritual *kolos* done on Easter Monday and Midsummer Night. The latter are usually performed round bonfires. In northern Serbia they also have versions of the *Lazarice* celebrated, as in the south, on Lazarus's Day (see p. 269). On St George's Day and at Whitsun women perform the *Kraljice* or 'queen's dances'. The dancers traditionally wear high, mitre-shaped head-dresses adorned with holy pictures, and carry handkerchiefs and banners of red silk decorated with various botanical motifs.

In the northern Vojvodina, near Subotica (see p. 313), one of the most famous dances is the *Momačko* or Bachelor's *kolo*. In this the men compete in front of the women who judge the best dancer. The music is normally provided by the *tambura*, a stringed instrument not unlike a lute.

The Serbs also have a dance in which the dancers are more or less in a straight line (as, I believe, do the Vlach, though I have never seen them do it) and hold on to each other by their belts. The styles vary from region to region. Among the better known variations are the *Šestovka*, the *Kolubara* and the *Vlasina*. Some of them are extremely swift, intricate and exciting.

Many of the dances in **Bosnia-Hercegovina** are done without musical accompaniment. They are warlike and spirited and reflect a tradition of militant independence. The *Trusa* and the *Dilber* are two of the better known. The *Glamoč* (see p. 355) named after the small town of that name is a very exhilarating measure.

Slovenia, as I have suggested, is more restricted. The Slovenes dance a lot and do it well, but the Bela Krajina, the border region between Croatia and Slovenia (see p. 366), is almost certainly the only area where the traditional *kolos* survive. Some are closed, some open and two of the better known are named after prominent towns: the *Metliško kolo* and the *Črnomelj kolo*. Otherwise, the more conventional couple dancing is popular all over Slovenia, and so is the *Polka*, the Bohemian nineteenth-century dance.

Costumes

The drawings on the next two pages are intended to give a general idea of a few of the more outstanding costumes you are likely to see in various regions. They include the most obvious features, on which there are innumerable variations. Some of the detail in the women's costumes is generalised. The minutiae vary from village to village. The variations run into hundreds, if not thousands.

SLOVENIA: 1 & 2, Bela Krajina region. Decreasing in use. 3, Bohinj region.
CROATIA: 4, inland generally. 5, Sisak region. Special occasions. 6, Dubrovnik
and Konavli regions. Married woman.
MONTENEGRO: 7, special occasions. 8, typical in the interior. Decreasing in use.
9, middle-aged and elderly men.

SERBIA: 10, Šiptar: Kosmet region and further south. 11, central and southern regions. Much varied. 12, general costume, much varied. Also found Macedonia, Montenegro and Bosnia-Hercegovina; BOSNIA-HERCEGOVINA: 13, simple peasant garb, throughout this area and Serbia. 14, Muslim. Many variants also in Macedonia and the Kosmet. 15, Bosnian traditional; clear Turkish influence. MACEDONIA: 16, typical heavy elaborate dress, particularly of Galičnik and other upland regions. 17, Southern regions, particularly Struga and Ohrid. 18, southern regions, Greek influence. Special occasions.

441

Hunting and Shooting

There is a great variety of game in Jugoslavia: from partridge to black bear. There are large numbers of hare, deer, foxes, lynx, chamois, wild boar, wild cat and almost every sort of bird. There are also many wolves, though they have decreased somewhat since the last war. The hunting of the bigger game is *extremely* expensive; in fact, only the very wealthy can afford it. For a permit you should apply to one of the official tourist agencies: Turistički Savez, in Belgrade, Ljubljana, Zagreb, Titograd, Sarajevo and Skopje. Some information about this can be obtained from the Tourist office in London and from Generalturist. The latter will provide details of costs.

If, like myself, you find that animals are much more interesting alive (as well as cheaper) than dead, it is better to take a camera and arrange with local authorities for a guide to take you on a photographic safari.

The following are the better known areas for hunting and shooting:

1. *Rog.* A mountainous area near Kočevje. The game available are deer (August 16—December 31); roedeer (April 1—December 31); wild boar and wolf (all the year round).

2. *Julian Alps.* The mountainous region round the lakes of Bled and Bohinj. Game: mountain goat (August 31—December 31).

3. *Risnjak and Velika Kapela.* The forests of the Gorski Kotar. Game: bear (November 1—December 31); wild boar (July 1—January 15); deer (August 1—December 31).

4. *Repaš.* A very good area on the left bank of the Drava near Koprivnica. Game: deer (August 1—December 31); hare (October 16—January 1); wild goose and wild duck (July 1—February 28).

5. *Durgutovica.* A low-lying region between Vinkovci and Osijek. Game: pheasant (October 1—January 15); hare (October 16—January 1); deer (August 1—December 31); wild goose and wild duck (July 1—February 28).

6. *Spačva and Merolino.* A low-lying region south and west of Vinkovci. There are big forests here full of deer, wild boar and other game. Deer (August 1—December 31); wild boar (July 1—January 15); wild goose and wild duck (July 1—February 28).

7. *Koprivnica.* A mountainous area near Bugojno. Most of the best hunting in Bosnia and Hercegovina is to be found in this region. Game: bear (October 1—December 31); wild boar (May 1—March 31).

8. *Prenj.* The district in the Prenj, Čvrsnica and Diva Grabovica

442

mountains south of Konjić. Game: bear (October 1—December 31); the exact dates for wild goat and partridge vary.

9. *Zelengora*. A forested and mountainous region west of Foča. Game: bear (October 1—December 31); wild boar (May 1—March 31); wolf (all the year round).

10. *Hutovo Blato*. A well-known district for game birds in the Neretva valley near Čapljina. Game: wild duck (August 1—January 28); wild goose (August 1—February 28).

Fishing

FRESH-WATER FISHING

There is a great variety of fresh-water fishing in lake, stream and river. Angling on the mountain rivers is particularly exciting. The principal fresh-water fish are: trout, grayling, char, pike, carp, chub, aspe, bream, barbel, tench, sheathfish and sterlet.

The permits vary from area to area and they can often be obtained at travel agencies and hotels. They cost between five and twenty-five new dinars a day. Their price, of course, will vary according to the kind of fish you want to catch and how rare or abundant they are.

The following are the centres for the main fishing areas:

1. *Bled*. The lake has pike and sheathfish. In the small River Radovna you can catch trout; grayling and char are to be found in the lower part of the Sava Bohinjka.

2. *Tolmin*. The rivers Soča, Idrijca and Vipava have plenty of brown trout and grayling.

3. *Bohinj*. The lake has trout and pike. Trout in the upper reaches of the Sava Bohinjka.

4. *Ljubljana*. Char, trout and grayling in the rivers Sora and Ljubljan-ica.

5. *Novo Mesto*. The centre for the River Krka which has plenty of pike, sheathfish, grayling and trout.

6. *Maribor*. The River Drava, especially the area near Mt Pohorje, has a variety of fish.

7. *Celje*. The upper reaches of the small River Savinja have plenty of trout, grayling and char.

8. *Zagreb*. A good centre for the River Sava which has a wide variety of fish.

443

9. *Varaždin.* On the Drava. A lot of pike and char. You can also fish in the lake at Trakoščan.

10. *Vinkovci.* On the small River Bosut. Carp, perch and small sheath-fish.

11. *Belgrade.* A good centre for fishing excursions. Near it is the big reservation called the 'Pančevački Rit'. Upstream of the Sava some of the best spots are at Ostružnica, Umka, Obrenovac (the mouth of the Kolubara) as well as the mouth of the Sava into the Danube. On the Danube the best places are Višnjica, Ritopek, Vinča, Grocka and Smederevo. The fish are varied: carp, tench, roach, pike, sheathfish and aspe.

12. *Novi Sad.* A good centre right on the Danube. Some of the backwaters provide excellent fishing for big pike and sheathfish, especially at Čurug and Titel.

13. *Apatin.* On the Danube. The waters are very deep and swift here and the fish are large, especially the sheathfish and aspe. The big pools near the banks and round the islands shelter pike.

14. *Paraćin.* Near the River Crnica which has trout. Farther away is the mountain river of Crni Timok. The best village centre for this is Lukovo.

15. *Pirot.* A good centre for a number of mountain streams, especially the Visočica. Most of them flow through deep gorges and rocky banks. Trout and chub abound here.

16. *Lake Vlasina.* A big man-made lake surrounded by pine woods. It has been stocked with trout of the same kind you find in Lake Ohrid.

17. *Skopje.* Centre for the Vardar river which has plenty of chub, carp and barbel. Near Matka the Treska river has been dammed to form a lake where there are trout and chub.

18. *Mavrovo.* The lake has plenty of trout and the River Radika and its tributaries are particularly well-known for their excellent trout fishing.

19. *Ohrid.* The lake is full of trout. The Crni Drim river provides trout and eel. The Sveti Naum end of the lake and where the Crni Drim flows out of the lake through Struga are particularly good areas.

20. *Prespa.* The lake is full of trout, chub and carp.

21. *Brod na Kupi.* Centre for the upper reaches of the River Kupa. There is an abundance of grayling, trout and char.

22. *Obrovac.* On the River Zrmanja. Plenty of trout.

23. *Šibenik.* Centre for the River Krka and the lake Visovačko Jezero. Trout, chub, barbel and eel are abundant.

24. *Split and Omiš.* Centres for the River Jadro which has plenty of trout.

25. *Titograd.* An excellent centre for several rivers: the Ribnica, the Morača and the Cijevna. All provide good trout fishing.

26. *Danilovgrad.* On the River Zeta. Several varieties of trout.

27. *Andrijevica.* A mountain town on the River Lim. The fishing on the Lim is mostly for trout, grayling and char.

28. *Kolašin*. On the upper reaches of the Tara, one of the most beautiful mountain rivers in Europe. Again there are plenty of trout, grayling and charr.

29. *Plav*. On the banks of a glacial lake surrounded by mountains. Several streams flow into it. Out of it flows the Lim into a big gorge. Trout, grayling, chub and char abound here. Four hours away on foot is Lake Ridsko, a most beautiful stretch of water where there are plenty of trout.

30. *Peć*. At the entrance to the Rugovo Gorge through which run the Pećka Bistrica and the Alagijina. Good trout fishing. At Dečani there is another stream, the Dečanska Bistrica, also with plenty of trout.

31. *Studenica*. Plenty of trout in the River Studenica and its tributaries.

32. *Novi Pazar*. Near the source of the Raška and its tributary the Ljudska. Trout fishing.

33. *Tutin*. High in remote mountains on the River Vidrenjak and near the River Ibar. Trout, grayling, char, barbel and chub are plentiful.

34. *Kraljevo*. A good centre for the Ibar and the Zapadna Morava. Sheathfish, chub and trout provide the best fishing.

35. *Višegrad*. On the Drina. The Drina Gorge is one of the loveliest in Europe. The waters are deep and swift and there are a lot of rapids. Very large char and barbel are caught here. But there are few trout.

36. *Ustiprača*. On the Prača river near where it enters the Drina. Grayling, trout and big char are plentiful.

37. *Šćepan-Polje*. At the confluence of the Tara and the Piva. The best fishing is for grayling, trout and char.

38. *Tjentište*. A lovely valley in the Mt Zelengora region, through which flows the River Sutjeska. Trout, grayling and char are plentiful.

39. *Plužine*. A village on Mt Durmitor which has several excellent streams in the locality. The best fishing is for trout and grayling.

40. *Pljevlja*. Near the River Cehotina, which is deep and swift and harbours grayling, trout and char.

41. *Žabljak*. The Mt Durmitor area. Trout fishing on the two lakes (Crno and Zmijsko) is good.

42. *Šavnik*. Near the rivers Pridvorica, Sinjac and Komarnica. Grayling and trout are plentiful.

43. *Banjaluka*. On the Vrbas river, which is rich in chub, char, trout and grayling.

44. *Jajce*. One of the best centres. The River Pliva is rich in trout and grayling. The nearby Plivsko Jezero has big trout and carp.

45. *Mrkonjić-Grad*. The small lake nearby has plenty of trout.

46. *Duvno*. The River Šujica has plenty of chub and trout.

47. *Livno*. The rivers Šturba and Plovuča are rich in trout.

48. *Sarajevo*. An excellent centre for excursions. The Bosna river is rich in char, grayling, chub, barbel and roach.

49. *Vlasenica*. Two good mountain streams in the locality: the Jadar and the Drinjaca. Plentiful trout, grayling, char and chub.

50. *Konjić*. The man-made Jablanica lake nearby, and the Neretva river are rich in trout and big chub.

51. *Boračko Jezero*. A lake near Mt Prenj with plentiful trout. The River Neretva is more interesting, especially near the village of Glavatičevo. The trout are big.

52. *Mostar*. Again on the Neretva. Trout.

53. *Čapljina*. On the Neretva and near the tributary Trebižat which also has plenty of trout.

54. *Karlovac*. Several rivers and streams in the area for pike, sheathfish, chub, trout and char.

55. *Plitvice Lakes*. Abundant trout. In the River Korana which flows out of the lakes there are big pike and chub.

56. *Martin Brod*. The best centre on the River Una. The trout, grayling and chub fishing is excellent here.

SEA-WATER FISHING

The Adriatic coast is particularly rich in a wide variety of fish, and the facts that it is so indented and has so many islands make it an ideal place for all forms of fishing—including under water. The sea is extremely clear and warm. Among the fish available are: mullet, tunny, swordfish, bass, bream, moray and conger eels, and dogfish.

You can make private arrangements at most ports and fishing villages or you can make them through the agencies. The Tourist office organises fourteen-day excursions from Rijeka and a small and very well equipped flotilla goes to the best fishing grounds. Ten-day fishing cruises on trawlers can also be arranged.

Fees have to be paid and permits are necessary. Fishing with hook and net costs about ten new dinars per day. A permit for underwater fishing costs about twenty per day. Tourists can join the Jugoslav Fishing Association for eighteen new dinars and then pay only half the fees. Boats can be hired almost anywhere on the coast for between twenty-five and sixty dinars a day. It is almost essential to have the advice and help of the local fishermen.

UNDERWATER FISHING

The main underwater fishing areas are as follows:

1. *Koper–Piran–Poreč–Rovinj*. In this region Savudrija, the Mirna cove, the islets Veliki and Mali Školj and the Črvar shoal are very good. The islands near Rovinj are also recommended and the entrance to the Lim fiord.

2. *Pula–Labin–Opatija–Rijeka*. The best places are Barbariga, Preman-

tura and Medulin and the southern cape of Istria. From Rabac to Rijeka there are few fish and the surroundings of Rijeka are not suitable.

3. *The Kvarner Islands–Bakar–Crikvenica–Senj.* Punta Križa on the island of Cres is the best spot in this area. All the seaward coasts of Krk, Cres and Lošinj provide excellent fishing. Near Rab the best places are the islands of Veliki and Mali Loganj.

4. *Jablanac–Karlobag–Pag–Paklenica.* The seaward coast of Pag provides the best places.

5. *Obrovac–Novigrad–Nin–Zadar–Biograd-na-Moru.* There aren't a great many fish on this part of the coast but you find mullet and bass at the mouth of the Zrmanja and good fishing grounds round Ugljan and Pašman.

6. *Northern Dalmatian Islands and the Kornati.* The Kornat islands provide easily the best underwater fishing in the Adriatic. There are a great many fish and even a beginner can hardly fail to catch something. Frequent excursions are organised from Zadar.

7. *Šibenik and its islands.* The islands are part of the Kornat group and are as good as those near Zadar.

8. *Rogoznica–Trogir–Kašteli–Split.* The coast from Primošten to the Bay of Marina provides good fishing, and so do the seaward shores of Brač, Šolta and Čiovo. The mouth of the River Cetina at Omiš is another reputed spot. Unfortunately the Makarska area is rather poor for this sport.

9. *Vis–Hvar–Korčula–Ploče.* The water round these parts is exceptionally clear. Sometimes you can see down as much as 150 feet. Vis and Korčula provide the best fishing, and the group of small islands off Hvar called the Pakleni Otoci.

10. *Pelješac–Lastovo–Mljet–Dubrovnik.* This is a very good area. There are a lot of fish and the water is very clear. Mljet and Lastovo are the best of the islands. But those nearer Dubrovnik, like Koločep and Lopud, also provide excellent fishing.

11. *Cavtat–Hercegnovi–Kotor–Budva.* The fishing between Cavtat and Hercegnovi is good, especially for dusky perch and moray eel. The islands of Mrkan and Bobara are good sites. There are plenty of fish in the Boka Kotorska but the coast provides better sport: particularly between the Gulf and Budva and the Traste bay. Near Budva the best places are Platamone and the little island Sv Nikola.

12. *Sveti Stefan–Bar–Ulcinj.* The coast is very rich in fish, especially between Bar and Ulcinj. There are no islands and most of the fishing has to be done by boat from Bar or Ulcinj.

Ski-ing

The mountain resorts of Jugoslavia lie in surroundings which are just as beautiful as those of any other ski-ing country, but they are not so well equipped as those in Austria, Switzerland, Italy or France. The main concentration is, of course, in Slovenia—in the region of the Julian Alps, where ski-ing has been practised for at least two hundred years. There are a few other places in Serbia, Bosnia and Macedonia.

I list here the main resorts—not in any special order of importance—with as much information about them as it has been possible to collect. I am particularly indebted to Mr Frank Hawkins for a number of facts.

Kranjska Gora. 2,700 ft. Eight lifts: six drag and two chair. One of the best known and most popular resorts. Ski-ing is concentrated on a difficult wooded mountain called Vitranc and is not a place for beginners. The difficulty of the descent from the top station to the middle is that much of the way is on a narrow path with a sheer drop on one side. Most of the runs are middle difficult and open. There is one slope of two hundred yards which is suitable for children. The other main slopes vary in length from 250 yds. to 1,500. The longest run drops 2,500 ft.

Accommodation: Hotel Erika, at the foot of the Vršic Pass, four kilometres from the ski-ing grounds. Hotel Prisank, on the ski-ing grounds. There is also a motel and the rather older Hotel Razor. Night-life limited but there is a small night-club. Not a sophisticated place but has character. Communication by bus is good.

Bled. 1,500 ft. The most famous Jugoslav mountain resort (see p. 376), with varied and good ski-ing over a number of slopes and several gentle runs for beginners. One chair-lift goes 900 ft to the Straža hill, from where there are two descents: one difficult, the other much easier. There is another 600 ft. lift to the Višelnica hill which has several gentle slopes.

Accommodation: at least sixteen hotels of various categories. I recommend the Toplice, the Jelovica, the Blegaš, the Bogatin and Mežaklja. Most of them are excellent. Night-life plentiful. Communications by bus and train are efficient.

Bohinj. 1,500 ft. Cable car to the Vogel Mountain, two chair-lifts, four drag-lifts. After Bled the best known lake resort in Slovenia (see p. 376). Snow conditions good until April. Some of the runs above the tree line are magnificent and you can do a limited amount of touring. West of Bohinj is Komna—a plateau, in places 6,000 feet up, also well supplied with lifts.

Accommodation: the hotels serve both areas. The Bellvue, the Jezero, the Pod Voglom and the Zlatorog are good. At the top station of the cable-car is a new hotel, the Na Voglu. The Mladinski Dom Bohinj is a well-equipped youth centre, with good accommodation. Transport to the cable-lift by minibus. Bus and train communications are efficient.

Krvavec. 6,000 ft. This is part of the Kamnik Alps nearer Ljubljana (see p. 368). The snow here lasts until April and it is a popular place for tournaments. There are several slopes of varying lengths and difficulties reached by drag lifts and a gondola from the village of Cerklje.

Accommodation: The Dom na Krvavcu on the high plateau. Night-life nil. Communications are by bus from Kranj.

Planica. 3,000 ft. Chair-lifts. A beautiful Alpine valley six kilometres long which has become a popular place for national and international contest. The world record for ski-jumping was broken at Planica several times between 1934 and 1948, and the main jumps are among the longest in the world and are served by chair-lift. For the average British skier jumping is, of course, a spectator sport. At Planica there are frequent displays of jumping, culminating every year in a special show at the end of March. Accommodation: Dom v Planici, twenty minutes from the ski-ing ground; and the Kača v Tamarju, two hours from the ski-ing ground. There is also a small village inn at Rateče nearby, the Gostilna na Zerjavu. Night-life very limited. Communications by bus are adequate.

Pohorje. 3,000 ft. A mountainous area near Maribor (see p. 382). There is transport from Maribor to the terminus of the drag-lift which takes you up to 2,300 ft. A cable-car continues the journey to the upper slopes. There are several good runs, some of which are difficult.

Accommodation: Bellevue Hotel, the Poštarski Dom, the Dom Miloša Zidanška and the Planinka. All well-equipped. Night-life negligible. Communications with Maribor efficient.

Platak. 3,000 ft. Near Rijeka (see p. 13), and one of the few places in Europe where you could combine a swimming and ski-ing holiday. The snow lasts late into April and even into early May when Opatija is beginning to fill up and the waters of the Kvarner Gulf are already warm. There are several drag and chair-lifts and a variety of slopes. In January and February ten-day courses for experienced skiers as well as beginners are held.

Accommodation: one hotel at Platak, the Dom na Platku. The ideal plan would be to stay in Opatija and drive to the ski-ing grounds.

Jahorina. 6,000 ft. It lies south-east of Sarajevo (see p. 326) and is the most popular ski centre of Bosnia. The winter season lasts from December to the end of March. A cable-car and a drag-lift take you to a variety of slopes, in magnificent forested country.

Accommodation: hotels Johorina and Šator. Bus communications from Sarajevo are quite efficient.

Kopaonik. 6,000 ft. This, near Raška and Novi Pazar (see p. 259), is the best of the Serbian ski-ing resorts, with a good variety of slopes. One drag lift. Accommodation: well-equipped lodges on the ski-ing grounds. Communications are poor. You first have to go to Raška by rail and then on by bus. **Popova Šapka.** 6,000 ft. The best known of the Macedonian resorts, lying west of Tetovo (see p. 210). More accessible than Kopaonik but still remote. Many excellent slopes. Two drag-lifts.

Accommodation: Well-equipped lodges at Popova Šapka; at Tetovo a decent hotel, The New. Bus and rail communications from Tetovo are adequate.

Spas

Jugoslavia is unusually rich in mineral and thermal springs. Not only does the country have an extraordinary number of them, they also produce most of the mineral waters known. Many were in use in the Illyrian period but the Romans were the first to exploit them systematically.

Some may be squeamish about the idea of a Balkan spa and perhaps imagine they are like eighteenth-century Bath where the English sank their class differences for a time while standing up to their necks in the democratic promiscuity of each other's filth. They would be wrong. Jugoslav spas are clean, well-organised and well-equipped. Below are brief details of a few of the principal establishments, some of which I have mentioned in the main text:

1. Bukovička Banja. Near Topola and Orašac in central Serbia (see p. 288). It has four springs; a pool and two dozen tubs for bathing in heated mineral waters. Open-air swimming-pool. Terraces for sun-bathing. Most agreeable park. Facilities for sport and gentle recuperative exercise on the wooded slopes of Mt. Bukulja. Cinema and night-club. Season: Feb. 1st to Oct. 15th. Accommodation: four comfortable hotels: Šumadija, Starozdanje, Zelengora and Beograd.

2. Dobrna. Slovenia, eighteen kilometres from Celje (see p. 380). Several springs, in use since the fifteenth century. The establishment stands in a large park ideal for walking. Several hotels, of which the best is Zdravíliški Dom. Entertainments are limited. Some concerts. The more energetic can fish and hunt. Open all the year round.

3. Guber. Near Zvornik (see p. 324) in Bosnia. Accommodation is a little

limited but there are some decent hotels at Srebrenica nearby. Surroundings are beautiful. Plenty of facilities for excursions, for hunting and fishing. Open all the year round.

4. Igalo. Next to Hercegnovi (see p. 136). Has well-equipped premises as well as a pleasant hotel, the Igalo. Good beach nearby and, of course, almost unlimited scope for excursions. Open all the year round; most suitable as a winter resort.

5. Ilidža. One of the most famous spas (see p. 338) and only 12 kilometres from Sarajevo. Four bathing establishments with tubs, pools and recreation rooms. Large and able staff minister to the sufferers. For entertainment one goes to Sarajevo.

Accommodation: the main hotel is the Srbija; large and comfortable.

6. Koviljača. One of the bigger Serbian spas; on the right bank of the river Drina, about twenty kilometres north of Zvornik (see p. 324). Well-equipped place with tubs, pools and departments for mud treatment, massage and recreation. The sulphurous springs, like those at Ilidža, are good for various forms of rheumatism. There are concerts, and you can hunt in the district and go rafting on the Drina.

Accommodation in large number of comfortable hotels and villas. Open from May to October.

7. Lipik. Near Zagreb (see p. 358), in the Pakra valley. Usual spa installations, several hotels, restaurants and cafés. Concerts, a cinema and a swimming pool provide most of the entertainment. Open all the year round.

8. Mataruška Banja. A few kilometres from Kraljevo. Delightful surroundings very near Ibar river. The buildings, scattered in a large park, provide several pools and sixty tubs. Comfortable accommodation in several hotels and annexes. Cinemas, concerts and variety shows provided. Excellent centre for excursions down the Ibar valley and along the Morava valley (see chaps. 16 and 17). Open all the year round.

9. Niška Banja. Ten kilometres from Niš. Very up-to-date spa with new pools and tubs, an inhalatorium and the latest equipment for physical therapy. Two good hotels (the Ozren and the Srbija). Plenty of scope for excursions. Niš itself provides a certain amount of entertainment (see p. 272). Open the whole year.

10. Rogaška Slatina. The countryside round this spa, thirty kilometres from Celje, is among the loveliest in Slovenia. The establishment is well equipped; various facilities for entertainment.

Accommodation: in four comfortable hotels, the Bohor, the Slovenski Dom, the Zdravilíški Dom and the Styria. Open all the year round.

11. Slatina Radenci. Also in Slovenia, in the Mura valley. Several comfortable hotels, a cinema, café and night club and amenities for sport. Good centre for Maribor and that district (see p. 382). Open May 1st to end of October.

12. Vrnjačka Banja. On the wooded slopes of Mt Goč in Serbia, off the main road between Kraljevo and Kruševac (see pp. 282-3). Biggest and best spa in Jugoslavia. Modern establishment that accommodates between two and three thousand people in hotels and private houses. I can recommend the Beograd, Park and Sloboda hotels. Wide variety of entertainments provided. An excellent centre for excursions to Ljubostinja, Žiča, Studenica, Sopoćani, Kruševac, Kalenić, Manasija and many other places. Activities like fishing and shooting are catered for. Open the whole year.

The Alphabets

Cyrillic		Latin		Pronunciation
А	а	A	a	'a' as in 'father'
Б	б	B	b	'b' as in 'bed'
В	в	V	v	'v' as in 'vet'
Г	г	G	g	'g' as in 'gate'
Д	д	D	d	'd' as in 'day'
Ђ	ђ	Dj	dj	'dj' as in 'midget'
Е	е	E	e	'e' as in 'pet'
Ж	ж	Ž	ž	's' as in 'pleasure'
З	з	Z	z	'z' as in 'zebra'
И	и	I	i	'i' as in 'machine'
Ј	ј	J	j	'y' as in 'yet'
К	к	K	k	'k' as in 'kitchen'
Л	л	L	l	'l' as in 'luck'
Љ	љ	Lj	lj	'lli' as in 'million'
М	м	M	m	'm' as in 'man'
Н	н	N	n	'n' as in 'name'
Њ	њ	Nj	nj	'ni' as in 'onion'
О	о	O	o	'o' as in 'rod'
П	п	P	p	'p' as in 'pear'
Р	р	R	r	'r' as in 'rat'
С	с	S	s	's' as in 'sea'
Т	т	T	t	't' as in 'toe'
Ћ	ћ	Ć	ć	't' (ty) as in 'picture'
У	у	U	u	'u' as in 'rule'
Ф	ф	F	f	'f' as in 'fate'
Х	х	H	h	'h' as in 'hat' but often almost silent
Ц	ц	C	c	'ts' as in 'hits'

Cyrillic		Latin		Pronunciation
Ч	ч	Č	č	'ch' as in 'chain'
Џ	џ	Dž	dž	'j' as in 'jack'
Ш	ш	Š	š	'sh' as in 'shell'

Phonetically the language is consistent and a letter always has the same pronunciation wherever it occurs. The stress in a word never falls on the last syllable and no word, unless it is a compound, has more than one stress. Distribution of stress varies.

Important Dates

This list is designed to fill in some of the historical details not mentioned in the main text and to give a sequence of events. It is to be taken as a *very* rough guide.

c. 1200 BC Illyrians settle in the region of modern Jugoslavia.

4th century BC Illyrian tribes form a kingdom. Greek merchants establish trading cities on the Dalmatian coast and on the islands; more especially at Epidaurus (Cavtat) and Trogir (Tragurion).
355 BC Philip II of Macedon conducts a campaign against the Illyrians.

280 BC Celtic tribes (Galatae) cross into the Balkans.
3rd century BC King Agron and Queen Teuta restore Illyrian kingdom.
230 BC Queen Teuta of Scutari (Skadar) pays tribute to Rome.
229 BC First Roman campaign against pirates on the Dalmatian coast. The coastal strip of Illyricum becomes a Roman protectorate.
220 BC Illyrians spread into Macedonia.

168-117 BC Six further Roman campaigns against the Illyrians.
148 BC Macedonia becomes a Roman province.
33 BC Final conquest of Illyria by the Romans. Illyrian tribes now become a source of troops.

AD 9 The Illyrians attempt an uprising which is crushed.
14 The death of Augustus.
1-100 Romans begin settling at Pula, Salona, Skopje, Stobi and Bitola.

243-315 Diocletian.

453

295 Division of empire. The imperial boundary runs along lower reaches of the Danube and Drina. The eastern empire gains increasing influence over the whole Balkan peninsula.

334 Constantinople founded by Constantine.

350 After the partition of the Roman Empire Byzantine influence in the Balkans increases.

379-401 West Goths move into Illyria.

450 Huns move through the northern province of Pannonia and the East Goths follow them.

489 Odwacer, and later Theodoric, become masters of Illyria.

490-568 The Langobards invade the lower reaches of the Danube.

500-700 The South Slavs from the Carpathian area and farther north move into the valleys of the Danube and the Sava. There is a constant move south and west. By the end of the seventh century they are finally settled.

565-570 The Avars found a state in lower Austria and Hungary and move south into the Balkans. They expel the Langobards and subdue the South Slavs.

570 Mahomet born in Mecca.

622-26 The Avars besiege Constantinople.

623-25 In defence against the Avars the Slavonic people put themselves under the rule of a Frankish merchant called Samo, who calls himself king. He establishes a big kingdom which stretches from the Carpathians to the Adriatic, from near Berlin to Skopje. This state lasts for thirty-three years. Samo dies. The state disintegrates.

8th century. Prince Višeslav is temporarily successful in uniting Serbian tribes in the Neretva, Tara and Piva valleys.

791-805 Frankish campaigns against the Avars. Slovenes and Croats come under Franconian influence.

809 Foundation of the Bokeljska Mornarica at Kotor.

830 King Vlastimir founds an independent Serbian state of Raška. This was to be conquered in 917 by the Bulgarians, and then re-established by a prince Časlav who enlarged the kingdom by incorporating Zeta (roughly the region of modern Montenegro) Hum and the coastal area near Dubrovnik and the Neretva valley.

825-85 St. Methodius.

826-69 St Cyril.

850 Vlastimir, ruler of Zeta and Raška.

852 Trpimir assumes title of Duke of the Croats.

864 At the request of the Moravian prince Rastislav, Emperor Michael III

of Byzantium send SS Cyril and Methodius to Moravia. Church Slavonic alphabet developed. The mission of the apostles to the South Slavs, probably a counter measure to Frankish Christianisation is suppressed by the Franks. Clement and Naum, two pupils of Cyril, move to Lake Ohrid where they establish monasteries and a university.

879-92 Prince Branimir frees Croatia from Byzantine dominance. Tomislav unites Dalmatia and Pannonian Croatia.

925 Tomislav becomes first king of Croatia, with a kingdom which corresponds roughly with that of modern Croatia.

925 and 927 Church Council in Split.

976 Csar Samuel becomes founder and emperor of the first Macedonian state.

c. 1000 Venice attempts to seize Dalmatian islands and coastal region.

c. 1025 Stefan Vojislav, king of Zeta.

11th century Bogomilism spreads into Bosnia. The Hungarians undertake several crusades against this Bosnian 'Church'.

1058-74 Krešimir IV considerably enlarges Croatia and now calls himself king of Dalmatia and Croatia.

1076-89 Zvonimir, king of Croatia.

1081-1101 Bodin, king of Zeta.

1091 Croat royal house ceases.

c. 1100 Dubrovnik founded.

1102 Twelve Croat tribes sign treaty with Hungarian king Koloman. An Hungarian *Ban* takes over. Croat union with Hungary widens gulf between Croats and Serbs, already divided in faith.

c. 1120 Serb tribes unite and with help of Hungary invade Byzantine territories. Kingdom of Rama, roughly equivalent to modern Bosnia, passes temporarily to Hungary.

1174-1235 Sv Sava, first archbishop of Serbian Orthodox Church.

1180-1203 Kulin, king of Bosnia.

1180 Citizens of Dubrovnik choose a ruler for the first time.

1190-96 Stefan Nemanja *Župan* of Raška. Foundation of Nemanjić dynasty.

1190 Dubrovnik secures its position by means of treaties against external enemies, especially Venice. Trading pacts with pirates at Omiš.

1199? Death of Stefan Nemanja.

1196-1228 Stefan *Prvovenčani*, son of Stefan Nemanja, brother of Sv Sava, first crowned king of Serbia.

1204 The Fourth Crusade conquers Dalmatian towns.

1205 Dubrovnik falls to Venice.

1219 Serbian Church autonomous with the Patriarchate at Žiča.

1228-34 Stefan Radoslav, son of Stefan *Prvovenčani*, king of Serbia.

1234-43 Stefan Vladislav, brother of Radoslav, king of Serbia.

1243-76 Stefan Uroš I, brother of Vladislav, king of Serbia.

1253 Serbian Patriarchate transferred to Peć.

1266 Vinodol Statute

1276-82 Stefan Dragutin, son of Uroš I, king of Serbia.

1282-1321 Milutin, Uroš II, brother of Dragutin, king of Serbia.

c. 1300 Serbs advance to the north of Macedonia.

1321-22 Constantine, son of Milutin, king of Serbia.

1322-31 Stefan Uroš III, brother of Constantine, king of Serbia (also known as Stefan Dečanski).

1331-55 Stefan Dušan, Uroš IV, son of Uroš III, Csar of Serbia. Dušan occupies southern Macedonia, Thessalia, Albania and Epirus. At Skopje he is crowned Csar of Serbs, Greeks, Bulgarians and Albanians. He undertakes compaigns against Byzantium.

1349 The *Zakonic*, Dušan's Code.

1353-91 Tvrtko I, king of Bosnia.

1355-72 Stefan Uroš V, son of Dušan, Csar of Serbia; the last of the Nemanja dynasty.

1358 Venetian governor of Dubrovnik asked to remove himself. Dubrovnik formally recognises Hungarian sovereignty.

1366-71 Vukašin (guardian of Uroš V, father of Marko) king of Prilep.

1367 Stefan Uroš V gives up bit by bit the territories conquered by the Nemanjić kings.

1371 Southern Macedonia comes under Turkish rule.

1371-89 Lazar, prince of Serbia.

1389 Battle of Kosovo.

1389-92 Sultan Beyazid advances to the Danube.

1389-1427 Stefan, Lazar II, Despot of Serbia.

1389-98 Vuk Branković, ruler of Prizren.

1396 Europe gathers forces for first campaign against the Turks, called a Crusade. Crusade defeated at Nicopolis.

1420 Venice occupies whole of Dalmatia.

1427-56 Djordje Branković, Despot of Serbia.

1430 Dubrovnik makes treaty with Turks which guarantees trading rights.

1433 Belgrade occupied by Hungarians.

1453 Fall of Constantinople.

1459 Serbia becomes a *pašalik*. Fall of Smederevo.

1463 Bosnia conquered by the Turks. Refugees trek to the north.

1463-1669 Croats fight numerous defensive battles against the Turks. Military boundaries established.

1466 Rijeka becomes Austrian.

1482 Hercegovina occupied by the Turks.
1493 First printing press set up in Montenegro.

1521 Sultan Suleiman expels the Hungarians from Belgrade.
1529 First siege of Vienna by the Turks.
1535 More refugees trek to the north.
1571 Battle of Lepanto.
1573 Peasant revolt in Croatia against the Austrians, led by Matija Gubec.
1582 Gregorian Calendar introduced.
16th century. The *hajduks* begin their long reign of terror against the Turks. Refugees join them as partisans. The *zadruga* system is strengthened.

1667 Dubrovnik earthquake.
1671 End of Zrinjski-Frankopan era.
1676 Last levy of Christian children for the Janissaries.
1683 Second siege of Vienna by the Turks.
1688 Belgrade captured by the Austrians from the Turks.
1696-1737 Danilo Petrović, *Vladika* of Montenegro. He founds a Church dynasty which is inherited from uncle to nephew until 1860.

1702-3 Montenegrin Vespers.
1737-82 Sava, *Vladika* of Montenegro.
1752 Karadjordje born.
1765-66 Patriarchy of Peć suppressed by the Sultan.
1782-1830 Petar I, *Vladika* of Montenegro.
1787 Vuk Karadžić born.

1802-3 First revolt of Karadjordje against the Turks.
1804-13 Karadjordje supreme chief of the Serbs.
1806 Dubrovnik occupied by Napoleon's troops.
1808 The Republic of Dubrovnik dissolved and annexed to the province of Illyria.
1815 Miloš Obrenović becomes Serbian leader. Dubrovnik ceases finally to be a republic. Bishop Strossmayer born.
1818 Murder of Karadjordje.
1828 Janissaries disbanded.
1830 Miloš Obrenović recognised as heriditary prince of Serbia.
1830-51 Petar II Njegoš, *Vladika* of Montenegro.
1848 Year of Revolution in Europe.
1856 Treaty of Paris. Serbian independence recognised.
1860 Death of Miloš Obrenović. Michael Obrenović succeeds for second time.
1878 Niš freed from the Turks.
1882 Milan Obrenović proclaims Serbia a kingdom.

457

1903 Murder of Alexander Obrenović. Peter Karadjordjević succeeds.

1905 King Nicholas of Montenegro gives his country a constitution.

1906 Austria begins 'Custom's War' against Serbia.

1908 Bosnia-Hercegovina annexed by force by Austria.

1911 *Komitadži* plots spread anarchist movement in Macedonia.

1912-13 First and second Balkan wars. Serbs, Greeks, Macedonians and Montenegrins fight against the Turks. The Turks are expelled.

1913 Peace Treaty at Bucharest. Southern Macedonia passes to Greece; northern Macedonia to Serbia.

1914 (June 28th) Gavrilo Princip assassinates Archduke Franz Ferdinand at Sarajevo.

1918 (December 1st) People of Jugoslavia meet to found a communal state: the kingdom of Serbs, Croats and Slovenes. It was not recognised by the Treaty of Versailles and lasted till 1941.

1921 Death of King Peter. Succeeded by Alexander.

1928 Stefan Radić, leader of Croat peasant party, murdered in Parliament. Constitution suspended. Military dictatorship under King Alexander.

1934 King Alexander assassinated in Marseilles. Regency under Prince Paul Karadjordjević. Peter II succeeds as king.

1939 Outbreak of Second World War.

1941 Germany invades Jugoslavia. King leaves the country.

1941-45 The Communists rise to power under the leadership of Tito.

1945 (November 29th) Popular Assembly established Federal People's Republic. Monarchy abolished.

1946 (January 31st) New Constitution adopted.

1947 Break with the Cominform.

1953 Redrafting of constitution. Tito president of Jugoslavia.

1966 Re-examination of principles, policy and personnel.

Suggestions for Further Reading

(those marked with an asterisk are recommended to the general reader)

History

(I have not included primary sources. Those who wish to consult them should refer to the bibliographies of scholars like Bury, Runciman and Von Ranke.)

Armstrong, H. F., *Tito and Goliath*, N.Y. 1951
Asboth, de, J., *An Official Tour through Bosnia and Herzegovina*, 1890
Auty, P., *Building of New Yugoslavia*, London, 1954
*Auty, P., *Yugoslavia*, London, 1954
Baerlein, H., *The Birth of Yugoslavia*, London, 1922
Barker, E., *Macedonia: its place in Balkan power politics*, London, 1950
Baynes, N. H., *The Byzantine Empire*, London, 1925
Brailsford, H. N., *Macedonia: its races and their future*, London, 1906
Buchan, J., *Yugoslavia*, London, 1923
Bury, J. B., *The History of the Roman Empire*, 1893
    The History of the Later Roman Empire, 1889
    The History of the Eastern Roman Empire, 1912
Byrnes, R. J., *Yugoslavia*, N.Y. and London, 1949
*Byron, R., *The Byzantine Achievement*, London, 1929
Castellan, Georges *La Vit Quotidienne en Serbie*, Paris 1967
Clissold, S. (ed), *Yugoslav Handbook*, Cambridge, 1965
    Whirlwind, 1949
Ciliga, A., *La Yougoslavie sous la Menace Intérieure et Extérieure*, Paris, 1952
Crankshaw, E., *Russia without Stalin*, London, 1956
Cvijić, J., *La Peninsule Balkanique* n.d.
Davidson, B., *Partisan Picture*, London, 1946
Degras, J. (editor) *The Soviet Yugoslav Dispute*, London, 1948
Dvornik, F., *The Slavs: their early history and civilisation*, Boston, 1956
*Eliot, Sir Charles, *Turkey in Europe*, London, 1908
Gibbon, E., *The History of the Decline and Fall of the Roman Empire*
Gimbutas, Marija, *The Slavs*, London, 1971
Graham, S., *Alexander of Yugoslavia*, London, 1938
Heppell, M., and Singleton, F. B., *Yugoslavia*, London, 1961
Hodgkinson, J., *East and West of Tito*, London, 1952
    The Adriatic Sea, London, 1955
Jireček, C., *History of the Serbs*, Gotha, 1911
Kerner, K. (Editor), *Yugoslavia*, California, 1949

Laffan, R. G., *The Serbs, Guardians of the Gates*, Oxford, 1918
*Lot, F., *Les Invasions Barbares*, Paris, 1937
Maček, V., *In the Struggle for Freedom*, New York, 1957
Obolensky, D., *The Bogomils*, Cambridge, 1948
Obolensky, D., *The Byzantine Commonwealth*, London, 1971
Ostrogorsky, G., *History of the Byzantine State*, Oxford, 1956
Pavlović, Stefan, R., *Yugoslavia*, London, 1971
Preveden, F. R., *History of the Croatian People*, Chicago, 1948
*Runciman, Sir Steven, *Byzantine Civilisation*, London, 1933
　　　　　　　　　　　The Medieval Manichee, Cambridge, 1955
Seton-Watson, H., *East European Revolution*, London, 1950
　　　　　　　　Eastern Europe Between the Wars, Cambridge, 1945
Seton-Watson, R. W., *The Southern Slav Question and the Hapsburg Monarchy*
　　London, 1911
Spinka, M., *Christianity in the Balkans*, New York, 1933
Stevenson, F. S., *History of Montenegro*, London, 1912
Temperley, H. W., *History of Serbia*, London, 1917
Tomasević, J., *Peasants and Economic Change in Yugoslavia*, London, 1955
Ulam, A. B., *Tito and the Cominform*, Cambridge (Mass.), 1952
Vlasto, A. P., *The Entry of the Slavs into Christendom*, Cambridge, 1970
Von Ranke, *History of the Serbian Insurrection*, London, 1853
Vojnović, L., *Historie de Dalmatie*, Paris, 1934
Waring, L. F., *Serbia*, London, 1917
Wiskermann, E., *Undeclared War*, London, 1939

Art and Architecture

*Adam, Robert, *Architecture of Diocletian's Palace at Spalato*, London, 1764
Bihalji-Merin, O., and Benac, A., *Bogomil Sculpture*, Belgrade, 1961
Bošković, Djurdje, *Medieval Art in Serbia and Macedonia*, Belgrade, 1945
Demus, O., *Byzantine Mosaic Tradition*, 1948
Deroko, A., *Architecture monumentale et decorative de la Serbie au Moyen Age*,
　　Belgrade, 1953
Hoddinott, R. F., *Early Byzantine Churches in Macedonia and Southern Serbia*,
　　London, 1963
*Jackson, Sir T. G., *The Quarnero and Istria with Cettinje and the Isle of Grado*
　　Oxford, 1887
Kašanin, M., *Yugoslav Medieval Frescoes*, 1953
Millet G., *La peinture au Moyen Age en Yougoslavie*, Paris, 1954
　　　　　L'ancien art Serbe: les églises, Paris 1919
　　　　　L'Art Byzantin chez les Slaves: Les Balkans, Paris, 1930
Radičević, B., *Serbian Peasant Tombstones*, Belgrade, 1965
Radojčić, S., *Yugoslavia: Medieval Frescoes*, Paris, 1955
Radovan, *Sculpture Yougoslave du XIIIe Siècle*, Zagreb, 1951

Rice, Talbot, *Beginnings of Christian Art*, Edinburgh, 1957
Stele, F., *Slovene Medieval Art*, Ljubljana, 1935
Uspenski, *L'Art Byzantin chez les Slaves*, Paris, 1930
Wilson, Duncan, *The Life and Times of Vuk Stefanović Karadzič*, London, 1971

Miscellaneous

Adamić, L., *The Native's Return*, New York, 1934
Aldiss, Brian, *Cities and Stones*, London, 1967
*Andrić, Ivo, *Bridge on the Drina* (trans. by Lovett Edwards) 1962
*   *Bosnian Story* (trans. by Joseph Hitrec) 1963
                   The Woman from Sarajevo (trans. by Joseph Hitrec) 1965
Avakumović, I., *History of the Communist Party in Yugoslavia*, University of Aberdeen Press, 1964
Blanqui, M., *Voyage en Bulgarie*, Paris, 1843
Brown, A., *Yugoslav Life and Landscape*, London, 1954
Bulatović, M., *The Red Cockerel*, London, 1963
Dayre, J., *Anthologie des conteurs Croates modernes*, Zagreb, 1933
Deakin, F. W. D., *The Embattled Mountain*, Oxford, 1971
*Dedijer, V., *Tito Speaks*, London, 1953
                   With Tito Through the War, London, 1951
Djilas, M., *The New Class*, London, 1957
                   Land Without Justice, London, 1958
                   Anatomy of a Moral, London, 1959
                   Conversations with Stalin, London, 1962
                   Montenegro, London, 1964
                   The Leper and Other Stories, London, 1965
                   The Unperfect Society, London, 1969
Durham, E., *Some Tribal Origins, Laws and Customs*, London, 1928
*Edwards, Lovett, *Introducing Jugoslavia*, London, 1954
                   Profane Pilgrimage, London, 1938
                   A Wayfarer in Yugoslavia, London, 1939
                   Yugoslavia, London, 1971
*Evans, Sir Arthur, *Through Bosnia and Herzegovina on Foot during The Insurrection, 1875*, London, 1876
Evliya Celebija, *Narrative of Travels*, trans. by J. Von Hammer, London, 1834
*Fitzroy Maclean, Sir, *Eastern Approaches*, London, 1949
*   *Disputed Barricade: the Life and Times of Joseph Broz Tito*, London, 1957
Footman, D., *Balkan Holiday*, London, 1935
*Fortis, Abbé, *Travels into Dalmatia*, 1778
Gardner Wilkinson, Sir J., *Dalmatia and Montenegro*, London, 1848
Graham, S., *St Vitus' Day*, London, 1930
                   Balkan Monastery, London, 1935

The Companion Guide to Jugoslavia

Halpern, J. M., *A Serbian Village*, New York, 1958
    The Triumphant Heretic, London, 1958
Harrison, H. D., *The Soul of Jugoslavia*, London, 1941
Higgins, John, *Travels in the Balkans*, London, 1972
Irving, Celia, *The Adriatic Islands and Corfu*, London, 1971
Kinglake, A. W., *Eothen*, London, 1844
Koljević, S., (Editor and trans.) *Yugoslav Short Stories*, London, 1966
Lamartine, A. de, *Voyage en Orient*, Paris, 1835
Lawrence, C., *Irregular Adventure*, London 1947
Lendvai, Paul, *Eagles in Cobwebs*, London, 1969
Lodwick, J., *Twenty East of Greenwich*, n.d.
Loti, P., *Fleurs d'Ennui*, Paris 1880
Lowe, D. H., *The Ballads of Marko Kraljević*, Cambridge, 1922
Macartney, C. A. and Palmer, A. W., *Independent Eastern Europe*, London, 1962
Manhattan, A., *Terror over Jugoslavia*, London, 1953
Marmont, Marshal, *Memoirs du duc de Raguse*, Paris, 1857
Millet, A. H., *A travers la Serbie libérée*, Paris, 1918
Morrison, W., *Revolt of the Serbs against the Turks* (trans. of heroic poems),
    Cambridge, 1942
Muir Mackenzie and Irby, *Travels in the Slavonic Provinces of Turkey in Europe*,
    London, 1867
Newman, B., *Albanian Backdoor*, London, 1936
    Tito's Yugoslavia, London, 1952
*Nickels, Sylvie, *The Travellers' Guide to Yugoslavia*, London, 1969
Ostović, P. D., *The Truth about Jugoslavia*, New York, 1952
Parmentier, E., *Turquie d'Europe*, Paris, 1890
Parry, M., Lord, A., *Serbo-Croatian Heroic Songs*, Cambridge (Mass.), 1954
Rootham, H., *Kosovo: a translation of the heroic songs of the Serbs*, Oxford, 1920
Rootham, J., *Miss Fire*, London, 1946
Sandys, G., *A Relation of a Journey Begun An:Dom: 1610*, London, 1615
Sommelius, T., *The Iron Gate of Illyria*, London, 1955
Subotić, D., *Yugoslav Popular Ballads*, Cambridge, 1932
Trouton, R., *Peasant Renaissance in Yugoslavia, 1900-1950*, London, 1952
Vivian, H., *The Servian Tragedy, with impressions of Macedonia*, London, 1904
Waterston, A., *Planning in Yugoslavia*, Baltimore, 1962
Waugh, E., *Helena*, London, 1950
Waugh, E., *Unconditional Surrender*, London, 1961
*West, R., *Black Lamb & Grey Falcon*, London, 1942
Whelpton, E., *Dalmatia*, London, 1954
White, L., *Balkan Caesar*, London, 1951
Wolff, R. L., *The Balkans in Our Time*, Harvard, 1956
*Zilliacus, K., *Tito of Jugoslavia*, London, 1952

Indexes

The index is in two sections: INDEX OF PLACES and INDEX OF PERSONS AND SUBJECTS.

For the convenience of English readers, entries beginning with c, ć, č, s, š, z and ž have not been separated but are treated as if they were *all* c, s or z. Figures in **bold** type indicate the principal references.

INDEX OF PLACES

Index of Places

465

Index of Places

Index of Places

Index of Places

Rudine, 101
Rudnik, 318
Rugovo Gorge, 163, 178, 435
Ruma, 292, **306,** 307, 421
Rumija, Mt., 157

Šabac, 306, 421
Salona, 68, 79, 84, **92-3,** 101, 234, 236
Salonika, 184, 203, 206, 209
Samobor, 366, 421
Samodreža, monastery, 258
Sana, river, 353
Sandžak, region, 250
Sarajevo, 225, 317, 318, **326-38,** 349, 421, 431
Šar Planina, 190, 193, 209, 210
Sava, river, 32, 292, 305, 338, 353
Savina, monastery, 138, 432
Savudrija, 398
Seget, 76
Selca (Brač), 102
Semur-en-Brionnais, 188
Senj, 23, 27, 32, **35-8,** 95, 98, 387, 406, 421
Senj Gate, 38
Senjski, Rudnik, 280
Senta, 313
Serbia, 11, 23, 66, 77, 116, 122, 129, 134, 144, 151, 159, chaps. 16, 17, 18 and 19, 392, 413, 415, 416, 431, 433, 436-7
Šestine, 346, 366
Sheep's Field, plateau, 242, 247
Šibenik, 54, 58, **59-64,** 67, 110, 263, 417, 421
Sinj, 67, **93-5,** 421, 431
Šipan, 117
Sisak, 317, 346, **353-4,** 421, 430
Šiševski, monastery, 204
Skadar, lake, 52, 151, 163, 164
Škofja Luka, 373
Skopje, 170, 179, 193, chap. 13, 212, 213, 215, 217, 225, 243, 266, 282, 421, 430, 431, 435
Skopska Crna Gora, 193, 198, 204, 248, 430
Skradin, 65
Skupi, 194, 233
Slančev Briag, 241 n.

Slavonski Brod, 317, 318, **421, 431**
Slavonski, Požega, 318, 321
Slovenia, 11, 366, chaps. 21 and 22, 416, 433, 438
Slunj, 356, 421
Smederevo, 51, 221, 266, **289-91,** 295, 302, 421
Sofia, 184
Šolta, 93, 98, 102
Sombor, 292, 312, 421
Sopočani, monastery, 168, 180, 250, **261-3,** 279
Sopot waterfall, 139
Split, 23, 27, 35, 39, 55, 67, 68, 74, 76, **79-95,** 98, 100, 101, 102, 188, 349, 355, 356, 415, 417, 421, 431
Spreča, river, 337
Srbobran, 312
Sremski Karlovci, 292, 307, **308-10,** 421
Sremska Mitrovica (Sirmium), 48, 203, 292, **306,** 317
Sremska Palanka, 288
Stari Bar, 146, **157,** 158, 160
Starigrad (Dalmatia), 39, 417
Starigrad-na-Hvaru (Hvar), 105, 108, 421
Staro Nagoričino, 206, 219, 233, **244-5,** 256, 401
Štimlje, 249
Štip, 170, 210, 233, 239, **240-1,** 243, 421
Stobi, 233, 234-5, 295
Stobreč (Epetion), 95, 103
Stogovo Mts., 203
Stolac, 341, 344
Ston, 98, 101, **115-16,** 122, 421
Štračin, 244
Struga, 208, 216, 222, 421
Strumica, 233, **239,** 240, 421
Studenica, monastery, 168, 180, 250, 256, 262, **263-4**
Subotica, 292, 313, 421, 437
Šumadija, region, 151, 266, 286, 287, 318
Supetar (Brač), 102, 103
Supetarska Draga (Rab), 30
Susak, 26
Sušak (Rijeka), 16, 19
Sušica, 202
Sutivan (Brač), 102
Sutjeska Gorge, 324

Index of Places

Index of Places

Index of Persons and Subjects

Index of Persons and Subjects

Index of Persons and Subjects

Index of Persons and Subjects